The Story of the United States-Nicaraguan Relationship

"Those who have been discriminating against dark-skinned people for years have nothing to tell me about human rights."

Nicaraguan President Anastasio Somoza, 1977

"The crisis in Nicaragua can be described as a simple problem: a mentally deranged man [Anastasio Somoza] with an army of criminals is attacking a defenseless population. . . . This is not a problem for the OAS; what we need is a psychiatrist."

Panamanian leader Omar Torrijos, 1978

"Avoid the early mistakes we made in Cuba, the political rejection by the West, premature frontal attacks on the bourgeoisie, economic isolation."

Fidel Castro's advice to the Sandinistas

"If you don't hold me responsible for everything that occurred under my predecessors, I will not hold you responsible for everything that occurred under your predecessors."

Jimmy Carter's advice to the Sandinistas

"Reagan has become an obsession for us, and we've become an obsession for him."

Nicaraguan Minister of the Interior Tomás Borge, 1983

"Your work will make a great movie one day."

Ronald Reagan to Lt. Col. Oliver North, November 25, 1986

CONDEMNED TO REPETITION

CONDEMNED TO REPETITION

The United States and Nicaragua

WITH A NEW EPILOGUE

ROBERT A. PASTOR

PRINCETON UNIVERSITY PRESS

PRINCETON, NEW JERSEY

Published by Princeton University Press, 41 William Street,
Princeton, New Jersey 08540

In the United Kingdom: Princeton University Press, Guildford, Surrey

Library of Congress Cataloging in Publication Data will be
found on the last printed page of this book

First Princeton Paperback printing, 1988

This book has been composed in Linotron Trump

Clothbound editions of Princeton University Press books
are printed on acid-free paper, and binding materials are
chosen for strength and durability. Paperbacks, although satisfactory
for personal collections, are not usually suitable for library rebinding

Printed in the United States of America by Princeton University Press,
Princeton, New Jersey

Designed by Laury A. Egan

To
Tiffin Margaret and Robert Kiplin,
indisputable improvements on the past

Contents

Part III: Relating to the Revolution

Part IV: Looking Back and Ahead

List of Illustrations

Map of Nicaragua
Chart of the Political Opposition to Somoza, August 1978

(following page 206)

Anastasio Somoza, Jr., his mother, Anastasio Somoza, Sr., and Luis Somoza

Cartoon by Oliphant

Carlos Andrés Pérez of Venezuela in a meeting at the White House

Omar Torrijos of Panama in a meeting at the White House

President Carter's meeting with William Bowdler, U.S. representative to the OAS mediation

Cartoon by Oliphant

Edén Pastora and Cyrus Vance

President Carter's meeting with three members of the Nicaraguan Junta

Cartoon by Bill Mauldin

President Ronald Reagan

President Reagan with three leaders of the Nicaraguan Resistance

The history of America's relations with Nicaragua well illustrates the truth that governments, no more than individuals, are all good or all bad. . . . At times, the United States has been a noble and unselfish hero to Nicaragua; at times, it has been the villain who would let nothing thwart his purpose. And often, it has been both hero and villain at once, as in its high-handed, yet absolutely necessary, enforcement of American supervision of the last Nicaraguan election [in 1928]. . . . As is usual in life, the United States has been punished the most severely when it was acting the most altruistically.

Harold Norman Denny, *Dollars for Bullets*, **1929**

I ask first for [the American people's] help in remembering our history in Central America so we can learn from the mistakes of the past.

Ronald Reagan, 1986

Preface to the Paperback Edition

I COMPLETED this book as the Congressional hearings on the Iran–Contra affair began in May 1987. U.S.–Nicaraguan relations were in a dismal state. The Reagan Administration and the Sandinista government seemed locked in a self-defeating and tragic struggle that was dividing both countries, killing Nicaragua's youth, and damaging U.S. prestige. At the end of the book, I developed a three-pronged proposal for pursuing U.S. interests in Nicaragua which included supporting a Central American peace initiative. But I concluded that, ultimately, the success of any peace effort in Nicaragua would depend on whether the government and its opposition would treat each other with respect rather than as tools of foreign powers, and whether they could agree on a political framework that would permit peaceful change. Because of the deep distrust among Nicaraguans and between the Sandinistas and Washington, the obstacles to peace were formidable.

In the eleven months since then, events have moved at a rapid pace, but they have essentially confirmed the basic outlines of my previous analysis and proposal. The hearings concluded with a report that accused "a cabal of zealots" in the Administration of supporting the contras despite Congressional prohibitions, and several former officials were indicted for conspiracy to defraud the government. But the pivotal event of the period was the signing of a peace plan by the five Central American Presidents on August 7. Proposed by Costa Rican President Oscar Arias, the plan offered an opening toward peace that the Central Americans struggled to widen.

With the most to lose by continued war, Nicaraguans moved toward peace, although not in a straight line and certainly not without reservations. For every two steps forward, the government and the contras seemed to take one step back and one step sideways. Nonetheless, on March 23, 1988, after two days of direct negotiations, the Nicaraguan government and the Resistance surprised the world by agreeing to a cease-fire and the beginning of a political dialogue. The agreement did not end the war or guarantee democracy; it only opened a door for Nicaraguans to continue their journey toward these goals.

The book has been reviewed by many magazines and newspapers, but as yet, no one has found any inaccuracies. Therefore, I have not changed the text, but I have added an "Epilogue" to review and analyze the important events in U.S.–Nicaraguan relations from May 1987 to April 1988.

April 1, 1988

Preface

MY FIRST CONTACT with Nicaragua was on a December morning in 1968, when I disembarked from a banana boat at the Caribbean port of El Bluff next to a small town called Bluefields. Most of the Nicaraguans were black and spoke English with West Indian accents. For a moment, I thought that during the days I had spent cleaning snakes out of the boat's hold, the boat had taken a wrong turn. It had not. Bluefields, inhabited by blacks and Miskito Indians and ruled indirectly by the British for more than a century, was the western part of the Caribbean but also the eastern part of Nicaragua. Tired of snakes and eager to see the country, I jumped ship.

A decade later, I found myself once again trying to avoid snakes in Nicaragua. This time, I was working on the National Security Council, and the United States was trying to find its way through Nicaragua's worst political crisis. The snakes were harder to find, but just as deadly. I was accused of being a dangerous leftist by Anastasio Somoza's press secretary and a "hawkish" cold warrior by the Cuban national press.

This book, however, is not about my journey. It is about the journey of two nations—the United States and Nicaragua—through the treacherous jungle of domestic and international politics. It is a story of how two nations have tried but failed to learn how to avoid being repeatedly bitten by the same snake.

The book is also a partial answer to a set of questions that I have carried back and forth with me between the university and the government. Questions of process: How is U.S. policy made? What accounts for the apparent repetition in U.S. policy in the Caribbean Basin? And questions of substance: Is it possible for a powerful, idealistic nation like the United States and small, poor nations on its periphery to establish fair and respectful relationships? Since I was a student, I have been attracted to Latin America and the Caribbean because it is the one region where, as Zbigniew Brzezinski put it, U.S. power and its commitment to principle most often collide. Is there not a way to integrate our ideals and our strategic concerns?

This work approaches that question indirectly, as it seeks to describe the formulation and impact of U.S. foreign policy toward Nicaragua; explain why the United States—and other governments and groups—have mismanaged the continuing crisis in Nicaragua; and, finally, offer some practical recommendations on how to address the current crisis and similar ones in the future.

After an introduction to the principal themes of the book, Chapters 2 and 3 describe the history of the U.S.–Nicaraguan relationship, the social and economic background to the revolution, and the different perspectives of its major protagonists. However, the thematic and substantive center of the book is Part II (Chapters 4-9), where the major decisions and events that occurred from 1977 to 1979 are discussed in detail. How did the Sandinistas come to power despite U.S. efforts? Part III (Chapters 10-13) describes the evolution of the U.S.–Nicaraguan relationship since Somoza's departure in July 1979.

Part IV (Chapters 14-16) steps back from the details to evaluate the whole. Chapter 14 recounts the seven stages of the U.S.–Nicaraguan relationship and offers an analysis and explanation for the policies and the mistakes. The question is not *who* lost Nicaragua but, rather, why has everyone associated with the tragedy of the last decade lost? Why did everyone's nightmare come true? In Chapter 15, I yield to the temptation of describing how it all could have been different and identify specific decisions at particular moments by different actors that could have produced a better outcome. In addition to rearranging the past, I offer an alternative U.S. policy toward Nicaragua and Central America for the future. Finally, in the last chapter, I suggest ways in which future succession crises and revolutions could be managed more effectively by the United States.

The United States has long been considered the determining political actor in Nicaragua, and this book emphasizes U.S. policy. Nonetheless, one of the work's conclusions is that neither the Nicaraguan revolution nor its subsequent radicalization can be explained solely by U.S. actions. The discussion therefore includes other important governments and groups—many of whose policies, interestingly enough, have also exhibited repetitive patterns.

In reconstructing the Nicaraguan case, I have two advantages. I was a witness to, and sometimes a participant in, the policy process, and I was granted access to review important classified government documents from the White House and the foreign policy agencies that are currently at the Carter Presidential Library. As the Director of Latin American and Caribbean Affairs on the National Security Council from 1977 to 1981, I am aware of all key government decisions during this period and was involved in most of them.

However, the advantage of having participated in making a policy often carries with it the disadvantage—from a scholarly standpoint—of having a stake in defending that policy. Although this book describes and explains the policy, it also tries to avoid defending it. This is neither a memoir nor an apologia for the Carter Administration's actions. Too often in memoirs, an Administration's successes tend to have occurred when the author's recommendations prevailed, and its mistakes have happened when the author's ideas were rejected. The hard choices that an Administration confronts are concealed from the reader. I have sought to avoid that syndrome by reconstructing as fairly as possible the options, debate, and choices made by the government and by taking a number of precautions to reduce the chance that this work would be a single or one-sided portrayal of the case. In particular, I have interviewed many of the key participants in the United States as well as in Nicaragua and elsewhere, and their perspectives are incorporated in what follows.

As one tries to reconstruct a specific event or an entire case, one encounters many truths or, rather, many partial truths. Statements made at the time may have been intended to serve a specific purpose other than to depict events or describe the speaker's real intention. For example, on September 1, 1978, both Somoza and the Sandinistas held separate press conferences. The Sandinistas accused the United States of sending mercenaries and CIA agents to prevent their victory; Somoza accused the United States of trying to overthrow him.[1] Newspapers tended to report one and discount the other, depending on their point of view. The purpose of both statements, however, was the same: to vent fears rather than to provide facts. Both were hoping their words would prove to be self-denying prophecies.

Another problem in reconstructing events is that most meetings and conversations are interpreted differently by the participants. In interviews as in memoirs, people usually remember events selectively and with the distorting prism of hindsight, which tends to reduce their role in failures and enhance it in successes. It is difficult to reconstruct an event even if one tries hard, and it is evident to the casual reader of books on Nicaragua that many authors do not try. For this book, I found government documents to be an essential foundation for the preparation of a chronology, which I then used both to jog the memory of participants and to ensure that they did not unintentionally revise events. (To assist the reader in following the narrative, a very brief chronology will be found on page 317, and a list of abbreviations on page 315.)

Readers will note an obvious difference in perspective and level of detail between my treatment of policy making during the Carter Administration and my examination of it in the Reagan Administration. That is partly because I have chosen to give more attention to the question of how to relate to a crisis of succession than how to relate to a revolution, but also, of course, because I did not have access to classified information or internal discussions during the Reagan Administration. This lack of firsthand knowledge has been somewhat offset by numerous interviews as well as by the large amount of classified material that has been disclosed, either intentionally or not, during the Reagan years.

Although this book is informed by the present, it seeks to avoid the illusion of inevitability, which only hindsight makes possible. From today's perspective, the overthrow of Somoza looks inevitable, and even in 1978, about a year before it occurred, the U.S. government thought it was probable. However, no one was certain when, or even whether, Somoza would fall. Four months before the triumph of the Sandinistas, as Venezuelan and Costa Rican support for them appeared to end, many observers predicted that Somoza had weathered the worst.[2] Reminiscent of Lenin's famous prediction in March 1917 that he would "probably not live to see the decisive battles of the revolution," Daniel Ortega has admitted that as late as July 1979, days before Somoza's departure, he doubted he would live to see the Sandinista victory.[3] Similarly, in examining the deterioration of U.S.–Nicaraguan relations after July 1979, I seek to explain why it occurred, but I do not believe this was at all inevitable.

Yogi Berra offered the best caveat against the temptation of asserting inevitability after the fact: "It ain't over till it's over." This book tries to recapture the uncertainty of the moment, which is the distinguishing characteristic of policy making.

Acknowledgments

BOTH BEFORE and after the Sandinista victory, Nicaragua has preoccupied me, as it has come to preoccupy many other North Americans, and just as we have always preoccupied Nicaraguans. I deliberately sought the distance of four years after the Sandinistas took power before beginning the research for this book. I needed another four years to write, revise, and rethink it. The facts of the case have remained the same, but I believe the additional time has deepened my understanding of them.

The author of a book with such a long gestation naturally accumulates numerous debts of gratitude. I could not have written it without the help of the many people whose interviews permitted me to understand dimensions of the case I missed the first time; they are listed at the end of the book. I am especially grateful to Jimmy Carter and Zbigniew Brzezinski, both of whom gave me the opportunity to see firsthand how and why policy is made, and who both, after leaving office, were so generous with their time and recollections. During the crisis, I admired Viron "Pete" Vaky, then Assistant Secretary of State, as he drew from vast reserves of patience and experience, but my appreciation for him grew as he read through this entire manuscript twice to ensure that it would represent the policy challenges faced by the U.S. government fairly and fully.

I consider myself especially fortunate to have scholarly friends who displayed no inhibition about slicing up previous drafts with rapier criticisms. Although not all of them will agree with the final product, I hope they all derive some satisfaction in recognizing how much better it is because of their efforts. Those who read and gave superb comments on the draft of the entire manuscript were Richard Ullman, Richard Millett, William LeoGrande, W. Anthony Lake, and David Ziegler. In addition, many people commented on individual chapters and sections: Jorge Domínguez, Richard Feinberg, Rodolfo Pastor, Joseph S. Nye, Jr., Robert Lieber, Jorge Castañeda, Carlos Rico, Rob Paarlberg, Manuel García y Griego, Cheryl Eschbach, and Carolyn Rose-Avila. I have benefited from competent and industrious research assistants over the years at the University of Maryland, El Colegio de Mexico, and Emory University: Charles Becker, Carola Weil, Frank Baitman, José Madrazo, and Francine Mizell. Leona Schecter's perseverance and the editorial skills of Sandy Thatcher and Elizabeth Gretz helped transform the manuscript into a book.

Donald Schewe, the Director of the Archives of the Carter Presidential Library, and Martin Elsey, his assistant, helped me locate important White House papers on Nicaragua. Brenda Reger, Director of the Office of Information Policy of the National Security Council, had the dubious honor of being the first to review the entire manuscript, and I am very grateful that she cleared it for you to read. I hope you will be as well.

I thank Austin Hoyt of Public Television in Boston (WGBH) for permitting me to read the transcripts of interviews that were done for the documentary he produced on Central America. Parts of the book also benefited from the State Department cables that have been declassified as a result of requests by Scott Armstrong and Peter Kornbluh of the National Security Archive.

My largest debt is to my wife Margy, whom I married in June 1979 as the Nicaraguan crisis was reaching a climax. It is hard for me to imagine writing this book without her encouragement, patience, and, most of all, her perceptive editorial judgment.

I completed the book as Congress began a Watergate-style investigation of the Iran–contra affair. The hearings began with the question of how the profits from the arms sale to Iran were diverted to support the contras, but the real questions at the center of the affair related to the causes of the war in Nicaragua and the nature of U.S. involvement. What led the Reagan Administration to support Nicaraguans trying to overthrow their government? Did the policies of the Carter Administration and its predecessors contribute to the current crisis? What alternatives exist for U.S. policy? This work responds to those questions.

THIS BOOK may be about the past, but it is for the future, and so I dedicate it with hope to my two children, Tiffin Margaret and Robert Kiplin.

June 1, 1987

Part I

SETTING THE STAGE

But don't you see that the whole trouble lies here.
In words, words. Each one of us has within him a
whole world of things, each man of us his own
special world. And how can we ever come to an
understanding if I put in the words I utter the
sense and value of things as I see them; while you
who listen to me must inevitably translate them
according to the conception of things each one of
you has within himself. We think we understand
each other, but we never really do.

**Luigi Pirandello, *Six Characters in Search
of an Author***

Chapter 1

DECLINING DICTATORS,

RISING REVOLUTIONS

> *'Revolution.'* In politics, an abrupt change in the form of
> misgovernment. Revolutions are usually accompanied by a
> considerable effusion of blood, but are accounted worth it—
> this appraisement being made by beneficiaries whose blood
> had not the mischance to be shed.
> **Ambrose Bierce, *The Devil's Dictionary***

"HE'S A SON of a bitch, but he's *our* son of a bitch." This comment
about Anastasio Somoza by President Franklin Roosevelt is widely
known and used.[1] The Somoza family referred to it—to show they
were tough, but their *partner*, the United States, was even tougher.
Moderate critics of U.S. foreign policy cite the remark to show the
myopia of a policy that supports right-wing dictators just because
they are anti-Communist. Radical critics of the United States use the
comment to show that U.S. assertions of idealism are hypocritical
and mask a hegemonic or imperialistic purpose. Latin Americans refer to it to show that they are different from Somoza; they are independent. The comment has been used by everyone to make so many
points that no one has bothered to find out whether it was actually
ever used by Franklin Roosevelt.

It probably wasn't. The first record of the statement is in a cover
article on Somoza in *Time* magazine on November 15, 1948—three
and a half years after Roosevelt died, and nine years after he was said
to have made the comment. Donald Schewe, an archivist who
worked at the FDR Library in Hyde Park for nine years, searched for
the citation but never found it. However, after reading through thousands of pages of Roosevelt's correspondence, press conferences, and
records, Schewe concluded "that was not the kind of language that
Roosevelt used."[2] "Son of a bitch" was, however, the kind of language that Somoza *always* used.[3]

Some have suggested that the essence of U.S.–Nicaraguan relations can be found in the words attributed to Roosevelt. The real clue
to the relationship, however, is in the way an apocryphal comment

has been used. Although few believed the many outrageous statements that the members of the Somoza family made, many wanted to believe this statement because it was comfortable. It reinforced two prevailing myths about the United States and of Somoza: Somoza existed *because of* the United States; the United States *prefers* vassals and right-wing dictators. Somoza enjoyed the remark because he viewed the myth as a source of power. The United States, hardly a victim, did not mind the comment when it supported Somoza, and could not dissociate from it when it did not.

Over time, as the Nicaraguan state developed, Somoza's myth backfired, antagonizing the nationalistic sensibilities of independent-minded people in Nicaragua and throughout Latin America. Indeed, the Sandinistas, who replaced Somoza, have chosen to use the mirror image of Somoza's myth—the United States as a hostile colossus—for the same purpose: to strengthen their regime. Instead of advertising U.S. friendship, the Sandinistas denounce U.S. imperialism in order to demonstrate their nationalist credentials and to attract youthful support.

"Nicaragua" and "the United States"—the ideas, not the nations—have often functioned as metaphors serving ulterior purposes. Among North Americans today, "Nicaragua" has become a metaphor for "Vietnam" or "Cuba," depending on one's political preferences, and to Nicaraguans, "the United States" represents either savior or Satan. Both nations, of course, are more complicated than these metaphors, and their relationship—the subject of this book—is even more so.

The Ghost of Cuba Past

On July 17, 1979, Anastasio Somoza Debayle* resigned from the Presidency of Nicaragua, and three days later, a new government led by the Sandinista National Liberation Front (FSLN, or Frente) took power. The Carter Administration had foreseen the possibility of a Sandinista victory about a year before it occurred. Viewing the key Sandinista military leaders as Marxist-Leninists who admired Cuba

---

*Spanish names have a second surname, which is the mother's family name. The patriarch of the Somozas was Anastasio Somoza García (1896-1956). García, his mother's name, will not be used, and sometimes he will be called Tacho I. He and his wife, Salvadora Debayle, had two sons, Luis Somoza Debayle (1923-67) and Anastasio Somoza Debayle (1925-80), who was also known as Anastasio Somoza, Jr., or Tacho II. His son is Anastasio Somoza Portacarrero (1951-   ) or Tacho III. In most cases, I will not use the maternal surname of Spanish names.

and despised the United States, the Administration aimed to preclude a military victory by the Sandinistas but not to support Somoza, who was seen as indefensible. Over the course of the year, a subcommittee of the National Security Council met nearly twenty-five times to formulate policies to facilitate a peaceful democratic transition in Nicaragua and thus avoid a violent takeover by the Sandinistas.

In the middle of the crisis, a group of young, well-groomed Americans arrived in Managua with a quiet determination to solve the conflict through transcendental meditation.[4] As it turned out, the U.S. government had about as much impact on the outcome of the Nicaraguan revolution as did this group.

How could that be? It was generally assumed by most Nicaraguans, ranging across the political spectrum from Somoza to the Sandinistas, that the United States was a crucial actor in Nicaraguan politics. While Nicaraguans were dying in Nicaragua, Somoza told reporters: "The battle is being fought in the U.S."[5] Most of those who have written about the Nicaraguan revolution share the assumption that the United States's role was decisive. If that was the case, why did it not prevent a Sandinista victory?

Two major critiques of U.S. policy answer that question, though their authors contradict each other in their description, interpretation, and judgment. Jeane Kirkpatrick, in two provocative essays written for *Commentary*, describes a consistent and deliberate policy by the Carter Administration "to weaken the government of Anastasio Somoza and to strengthen his opponents." Her judgment is that Carter's policy "brought down the Somoza regime."[6]

An alternative view is offered by William LeoGrande in an article in *Foreign Affairs*. He criticizes the policy for always being several steps behind events, as it "labored mightily . . . to prevent the accession of a Sandinista government in Nicaragua." LeoGrande, Tom Farer, Shirley Christian, and others who have written about U.S. policy and the Nicaraguan revolution reach a conclusion the opposite of Kirkpatrick's—that the Carter policy failed precisely because it *did not* try to bring Somoza down.[7]

Ironically, both sides agree that the Administration set an objective—in the first case, to bring down Somoza; in the second case, not to overthrow him—and achieved that objective, even though it was mistaken.

Analysts also differ on the causes of the policy failure. Whereas Kirkpatrick suggests that the Carter Administration was insufficiently alert to the Communist involvement in the Nicaraguan opposition, Richard Fagen writes that the policy failed for the opposite reason—that the Administration's "twisted perceptions . . . [of a] Cuba–Sandinista connection" prevented it from taking the actions necessary to topple Somoza.[8] William LeoGrande also attributes the failure to misperception: "the fear of 'another Cuba,' and the questionable conviction that the radical opposition was intent on creating one."[9]

LeoGrande is correct that the Carter Administration feared "another Cuba," and that this concern influenced policy. Despite it, however, the Nicaraguan revolution evolved in ways that were strikingly reminiscent of the Cuban revolution twenty years before. Both revolutions were propelled by broad-based opposition to long-standing dictators who were not only despised by their own citizens but by much of the international community. Rather than oppose the revolution, the middle class and the business community in both countries played leading roles, first in organizing general strikes, then in waiting for the United States to find a solution, and finally in ignoring U.S. advice and supporting the rebels. The United States deliberately withdrew support from the dictators and searched in vain for a middle, democratic option. Democratic leaders in Costa Rica and Venezuela passed arms covertly to rebel leaders in both cases.

In their memoirs, which were written for a North American, English-speaking audience, both dictators blamed the United States rather than themselves for their fall. A sense of *déjà vu* is perhaps most vividly conveyed, however, in the titles of those memoirs: *Cuba Betrayed* by Fulgencio Batista, and *Nicaragua Betrayed* by Anastasio Somoza, Jr.[10]

After the Sandinista triumph, many leaders—including even Fidel Castro—expressed their hope that Nicaragua would not become another Cuba.[11] In Nicaragua and throughout the region, most hoped that the United States would support the revolution rather than confront it, and that is what the United States did at the beginning. But within eighteen months, the United States stopped supporting the Nicaraguan government and, one year after that, was financing a covert war to overthrow it. In the same period, the Sandinista government accelerated its revolution and became more dependent on Cuba and the Soviet bloc for military and economic aid.

On June 8, 1986, outside the White House, an estimated crowd of about 2,000 people, mostly Cuban-Americans, listened and cheered Reagan Administration officials who demanded more aid for Nicaraguan contras trying to overthrow the Sandinista government in a program that increasingly resembled the Bay of Pigs invasion of Cuba. One speaker read a personal message from Ronald Reagan, who promised: "There shall be no more Cubas in our hemisphere."[12]

Despite Castro's advice and Reagan's best effort, Nicaragua, while not Cuba, resembled it more at that time than in any previous year.

The most fascinating and puzzling aspect of the Nicaraguan story was that all the key leaders in the United States, Nicaragua, and the neighboring countries were not simply aware of the Cuban events; they were preoccupied with the parallels. With the exception of Castro and the Sandinistas, they kept reminding each other during the revolution to avoid repeating the mistakes made in Cuba two decades before. "Those who cannot remember the past," George Santayana wrote in a much-quoted sentence, "are condemned to repeat it."[13] In the case of Nicaragua, however, the actors remembered the outlines, if not the details, of the history, and yet they could not avoid repeating it. This was not only true of the United States, but of Venezuela, Costa Rica, the middle-class leadership in Nicaragua, and especially Anastasio Somoza.

The Cuban Drama in Seven Stages

What images of Cuba did decision makers have in mind as they addressed the Nicaraguan crisis? In the first two decades of this century, the United States intervened militarily in Cuba, Nicaragua, and several other countries in the region. By the late 1920s, however, at the height of its global power, the United States turned inward and withdrew not just from Europe but even from the Caribbean Basin. By the mid-1930s, U.S. intervention had been replaced with a rigid noninterventionism. Few in the region understood the change or thought it would last.

When the President of Cuba, Gerardo Machado, changed the constitution to permit his reelection in May 1929, many Cubans asked the United States to force Machado to resign. Secretary of State Henry Stimson rejected the request, saying: "It would be a very serious intervention for us to advise the President of Cuba to resign." Although Havana remained the victim of terrorism and bombings, President Franklin Roosevelt made the same point when he came into office: "Certainly, we cannot be in a position of saying to Machado, 'you have to get out.' That would be obvious interference in the internal affairs of another nation."[14]

Roosevelt rejected two requests by Ambassador Sumner Welles to intervene, but Welles continued to pressure Machado and conspire with the military, and on August 12, 1933, Machado left Cuba. The immediate effect was a period of instability and a political vacuum, which was filled by Sergeant Fulgencio Batista. Batista became Chief of the Army and ruled from behind the scenes until his election as President in 1940. By then, the United States was prepared to over-look the dictatorship because of the stability he brought to Cuba dur-ing a time of world war.

Batista relinquished power at the end of his term in 1944, but in 1952, he ran for President again. Behind in the polls, Batista staged a military coup in March of that year. On July 26, 1953, Fidel Castro led a group in a futile attempt to overthrow Batista.

Castro was imprisoned, but Batista permitted him to leave the country.[15] By Christmas of 1956, however, he returned to Cuba and, with twenty followers, had launched his revolution in the moun-tains of the Sierra Maestra. U.S.–Cuban relations then passed through seven stages.

1. IDENTIFICATION. U.S. Ambassador Arthur Gardner (1953-57) was effusive in his praise of Batista, and in the first stop of a Latin American tour, Vice President Richard Nixon reinforced the impres-sion that the United States stood firmly behind the dictator. The op-position to Batista therefore tended to identify the United States with the dictator, although at the same time it tried to persuade the United States to change its position.

In order to be recognized among all the opposition groups, Castro had an interview arranged for him with Herbert Matthews of the *New York Times* in February 1957 in the mountains. Awed by Castro and by what he thought was a band of about 200 (although it actually numbered 18 at the time), Matthews wrote a series of articles that made Castro an international figure. On July 12, 1957, Castro issued a manifesto calling for free elections, agrarian reform, a constitu-tional government, and an end to all forms of foreign intervention.

2. DISTANCE AND DISSOCIATION. The State Department was increasingly worried about the deterioration in Cuba and attributed it to Batista. The United States pressured him to hold free elections in 1958, hoping that they would provide an escape valve for the po-litical pressures that were building. Earl Smith, an investment banker, arrived as the new U.S. Ambassador in mid-July, and he made a good impression in the country by criticizing "excessive police ac-tion."[16]

The Catholic Church also contributed to Batista's isolation. On March 1, 1958, Cuban bishops called for an investigation of the re-gime's brutality and asked Batista to step down in favor of a govern-ment of national unity. The statement influenced public opinion against Batista in the United States, forcing the U.S. government to reevaluate its military aid program. On April 8, 1958, Secretary of State John Foster Dulles announced an arms embargo against Batista, saying: "We don't like to have them [arms] go where the purpose is to conduct a civil war."[17] This was the clearest sign of U.S. dissociation from Batista. Hugh Thomas described the State Department's dilemma: "As democrats, they would have liked an alternative to Castro as a successor to Batista; but hostile to the idea of intervention, they shrank from any positive action to unseat Batista. The arms embargo seemed then the most positive form of negative action."[18]

3. THE LEFT LEGITIMIZED BY THE MIDDLE. Castro announced a general strike on April 9, 1958, and although it failed to unseat Batista, it added to his image as the center of the opposition. On July 20, 1958, representatives of all the opposition groups, including Castro's 26th of July, signed an agreement in Caracas—the "Caracas Pact"—which named an opposition government, with a moderate judge as president and Castro as commander-in-chief.

The Caracas statement represented a decisive shift in the balance of power within Cuba, as many in the middle class aligned with Castro. The Venezuelan site was as important as the message, because it connoted a new alignment of Latin American democratic forces behind Castro. Just six months before, Venezuelan dictator Marcos Pérez Jiménez had been overthrown, and the country was eager to demonstrate its solidarity with other democratic movements. Several democratic leaders from the region had already given covert support to Castro. José Figueres, Costa Rica's President, sent him a planeload of arms on March 30, 1958, and Carlos Andrés Pérez, who would become President of Venezuela during the Nicaraguan crisis, noted that, on behalf of Acción Democrática, he sent arms to Cuba as well.[19] Figueres later explained why Castro received so much help from democrats in the region:

> I helped Fidel Castro as much as I could because what was involved was the overthrow of a military dictatorship. . . . In the U.S., there's not enough knowledge of the fact that in Latin America for a long time, we have been trying to gather forces to establish a uniform political system based on the electoral system. . . . We were completely willing to help overthrow all military dictatorships. We didn't know, and I think nobody knows, what were Fidel Castro's ideas regarding Communism at the time.[20]

Batista could not fail to recognize his international isolation and, using a psychological tactic familiar to the Somozas, he tried to change U.S. policy by blaming the United States for helping the rebels. Castro used the same tactic in reverse; he condemned the Eisenhower Administration for remaining too committed to Batista.[21]

4. THE SEARCH FOR A THIRD FORCE. The hope that Cuba's elections of November 1958 would offer an exit from the instability proved empty. Most of the opposition leaders refused to participate, and the results were manipulated by Batista. In late November 1958, senior officials in the Eisenhower Administration, realizing that time for finding an alternative to Castro was growing short, asked William Pawley, an American businessman with experience in Latin America, to undertake a secret mission. Pawley said its purpose was to "get Batista to capitulate to a caretaker government, unfriendly to him but satisfactory to us, whom we would immediately recognize and give military assistance to in order that Fidel Castro should not come to power."[22] Pawley went to Havana and proposed that Batista transfer power to a provisional government involving Colonel Ramón Barquín, who was in prison for having led an unsuccessful coup against Batista in 1956. Batista refused, saying to an aide that he was inclined to "kick out this Pawley."[23]

In the last month before Batista fled, the Eisenhower Administration desperately sought to locate and support a "third force." Batista too realized his end was near, but tried to pretend that it was not, lest his own armed forces overthrow and kill him. The CIA wanted to get Barquín released and to link him with Justo Carrillo and other moderate civilians. Castro, wary of these plots, was concerned that the replacement of Batista by someone credible and independent like Barquín could bring a premature halt to his revolution. But Castro was saved by Batista. On New Year's Eve, 1958, Batista fled after handing power to one of his staff, General Eulogio Cantillo.

Cantillo decided it was futile to hold the Army together, and he handed power to Barquín, who had just been released from prison. Barquín then surprised everyone by telephoning Castro and surrendering the Army, giving up "what chance there was of a government of the center," according to Hugh Thomas.[24] The Cuban military disintegrated in a matter of days.

5. RELATING TO THE REVOLUTION. The United States recognized the revolution, but both the Eisenhower Administration and Castro had ample grounds for suspecting each other's motives. Castro knew that the United States had desperately tried to keep him

from power, and the United States suspected that Castro's support for elections and the 1940 constitution concealed a more radical proclivity. Castro knew the power the United States had exercised in Cuba through nearly $2 billion of investments, and the United States could not doubt Castro's enormous popularity. Ambassador Smith was replaced with a liberal-minded professional, Philip Bonsal. The new Ambassador sought to meet with Castro to develop a good relationship, but Castro did not want to appear to be like other Cuban leaders who took their orders from the U.S. Embassy, and he kept his distance.

Castro traveled to the United States in April 1959 at the invitation of the American Society of Newspaper Editors. Eisenhower decided to leave Washington, believing it would be more appropriate for Castro to meet with Vice President Nixon and Secretary of State Christian Herter. The United States was prepared to discuss aid to Cuba if Castro raised the issue, but he did not. Both sides tested the other, and both received poor grades.

Castro's revolution did not stop for breath. In March, he decreed a sweeping land reform law, lowered rents by 50 percent, denounced the United States, and nationalized the Cuban Telephone Company, which had been owned by Americans. By the fall, moderates within the government were replaced by radicals, and the independent revolutionary leader Hubert Matos was imprisoned. Castro's denunciations of the United States as Cuba's enemy increased in number and virulence.

6. DISTANCE AND NEGOTIATION.   Bonsal continued to counsel caution, but another group in the Administration, led by Richard Nixon, urged a tougher approach so that other Latin Americans would not think the United States could be defied with impunity. Castro's own actions served to strengthen Nixon's arguments, and Nixon undoubtedly offered Castro a persuasive example that the United States was unwilling to accept the Cuban revolution. Nonetheless, in January 1960, Bonsal persuaded President Eisenhower to issue a statement that was both firm and conciliatory, urging Castro to begin talks with the United States and negotiate differences. Cuba accepted the offer in principle but continually delayed the talks. In the meantime, Castro hosted the visit of Soviet First Deputy Premier Anastas Mikoyan. And on March 4, 1960, Castro accused the United States of blowing up a French ship in the Havana harbor.

7. CONFRONTATION.   The United States expressed shock at the charge, which it denied, but two weeks later, Eisenhower secretly au-

thorized the Central Intelligence Agency to begin recruiting Cuban exiles for a possible attempt to overthrow Castro. Reports of CIA recruiting soon reached Castro, who responded by improving his nation's defenses, expanding the Army, and denouncing the United States.

Each action provoked a reaction by the other. In June 1960, after U.S. oil companies refused to refine Soviet oil, Cuba nationalized them. The United States then cut Cuba's sugar quota, and Cuba responded by increasing its sugar sales to the Soviet bloc and nationalizing most of the U.S. property in Cuba. Finally, on January 2, 1961, Cuba insisted that the United States reduce the size of its embassy, and Eisenhower, in one of the last acts of his Administration, responded by closing it. Three months later, the United States sponsored an unsuccessful invasion of more than 1,000 Cuban exiles at the Bay of Pigs. By the end of 1961, Castro had declared himself a Marxist-Leninist.

After the Cuban missile crisis in October 1962 brought the world to the brink of nuclear disaster, Cuba deepened its relationship with the Soviet Union and created a one-party Communist state. The United States continued to try to undermine the revolution, but with little effect. The worst fears and suspicions of both sides, however, continued to be confirmed, having achieved, in the words of one analyst, "a self-perpetuating momentum."[25]

All the participants in the Nicaraguan drama twenty years later continuously reminded each other of this history.[26] Needless to say, few if any of the key actors either knew or remembered the details, but the outline of what had happened was imprinted in their consciousness. And three men—Carlos Andrés Pérez, José Figueres, and Fidel Castro—did recall many details, since they were involved in both episodes.

Insurrection and Revolution: Separate Challenges

If U.S. policy appears repetitive, so too are the questions that the public asks: Why can't the United States live with Latin American revolutions? How can events in such small countries affect U.S. national security?[27] These questions are not unique to Cuba and Nicaragua. The United States has wrestled or is wrestling with similar problems of declining dictators and rising revolutions in the Dominican Republic, Haiti, Vietnam, the Philippines, Chile, and, in a sense, South Africa. Answers to these questions have proven unsatisfactory, however, and a consensus has been elusive. Perhaps the time has come to inquire whether these are the right questions.

The answer is that these questions do *not* help us to understand the patterns or the ineffectiveness of U.S. policies. Part of the confusion stems from a misunderstanding of the word "revolution." Walter LaFeber describes "revolutions" as "virtually the only method of transferring power" in Central America, and thus comparable to elections in the United States.[28] LaFeber's thesis is that the United States fears and resists all revolutions, but his definition would include every coup d'état in the region—most of which the United States accepted, and some of which it encouraged.

An alternative definition of revolution is a purposive, violent, and fundamental change in society in which power is transferred across social classes, or rather from one elite, representing the middle or upper class, to another, oriented toward a lower class.[29] An insurrection, by contrast, is a major uprising against political authority by many diverse groups, including, for example, businessmen and revolutionaries.

The distinction between insurrections and revolutions is significant because each poses a different challenge for U.S. policy makers. The first—insurrection—is by far the more difficult and common problem. Essentially, insurrections are born as crises of political succession. Political violence is endemic when there are no clear, legitimate, and acceptable procedures for transferring power in a country, and, of course, this has been the norm for most of Latin America in the last century. Most often, the change is quick—a coup d'état in which one ruling faction ousts another.

Though some have suggested that revolutions are inevitable, in fact they are exceptional, occurring in only three countries in Latin America in the last fifty years. And it is significant that all three great Latin American revolutions—in Mexico, Cuba, and Nicaragua—began as crises of political succession and only succeeded because virtually the entire nation agreed that the problem was the dictator. Moreover, the thesis that the United States and its "bourgeois lackeys" reflexively resist revolutions is disproven in these three cases, which succeeded in large part because the middle class supported and legitimized the revolt and because the United States did not forcefully resist it.[30]

It is true, however, that the United States has tried to prevent Marxist-Leninist revolutionaries—or groups perceived as such—from seizing power. This is because once such a group takes power, it can legally invite a powerful, hostile government to defend it (or expand its influence). If such groups define the United States as their implacable enemy and the Soviet Union and Cuba as their friends, the probability is that they will seek a military relationship with the Soviet Union for defense against U.S. imperialism.[31] The U.S. government has long believed that its influence is greater, and the risks to world peace fewer, in preventing a hostile group from coming to power than in preventing a hostile government from asking the Soviet Union for help. Problems arise when the hostile group either disguises its intentions or has diverse, complicated, or obscure goals.

During a succession crisis, the main challenge and preoccupation of U.S. policy makers is not with the revolutionaries but with the incumbent dictator. The problem is not managing revolutionary change but, rather, trying to promote a negotiating process between parties that refuse to talk with one another.

If the revolutionaries come to power, as they have done in Cuba and Nicaragua, policymakers face a different challenge: how to promote U.S. interests to a regime that views the United States as opposed to its principal goals. But here again, in the cases of both Cuba and Nicaragua, the United States did not reflexively resist the new revolutionary government.[32] In Nicaragua, the United States was the major financial supporter of the revolution in its first stage. U.S. support did not end because of Nicaragua's internal policies but rather because of Nicaragua's support for international subversion.

The Thesis in Brief

One purpose of this study is to explain why the Nicaraguan revolution occurred, why it was radicalized, and why the United States and other actors repeated much the same unsuccessful policies that each had pursued twenty years before in Cuba. Each question has its answer, but the thread that connects the answers is that mistrust between the United States and its friends—an attitude born of different histories, interests, and perceptions—undermined their common objectives.

One reason for the Sandinista victory is that many thought the United States would prevent it, but no one acted on that assumption. All the key actors in the region thought the United States could control everyone else's behavior—except their own. The United States was perceived to be at the center of events, but that was an illusion—to which even the United States fell victim.

Although much of the literature on the Nicaraguan revolution views the United States as the actor and Nicaragua as the object, a much more complicated interaction occurred. The United States was at the center of the region's consciousness, but Nicaraguans always remained at the center of events. Though the United States is vastly more powerful than the nations of Central America, one should not assume that such power automatically translates into influence or control. Indeed, such power is sometimes reversible, with leaders or groups in the region using the United States to further their own political or economic ends, while ignoring U.S. attempts to influence them.

Some have found this role reversal difficult to interpret. For example, in summarizing U.S.–Nicaraguan relations over a forty-year period, one historian concluded: "As every President after Hoover knew, [the] Somozas did as they were told."[33] It is true that in order to strengthen their internal position, the Somozas cultivated the myth that they were working for the United States, but it was only a myth. The Somozas were no one's fools or servants. They cooperated with the United States only when it was in their interest to do so. To understand the revolution, one must begin by recognizing that the United States is only one of many actors.

The roots of the revolution's radicalization were in the minds of the Sandinista and North American leaders. The different histories and deep suspicions each had of the other led each to perceive defensive actions as provocative ones. Both sides made policies that consistently evoked the worst in the other.

The repetitive policies of each of the actors also grew out of their national experience—each nation's history and political culture. For each nation, there was continuity—repetition—in many of the policies, but there were also some important changes over time, due in part to different leaders with markedly different perceptions of the nature and intensity of the threat to their national interests.

The clue for understanding both the mistakes of the past and the possibilities for the future lies at the *intersection* of U.S. and Latin American policies. The psychological baggage that both sides have brought to the relationship has distorted visions so much that it is a wonder there have not been more accidents and tragedies. By analyzing the Nicaraguan case, I hope to explain the origins of the psychological divergence and how it has affected relationships. By keeping U.S. policy at the center of this book, I shall try to show how it actually works and why that does not always matter.

Chapter 2

A FRACTURED HISTORY

Peaceful changes between different factions of the ruling classes, which have been rather frequent in other Latin American countries, have not taken place in Nicaragua. This traditional experience predisposed the Nicaraguan people against electoral farces and in favor of armed struggle. There is no doubt, then, that the Nicaraguan people have a rich tradition of rebellion.[1]

Carlos Fonseca Amador

The Subterranean Rhythm

ON A NARROW ISTHMUS between the world's two great oceans, Nicaragua and its Central American neighbors share a geopolitical burden worthy of Job. Not only does the Isthmus hold together two large and proud continents that sometimes appear to move in opposite directions, but it does this while being squeezed between two tectonic plates. The seismic pressures created as these two plates rub against each other turn rock into magma and ignite gases that search for vents or weaknesses in the earth's crust. Not just life but also the earth itself is hard in the Isthmus, and there are few vents to permit the gradual release of the pressure. The result is volcanic eruptions or earthquakes of great severity. Nicaragua alone has been jolted in 1885, 1931, and 1972.

By some metaphysical law, Nicaraguan politics have conformed to nature's tantrums. Like its geology, its politics have been irregular, impulsive, and often explosive. Changes are more appropriately measured on the Richter scale than by election results. A survey of the history of Nicaragua reveals a tragic chronicle of a people compelled to adapt to natural and political disasters.

The Spanish, who arrived in 1522, left an unequaled legacy of exploitation and cruelty. Of the nearly one million Indians estimated to be in the area now known as Nicaragua, Conquistador Gil González de Avila and his successors converted about 30,000 to Catholicism and sent nearly 500,000 to other parts of the empire as slaves. Diseases took their toll on those who survived the wars, poverty, and slavery. The little gold that Nicaragua yielded was shipped to Spain.[2]

Nearly three hundred years later, as the region emerged from colonialism, the population of Nicaragua was approximately 200,000, still less than one-fifth the precolonial level. With the exception of a limited trade in indigo and cacao (chocolate), the economy, according to one scholar, was "static," the Spanish being uninterested in development.[3] There were hardly any schools and few roads. The little wealth created by the primitive economies was concentrated in the hands of a few families, and the region had no experience with democracy and little with self-government.

In 1821, Agustín Iturbide, the Mexican who declared himself Emperor, proclaimed independence for New Spain (Mexico and Central America) from old Spain. At the same time, on behalf of Central America, the Captain-General in Guatemala City declared independence from *both* the old and the new Spain. Only when colonialism became a chapter in the region's history did its single virtue become apparent: it had kept small, fragile political entities like those in Central America united. Independence in the early nineteenth century brought continual military struggles among families, cities, and the nations of Central America. Many of the conflicts were connected.

Within Nicaragua, two political parties emerged to represent the interests of a few families in two cities: Liberals from León and Conservatives from Granada. Initially, the parties had distinguishable philosophies reflecting the different economic interests of the two towns: León more commercial and open-minded and Granada more agricultural, clerical, and orthodox. (The labels remained in the twentieth century long after the philosophical differences had eroded.) Each town sought an international ally, with León looking to Mexico and Granada seeking help from Guatemala.

In 1823, before he could unite the region under Mexican hegemony, Emperor Agustín was overthrown. With Guatemalan leadership, Central America established a federation, but it was so loose that each state remained "sovereign," and the President of Central America was denied the power to enforce compliance with the government's statutes. The federation formally dissolved on May 30, 1838, but the "idea" of Central America persisted with an ironically perverse effect: it has tempted powerful leaders in one nation to overthrow neighboring governments in the name of unity. The result has been more fragmentation and instability.

Within Nicaragua between 1824 and 1842, Conservatives and Liberals fought seventeen major battles, and power changed hands eighteen times.[4] In 1845, Nicaragua's Conservatives, aided by Conservative leaders from El Salvador and Honduras and led by Fruto

Chamorro, the great-grandfather of Pedro Joaquín Chamorro, defeated the Liberals, led by Bernabé Somoza, the great-uncle of Anastasio Somoza García. Somoza had received some help from Liberals
in other Central American countries, and had requested aid from the
United States, which denied it because he was considered "a noto-
rious bandit."[5] In 1851, after sacking each other's capitals several
times, the Conservatives and the Liberals finally compromised on a
new capital, Managua, which was about half the distance between
León and Granada.

U.S. interest in the region until then had been marginal and sporadic. With the end of the U.S.–Mexican war in 1848 and the discovery of gold in California the same year, however, there was a resur-
gence of interest in the Isthmus as a transit between the two oceans.
The United States had previously acquiesced in the expansion of
British influence on the eastern (Mosquito) coast of Central America,
but in 1850, with the signing of the Clayton-Bulwer Treaty, the
United States insisted on equal access to the Isthmus. Great Britain
and the United States agreed that any future isthmian railway or
canal would be jointly controlled and neutral and would charge the
same tolls for ships from both countries. The treaty was symbolically
important for two reasons: first, no Central American nation signed
it or was even consulted; and second, the most powerful nation in the
world at the time accepted parity in Central America with the
United States.[6]

With the Isthmus secured, Cornelius Vanderbilt developed a
transit route across Nicaragua in 1851, using a stagecoach and
steamer. The U.S. government was too preoccupied with the sec-
tional feud that would soon tear apart the Union to become involved
in Nicaragua's internecine disputes, but this did not deter individual
Americans.

One such adventurer, or "filibuster," to use the term of the times,
was William Walker, a Tennessean who was small in stature but possessed a towering ambition. In 1855, the Liberals invited him to Nicaragua to help defeat the Conservatives. The U.S. government actively tried to discourage filibusters, and President Franklin Pierce
issued a proclamation specifically aimed at Walker, which directed
Americans not to join him in Nicaragua.[7]

Walker and fifty-seven American soldiers of fortune ignored the
warning. Together they quickly defeated the Conservatives and
burned their capital in Granada. Walker allowed a Liberal leader to
function as a nominal president for a short time while he kept control of the Army. Then, in July 1856, he named himself President of
Nicaragua, legalized slavery, and made English the official language.

To the surprise of many Nicaraguans and other Central Americans, who viewed Walker as a Trojan horse for U.S. imperialism, the State Department reprimanded the U.S. Minister to Managua, who had recognized Walker's government, and the United States officially withdrew recognition. When Walker sent a representative to Washington to seek recognition and support, Secretary of State William Marcy refused to see him.[8]

Yet Walker stirred deep and contradictory feelings in the United States on the divisive issues of slavery and manifest destiny. One year later, in a weak position politically, Pierce tried to gain Southern support for his renomination by recognizing the Walker government. After the Democratic convention passed him over, he again withdrew recognition.[9]

If Walker divided the United States, he succeeded in unifying both the Conservative and Liberal parties against him, a feat not duplicated in Nicaraguan history until the 1980s. Moreover, by seizing Vanderbilt's transit company, he made a formidable foreign enemy. With the support of the British, the combined armies of all the countries of Central America, and Vanderbilt's financial assistance, the Nicaraguans drove Walker out of the country in 1857. (When he returned in 1860, he was captured by the British, who delivered him to the Hondurans to be executed.)

The experience with Walker and the fear that Costa Rica might exploit Nicaragua's weakness to occupy the southern part of the country provided a stimulus for Nicaragua's two parties to declare a truce and jointly rule while drafting a new constitution. In August 1858 Nicaragua became a republic, with a president elected for a single, four-year term and a bicameral legislature. Because the Liberals were discredited by having invited Walker, the Conservative Tomás Martínez captured the Presidency.

The Conservatives were able to stay in power for thirty-five years because the party developed a system to rotate its leaders. When the Conservatives divided in 1893, however, the Liberals quickly seized the opportunity. José Santos Zelaya, a Liberal from León, took power. By rewriting the constitution, he was "reelected" twice and served sixteen years.

During these fifty years of Conservative and then Liberal rule, only the forms of democracy were maintained. The opposition was ignored or suppressed, and elections were rigged. Still, these were years of relative peace, and particularly under the Liberal Party rule of Zelaya, Nicaragua began to modernize and develop. A railroad was built connecting the major cities in the western part of the country; some agricultural diversification occurred; and the number of schools was increased and their quality improved. However, compared to the other countries of Central America, Nicaragua received little foreign investment and made little economic progress.[10]

Zelaya modernized the Army and established a military academy, staffed by a German captain, a Nicaraguan colonel, and several Chilean officers.[11] Shortly after taking power, Zelaya assisted a group of Honduran Liberals to take power there. Later, he tried to replicate his success in other Central American countries as well as in Colombia and Ecuador, but he failed.[12] Nevertheless, Zelaya transformed Nicaragua into the premier military power in Central America for the first time in its history.

U.S. Entry into the Caribbean

By the end of the nineteenth century, the U.S. frontier had been reached, and North Americans, exuding the confidence and strength of a new, world-class power, sought new areas for expansion. A rebellion in Cuba provided the perfect opportunity to both defeat a European nation and serve a just cause—independence for a neighbor.

After the war with Spain, the United States turned its attention to excluding other powers from the Isthmus and building a canal. U.S. and Nicaraguan interests coincided in expelling Great Britain from the Mosquito Coast. For this, Zelaya expressed his gratitude to the United States as the "natural protector of all the small Republics of the Americas."[13] Next, the United States negotiated the Hay-Pauncefote Treaty of 1902 with Great Britain, which granted the United States the unilateral right to construct and defend an isthmian canal. The Clayton-Bulwer Treaty, which was repealed, had recognized a balance of power fifty years before; the new treaty was "the token of Great Britain's real decision to leave to the United States mastery of its own continental life-line."[14]

After the United States selected Panama to build a canal, however, the relationship with Nicaragua deteriorated. It grew worse in 1907 when Zelaya invaded Honduras, replaced its President, and prepared to invade El Salvador.

Whereas internal instability and cross-border intervention in the region was hardly noticed by the United States in the nineteenth century, it generated profound disquiet and occasionally direct military action by the United States in the twentieth. The area had not changed; the reach and the investment of the United States had. The most important investment, of course, was the Panama Canal. The U.S. concern with stability in the Caribbean Basin was especially pronounced in Nicaragua, because it was chronically unstable and because it offered the only alternative canal route to that of Panama.

Nonetheless, Theodore Roosevelt, whose famous corollary to the Monroe Doctrine justified U.S. intervention in the Caribbean, preferred a different approach in Central America. He joined with the President of Mexico in inviting all five Central American governments to a peace conference in Washington, beginning on November 14, 1907, to negotiate treaties to resolve the region's disputes. Although the participants failed to rejuvenate a Central American federation, all parties did agree to a ten-year Treaty of Peace and Amity and to seven conventions, including one establishing a Central American court of justice with compulsory jurisdiction and another denying recognition to any government that came to power by violent means. All parties also obligated themselves to prevent the use of their territory as a base for the organization of revolutionary movements against other Central American states. By the middle of 1908, all the conventions were ratified. Implementing them was another matter.[15]

The Washington conference did not affect Zelaya's ambitions or behavior any more than it inhibited the United States. In addition to threatening his neighbors and forcing U.S. companies to renegotiate their concessions, Zelaya also contracted with a German company to build a railroad to the Atlantic and was reported to have opened separate negotiations with Japan and Great Britain for a new canal.[16] The United States was therefore pleased when the Conservatives launched a revolution in October 1909 in Bluefields (on the Atlantic coast). The revolution, which was financed by U.S. companies and other Central American governments, recruited the governor of the province, General Juan Estrada, as its leader. The U.S. government did not take an official position on the revolution, but it viewed the uprising sympathetically.

Zelaya quickly dispatched troops to the eastern coast, and the rebels, who were outnumbered, sought U.S. intervention. Under the guise of protecting American citizens in Bluefields, 400 Marines landed.[17] General Estrada was mistakenly encouraged by the arrival of the Americans, and he led his army to defeat against Zelaya's. Estrada then retreated to Bluefields and Marine protection, but not before two of his North American demolition experts were captured and executed by Zelaya's troops.

U.S. public opinion was outraged by the executions. The State Department condemned Zelaya's regime as "a blot upon the history of Nicaragua" and broke diplomatic relations. Zelaya succumbed to the pressure on December 16, 1909, when he tendered his resignation to eliminate a "pretext" for U.S. intervention.[18] This would not be the last Nicaraguan government the United States would overthrow, but it was the first. Twenty years later, a correspondent for the *New York Times* noted: "In 1909, the U.S. took a bear by the tail, and it has never been able to let it go. . . . Once in, [the United States] found that it could not get out. It tried to get out, and disaster struck Nicaragua, and dragged it in again."[19] The United States had become the arbiter of Nicaraguan politics.

The Nicaraguan Congress selected one of Zelaya's men, José Madriz, as President, but he was unsatisfactory to the United States, which withheld recognition until the rebels overthrew him. The new government of Juan Estrada was born with serious defects, not the least of which was that it enjoyed little, if any, popular support. The Liberals opposed the government, and so too did many Conservative generals, who considered themselves better qualified for the Presidency than either Estrada or his Vice President, Adolfo Díaz. As a result, the United States was pulled deeper and deeper into the details of constructing a stable and solvent government. This, in turn, caused the Nicaraguans, alternately to rely on the United States and to resent and resist it. Rebellions by Conservative and Liberal generals increased in number and scope.[20]

By August 1912, Díaz, who had replaced Estrada as President, found himself so weak that he requested military support from the United States. Marines landed at Corinto on the Pacific side and at Bluefields on the Atlantic. With the exception of an eighteen-month period (August 1925–January 1927) when the Marines left Nicaragua, the intervention of 1912 lasted until January 1933. In the first phase, the United States used 2,700 troops and defeated the rebels by October 1912. The United States then withdrew all but 100 men, which was still a sufficient force to deter the Liberals from trying to overthrow the government. In defending the Conservatives from 1912 to 1925, however, the United States was accused of using them as surrogates, and they were accused of being puppets.

To build a secure economic foundation for political stability, the United States organized the nation's finances, supervised the budget expenditures, and collected customs revenues.[21] U.S. banks managed the Nicaraguan railroad and national bank and nominated the collector general of the customs, subject to the State Department's approval.[22] An extended period of political stability permitted investment and some economic growth, and by 1920, the Nicaraguan government had paid off some of its international debt.

In 1921, though it was the most powerful nation in the world, the United States decided against joining the League of Nations and decided to withdraw its military forces from most of the Caribbean area. The challenge for U.S. policy in Nicaragua, according to the State Department, was "to create a situation where the legation guard [the Marines] could be safely withdrawn" without provoking another revolution.[23] The department judged that this objective could only be achieved by a government with broad support, and that the only way to find such a government would be in a free Presidential election in 1924. The United States persuaded the Nicaraguan government to employ Harold Dodds of Princeton University to draft a new electoral law. Dodds did so, but he insisted that outside supervision by the United States was necessary to guarantee a free election. Nicaragua rejected that stipulation.

A coalition ticket with a Conservative, Carlos Solórzano, as President and a Liberal, Juan Sacasa, as Vice President won a fraudulent election, and the two were inaugurated on January 1, 1925. Solórzano asked the Marines to stay, but President Calvin Coolidge was determined to bring them home, and he did so on August 1, 1925. Within one month, the government coalition began to come apart, and within a year, Nicaragua was engulfed in another civil war.

In the year before the Marines returned, Nicaragua's politicians continued to look to Washington for direction, but the United States had decided in principle to limit its involvement. In practice the United States was ambivalent, sometimes saying that Nicaragua should solve its own problems, sometimes sending ambiguous signals, and infrequently sending a clear message. The ambivalence stemmed from a contradictory mission: although the State Department wanted to limit its role, U.S. diplomats in Managua were major actors in Nicaragua's politics, and their job was to prevent instability and avoid losing control of events.

The United States was also constrained by the results of a second meeting with Central American governments, which began in December 1922, to discuss ways to make the 1907 treaties effective. The conference agreed to another Treaty of Peace and the establishment of "tribunals of inquiry" or fact-finding missions. The United States proposed arms limitations, but the Central Americans were not interested. The conference also agreed on an elaborate formula to withhold recognition from revolutionary governments or leaders as a way to discourage revolutions.[24]

This conference did not bring peace to Central America any more than the previous one had. The Conservatives in Nicaragua took control of the government but could not defend themselves from attacks by the Liberals, who were then led by Juan Sacasa and José María Moncada. The Liberals were receiving arms from the Mexican gov-

ernment at a time when U.S.–Mexican relations were strained, and
the Coolidge Administration suspected that the Mexicans were supporting Communist activities in Latin America. Therefore, when the
Nicaraguan President urgently appealed for help and was seconded
by the British, Italian, and U.S. embassies, President Coolidge dispatched 160 Marines on January 6, 1927. They were insufficient, and
within a few months, U.S. forces were expanded by over 5,000 Marines and eleven cruisers and destroyers.[25]

Coolidge defended the action, which was a departure from his pol-
icy of noninterference, by stressing the covert support that the rebels
were receiving from Mexico and the "proprietary rights" of the
Bryan-Chamorro Treaty, which in 1914 had granted the United
States exclusive rights to build a canal in Nicaragua.[26] At the same
time he wanted a solution that would bring the troops home, and on
March 31, 1927, Coolidge dispatched former Secretary of War Henry
L. Stimson to Nicaragua "to investigate [the problem] and report." "If
I should find a chance to straighten the matter out," Stimson recalled
as Coolidge's instructions, "he wished I would try."[27]

After arriving in Nicaragua, Stimson met with many Liberal and
Conservative leaders. His conclusion, which he believed they
shared, was that the cause of the problem was "that Nicaragua had
never had a really free election; that the government habitually controlled the result and that the habit was so inveterate and ingrained
that they could only hope to obtain a free, fair start through outside
assistance in supervising the conduct of the polls."[28] Nicaragua was
weakened by the war, and both sides had concluded that they could
not win. It was also clear that both sides trusted the United States,
but not each other, and believed that the United States alone could
enforce a settlement.

With the exception of one Liberal general, Augusto César Sandino,
the armies of both sides deposited their arms with the U.S. Marines.
Sandino withdrew to the northeast of Nicaragua with 150 followers
and continued the fight against his own government and the U.S.
forces. The U.S. government considered Sandino a "bandit," robbing
and killing poor people and harassing small outposts,[29] but he was
perceived differently in much of Latin America. Although there was
never any possibility Sandino would overthrow the government, he
did succeed in capturing the popular imagination as a nationalist
David—one of Latin America's first—struggling against the U.S. Go-
liath.[30]

From the U.S. perspective, Sandino was irritating, but the larger
problem was to establish a nonpartisan constabulary and ensure free
elections. On November 4, 1928, the United States supervised the

first "free" Presidential election in Nicaraguan history.[31] The Liberal José María Moncada won the election by a vote of 76,676 to 56,987. On January 1, 1929, for the first and only time in Nicaraguan history, power was transferred peacefully from a leader of one political party to another in an inauguration ceremony in which both leaders participated. After the election, the United States reduced the number of Marines in Nicaragua from 5,000 to 1,300, but Sandino pledged to continue fighting until all U.S. troops were withdrawn.

Henry Stimson became Herbert Hoover's Secretary of State, and he was determined that after supervising Nicaragua's elections in 1930 and 1932 as he had promised, the Marines would be withdrawn. Stimson's motives for advocating withdrawal were unambiguous. First, he believed that one of the U.S. objectives in Central America should be to secure the independence of the countries, and that meant using force only in exceptional and temporary circumstances. Second, he was sensitive to the mounting opposition to U.S. intervention in the United States and abroad. And third, he wanted to mobilize international opinion against Japanese aggression in Asia ("the Stimson Doctrine"), and the U.S. occupation of Nicaragua was obviously inconsistent with his own doctrine.

Liberal leader Juan Sacasa won the Presidential election in 1932, and on January 1, 1933, moments after the inauguration, General Calvin B. Matthews, the head of the Marine legation and the National Guard, "departed, leaving in such a rush that his Chief of Staff doubts that [Matthews] had time to finish packing."[32]

The First Somoza

Some in the State Department viewed the creation of a National Guard as an essential exit out of Nicaragua's intermittent partisan wars. Others, including the U.S. Minister to Managua, predicted that the National Guard would become the army of the party in power as soon as the Marines left.[33] The two predictions were not incompatible, and indeed both came true. The United States helped create a modern military instrument that brought an end to partisan warfare, but when the United States departed, the party in power, the Liberals, quickly turned the Guard into their partisan army. After consulting with his predecessor, Moncada, and with the U.S. Minister, President Sacasa appointed Anastasio Somoza García, the ambitious and shrewd young husband of his niece, as the Director-General of the National Guard. Somoza, who had been Stimson's interpreter used

the Guard first to defend Sacasa, then to take power in 1936, and finally to keep power until he was assassinated in 1956.

Sandino ended his campaign after the Marines departed. He
reached a peace agreement with Sacasa, and warned the President
that the Guard was his greatest threat. Somoza and his force, in turn,
feared that Sacasa might find the warning credible. On February 21,
1934, after dining with Sacasa at the Presidential palace, Sandino was
arrested by a Guard patrol and executed.

Sacasa pledged an investigation of the murder, but Somoza, using
his allies in the Nicaraguan Congress, effectively blocked any investigation. Evidently believing that if he could share the responsibility,
he could lessen his culpability, Somoza claimed that the execution
was approved by the United States, which also, he said, supported his
political ambitions. Both statements were untrue, but that did not
stop Somoza from repeating them. After several efforts, U.S. Minister Arthur Bliss Lane finally persuaded the Department of State to issue a public statement on June 25, 1934, rejecting both insinua-
tions.[34] Somoza, however, was unfazed.

Somoza was the first Nicaraguan leader to recognize that the
United States had really decided to withdraw from Nicaragua's internal political affairs. Sacasa did not understand this. Lane accepted the
policy, but he did not know how to implement it. Nicaraguans had
become so accustomed to U.S. control that the psychology of their
dependent relationship continued long after direct U.S. involvement
ended. Somoza, having begun as an interpreter, proved most adept at
manipulating the image of the relationship and made it appear that
the United States condoned, approved, or even instructed him. For
example, in the week before the murder of Sandino, Somoza made
certain he was repeatedly seen talking with the U.S. Minister and
even joining him at a baseball game.[35]

Somoza's attempt to identify himself and his cause with the
United States infuriated his opponents and exasperated the United
States. But the United States was deliberately trying to remove itself
from Nicaragua's internal affairs, and it went to extremes to avoid
even setting the record straight. When the U.S. Minister recommended that the United States block Somoza's attempts to take over
the government, Secretary of State Cordell Hull, anticipating the debate that would divide the Carter Administration forty-five years
later, endeavored to explain the basis of the new policy:

> it has for many years been said that the United States has sought
> to impose its own views upon the Central American states, and
> that to this end, it has not hesitated to interfere or intervene in

their internal affairs. This criticism has been made particularly in regard to our relations with Nicaragua. We therefore desire not only to refrain in fact from any interference, but also from any measure which might seem to give the appearance of such interference.[36]

From 1934 to 1936, the United States agonized over defining and justifying its policy of noninterference, as Somoza gradually took control of the Liberal Party and solidified his hold on the Guard. Many people, both within and outside the Nicaraguan government, urged the United States to stop Somoza. President Sacasa personally argued that the United States had a "responsibility" to do so because it had created the Guard, but the State Department rejected that argument, saying that U.S. intervention ended in January 1933, and "in seeking advice . . . and requesting our opinion, Dr. Sacasa was in fact seeking to prolong or revive the intervention." Sacasa rebutted that "a word of advice or an opinion would not constitute intervention," but State insisted it could be interpreted as such. Sacasa pressed, saying "silence at this time might also be interpreted as a kind of intervention."[37] The Mexican Chargé in Managua warned that if Somoza, the man "responsible for the death of Sandino, a hero in Latin America yet a mortal enemy of the United States" took power, it would appear as though the United States "had put him in power as a reward for having killed Sandino."[38]

The State Department would not respond, believing that Nicaragua could only learn self-government if the United States resisted efforts to be drawn into internal disputes. Although it was not the intention of the U.S. government, the effect of this policy was to permit Somoza to have a clear path to the Presidency. The United States had gone from one extreme—U.S. Marines—to another—silence. The Roosevelt Administration could have stated its public opposition to Somoza's takeover clearly and openly. Even if that had failed to divert Somoza, it might have scotched subsequent allegations that the United States wanted Somoza as Nicaragua's President.

In June 1936, Somoza pushed his uncle out of office and the country. Somoza then quit his command of the National Guard in November, and with his opponent in exile, he ran for the Presidency. The opposition first asked the United States to stop the December 8 election. When the United States restated its policy of noninterference, the opposition decided not to participate. His landslide victory was no more surprising than his resumption of his post as Chief of the Guard two weeks later. When his term ended, Somoza changed the constitution to permit him to have a another "transitory" term until May 1947.

Like his predecessors, but much more so, Somoza used his office for profit as well as for power. Just as he had modernized the military, he also developed new sources of wealth. Most of his investments were in Nicaragua, and in almost every sector. He also used his investments as an additional means of securing his control of the Guard, by graduating senior officers into his companies. His officers therefore were given a powerful additional incentive for remaining loyal to him.

As World War II ended and dictators fell in Guatemala, El Salvador, and Venezuela, Nicaraguans hoped they would be next. U.S. policy remained one of noninterference, but with the death of President Roosevelt and the departure of Secretary of State Hull, the State Department chose to interpret policy more broadly to permit some opportunities to influence Nicaraguan politics. On August 1, 1945, the Assistant Secretary of State for Inter-American Affairs, Nelson Rockefeller, requested a meeting with the Nicaraguan Ambassador and told him that "should Somoza run for re-election, it might create difficulties for him which would seriously affect relations between the two countries."[39] When he heard this, Somoza suggested the U.S. Ambassador join him in selecting a successor, but his supercilious offer was rejected.

Somoza nominated Leonardo Argüello, a previous opponent who was now 70 years old, as the Liberal candidate. Argüello won an election that was reportedly stolen by the Guard.[40] However, on May 2, 1947, the day after his inauguration, Argüello reorganized the General Staff of the Guard and began replacing some of the officers, without consulting Somoza. Argüello informed the U.S. Embassy that he intended to assert control over the Guard despite Somoza's vigorous protests. Somoza then called the Chargé to inform him of his views of Argüello: "Can you imagine what a stupid bastard? I took him out of León where he couldn't earn a dime, and he does something crazy like that."[41] On May 24, Argüello told the U.S. Chargé that he was asking for Somoza's resignation; two days later, he was deposed by Somoza.[42]

The United States deliberately withheld recognition from Somoza and the government he was trying to install. It stepped up the pressure by demanding the return of all ammunition belonging to the military mission and withdrawing the chief of the U.S. military mission and the American director of the Nicaraguan Military Academy. Internationally, the United States indicated to the Latin American governments that were then negotiating the Rio Pact that the "oppressive" Nicaraguan regime, which was "a puppet one and a creature of Somoza," should not be recognized, although the United States agreed to "follow the majority" of votes on the issue.[43]

By August 7, 1947, worried about economic sanctions, Somoza suggested to the United States a number of steps he could take—short of stepping down from the Guard—that could permit U.S. recognition. The United States did not respond then, but in a meeting with Assistant Secretary of State Norman Armour on August 24, 1947, at the Rio conference, the Nicaraguan Ambassador to Washington "wondered . . . whether the departure of Somoza would not help in clearing up the situation and making recognition easier." Armour "entirely agreed," but only if the government was broadened after Somoza's departure to include "representatives of certain of the other groups."[44] Needless to say, Somoza did not agree or leave. He felt the pressure from the United States but knew that his power ultimately derived from his control of the Guard. Thirty years later feeling similar pressures from the north, his son recalled this period and kept firm control over the military.

In April 1948, at the Bogotá conference, the foreign ministers of the American states adopted a resolution urging the continuity of diplomatic relations among OAS (Organization of American States) nations as a general principle. As a result of that resolution, the United States extended recognition to the government of Víctor Manuel Róman y Reyes, Somoza's elderly uncle, who had been appointed President by a new constitutional convention.[45] He died on May 6, 1950, and a new constitution (Nicaragua's tenth) allowed Somoza to seek and win election as President. He was inaugurated on May 1, 1951. The new constitution guaranteed the opposition party one-third of the seats in Congress.

Democrats vs. Dictators vs. Communists

After World War II, a new three-sided ideological struggle involving dictators, democrats, and Communists was grafted onto the traditional Central American landscape of mutual intervention. In October 1944, the democrats of Central America received a boost from a successful democratic coup in Guatemala. The new President, Juan José Arévalo, invited democrats from the region to Guatemala City on December 16, 1947, to sign a "Caribbean Pact" to help each other bring democracy to the region.[46]

In the Presidential elections in Costa Rica in February 1948, Rafael Angel Calderón ran against Otilio Ulate, a popular newspaper editor. Two of the three members of the Electoral Tribunal announced that Ulate had won the election, but Calderón's party, which controlled the Congress, annulled it. With help from the democratic "Caribbean Legion," José Figueres, a young follower of Ulate, launched a six-week guerrilla war and defeated Calderón. He then established an eighteen-month junta that inaugurated a second republic. In November 1949, as proof that he was a different breed than the traditional *caudillo*, Figueres passed the Presidency to Ulate. At the same time, Figueres honored an agreement he had made with Rosendo Argüello, Jr., a Nicaraguan leader, to help him overthrow Somoza after Argüello had helped Figueres overthrow Calderón.

Before Figueres and Argüello could attack Nicaragua, however, Calderón, who had received help from Somoza, led his small army from Nicaragua into Costa Rica in December 1949. The United States demanded Somoza stop supporting Calderón, and the Costa Ricans defeated the invasion.

Somoza had been trying desperately to obtain renewed U.S. military aid, which he had received during the war in exchange for bases. With the emergence of a leftist government in Guatemala, Somoza saw an opportunity. He sent his Ambassador to the State Department on September 29, 1952, to seek "urgent" military aid and U.S. cooperation for a plan to overthrow the Guatemalan government. Somoza also expressed concern about two other "leftists" in the area, Figueres and Rómulo Betancourt. The Truman Administration was noncommittal about military aid, but precise in discouraging any conspiracies against Guatemala or Costa Rica.[47] In a memorandum to Truman, Secretary of State Dean Acheson acknowledged that Somoza was friendly to the United States but also described him as greedy ("his desire for personal gain is very great") and as "a one-man show."[48]

The view of Nicaragua and Guatemala changed with Administrations. The Eisenhower Administration viewed the existence of Communists in the government in Guatemala as a serious threat to the United States, and it gave less weight to the criticisms of Somoza as a dictator and more to his loyalty. In a telegram to the Department of State on March 6, 1953, Ambassador Thomas Whelan argued that the United States should sign a military aid agreement with Somoza, who Whelan asserted was "not a dictator in the true sense of the word." Whelan wrote that Somoza was prepared to be helpful against Guatemala and had promised not to "take any action" against Costa

Rica, where Figueres had just been elected.[49] The Administration accepted the proposal and negotiated a military aid agreement with Nicaragua at the same time that the CIA began using Nicaraguan territory to train Guatemalan rebels.[50]

In August 1953, twenty years after a Republican President had withdrawn U.S. troops from Nicaragua, President Eisenhower decided to overthrow the Guatemalan government. The United States was motivated by its concern about Communist participation in the Guatemalan government, but the U.S. action was interpreted in the region in more traditional ways. Somoza, in addition, saw his new alliance with the United States as permitting him to secure another term for the Presidency and overthrow Figueres, who continued to sponsor plots against him. As soon as the Guatemalan government was overthrown in June 1954, Somoza provided weapons and training to a group of 500 Costa Rican exiles, the Authentic Anti-Communist Revolutionary Army, under the leadership of Teodoro Picado, Jr., the son of a former Costa Rican President. Assistance also came from Dominican dictator Rafael Trujillo and Pérez Jiménez of Venezuela.

The United States tried to defuse tensions between Costa Rica and Nicaragua, but by August 12, 1954, it was clear that such efforts had failed. The Acting Secretary of State then decided to "let it be known to Somoza by appropriate means that he had impaired his position with the United States." This warning also failed to deter Somoza. On January 11, 1955, Picado's army entered Costa Rica and was aided by air drops of war matériel by the Nicaraguan Air Force.[51]

The United States acted quickly to halt the war. As a symbol of its support for Figueres, the United States airlifted fifteen tons of light arms to San José and sold four P-51 fighter planes to the Costa Rican government for a dollar each. The OAS immediately sent a team to the border to establish a buffer zone. The crisis was over, but Somoza had jeopardized his relationship with the United States, which reduced aid. Somoza, who had helped the United States on Guatemala, complained: "What advantage do we get from being friendly? You treat us like an old wife. We would rather be treated like a young mistress."[52]

In September 1956, after receiving his party's nomination to serve another Presidential term, Anastasio Somoza García attended a Saturday night dance in León. There Rigoberto López Pérez, a young Nicaraguan poet, shot him five times before being killed by Somoza's bodyguards. With U.S. help, Somoza was flown for emergency treatment to the Canal Zone, but within a week, he was dead.

Recurring Themes

Throughout Nicaragua's history, the vast majority of the people have scraped a meager living from a rich earth while a few wealthy families controlled most of the economy and fought for power. Force remained the currency of political change. Stability was imposed by either dictators or U.S. Marines, but freedom could not be imposed, and no government would guarantee it. For almost every local battle, a Nicaraguan faction sought help from abroad.

The scars left by North American adventurer William Walker remain on the Nicaraguan body politic as the first mark of U.S. intervention. What is often forgotten is that Walker was invited by Nicaraguans and discouraged by the U.S. government. Zelaya also invited the United States to help him expel the British. When the United States turned against him, he looked for help from Britain and even Mexico, but to no avail. From 1912 to 1933, U.S. support was sought first by the Conservatives and then by the Liberals. Only Sandino fought the United States, but he too invited aid from Mexico and was the first to recruit international public opinion for his cause.

U.S. policy was shaped by its internal politics and its self-perception. U.S. policy toward Walker had much less to do with Nicaragua than with internal issues like slavery and manifest destiny. Its involvement in the Caribbean Basin and intervention in Nicaragua during the first three decades of the twentieth century were driven by strategic concerns regarding the Canal, but the character of U.S. involvement was shaped by ambivalent and contradictory ideas of its proper role. The United States did not want to control Nicaragua or the other nations in the region, but it also did not want to allow developments to get out of control. It wanted Nicaraguans to act independently, *except* when doing so would affect U.S. interests adversely. When it did intervene in Nicaragua's internal affairs, it did so thinking its involvement would be brief—but it was not.

The establishment of the National Guard and the supervision of "free" elections were the clearest examples of what happens when two such different nations interact. Both were done with the best of intentions—providing a framework for peaceful democratic change and facilitating the exit of the Marines—but with the worst of consequences—the beginning of the Somoza dynasty.

The complex psychology that accompanies a relationship between a powerful occupation force and a small nation was fully developed in Nicaragua. The United States became impatient with Nicaraguan greed and tyranny, and Nicaraguans became angry with U.S. arrogance. When the U.S. Marines left, Nicaraguans felt a combination of both pride and uncertainty about themselves, and admiration and resentment for the United States.

Only Anastasio Somoza García grasped the full implications of a United States that swung out of Nicaragua so fast it feared raising its voice about Nicaraguan politics lest the pendulum of intervention swing back. And so Somoza manipulated the absence of the United States as much as the U.S. presence had previously manipulated Nicaragua. Somoza's venality and his pretense of being a U.S. surrogate obscured a significant historic development: the expansion of the region's autonomy, its growing ability to control its own destiny. With minor exceptions or retreats, the governments in the region, whether friendly to the United States or not, had gradually but inexorably widened their area for decision making. In 1910, the United States could overthrow a government merely by withholding recognition; in 1947, the same tactic failed. In 1954, the United States could arm fewer that two hundred Guatemalans and topple the government; thirty years later, 20,000 contras could not shake the Sandinista government.

Anastasio Somoza had learned to dodge or ignore U.S. pressures, but in the end, he could not ignore Nicaragua's subterranean rhythm. He capped the pressures for political change for twenty years and met his end with a lethal blast, the volcanic fate of Nicaragua's geology and its politics.

Chapter 3

ROADS TO REVOLUTION

> We are usually told that revolutions are set in motion to
> realize radical changes. Actually, it is drastic change which
> sets the stage for revolution. . . . Where things have not
> changed at all, there is the least likelihood of revolution.
> **Eric Hoffer**

The Brothers Somoza

THE DYNASTY began with the death of the old man. His two sons
had been taught to view their country as their estate, and they moved
rapidly and expertly to replace their father. Luis Somoza, 34, a graduate of Louisiana State University, was President of the Nicaraguan
Congress at the time of the assassination, and he was chosen to
complete his father's term and to receive the party's nomination for
the Presidential election in February 1957. He was elected over-
whelmingly.

Anastasio Somoza, Jr., 31, who was called "Tachito," had graduated from West Point and was Acting Director of the Guard and the
Commander of the Nicaraguan Air Force. He was promoted by his
brother, and his first decisions were to arrest hundreds of opposition
leaders in Managua and to replace all officers of potential ambition
or questionable loyalty.

The feud with Figueres was passed on to the next generation of
Somozas, who suspected, incorrectly, that the Costa Rican leader
had been involved in the murder of their father. In May 1957, three
gunmen were arrested in San José and charged with plotting to kill
Figueres. A few months later, Figueres reported that he had uncov-
ered a new Nicaraguan-supported plot to overthrow him. Two years
later, in May 1959, Figueres equipped an expedition led by Pedro Joaquín Chamorro and Enrique Lacayo and airlifted them and two
planeloads of rebels into Nicaragua to link up with another group
that entered by land from Costa Rica. The Somozas defeated the expedition and imprisoned Chamorro and his followers.[1]

By 1961, the Somoza–Figueres feud was eclipsed by the geopolitical struggle between the United States and Cuba. The Somoza brothers became a target for a few unsuccessful raids from Cuba by Nicara-

guan rebels, and the United States, in turn, enlisted the Somozas in their effort to overthrow Castro. Luis Somoza eagerly volunteered facilities on Nicaragua's Caribbean coast to serve as a staging area for the Cuban exiles destined for the Bay of Pigs.

Nicaraguan guerrillas had long been trying to overthrow Somoza, but "revolutions" were different after Castro's success. Prior to 1959, most revolutions were aimed at overthrowing dictators. Castro mixed Marxism, nationalism, and anti-Americanism in a new recipe that created problems for the United States and inspired leftists throughout Latin America. In Nicaragua, Carlos Fonseca Amador and Tomás Borge quit the pro-Moscow Nicaraguan Socialist Party because of its reluctance to pursue an armed struggle. They went to Havana, where they organized the Frente Liberación Nacional (National Liberation Front). The FLN then merged with several other groups, including the Frente Revolucionario Sandino led by Edén Pastora, who had been fighting Somoza since 1958. Together, in July 1961 in Honduras, these groups established the Frente Sandinista de Liberación Nacional (FSLN).[2] Fonseca, the leader of the new group, was clear on the source of inspiration of the FSLN: "With the victory of the Cuban Revolution, the Nicaraguan rebels' spirit recovered its radiance. The Marxism of Lenin, Fidel, Che, Ho Chi Minh was acquired by the Sandinista National Liberation Front, which had undertaken again the hazardous and difficult guerrilla path."[3]

The Sandinistas, however, posed no threat to the Somozas in the 1960s. With increasing investment in Nicaragua as a result of the Alliance for Progress and the Central American Common Market, this was a period of unprecedented economic progress. Luis Somoza, an ostensibly more genial and accommodating politician than his father or brother, began to relax political restrictions and decided not to seek another term. Instead, in February 1963, he had René Schick, a lawyer who had served the elder Somoza as a private secretary, nominated as the Liberal candidate. However, when the Conservative candidate Fernando Agüerro did not receive guarantees of a free election and Luis Somoza refused to invite OAS observers because it would constitute "foreign interference" in Nicaragua's internal affairs, Agüerro withdrew. Schick won by a margin of more than ten to one. Luis Somoza, while retaining real power, did allow Schick more autonomy than his father ever considered. Schick was even allowed to implement several decisions against the wishes of the Guard, including trying one officer for murder and exiling rather than imprisoning or executing Carlos Fonseca Amador after his capture in July 1964.[4]

Brother Anastasio Somoza concentrated on securing the Guard's support before obtaining, on August 1, 1966, the nomination of the Liberal Party for the next Presidential election. The constitution required that he resign from the Guard, which he did, although he did not move out of his office. The opposition united again behind the candidacy of Fernando Agüerro, and he mobilized a large demonstration in Managua in January 1967 to seek guarantees for a free election. The Guard put down the demonstrations ruthlessly, and Somoza won the election on February 5 with 70 percent of the vote. Like his father, Anastasio Jr. insisted on maintaining formal control of the Guard and the government simultaneously. In April 1967, Luis Somoza, who was said to have been a moderating influence on his younger brother, had a heart attack and died.

The election of Richard Nixon brought to the White House a man who saw the Communist threat in the hemisphere much as Anastasio Somoza did.[5] Nixon named as Ambassador Turner Shelton, who became a confidant of Somoza. Like Thomas Whelan, Shelton could not speak Spanish, and he made no effort to communicate with the opposition.

As his term was coming to an end in 1971, Somoza conspired to remain in power. He first reached an agreement with his former rival Fernando Agüerro to dissolve Congress, call a constituent assembly, and appoint a three-member ruling junta, composed of Agüerro and two of Somoza's representatives. The junta governed the nation from May 1972 until Presidential elections in December 1974. Other opposition leaders rejected the agreement, and for the first time the Church, led by Archbishop Miguel Obando y Bravo, issued a statement denying the pact had any Church sanction.

If the Archbishop's statement did not shake Managua, nature succeeded where he failed. On December 23, 1972, the streets of Managua were lifted by a powerful earthquake, then dropped, and finally burned by a storm of fire. When the streets settled and cooled, the city was rubble, 8,000–10,000 people were dead, and hundreds of thousands of people were left homeless. For a moment, the regime also shook, as many members of the National Guard deserted either to help their families or to loot. With the moral support of Ambassador Shelton and the offers of aid from the United States and the international community, Somoza steadied himself and transformed a tragic national loss into a personal financial gain. He accomplished this by channeling aid through his companies and purchasing the parts of the city where he planned to undertake reconstruction. He also encouraged Guard leaders to profit from the foreign aid and the reconstruction opportunities in the city. The acts of the Guard further isolated them from the Nicaraguan population even while tying them closer to Somoza. The business community's deep-seated contempt for Somoza stemmed to a great extent from his exploitation of the earthquake. After this event, some of the children of the middle and upper classes began to leave school to join the Sandinistas.

Except for the Ambassador, most of the U.S. Embassy staff in Managua recognized the earthquake as a turning point politically; they recommended that the United States distance itself from Somoza. But Shelton continued to support Somoza as the latter maneuvered into position for another presidential term.[6] Once again, Somoza rewrote the constitution and feigned resignation from the Guard. Once again, the opposition, this time united by Pedro Joaquín Chamorro, refused to participate in the election and recommended abstention. Although 40 percent of the voters stayed away from the polls on September 1, 1974, 815,758 votes were counted, and Somoza won 748,985 of those. The bishops and the opposition refused to participate in his inauguration, on December 1, 1974, for a seven-year term. Years later, Somoza would confide to an aide: "My single biggest mistake was running for reelection in 1974."[7]

As a head of state, Anastasio Somoza was a most unusual hybrid, an American-Nicaraguan. Except for four years, all of his schooling had been in the United States. "I know the U.S. better than my country," Somoza once said.[8] A more accurate statement would have been that he knew some parts of the United States in the 1930s and 1940s better than he knew Nicaragua. "Next to Nicaragua, I loved the U.S. more than any place in the world," he wrote in his memoirs.[9] Several have suggested that he felt a greater affection and affinity with North Americans than he did for Nicaraguans, whom he treated either formally or with contempt.[10]

Although there was an obvious political motive in the title of his memoirs, *Nicaragua Betrayed*, the title also reflected a theme of the book and a personal obsession of its author.[11] He saw the world, as many conservative Americans did, as divided between Communists and non-Communists. When the United States deserted him, he viewed himself as a victim of an "international conspiracy" as vast and incredible as Joe McCarthy's, including not just Cuba but Venezuela and Costa Rica and people like Rómulo Betancourt ("a self-declared Communist"), Jimmy Carter, Edward Koch (then a liberal Congressman from New York), Edward Kennedy, and Jack Anderson.[12]

Somoza also saw himself as a shrewd politician and businessman; he viewed his political opponents as incompetent and other Nicaraguan businessmen as jealous of his success. He ruled with an iron hand and was not averse to having the Guard abuse and torture political prisoners. Still, he would suggest to Americans that his Liberal Party was comparable to FDR's Democratic Party, and that his political machine was no worse than Richard Daley's in Chicago. His grasp of the truth was tenuous, at best.[13]

Using American terms and counting on American disinterest in Nicaragua, Somoza believed he could persuade most Americans that Nicaraguan politics were not that much different from U.S. politics, except that Nicaragua was threatened by Castro and the Communists. When pressed to resign, Somoza would insist on the importance of respecting the constitution. He expected that Americans would be unaware of the numerous times the Somozas had changed the constitution to serve their purposes.

The United States: From Identification to Neutrality

Although Nicaragua's middle class generally dates the beginning of Somoza's downfall to the 1972 earthquake, the protagonists—Somoza and the Sandinistas—use different benchmarks. Characteristically, Somoza dates the beginning of his downfall to a change in U.S. administrations. However, it was not the arrival of Jimmy Carter that first troubled Somoza, but "Nixon's departure" and the subsequent replacement of Ambassador Shelton.[14]

Somoza was correct that U.S. policy changed after Nixon's resignation. The very next day, Secretary of State Henry Kissinger phoned William D. Rogers, a Washington attorney and formerly Deputy Coordinator of the Alliance for Progress in the Kennedy Administration, and asked him to become Assistant Secretary of State for Inter-American Affairs.[15] When Kissinger had been appointed Secretary of State in 1973, he had asked Rogers to take the same position, but Rogers declined to work under Nixon. This time Rogers accepted, subject to two conditions: first, the CIA would not do anything serious in Latin America, as had occurred in Chile, without his knowledge; and second, he wanted to make basic changes in policy and personnel, particularly with regard to several ambassadors.

Turner Shelton was one of those he had in mind. In appointing his replacement, however, Rogers had to defer to Vice President Nelson Rockefeller, who proposed James Theberge, a conservative Latin Americanist from Georgetown University.

To ensure a change in policy, Rogers drafted and cleared detailed instructions, and then he delivered the new policy directly to Somoza with Theberge present to underscore two points for both. First, "the U.S. was [henceforth] absolutely neutral both publicly and privately in all its actions" with regard to Somoza and the opposition, and the United States would begin a dialogue with the opposition. Second, the United States was going to be watching the accounts of the Agency for International Development (AID) much more closely to ensure that the money was not misspent.[16]

Somoza received the message, and later wrote that it:

> came as a shock, and it was hard to take. . . . There were more surprises. Ambassador Theberge began to associate with Pedro Joaquín Chamorro, a known Sandinista. He was entertained by those people [Conservatives] in Granada and . . . was bent on establishing a close relation with the wrong side—an opposition coalition. It seemed to me that . . . my country and I were in for trouble.[17]

Actually, Rogers had replaced the collaborationist policy of Shelton with a variation on the policy of noninterference and neutrality as it had been developed during the Roosevelt–Truman years.

The Sandinistas

The Sandinistas celebrate the anniversary of their first spectacular raid as the first glimpse of light at the end of a tunnel leading to victory.[18] Soon after Christmas in 1974, José María "Chema" Castillo Quant, a wealthy friend of Somoza and former minister of agriculture, hosted a farewell party for Ambassador Shelton. At about the same time, the Sandinistas had decided to do something to show they were a viable threat to the Somoza regime. Tomás Borge, who had received two years of military training in Cuba, prepared a small group of Sandinistas to capture prominent officials at an Embassy reception, but when they heard about the Castillo party on the radio, they changed their plans. Shelton had departed by the time the Sandinistas arrived, but many guests were still there, including Nicaragua's Foreign Minister, Managua's Mayor, and Somoza's brother-in-law, Guillermo Sevilla-Sacasa, who was also Ambassador to the United States.

The Sandinistas killed Castillo, held the rest of his guests hostage, and demanded that Archbishop Obando act as mediator. On December 30, after tense negotiations, Somoza agreed to release fourteen imprisoned Sandinistas, including Daniel Ortega; provide $1 million in cash; and publish the FSLN's 12,000-word communiqué denouncing Somoza and U.S. imperialism and asking the people to rise up and join the Frente to overthrow Somoza. The Sandinistas then flew to

Cuba. The raid, according to Borge, was a tremendous success: "It put the Sandinista movement in the spotlight world-wide, and our organization started to be recognized internationally."[19]

The raid helped to attract and recruit young people to the Sandinista movement, including the daughter of Chema Castillo and a young businessman, Alfredo César, who secretly began organizing a small group of his colleagues to help the movement.[20] But these rewards were more than offset by the repression that Somoza unleashed to take revenge for the raid. At that time, the FSLN was estimated by Henry Ruiz, one of its leaders, to have about 150 cadre. In the next two years, the Guard arrested Tomás Borge and killed much of the Frente leadership, including Eduardo Contreras, Carlos Agüerro, and on November 6, 1976, its founder, Carlos Fonseca Amador.

Still, there remained enough Sandinistas to make a revolution. Who were they? The Sandinistas' view of Nicaragua's history had much in common with Somoza's Manichaean vision of the world, except that the saints and the sinners exchanged uniforms. Where Sandino is a bandit in Somoza's passion play, he is the Christ for the Sandinistas, and "the crime of February 21"—the date in 1934 when Sandino was murdered—is the date of his crucifixion. The United States is Pontius Pilate, who gave the instructions to Somoza to kill Sandino and then washed its hands of the crime. According to Carlos Fonseca Amador, Nicaragua had been "a victim of Yankee aggression for more than a century," and Nicaragua's history can be described most concisely as a list of U.S. interventions, beginning with William Walker. Every Nicaraguan who collaborated with the United States, like Adolfo Díaz, is a "traitor," and everyone who fought or defied the United States like José Santos Zelaya, is a patriot. Also central to the Sandinista outlook are the Marxist interpretation of history as a class struggle and the view of Nicaragua as a victim of U.S. transnational corporations and the Nicaraguan bourgeoisie.[21]

Given the importance of the theme of the United States dictating to and exploiting Nicaragua, the origins of the modern Sandinista movement are as strangely ironic as Somoza's dual personality. The principal founders of the FSLN—Fonseca, Borge, and Silvio Mayorga—left the Nicaraguan Socialist Party, which was established in 1944, according to Fonseca, by a directive from Joseph Stalin sent through the leader of the American Communist Party, Earl Browder. Stalin had issued orders to all the Communist parties in the world to form a united front with all those who declared war against Hitler. That included Somoza, who had followed the lead of the United States and declared war against Germany. Therefore, the first act of the new Nicaraguan Socialist party was to proclaim its support for Somoza's government—on the instructions of an American, who was acting as a surrogate for Stalin.[22]

The Sandinista movement tried to marry a Marxist interpretation of history with a visceral hatred of Somoza, the National Guard, and the United States. Sandino—the great anti-Yankee Nicaraguan revolutionary—was a natural symbol for the movement, except that the Marxists had difficulty locating "class consciousness" in Sandino's actions and writings. Sandino welcomed "Internationalists," but he rejected all ideologies, calling his movement "essentially a nationalist thing."[23]

In 1973, after years of arguing with Borge and Ruiz, Pastora, who believed that Sandino was a nationalist and not a Marxist and that Marx was a democrat and not a Leninist, finally left the movement. He had recommended that the Sandinistas "should discontinue implementing a Marxist-Leninist revolution and should implement a nationalist revolution of Sandinista character." His main argument for changing direction, however, was pragmatic: "A long time had gone by, and we had still not convinced the Nicaraguan people of a Cuban revolution, which they were trying to copy."[24] Pastora went to Costa Rica and started a shark-fishing business.

The formative experience of many of the leaders of the Sandinistas was a traumatic act inflicted on them or their families by Somoza's Guard. Both parents in the Ortega family were jailed by Somoza. "Family conversations and discussions," Daniel Ortega recalls, "always were anti-Somoza, and included criticisms of the U.S. for its permanent complicity with the Somoza government." All the Ortega brothers joined the FSLN, and one, Camilio, was killed. Daniel Ortega was imprisoned five separate times; the first in 1959 when he was 14, and the last from 1967 to 1974.[25]

Originating in Marxism, but driven by nationalism and hatred for the Somoza dynasty, the Sandinista philosophy naturally evolved as its membership changed. After the earthquake, a young group of idealistic Christian students from El Colegio de Centro America joined the movement, despite resistance by Henry Ruiz, who had been trained in Moscow. Radical priests like Ernesto Cardenal reinforced the Christian current in the movement.

The repression forced the movement to reconsider its strategy. In 1975, Humberto Ortega was completing his manuscript, *50 Años de Lucha Sandinista*, and he admitted that "we were in a precarious situation."[26] By its own account, the FSLN had failed in the 1960s, because of its inability to adapt to the jungle, and in most of the 1970s, because of the military power of the Guard.[27] After the decapitation of the Frente leadership, the next tier of leaders divided into three "tendencies" or groups. These reflected traditional Nicaraguan factionalism but also different strategies and constituencies. When interviewed in the fall of 1978, representatives of each faction called for unity but did not conceal their criticism of the other. Their only point of agreement was their fear that the bourgeoisie and the imperialists could overthrow Somoza before the revolution succeeded.[28]

The original group, which included Borge and Ruiz, was called the "Prolonged Popular War" (GPP), and they remained wedded to the strategy of organizing the peasants from the mountains. After their Cuban "foco" strategy failed, they adopted the prolonged-war strategy of General Vo Nguyen Giap of Vietnam. They criticized the "Tercerista" faction for expecting a "great surge" to sweep away Somoza. They felt there was no alternative to working methodically with the peasants to build a guerrilla movement. Their weakness was that they could point to few peasants who had been converted.

A second group, "Proletarian Tendency" (TP), led by Jaime Wheelock Román, was younger, more intellectual, and concentrated its efforts on the workers in the urban areas. When asked about the difference between his movement and the other tendencies, Wheelock described the others as "currents of interest whose objectives, strategies, allies, and tactics are divergent and even contradictory." His group saw the road to revolution in organizing strikes.

The third group, "Terceristas" ("third force"), led by the Ortegas, was the least educated and the most pragmatic. They had absorbed the young, idealistic Christian recruits and had less patience for debates over Marxist purity. Asked to explain the differences between the tendencies, Daniel Ortega said: "Since 1973, we have forced ourselves to search for ideological-organizational ways to overcome within our ranks programmatic tendencies on the one side, and pseudo-theoretical tendencies on the other."[29]

In other words, the Terceristas were tired of talk, perhaps because they were not good at it. They wanted to overthrow Somoza and realized this could only be done by concealing their Marxist rhetoric and looking for allies everywhere. Their strategy was to undertake a few armed attacks and advertise them as major assaults on the dynasty. The Terceristas criticized the GPP for isolating themselves in the mountains and the TP for being "a small group of people of academic formation"; they saw themselves as "the front of the popular insurrection."[30]

In late 1976, Humberto Ortega persuaded Pastora and Carlos Coronel, a politically astute entrepreneur, to join the Terceristas. Had this new alliance and others that the Terceristas established not been formed, it is doubtful that the Sandinistas would have emerged from the wilderness. As a result of their strategy, however, the Terceristas *did* become the vanguard of the revolution, and the other two groups followed behind them.

The Revolution before the Revolution

The Sandinista view of the Nicaraguan economy was that it was approaching crisis in the mid-1970s, the culmination of decades of neocolonial Yankee exploitation.[31] However, a closer look at the economic and social data of Nicaragua suggests that this revolution, like others, was the result not of poverty and backwardness but of economic growth. In the two decades preceding the Nicaraguan revolution, the social and economic progress was more profound than it had been for the previous two hundred years. The economic growth created new groups that placed pressure on an anachronistic political system.[32]

During the Alliance for Progress, from 1962 to 1970, Nicaragua received, on the average, about the same as each of its Central American neighbors: $92.5 million in economic aid (loans, grants, PL 480-II) and $11 million in military aid. During the next six years, owing to the earthquake, Nicaragua received nearly three times as much in economic aid, but less military aid.[33]

Loans from the World Bank and the Inter-American Development Bank also increased in number and value and, together with U.S. aid, provided the stimulus for an unprecedented surge in development. The average annual growth rate for Nicaragua from 1960 to 1970 was 7.2 percent, and from 1970 to 1978, 5.8 percent; this was almost double the rate for the United States during the same period, and among the fastest in the world.[34] Although agriculture in most developing countries declined sharply, Nicaragua's agricultural base remained strong and dynamic, particularly in exports, but food for local consumption was not neglected. Food imports as a percentage of total imports actually declined from 9 percent in 1960 to 8 percent in 1977.

Trade, which grew in the 1960s at about 10 percent annually, was a major engine of growth and diversification. Nicaragua is dependent on agricultural exports, but it is hardly a banana republic. It also exports beef, cotton, and coffee, and its overall dependence on these commodities declined from 95 percent of its exports in 1960 to 82 percent in 1977. Similarly, its dependence on the United States and the other industrialized countries as the source of all of its imports also declined during this period—from 91 percent of its trade in 1960 to 69 percent in 1978. The U.S. share of Nicaragua's exports fell from 43 percent in 1960 to 19 percent in 1974.[35]

The major cause of the shift in trade and stimulus for growth came from the Central American Common Market, which was established in 1960. Trade among participating countries mushroomed from $32 million in 1960 to over $900 million in 1978, with manufactures accounting for 95 percent of the total.[36]

Population expansion, due to improved health conditions, was probably the major source of change, however. The population doubled in twenty years from 1.1 million in 1950. By 1975, over 50 percent of the population was under the age of 15.[37] The number of doctors as a percentage of the population increased. The infant mortality rate declined, and life expectancy increased from 47 years in 1960 to 55 years in 1980.

Education also improved and was extended to a wider segment of the population. The proportion of Nicaraguan children enrolled in primary schools as a percentage of all Nicaraguan children of that age group was 66 percent in 1960 and 92 percent in 1977; the figures for secondary schools were 7 percent and 29 percent.

In short, the growth in production and trade and the improvements in health and education were nothing short of revolutionary. Although per capita income was only $840 in 1978, this represented more than a four-fold increase for a population that more than doubled since 1950; it also reflected a doubling in income in the previous eight years. Put another way, if the total population had remained the same, per capita income would have increased nearly ten times between 1950 and 1978. New middle and working classes emerged, better educated, healthier, and more likely to live in the urban areas than their parents.

These changes and improvements, however, should not obscure the gross inequities that existed and that, in some cases, were exacerbated by the new growth. The most visible disparities were between the urban and rural areas and between the new wealthy and the new poor in the urban areas. But the most frustrating gap of all was the one that separated the Somoza family from the rest of the country. The Somozas not only controlled the nation's military and politics but had an expanding share in the nation's economy. They owned cattle, cotton, sugar, and rice farms, an airline, a shipping concern, a fishing fleet, a cement plant, a slaughterhouse, a construction company, and vast real estate holdings. There were no precise data on the Somoza family's wealth, but Anastasio Somoza reported his worth in July 1979 as $100 million. Other sources suggested it was closer to $900 million.[38]

The economy had grown and diversified; the population had grown and become better educated. People hoped that the time had also come to change the dynasty. But it did not change. New young, educated leadership pushed up against an immovable political system, like volcanic gases and magma pushing up against a mountain peak. The pressures did not dissipate; they grew stronger, searching for vents to escape or a section of rock to detonate.

Part II

THE SUCCESSION CRISIS,

1977-1979

> Our life is managed from behind the scenes;
> we are actors in dramas we cannot interpret.
> Of almost no decisive event can we say: this
> was of our choosing.
>
> **Walter Lippmann,** *Drift and Mastery*

Chapter 4

HUMAN RIGHTS AND

NICARAGUAN WRONGS

Those who have been discriminating against dark-skinned
people for years have nothing to tell me about human rights.
Anastasio Somoza, April 23, 1977

As JIMMY CARTER was taking the oath of office, Anastasio Somoza
had more reason to be concerned with his weight than with the Sandinistas. At 267 pounds, Somoza was considerably heavier than his
brother Luis was when he died of a heart attack in 1967. Moreover, as
Somoza's girth was expanding, the Sandinista threat was shrinking.
Since Somoza had decreed martial law in December 1974 after the
Christmas party raid, the National Guard almost destroyed the
FSLN. In June 1977, the Department of State estimated total Sandinista guerrilla strength at 50 fighting men.[1]

In the absence of any threat more serious than Somoza's weight
problem, and with an ambitious domestic and international agenda,
the Carter Administration had little time for Nicaragua at the beginning. The lack of high-level attention, however, did not mean that
Nicaragua was neglected or that the United States did not have a policy. The U.S. approach was fashioned via a classical, deductive
method: general policies, which were formulated at a high-level at
the beginning of the Administration, were adapted by middle-level
officials to the specific circumstances of Nicaragua.

Unlike most of his predecessors, Jimmy Carter had a deep personal
interest in Latin America, and this was reflected in his choice of his
first state visitor (from Mexico), his second foreign policy address (at
the OAS), his highest priority in the first eighteen months (the Panama Canal treaties), and the six-country tour of Latin America and
the Caribbean by his wife (May-June 1977).[2] In the overall policy that
he developed toward the region, three specific themes had a special
impact on Nicaragua.

First, his commitment to new Canal treaties with Panama communicated a willingness on the part of the United States to take the
concerns of a small Central American country seriously. It also led

Carter to develop close relationships with Panamanian leader Omar Torrijos and Venezuelan President Carlos Andrés Pérez, both of whom had strong views on Nicaragua. Second, Carter had criticized the Nixon Administration for destabilizing the democratically elected government in Chile and then embracing the Pinochet dictatorship that overthrew it. In his inaugural address, Carter stated his opposition to overthrowing established governments: "We will not act abroad in ways that we would not tolerate at home." His third theme was the most central and personal: the advancement of human rights and democracy. In a speech at Notre Dame in May 1977 on his vision of the United States using its global power and influence "for humane purposes," Carter made a remark that had obvious if not specifically intended consequences for Somoza: "Being confident, we are now free of that inordinate fear of Communism, which once led us to embrace any dictator who joined us in that fear." Given the repressive, authoritarian rule of Anastasio Somoza, and the relative absence of a threat to the United States, human rights was the general policy that was initially judged to be most relevant to Nicaragua.

Human Rights Policy: Theory and Application

The Carter Administration's human rights policy had both a moral and a national security premise. By supporting a dictator, the United States would lose the support of his nation and especially of its youth, which would identify the United States as part of its national problem. This, of course, is what had happened in Nicaragua. There were risks in withdrawing support from dictators, but the Administration believed that the prospect of violent revolutions would be greater in the long run if possibilities for peaceful change were precluded.

Applying the theory to the Somoza regime, the Carter Administration viewed the dynasty's "continuismo" and repression as the cause of the nation's instability. The Sandinistas were the symptoms of this problem, not the cause. Remote threats like the Sandinistas were less likely to become real if the political system were opened gradually than if the system remained closed. Therefore, the issue was how to promote human rights.

The way a government defines an issue determines the forum in which the issue will be debated. When Nicaragua was defined as a human rights issue, the central forum for debating how the United States should relate to Nicaragua became the Interagency Group on

Human Rights and Foreign Assistance, under the chairmanship of Deputy Secretary of State Warren Christopher. The policy became the sum of the committee's specific decisions on when and whether to increase or reduce foreign aid.

The Carter Administration's policy grew in part out of Congressional initiatives begun in 1973 to reduce foreign aid to countries violating human rights. Because the Nixon and Ford Administrations gave low priority to human rights, Congress passed laws requiring the President to take it into account in a wide range of aid programs.[3] The Carter Administration took office committed to Congress's priorities yet found translating the laws into effective policy difficult, partly due to inherent contradictions. For example, are human rights promoted by denying aid to poor people in countries ruled by dictators? Congress recognized the contradiction but walked around it, instructing the United States to reduce aid and vote against loans to countries that violated human rights "unless such assistance will directly benefit the needy people." One could argue either that aid should be approved because it would always benefit *some* needy people, or that aid should be denied because it would legitimize a repressive regime and prolong suffering. The Administration agreed that such questions could not be answered by any single formula; what was needed was a framework for case-by-case decision making that could also take into account other interests and review the kind of strategy that would be most effective for each country.

The Christopher Committee was established by Presidential directive on April 1, 1977, to address these specific cases. Its mandate was to ensure that the aid program was used to promote human rights. The objectives were to discourage human rights violations, to encourage improvements in human rights, and to promote democratic institutions that could permanently guarantee human rights. Different instruments would be used, depending on the severity of the violation and other U.S. interests. If private diplomacy, the preferred method, failed to achieve its objective, the United States would raise the stakes by going public and demonstrate its seriousness by reducing aid.

The committee debated specific human rights objectives and whether to provide aid to encourage good performance, deny aid to penalize bad performance, or use a combination of carrots and sticks. Participants included representatives from all aid-granting agencies as well as those with human rights or geographical responsibilities. Each agency generally had a vested interest in one of the options. By and large, aid-granting agencies and the regional bureaus, like the Bureau of Inter-American Affairs (ARA), would argue in favor of the carrot, insisting that only with good relations and the option to with-draw the carrot could one induce improvements in human rights performance. To deny aid would be counterproductive, they would argue. On the other side, the Bureau of Human Rights (HA) generally argued on behalf of the stick—denial of loans, reduction of aid—insisting that dictators would only take U.S. policy seriously if they had to pay a price. (HA did try to obtain additional aid to reward positive performance, but such efforts generally foundered because of budgetary constraints.) HA was led by political appointees, whose experience reflected both the domestic and the international origins of the Administration's concern for human rights. Assistant Secretary of State Patricia Derian had experience in the civil rights struggles in the South; her Deputy, Mark Schneider, had served as Senator Edward Kennedy's principal Latin American adviser and had drafted many of the human rights amendments. Derian was the articulate public voice of the policy, and Schneider, the adept bureaucratic operator.

The power of their small bureau derived from the personal skills of these two individuals and their colleagues, Carter's commitment, and most of all, from Warren Christopher, who transformed Carter's commitment into policy. Christopher judged that the best way to implement the policy was to combine both carrot and stick—denying aid for bad performance and supplying it for good performance, but because it was sometimes difficult to overrule the regional bureaus' argument that a particular strategy would be ineffective, he had to rely on the views of other regional specialists who worked in the State Department's Policy Planning Staff (PPC) and the National Security Council (NSC). These individuals were often political appointees, who shared the President's commitment to human rights but also had the regionalists' sense of the constraints of effecting change in a foreign country. After listening to the debate, Christopher would make a decision. The division that was built into the decision-making process was constructive, but when it spilled over—or rather leaked—into the public arena, it frequently left the impression of incoherence and inconsistency.

In brief, there was no specific policy toward Nicaragua early in the Carter presidency; there were only human rights policies that applied to Nicaragua. Outside of this framework, U.S. relations with Nicaragua received low priority. The new Ambassador, Mauricio Solaun, a Cuban-American professor of sociology from the University of Illinois, was not sent to Managua until August. Although among the more intelligent and informed of the Administration's ambassadors, Solaun was not particularly suited for the Nicaraguan post. He was a modest and unassuming individual who was well liked but not a good match for Somoza's gruff personality. Alfonso Robelo, a business leader and friend of Solaun's, recalled that the Ambassador "trembled when he went to see Somoza."[4]

There was a special poignancy in Solaun's service in Nicaragua. As a Cuban-American he, more than anyone, knew the cycle of events that had led to Castro's triumph and wanted to avoid a repetition. Yet Solaun could do little as he watched the worst-case scenario unfold before his eyes.

The Impact on Nicaragua

While some debated whether the human rights policy was having any effect, Somoza already felt it. In the words of one of his closest friends, U.S. Congressman John (Jack) Murphy, Somoza "knew that he was in deep trouble five days after the Carter Administration took office because it cancelled export licenses for the sale of ammunition for sporting arms. That was a message . . . [that Somoza] was out of favor with the United States. So early in 1977, he knew he would have difficulty with the Carter Administration."[5]

The press played a central role in publicizing human rights violations. Alan Riding, who had been covering Mexico and Central America for a decade for the *New York Times*, recalled that at the beginning of the Carter Administration he suspected that the purpose of the human rights policy was "just to needle the Russians." He sought a good test in Latin America, and in his mind, there was no better case than Nicaragua.[6] His articles on Guard repression therefore had a dual purpose—to criticize Somoza and to test the Administration.[7]

When the human rights reports were issued in Washington in April 1977, Somoza denounced the one on Nicaragua as "unacceptable," saying it "constituted interference in the internal affairs of Nicaragua." The report was brief and descriptive, citing the state of siege, the many reports of disappearances and torture, and summarizing the reports issued by other human rights organizations.[8] Five Latin American military governments protested the reports by renouncing U.S. military aid, but that was not Somoza's style. He hired lobbyists and public relations firms in Washington to try to change the policy.[9]

Somoza's objective was to defeat an effort led by Rep. Edward Koch to eliminate the military aid program for Nicaragua. In this he achieved some success, although the lobbyists were much less helpful than two influential Congressmen, Jack Murphy and Charles Wilson. Murphy and Somoza had been classmates at LaSalle Military Academy and West Point; their friendship had begun when they were 13 years old. From 1977 to 1980, according to Murphy, he spoke with Somoza "maybe two or three times a week. And I made many visits to Nicaragua."[10]

Charles Wilson, a flamboyant, conservative Democrat from Texas, became one of Somoza's most effective supporters even though he was not particularly fond of him. His reasons were related to policy, politics, and power. Wilson, like Murphy, thought the Carter Administration—particularly the State Department—was too liberal, too hostile to conservative regimes like that of Somoza, and blind to the Communist menace in the Third World. Politically, he thought Carter's foreign policy would make southern Democrats like himself vulnerable. Wilson therefore used his influence as a swing vote on the critical Foreign Operations Subcommittee of the House Appropriations Committee to try to change the Administration's policy on Nicaragua.[11]

Although the Appropriations Committee narrowly supported Koch's amendment to delete military aid to Nicaragua, Murphy and Wilson succeeded in restoring the funds on the House floor. Their victory was short lived and pyrrhic, however, because the Carter Administration undercut the vote by publicly assuring the House Appropriations Committee on June 22, 1977, that it would not sign a military aid agreement unless there was "an improvement in the human rights situation."

Somoza understood that over the long term he could not influence the United States unless the human rights situation improved, and in the spring of 1977, he instructed the National Guard to curb such abuses. The U.S. government learned of this directive, but many were skeptical of its significance until it was later confirmed by Amnesty International and the Catholic Church.[12]

On July 28, 1977, while visiting his mistress Dinorah Sampson, Somoza felt, in his words, "deep burning heat run across my chest." His doctors advised him to go to the Miami Heart Institute, which diagnosed the attack as angina.[13] Although he commanded an air force and owned Nicaragua's private airline, Somoza requested emergency evacuation by the U.S. Air Force. Aware of his condition but also of his family's long-standing tactic of trying to get the United States to identify with them at moments of vulnerability, the Administration said it would provide a plane, but he would have to pay for it. Somoza claimed to be "shocked and bitter" at the U.S. reaction, but he paid.[14]

His heart condition prevented him from his only opportunity to have a personal meeting with President Carter. In order to try to gain support for the Panama Canal treaties by showing the American people the treaties' importance to Latin America, Carter invited all the heads of state to the signing of the treaty on September 7, 1977. He met individually with each of the eighteen leaders who attended. Somoza's doctors insisted that instead of going, he return to Nicaragua to rest and begin a strict diet and regimen of exercise.

Just as he and his brother had stepped in quickly to fill the vacuum created when his father was assassinated, his son, Anastasio Somoza Portocarrero ("Tacho III"), assumed a more visible role in the government when his father was incapacitated. Tacho III was born in 1951 in the United States and was educated at Harvard University. On returning to Nicaragua, he enlisted in the National Guard and, as one would expect, rose rapidly. By 1977, he was commissioned a major and appointed Director of the Basic Infantry Training School, an elite group modeled on the U.S. Special Forces. As he shuttled between Managua and the Miami Heart Institute to pass messages to his father and return with instructions, Tacho III served as a visible reminder that the Somoza dynasty could extend another generation.

When Somoza returned to Nicaragua in September 1977, his colleagues urged him to step down. Luis Pallais, who was Somoza's cousin and president of the Nicaraguan Congress, argued that if Somoza transferred power to a unity government, he could undermine the opposition and preserve his interests. Pallais believes that he almost convinced Somoza, but as his health improved, so too did his interest in remaining in office. He finally put off Pallais by saying that he could "ride the waves" and remain in power, much as his father had done in 1947.[15]

Somoza was also visited by Costa Rican President Daniel Oduber, who suggested that the time was opportune for Somoza to step down from the Guard and the Presidency. Somoza rejected the idea. As the conversation shifted to Somoza's cool relationship with the United States, Somoza insisted that he still had friends there. Oduber, drawing on fragments of a brief conversation I had with him on May 30, said that the Carter Administration would not support him. Somoza said that this was not the first time that chilly winds had blown down on the Somozas from the north, and he would do as his father and brother had done, "crawl into his shell like an armadillo and wait for the wind to pass." He ended the conversation by saying he would remain President until the end of his term.[16]

Although unwilling to give up power, Somoza was prepared to take a number of steps to try to deal with the human rights problem. First he changed his Cabinet to make it more broadly representative and then he responded to the most pressing U.S. objective at that time:

on September 19, 1977, he ended censorship and lifted the state of siege that had been imposed since the Sandinista raid in December 1974. Immediately *La Prensa*, the only independent, antigovernment newspaper in Nicaragua, began publishing acerbic criticisms of the Somoza regime, and its editor, Pedro Joaquín Chamorro, the leader of a coalition of opposition parties called the Democratic Union of Liberation (UDEL), explored ways to democratize Nicaragua.

Somoza's decision to lift the state of siege put the human rights policy to a second test. Having withheld aid as an inducement to liberalize the political process, the United States should theoretically have released the aid after he took the step, and the Bureau of Inter-American Affairs argued that position. But the Human Rights Bureau argued that this was a small, insignificant step on the path toward a long and difficult dialogue. If the United States granted aid, the opposition would be demoralized and Somoza would have no incentive to pursue the dialogue. The classic division occurred, with ARA arguing to give the carrot and HA arguing to withhold it.

If the fiscal calendar had not forced a decision, the Administration would probably have avoided it, especially because the laws on economic and military aid were different, confusing, and easily subject to misinterpretation. After listening to a heated debate, Christopher decided that having achieved the U.S. objective of getting Somoza to end the state of siege, the United States could not disapprove aid to Nicaragua. On the other hand, the Administration did not want to approve aid and lose important leverage to try to obtain free elections. Christopher chose to keep the options open: the United States would neither approve nor disapprove aid. The United States announced it would not provide any military aid *until* further progress was made in human rights; however, the law required the Administration to sign the 1977 military aid agreement before the end of the fiscal year, or the money would revert to the Treasury and future leverage would be lost. There were no similar constraints built into the economic aid laws, so the Administration merely postponed that decision.

In announcing the continued suspension of economic aid and military aid, the State Department said that the signing of the military aid agreement was required by law, but that it did not mean that the United States was sending military aid. Nevertheless, the *Washington Post* reported: "In a confusing turnaround, the Carter Administration has decided to withhold economic aid while approving military assistance."[17]

The Sandinistas were the last to see the significance of the human rights policy, but their view of it was the clearest. Humberto Ortega, a leader of the Terceristas and Minister of Defense when the Sandinistas later triumphed, recalled:

> In mid-1977, there was great political activity among the bourgeois opposition resulting from the shift given to U.S. foreign policy by the Carter Administration. Imperialism and reaction were seeking ways of making changes in the regime without touching the basic strings of power: the tremendous economic and repressive power of the National Guard.[18]

The Sandinistas viewed the end of martial law and the U.S. effort to democratize Nicaragua as a threat, not an opportunity. The principal lesson that Latin American leftists had learned from the military coups against Guatemalan President Jacobo Arbenz in 1954 and Chilean President Salvador Allende in 1973 was that a revolution would fail unless the old military were replaced with a revolutionary army. The Sandinistas had learned this lesson well and, in Borge's words, remained "focused on the destruction of the National Guard and its replacement with a new armed force that would respond to a new program."[19] Indeed, they alone in Nicaragua preferred Somoza to remain in power until the Guard could be defeated.

Fearful that their revolution could be preempted, the Terceristas therefore accelerated a two-part strategy they had been developing since the Ortegas first contacted Edén Pastora in San José in 1976. Humberto Ortega said they "took note of the fact that the enemy had taken a step forward by lifting the state of siege and was considering an amnesty, and saw that if this happened, we would be in a difficult position. So we decided to speed up the offensive."[20]

On October 13, 1977, Pastora led a small group of Sandinistas in an attack on the Guard barracks in San Carlos, which was directly across the Costa Rican frontier. Simultaneously, other groups of Sandinistas attacked the police stations in Masaya (south of Managua) and at Ocotal in the northern part of Nicaragua.[21] The raids were "daring," in the words of Somoza, who also admitted surprise when he learned that the "sons of solid Conservative families participated in the battles."[22]

More significant was the Sandinistas' new public message: their goal was "not to install a Communist government but merely to overthrow the long-ruling Somoza regime and establish democracy" through free elections. The Sandinistas also insisted that they received "no money or weapons from the Castro regime and that no Nicaraguan guerrillas have been trained in Havana since" 1970.[23] They had learned the lesson Castro had learned from José Martí: "There are things which must be hidden if they are to be obtained."[24]

On October 15, 1977, two days after the raids, a group of twelve prominent Nicaraguan businessmen, lawyers, priests, and educators issued a statement in San José and in Washington, D.C.: "There can be no permanent solution to the escalating armed conflict, which now threatens to envelop all of Nicaragua, without the participation of the Sandinista National Liberation Front."[25] The group, which became known as the Group of Twelve, seemed authentic and independent of the FSLN. Prior to this statement, the Sandinistas were generally viewed by the moderate opposition as a few Communist guerrillas. The three attacks demonstrated they were a viable threat, and the Group of Twelve announcement offered them the legitimacy to be taken seriously by the country's moderate opposition.

Only a few people then knew that the Group of Twelve was created by the Terceristas. In early 1977, Daniel and Humberto Ortega had asked Sergio Ramírez, a Nicaraguan novelist who had recently returned from studying and teaching in Europe, to organize "an alliance with the democratic sectors of the national bourgeoisie" to urge the recognition of the FSLN.[26]

In one case, Joaquín Cuadra Lacayo, who had been fighting with the Sandinistas since 1974, recruited his father, one of Nicaragua's wealthiest and most respected lawyers. Another person who joined the Twelve was Arturo Cruz, a Nicaraguan who was working at the Inter-American Development Bank. Cruz was brought to San José before the attack on San Carlos, and Ramírez told him "we would announce the installation of a provisional government on Nicaraguan territory headed by the Group of 12."[27] When the Sandinistas failed to hold any territory, the Twelve issued its statement in San José.

In repelling the attack against San Carlos, the Nicaraguan Air Force fired across the Costa Rican border at three boats on the San Juan River. On one of those boats was the Costa Rican Minister of Public Security, Mario Charpentier, who was nearly killed. The Costa Ricans protested to the OAS, and the sentiment in Costa Rica, always unfriendly to Somoza, became hostile and, for the first time, sympathetic to the Sandinistas. Prior to the raid at San Carlos, the Sandinistas had purchased their small supply of arms on the black market; afterward, they received support from Costa Rica. According to Pastora, José Figueres became the main source of arms and supplies: "He immediately gave us 300 M-1 rifles, rockets, bazookas, 50 machine guns, 30,000 bullets."[28] Figueres said that he opened his farm, "La Lucha Sin Fin" (The Endless Struggle), to the Sandinistas: "We did everything that was possible to do to help the Sandinistas."[29]

The moderate opposition reacted in different ways to the events of October. Pedro Joaquín Chamorro met secretly with a group of Sandinistas in an effort to get to know them better and perhaps develop a common strategy with UDEL. Others tried to use the vitality injected in the anti-Somoza movement to begin a dialogue with Somoza on the question of a peaceful transition. A committee was established, composed of Archbishop Obando and Monsignor Pablo Vega from the Church, Alfonso Robelo and Felix Esteban Guardicki from the private sector, and Francisco Fiallos, a lawyer. With U.S. encouragement, Somoza agreed to meet with them in December 1977, but they found Somoza "completely stubborn" in his insistence that he finish out his term ending in 1981. They tried to persuade Somoza to begin a national dialogue on a transition before 1981, but he was unmoved.[30]

The Death of Chamorro

On January 9, 1978, in the Iranian city of Qom, the Shah's police opened fire on a demonstration, and the Iranian "revolution had begun."[31] The very next day, on the other side of the globe, the undisputed leader of the Nicaraguan opposition, Pedro Joaquín Chamorro, was assassinated, and another revolution had really begun. More than any other individual in Nicaragua, Chamorro, the descendant of three Nicaraguan Presidents, represented the moderate opposition. His death energized the nation and had a profound effect on Nicaragua's neighbors.

His son, Pedro Joaquín Chamorro Barrios, is convinced that Somoza was not responsible for the assassination,[32] but practically no one in Nicaragua believed that at the time. Thousands marched in the funeral procession, and the businessmen decided that the time had come to split decisively with Somoza. Alfonso Robelo, the president of the major business association in Nicaragua (COSEP), directed and organized a general strike from January 23 until the second week in February. It was 90 percent successful. For the first time, businessmen, as an organized and cohesive political group, issued a public demand for Somoza's resignation. If the earthquake was a watershed in the private sector's view of the venality of the Somoza dynasty, the killing of Chamorro was the catalyst that moved the private sector toward political action.

Chamorro's death also had a profound effect on his close friend, Carlos Andrés Pérez, the President of Venezuela. After Pérez took office in 1975, Chamorro, who had been in exile in Costa Rica with Pérez in the 1950s, visited and told him excitedly: "Carlos Andrés, look, now you can do something for my country." Pérez responded much as the United States would have done: "Pedro Joaquín, you are the one who has to do it, and if you do it, I will support it." Pérez did give him moral and political support, but the death of Chamorro "made me compromise my previous position." He began to play a more direct and active role.[33]

Pérez's Presidency (1974-79) coincided with the sudden rise in the price of oil, which provided a windfall for Venezuela and gave Pérez the resources to assert leadership internationally. In December 1974, he launched a program to provide aid and oil at subsidized prices for most of the countries of Central America and the Caribbean. With aid came influence, and Pérez, the quintessential activist, used it. A strong advocate of human rights and arms control in Latin America, Pérez was delighted by the election of Carter, whom he viewed as dedicated to the same goals. For the first time since his mentor Rómulo Betancourt had established a relationship with John F. Kennedy, Venezuela's President seemed positioned to establish a new cooperative relationship with a U.S. President. And just as Betancourt was obsessed with eliminating Dominican dictator Rafael Trujillo, Pérez had a similar preoccupation with Somoza.

Venezuela, unlike Nicaragua, was relatively high on the Carter Administration's list of priorities, and Pérez was the first South American President invited for a state visit. In late June 1977, Carter met with Pérez for two days of meetings that covered almost every important international issue—human rights, arms control, North–South relations, energy and OPEC, the Middle East (Venezuela's OPEC membership offered it a window for following the Arab-Israeli conflict), Cuba, Zimbabwe, and the Caribbean. No other Latin American President discussed as extensive an agenda with Carter. By the time the two met again in September 1977 after the signing of the Panama Canal treaties, Carter would refer to Pérez as "one of my best personal friends and a great counselor and adviser to me on matters that concern the nations of the Caribbean and Central and South America."[34] Pérez and Carter covered a wide agenda again and agreed to coordinate strategies on a number of issues, but in neither June nor September did they talk about Nicaragua.

Their first exchange on the subject occurred when Pérez sent Carter a letter on January 31, 1978. Pérez had just consulted with Omar Torrijos and Daniel Oduber on a joint strategy to overthrow Somoza, though he did not mention that in the letter. Instead, he described the situation in Nicaragua in dire terms and proposed joint action. Pérez gave the letter personally to the U.S. Ambassador, Viron Peter Vaky, in order to convey the importance he attached to receiving a quick response from Carter. In a classic case of diverging priorities, Carter was just then sending Pérez a letter on the Horn of Africa.

The First Policy Review

By January 1978, virtually all of the initiatives that Carter had begun a year before were beginning to create conflicts within the Administration and political friction with Congress. Carter was deeply worried that his first major initiative—the Canal treaties—could fail, and he devoted much of his time to persuading uncertain Senators. The centerpiece of his domestic policy—the energy legislation—was stuck. Delicate negotiations on SALT and China were beginning to strain the relationship between Secretary of State Cyrus Vance and National Security Adviser Zbigniew Brzezinski.

Although many political analysts predicted a fight between Brzezinski and Vance from the beginning of Carter's term,[35] both entered the Administration in agreement on priorities and the basic outlines of the Administration's approach to foreign policy. In his book *Between Two Ages*, written at the end of the 1960s, Brzezinski had recommended that the United States abandon the Monroe Doctrine and the "special relationship" with Latin America, place relations with the region "on the same level as its relations with the rest of the world," and approach revolutionary change in "the developing countries with a great deal of patience."[36] Brzezinski had also thought about Central America: "American long-range interests would be harmed by continuing indifference to the mounting desire in Central America for greater social justice and national dignity, as our indifference will only make it easier for Castro's Cuba to exploit that desire. Much of Latin America could be antagonized by any resulting conflicts."[37] Vance's views on Latin America were strikingly similar.[38]

On the other hand, there was no denying their different temperaments and perspectives, and their positions at State and the National Security Council reinforced these differences. Vance, a corporate lawyer and skillful negotiator, had the patience and tolerance that made him well suited to be Secretary of State. As National Security Adviser and as a Polish-born professor of Soviet politics, Brzezinski was more conservative and apt to evaluate an event more in terms of its implications for the U.S.–Soviet strategic relationship than was Vance. Although some believed that Brzezinski's Polish background led him to see everything in anti-Soviet terms, it also made him more sensitive to recognizing that Latin America's view of the United States and its need for self-respect had much in common with Poland's view of Russia.

The first important issue that separated Carter's two senior foreign policy advisers was the question of how to respond to the Soviet–Cuban military intervention in the Horn of Africa. Vance argued that it would be counterproductive to approach the crisis as an East–West issue because this could embolden the Somalis and provoke the Soviets, and the United States would be in a weak position to respond. Brzezinski felt that the Cuban–Soviet involvement had injected an East–West dimension into a regional conflict. He insisted that the United States respond for strategic reasons, to raise the costs of intervention to the Soviets and Cubans lest they consider it again, and for political reasons, to counter criticism that Carter was soft on the Soviets.[39]

Much of this criticism stemmed from the nature of the agenda Carter was addressing—"giving away" the Canal treaties, arms control, normalization of relations with China, cancelling the B-1 bomber—but there was no question that conservatives in the Democratic as well as the Republican party were increasingly bothered by the direction of Carter's foreign policy. Indeed, the Murphy–Wilson defense of Somoza was, in part, a reaction by conservative Democrats against the perception that Carter was tilting away from their world view. The disagreement between Brzezinski and Vance on the Horn was the first time this difference within the Democratic Party was aired within the Carter Administration.

In January 1978, Carter decided to consult with a number of world leaders about issues related to the Horn, and he sent a letter to Carlos Andrés Pérez. The letter requested Pérez's advice about the most appropriate response to Cuba's violation of the principle of nonintervention, a principle Latin America had championed. A week after Carter sent the letter, I tried to interest Brzezinski in the various issues raised by Pérez on Nicaragua, but he asked instead about Pérez's response to the letter on the Horn. I called Vaky in Caracas, and learned that Pérez would not receive our Ambassador or the letter until he had received a response on Nicaragua. When I relayed this to Brzezinski, he suddenly took an interest in Nicaragua and asked for a memo and a draft letter for the President, on an urgent basis.

The letter from Pérez, therefore, served its purpose: for the first time, the Carter Administration was forced to address the Nicaraguan situation as a political issue. Simultaneously, the moderate opposition in Nicaragua asked the U.S. Ambassador in Managua for a position, and he proposed a statement of support for democracy.

Warren Christopher, who had gradually assumed primary responsibility for Latin America and human rights on behalf of Vance, convened a small meeting to discuss what role the United States should play in Nicaragua and to review drafts of a statement and a letter for Carter. The Bureau of Inter-American Affairs suggested the United States directly mediate a dialogue between Somoza and the opposition. The representatives of Policy Planning and the Bureau of Human Rights and I, representing the NSC—all political appointees— argued that we should reaffirm our support for democracy, which the State Department did in a statement on February 6, 1978, but avoid becoming an intermediary. Christopher agreed.

Carter's letter, signed on February 17, pledged him to work closely with President Pérez on human rights issues and, as Pérez had suggested, to try to obtain Somoza's acceptance of a visit by the Inter-American Human Rights Commission (IAHRC). Second, with regard to Nicaraguan politics, Carter wrote: "We can and will voice our preference for increased democratization. . . . But we will not intervene or impose specific political solutions for individual countries." Ambassador Solaun was also instructed to encourage Somoza to accept a visit by the IAHRC.

Events in Nicaragua did not wait for the U.S. government to complete its abstract discussion on its proper role. The death of Chamorro unleashed a torrent of hatred against Somoza. Demonstrations were organized in most of the major municipalities and in several cases, as on the small island of Monimbó, a spontaneous, violent riot occurred.

The opposition united behind the business community during the general strike, and its organizer, Alfonso Robelo, soon found himself at the head of a mass and middle-class movement to unseat Somoza. Robelo, born in 1940 and educated as a chemical engineer at Rensselaer Polytechnic Institute, owned 10 percent of an agrobusiness that processed cotton seed for cooking oil. His real interest, however, was politics. At the age of 32, he became president of the Chamber of Industry, and by 36, he was elected president of the Nicaraguan Development Institute (INDE) and the Higher Council of Private Enterprise (COSEP), the two major business associations in Nicaragua. Because of this role, as already mentioned, he had participated in the stillborn dialogue with Somoza in December 1977.

The personal experience of leading the general strike whetted his political appetite. On March 16, together with a group of about a hundred young professionals, he established the Nicaraguan Democratic Movement, which then immediately tried to bring other groups under a new umbrella organization, the Broad Opposition Front (FAO). In May 1978, most of the moderate opposition agreed to associate with the FAO, and in August 1978, the Group of Twelve also joined. The Twelve also arranged meetings between Robelo and the Tercerista leadership in San José, Costa Rica, in April 1978. This was the first time he had met the Ortegas, and they impressed him as pragmatic, leftist Social Democrats. He did not think they were associated with Cuba, but he did not ask because he was not concerned with this issue.[40] The Group of Twelve also met with officials and organizations throughout the United States, Latin America, and Europe. A human rights organization, for example, arranged for Miguel D'Escoto, a Maryknoll priest and member of the Twelve, who would later become Nicaragua's Foreign Minister, to meet with me on November 11, 1977. His message was simple: the Sandinistas enjoyed wide support. They were not Castroite Marxists, though they included some radical elements. Nicaraguans were tired of living on Somoza's "national farm" and would overthrow Somoza and his regime. He also said that he hoped the United States would take a neutral position.[41]

Somoza recognized the growing power of the opposition and although he was not reluctant to confront it, he was shrewd enough to try other approaches as well. In a press conference on February 26, 1978, he announced for the first time his intention to leave both the Presidency and the National Guard at the end of his term. He established a special commission to investigate the Chamorro assassination. He also promised that new political parties could register, and he offered a dialogue on whether to reform the television and radio code, expand rights of labor unions, and restructure the National Guard. A measure of the crisis within Nicaragua was that people were disheartened to hear Somoza say he would step down in 1981, because that meant he would remain until then. The reaction was expressed in continuing riots and gun battles in various parts of the country.

Washington was still focused on other issues, but Carter had an opportunity to review events during his trip to Venezuela and Brazil. On March 28, 1978, in Caracas, Carter and Pérez talked about Nicaragua for the first time, although it was neither the first nor the most important issue they discussed.

Pérez raised the issue and posed the problem: "Somoza's authority was diminished. . . . The danger is the increased strength of the Sandinistas. It is very similar to the fall of Batista." During the discussion, Pérez kept returning to the Cuban case, and Carter, who said he agreed with the analysis, tried to focus on what could be done. "As you have requested," Carter said, "we have encouraged Somoza to let in the Inter-American Commission on Human Rights, and we have frozen our aid program. But we have a difficult time proposing direct action by the U.S. to bring about Somoza's downfall." Carter reiterated his commitment to nonintervention and said that he did not believe the United States should engage in a policy of changing the governments of small nations.

Pérez could have disagreed; he could have explained that stating a principle and practicing it were different or he could have argued that Somoza was an exception, but he did not, even though his actions implied that was what he believed. Instead, he accepted Carter's point and urged multilateral pressure on Somoza using the OAS and other forums, though he could not stop repeating the Cuban case and said he was convinced Somoza would not last until 1981. Carter suggested that if Pérez could persuade Somoza, perhaps Somoza would step down.

Pérez was disappointed by the response and decided to press ahead independently without consulting or even informing Carter. In 1977, Pérez had established a National Security Council in the Venezuelan government. It was composed of a few military officers to coordinate and manage crises and to undertake special projects for the President. Their first task was a study of Nicaragua. As the study evolved, Pérez defined its objective as the overthrow of Somoza and decided to use Venezuelan funds and arms to increase his country's influence with the Sandinistas and to serve as an incentive to unite the Sandinista factions.[42] However, the principal recipient of the weapons and monthly financial allotments was Pastora.[43]

The United States unintentionally moved in the opposite direction. In May, after one year of delays, the Administration reluctantly approved two basic human needs loans to Nicaragua: $3 million for education and $7.5 million for nutrition. Congressman Charles Wilson forced a decision, and the Administration felt it could no longer justify a delay.

Most members of Congress are unable to locate the point in the Executive Branch where effective leverage can translate into a deal, but Wilson found that point in the person of Henry Owen, who had been appointed the President's Coordinator for the International Summits but soon became a virtual czar of U.S. foreign economic policy during the Carter Administration. Owen was sensitive both to the tenuousness of the aid program on Capitol Hill and to the pivotal nature of Wilson's vote. When Wilson told Owen that he would block the aid bill until the two Nicaraguan loans were signed, Owen judged that a credible threat.

In general, the Administration approved basic human needs loans, except in the most egregious cases of human rights violations. Although the response by the Guard to the riots represented a serious concern, Somoza did not reimpose martial law or censorship of the press. His subsequent concessions made it difficult to argue that the situation in Nicaragua at that moment was bad enough to justify a further aid postponement, particularly because the United States had made such loans to countries with worse human rights records. Somoza had taken many of the steps that the Administration had been demanding, and it was hard to argue against the loans without making it sound as if the Administration was pursuing a vendetta against him. Owen persuaded Christopher to go ahead.

In its announcement of the loans, the Administration sought to correct the impression of inconsistency conveyed by news reports of the September 1977 decisions. First, the Administration noted it had not given any military aid to Nicaragua since it came into office, and it did not even request fiscal year 1979 funding.[44] Second, to preclude Somoza's trying to use the loans to indicate U.S. support, the State Department issued the following statement on May 16 in Washington and in Managua: "The U.S. reiterates its policy of strict non-intervention in the internal political affairs of Nicaragua and our continuing desire for a steady non-violent transition to genuine democratic rule. Approval of A.I.D. projects for the needy is not intended as an expression of political support." The effort failed; the *Washington Post* reported it as another "policy reversal."[45]

The Carter Letter

On June 19, Somoza held a press conference and promised to invite the Inter-American Human Rights Commission and allow the return of the Group of Twelve to Nicaragua. In addition, he said he would consider signing the American Convention on Human Rights and declaring an amnesty for political prisoners. The Carter Administration had attached priority to obtaining Somoza's agreement to each of these points, and several were pursued on the initiative of Venezuela.

Neither the *Washington Post* nor the *New York Times* covered that conference, but the Embassy routinely reported it. The key points were included by the White House Situation Room in its June 21 summary of events of the previous day. Carter read it and was impressed that Somoza had conceded most of the points the United States had been making. He instructed Brzezinski to prepare a letter for him to send to Somoza to express his support for the steps. Brzezinski asked me to do the draft. When I protested, he cut me off: "Write it. Put your concerns in the memo to the President and clear it with State."

Although I was uneasy about sending a letter to Somoza, I never guessed that it would turn out to be so controversial. The case is an interesting study of both the effect of the press on policy and the way in which the psychology of the U.S.–Nicaraguan relationship could transform something inherently insignificant into a major event.

Carter had sent similar letters to other heads of state in Latin America and elsewhere. His style was to encourage progress gently and to reinforce it when it occurred,[46] hardly a novel idea. Generals Pinochet of Chile and Videla of Argentina—leaders responsible for much worse repression than Somoza—had received such letters. Moreover, Carter had just returned from Panama, where he had met with five heads of state, and in the communiqué they jointly issued, no one had suggested singling out Nicaragua. In short, Carter had no reason to believe that Somoza should be an exception to his policy.

The letter I drafted noted each of Somoza's promises, as well as others he had previously made to reform the electoral system. The letter sought to encourage Somoza to fulfill his promises by explaining the importance Carter attached to each of them. For example, Carter expressed his "hope that your government can rapidly reach agreement with the [Human Rights] Commission on a date for their visit," and he underscored its importance by noting that "multilateral institutions can be a most appropriate and effective means of protecting human rights." The letter concluded: "I look forward to hearing of the implementation of your decisions."

I then sent the draft to the State Department. ARA joined HA in opposing any letter from Carter to Somoza, because they felt it could be misinterpreted to indicate that the United States was not serious about its human rights policy. Christopher asked about the origin of the letter, and I told him that the President had requested it. I did not offer my views about whether to send it because I did not feel strongly about the issue, and I had not yet made up my own mind. State then formally returned the letter to the National Security Council with marginal changes and a recommendation that it be delayed for a week, pending the negotiations between Nicaragua and the Inter-American Commission over a visit.

My job then was to prepare a cover memo for Brzezinski to send to the President, and I recommended against sending the letter for two reasons. First, Somoza did not have a good record of keeping his promises. Second, I feared Somoza would use the letter—"not necessarily the substance, just that you sent him a personal note—in a way which will lend support to him for partisan political purposes." Brzezinski, who at that time had more substantial disagreements with the State Department, decided to delete my argument against sending the letter and submit a simpler memo concurring with the department's recommendation. On June 26, Carter revised the letter to make the same points more gently and personally, expressing his "appreciation" for the steps. He also accepted the recommendation to delay sending the letter until June 30.

After the President signs a letter, the standard operating procedure is for the State Department to cable the text to the appropriate ambassador for delivery. This time, State procrastinated, finally cabling it on July 8. Ambassador Solaun presented it orally on July 11. On July 14, he informed the State Department that the Broad Opposition Front was planning a general strike on July 19, and fearful of the letter's possible impact, he asked permission not to deliver the physical letter when it arrived. Pete Vaky, the new Assistant Secretary of State for Inter-American Affairs, agreed with Solaun.

I was surprised to learn that Solaun had delayed implementing the President's decision for two weeks without informing the White House. I suggested that Vaky try to persuade Vance to ask the President's permission not to deliver the letter. Neither Vance nor Brzezinski thought it was worth the President's time or temper, but they accepted my recommendation that Solaun be told to stress the confidential aspect of the letter. If Somoza chose to use the letter and violate the confidence of President Carter, then that would tell us something about our ability to communicate sincerely with him. It did.

On July 21, Solaun delivered the letter, and after he left, Somoza was startled and confused. The letter arrived, Somoza later recalled, "at a time when I needed encouragement, and particularly from the U.S."[47] Somoza felt that he was finally "making headway," and for the first time, was communicating with "the middie" (midshipman), as he referred to Carter in his conversations with Representative Jack Murphy and Max Kelly, a personal aide and another fellow West Point graduate.[48]

Though Solaun had stressed the need for confidentiality, Somoza wrote in his memoirs of his first reaction: "The contents of that letter, if publicly known, could assist me greatly in warding off my other enemies. I was not interested in a collector's item, and without being able to use the letter, that's what it was."[49] He knew by then what the United States did not, that Pérez was the principal source of arms and funding to the Sandinistas, and he decided to use the letter on him first.

He immediately arranged a meeting with Pérez on a small island, La Orchila, off the coast of Venezuela. Both flew there for a tough and uncompromising four-hour confrontation in late July 1978.[50] Somoza surprised Pérez with the letter, and claimed he enjoyed the support of President Carter. Pérez was annoyed but not diverted: "I don't care what Carter says. Our position is firm. You have to go."[51] They talked about several possible solutions to the crisis, and Pérez offered to ease Somoza's exit by purchasing Somoza's property in Nicaragua and ensuring his security. But Somoza claims he insisted on the need to stay to forestall a Communist victory. At this, Pérez responded forcefully, as he recalled in a later interview:

> Somoza, if you don't accept my advice to leave Nicaragua and give way to a democratic solution and to an agreement between the National Guard and the guerrillas for the rise of a government that would grant liberty in Nicaragua, you will be the greatest criminal in Latin America. Everyone is against you. You will not be saved from being overthrown.[52]

At the conclusion, they returned to where they started. "Regrettably," Pérez recalled, "he received all my advice with incredible cynicism, and we did not get any agreement." The letter had failed to serve Somoza's purpose.

A few days later, on August 1, the *Washington Post* published a front-page article, headlined "Carter Letter to Somoza Stirs Human Rights Row," by John Goshko. The lead paragraph read: "President Carter, overriding State Department objections, has sent a personal letter congratulating Nicaraguan President Anastasio Somoza for promises to improve the human rights situation in his country." Goshko wrote that the NSC had originated the letter "to give Somoza an encouraging pat on the back" and then forced the State Department to deliver it. The article indicated that "State Department officials are concerned that revelation of the letter . . . will raise questions about the credibility and sensitivity of the Administration's human rights policy." The article concluded that the human rights policy "seemed to veer back and forth, drawing charges that its policy toward Somoza is confusing, inconsistent, and ineffective."

In large part because of this article, Carter noted in his diary the next day: "The editorial policy of the *Washington Post* has been very good. The news policy abominable."[53] Carter was so angry with the distorted leak of the letter that he "came down on the State Department like a ton of bricks" and tried to get the leaker dismissed.[54] The source was not found, but Goshko later told me that it was a senior pro–human rights official in the Bureau of Inter-American Affairs. Goshko never saw the letter.

During the next two days, the White House provided a detailed briefing of the purpose and the contents of the letter. Rex Granum, the White House Deputy Press Secretary, emphasized that the letter's purpose was to encourage Somoza to implement his announcements, not to "congratulate" him on his progress. A brief clarification in the *Washington Post* the next day reported that Granum had said that both the State Department and the NSC had recommended the letter—which was technically correct—but the report still characterized the letter as "congratulating" Somoza, and that perception remains.[55]

The U.S. Chargé met with Somoza the day of the Goshko article, and Somoza promised that "no one has seen President Carter's letter." (The United States did not know he was lying; it was not aware of his meeting with Pérez.) As Somoza read the letter more closely, his initial reaction of it as "a nice, friendly letter," gave way to a feeling that it was a devious trick and that Carter was "stepping up his attack" against him.[56] At the same time, because of the letter, Somoza acknowledged in his memoirs that he did permit the Group of Twelve to return and the Inter-American Commission to visit. The latter would seriously and adversely affect his position in the OAS.

The letter also represented a watershed for U.S. policy, although an ironic one in some ways. First, it impelled Brzezinski and Carter to focus on Nicaragua for the first time. Before the incident, my memos on Nicaragua were returned as too long; afterward, they were requested. On August 8, I offered a detailed analysis that Somoza's strategy was to play for time until 1981, but by then, the United States might have "to deal with a real possibility of a strong leftist revolutionary movement and an evaporating political middle." I recommended a formal Presidential Review Memorandum to develop a long-term strategy, but Brzezinski was not yet that interested, and Vaky, who wanted State to manage the process, also opposed the idea.

Second, the letter represented the last time Nicaragua would be defined solely in the bureaucratic context of the human rights policy. After the letter and the Sandinista takeover of the National Palace in August, the United States approached Nicaragua as a political-security crisis, and the Human Rights Bureau was excluded from the central deliberations, although it continued to play a role in defining the State Department position. In addition, as in many leaks directed at the White House from a department, the leak of this letter served to divide the two from one another, heighten mutual suspicions, and shrink the number of people who would have access to policy-making meetings or decisions.

The strongest argument against sending the letter was that Somoza might disclose it in a way that associated himself with Carter. Therefore, the most exquisite irony of the entire episode was that it was leaked not by Somoza, but by a State Department official who was reportedly committed to Carter's human rights policy, even though the letter was Carter's idea and the leak enraged him. Moreover, this official described the letter incorrectly as "congratulating" Somoza for improving human rights, rather than encouraging him to fulfill his promises. And that description of the letter—rather than the letter itself—confused or angered Carter's friends in Latin America and the moderate opposition in Nicaragua.

The letter accomplished Carter's purpose of encouraging Somoza to fulfill at least some of his promises. Somoza tried to use the letter on Pérez, but failed. The leak by a State Department official accomplished what the letter and Somoza failed to do: it associated Carter with Somoza in a way that the actual letter did not.

The Takeover of the National Palace

Nicaragua's political landscape was not changed by the letter, however, but by the bold act of Edén Pastora and a group of twenty-five Sandinistas on August 22, 1978. Pastora captured the National Palace and 1,500 people in it![57] For the next two days, Pastora negotiated with Somoza with the aid of Archbishop Obando. Somoza was under considerable pressure by some of his officers to storm the palace, but instead he accepted most of the Sandinistas' demands. He released 59 political prisoners, including Pastora's old rival, Tomás Borge; paid $500,000 in cash (Pastora had asked for $10 million); and permitted their long communiqué to be published in the newspapers and read (105 minutes) over the radio three times a day during the next two days. The communiqué called on the Guard to rebel and the people to join them in overthrowing Somoza. Although describing the conflict as a class struggle, the Sandinistas welcomed capitalists to participate in the "anti-Somoza fight," provided they understood that they could not "try to impose formulas in which their personal interests come before those of the populace."

Somoza guaranteed the Sandinistas safe exit, and their trip to the airport was described by reporters as a "victory parade" because of the crowds cheering for the FSLN.[58] The Carter Administration was aware of the nation's distaste for Somoza, but it was startled and unsettled at how easily that hatred was transformed into support for the Sandinistas. An additional sign of their increasing legitimacy was the plane's destination. After the raid in 1974, the Sandinistas flew to Cuba; in 1978, they flew to Panama and Venezuela on planes provided by those two governments.

Tad Szulc, a former reporter of the *New York Times*, interviewed Pastora in Panama and reported that the Carter letter had provoked the palace takeover. Pastora told him: "How could [Carter] praise Somoza while our people were being massacred by the dictatorship?"[59] In an interview five years later, Pastora acknowledged that the letter had not provoked the raid. Pastora, like most of the Sandinista leadership, was aware that Somoza had lost U.S. support from the beginning.[60] Pastora used the letter to try to stimulate the Administration's critics and neutralize the policy.

Humberto Ortega later revealed the real reason for the palace takeover. The raid, he said, was taken "to foil the imperialist plot which consisted of staging a coup in August to put a civilian-military regime in power, and thus put a damper on the revolutionary struggle."[61] The Sandinistas knew that Somoza was the key to their victory; if the Guard replaced him, the Sandinistas would lose much of their popular support. The purpose of the raid was to preempt and thus prevent a coup against Somoza.

The Sandinistas were correct about the coup plot, but they overestimated the role played by the United States. Washington had no information—and certainly no policy—about a Guard coup. On August 28, however, eighty-five members of the National Guard, including Lieutenant Colonel Bernardino Larios and a dozen officers, were arrested for plotting a coup.[62] On September 9, General José Ivan Alegrett and several others, who had conveyed to reporters their anger over Somoza's surrender of the National Palace, died in a plane crash. There was widespread speculation that Somoza had them killed to discourage further plots.[63]

The Sandinistas feared a coup, but they also were determined to stay in front of the anti-Somoza movement. A second reason for the palace raid was simply to leapfrog others who laid a claim to a post-Somoza Nicaragua. In the two weeks before the raid, Archbishop Obando issued a declaration urging the establishment of "a national government of transition."[64] A few days later, the private sector led by Robelo's INDE issued a statement supporting the Church and urging Somoza to withdraw from the government.

The raid fulfilled the Sandinistas' most optimistic expectations. It placed them in the "vanguard" of an increasingly broad-based opposition and captured the excitement and support of Nicaragua's youth—"los muchachos." After the raid, on August 25, the FAO called for another general strike to seek Somoza's resignation. This sparked another uprising. Matagalpa was seized by "los muchachos," and they held it until the Nicaraguan Air Force began aerial bombing three days later.

The FSLN and some elements of the business community began, for the first time, to coordinate their plans for an insurrection in September. The United States was unaware of such cooperation, although Somoza was. Indeed, throughout much of this period, the three key sets of actors—the Sandinistas, the FAO, and Somoza's Guard—all assumed that the United States knew at least as much as they did about their adversaries' plans and may actually have been orchestrating events. Neither assumption was accurate.

Somoza and the Sandinistas knew more about each other than the United States knew about either. Somoza knew the Sandinistas were planning a takeover of the palace, and although he did not know when it would occur, he had readied a special force to resist the attack. When Pastora struck, the force was inexplicably not at the palace.[65] One of the reasons Pastora gained entry so easily was precisely because the Guard stationed at the palace thought Pastora's group was the special force. Similarly, as Humberto Ortega noted, the Sandinistas planned the takeover to preempt a coup against Somoza. The U.S. government was not only unaware of the coup plot beforehand, it did not consider its implications afterward.

In September 1978, fighting spread to five major cities in Nicaragua. The FSLN struggled to stay in front of the prairie fire, but as Humberto Ortega would later admit: "The mass movement went beyond the vanguard's capacity to take the lead. . . . It was a spontaneous reaction on the part of the masses which, in the end, the Sandinista Front began to direct through its activists and a number of military units."[66]

The pressure for U.S. involvement increased dramatically. Many in the moderate opposition feared the violence and the polarization, and pleaded with the United States to replace Somoza. Venezuela and Panama pressed the United States to the same end. On September 1, 1978, both Somoza and a leader of the Sandinistas held press conferences. The FSLN accused the United States of intervening in Nicaragua to defend Somoza, and Somoza accused the United States of trying to overthrow him. Somoza said the Carter Administration was "in the hands of leftists and communists."[67] The State Department spokesperson was asked about Somoza's allegation: "Our policy re-

mains one of non-intervention in the domestic politics of other countries. . . . We are not in the position of suggesting the overthrow or
downfall of any government."

The Frontier

The inauguration of Carter, Somoza's heart attack, the murder of
Chamorro, the establishment of the Group of Twelve, and the palace
raid—these five events between January 1977 and September 1978
shook the foundation of the Somoza dynasty. The crisis in Nicaragua
forced a distracted Carter Administration to confront some hard policy choices—not between human rights and security, as some have
suggested, but whether, and if so how, the United States should influence the process of political change in a small Central American
country.

The Carter policy succeeded in opening Nicaragua to genuine debate though the lifting of martial law, the end of censorship, the re-
straints on the National Guard, the invitation to the Inter-American
Commission, and the return of political exiles. Somoza was constrained, and the opposition had more space. As one observer noted
during the 1977 insurrection: "For fear of alienating Washington,
General Somoza has been unable to respond to the new offensive
against his regime by declaring a state of siege and unleashing a wave
of repression against his opponents."[68]

Although effective in Nicaragua, the policy had become increasingly controversial in the United States, with liberals criticizing the
Administration for being too easy on Somoza and conservatives condemning it for picking on old friends. There was some validity to
both criticisms. U.S. policy was deliberately reformist and gradual-
ist. It would neither accept Somoza nor aim to overthrow him. In
choosing this line, the Carter Administration drew unconsciously
from elements of a political culture that reflected a wariness of sharp
breaks and a preference for gradual change.

The issue for Nicaraguans, who were responding to a very different, volcanic political culture, was not how to get Somoza to democratize, but how to get him out. Nicaraguans were impatient for a
sharp break with the past. Though the United States had the potential power, the struggle was among Nicaraguans, and the United
States was forced to adjust to a process of revolutionary change for
which it was philosophically and temperamentally ill equipped.

By September 1978, the frontier of U.S. human rights policy had
been reached. As the war worsened in Nicaragua, this policy proved

to be less of a constraint on Somoza's behavior and less useful as a tool for pursuing U.S. interests. The issue became what role the United States should play as Nicaragua became engulfed in civil war. The people of Nicaragua, however, were in the lead; they forced the pace of events, and the United States reluctantly reexamined the premises of its policy and adapted.

Chapter 5

TO MEDIATE

OR NOT TO MEDIATE:

THE POLICY QUESTION

> The crisis in Nicaragua can be described as a simple
> problem: a mentally deranged man [Anastasio Somoza] with
> an army of criminals is attacking a defenseless population.
> . . . This is not a problem for the OAS; what we need is a
> psychiatrist.
> **Omar Torrijos, September 22, 1978**

THE CHEERS that greeted Edén Pastora on his way to the airport after the palace raid were the political equivalent of the tremors that seismologists detect before earthquakes or volcanic eruptions. Scientists can now judge with a high degree of probability whether there will be an eruption or an earthquake. What they don't know is when and how severe it will be. It could be one month, three years, or a decade.

The science of politics is even more inexact. In a recently declassified hearing of the Senate Foreign Relations Committee on the prospects of the Shah of Iran, Senator Frank Church warned: "All I know about history says he is not long for this world, nor his system. And when he goes down, boom, we go with him." The prognosis was perfect, but the timing was off by eighteen years. The hearing was held in 1961. In that interim, four U.S. Presidents came and went.[1]

The Carter Administration knew that Nicaragua would soon be jolted by a political earthquake; it just didn't know when. It might be one year, three, or more. Therefore, like the people who live in San Francisco today, the Administration was uncertain how or how much to prepare for the inevitable. Once again, however, Nicaraguans set the pace. With each tremor inside the country, everyone grew anxious and turned to the United States for help, just as they had after Nicaragua's natural earthquake in 1972.

There are procedures for responding to natural disasters, but no such formulas exist for political disasters. Nonetheless, the United States devoted considerable energy to try to find one. Between September 1978 and January 1979, a senior committee of the National Security Council met eleven times to debate what role the United States should play to resolve the crisis while serving its long-term interests. This chapter will focus on the evolution of U.S. policy from noninterference in September 1978 to multilateral mediation in November 1978.

A Motive for Movement

On September 9, the Sandinistas launched coordinated attacks on National Guard detachments in Nicaragua's major cities. Fighting for his political life, Somoza overcame whatever inhibitions he had acquired in the previous year and fought with the brutality a nation usually reserves for its enemy, not for its own people (and certainly not for its youth). But it still took nearly a month for the Guard to regain control of the towns.

As the demands increased for his resignation, Somoza became more intransigent. Using an old family tactic, he claimed that the only choice was between the Communists and himself.[2] The depth and breadth of the opposition in Nicaragua belied Somoza's description of the options. However, on August 29 Somoza began to take a series of steps that the United States interpreted as trying to make his false description true. He revoked the charter of the largest business associations and instructed the Central Bank to recall loans previously made to business leaders who organized the strike. Within a week, Somoza arrested about 50 leaders of the moderate opposition, including Adolfo Calero, a leader of the Conservative Party and manager of the Coca-Cola bottling franchise. Eventually 600 to 800 people were imprisoned.

Somoza's decision to strike at the moderate opposition was one of the major factors motivating the United States to review its previous policy of strict noninterference in Nicaragua's internal affairs. Until then, the senior officials in the Carter Administration—Carter, Vance, Brzezinski, and Christopher—had a clear vision of the role the United States should not play as well as the one it should. The United States should avoid, in their view, a posture of paternalism in which the United States, acting alone, would dictate political solutions.

Carter's preferred policy had two dimensions. First, the United States should encourage democracy and dialogue among competing groups within a country but should not mediate or arbitrate that dialogue. Decisions on the political future of Nicaragua should be made by Nicaraguans, not by the United States. The Carter Administration realized that the history of interventionism had left many in the region psychologically dependent on the United States to resolve their nations' problems, but the Administration, like Franklin Roosevelt's, wanted to avoid being drawn into those quarrels. The goal was to seek more balanced relationships. The United States would state its concerns, for example, on human rights, but it would not determine who should govern.

The second dimension stemmed from the same interest in balance, but it was aimed at international rather than national politics. The United States sought to forge regional relationships that were respectful and allowed greater autonomy, even for the small nations of the Caribbean Basin. This meant that if the Nicaraguan crisis required international help, the United States should consult and coordinate its response with friendly democratic governments in the region.

The vision of U.S. policy based on these two elements was impaired by Somoza's strategy to eliminate a reformist, middle option, and it was impugned by the pragmatism of the new Assistant Secretary of State for Inter-American Affairs, Pete Vaky.

A decision to replace the Administration's first Assistant Secretary, Terence Todman, was made in February 1978 after he gave a speech that sounded more like it was given by an Administration critic than by one of its officials. Todman, like many competent foreign service officers, was a charming and effective Ambassador, but in making policy, he was not effective and did not appear comfortable. Vance appointed Vaky to replace Todman.

Vaky was the Foreign Service's first choice because he was the diplomat's diplomat—he was aggressive, but he achieved his objectives in a smooth, gentle manner that almost appeared deferential. He combined long experience in Latin America with a number of policy-making assignments in Washington. Having served on the National Security Council during the first year of the Nixon Administration, he understood, as his predecessor did not, how the process worked under a strong President. Having served most recently as Ambassador to Costa Rica, Colombia, and then Venezuela, he understood how the Nicaraguan crisis was viewed by three of its democratic neighbors.

Like the political appointees of the Carter Administration, Vaky shared a distaste for the Somoza regime and a commitment to Carter's core principles—human rights, nonintervention, and regional cooperation. But the experience of working through hundreds of diplomatic problems under seven different Presidents had led him to be wary of the slogans, "principles," or ideology of any particular White House occupant. Vaky thought only the United States could solve the problem of Somoza, and that it should use whatever force necessary—barring assassination—to remove him.[3]

On August 29, 1978, Vaky called the first interagency meeting to address the political crisis in Nicaragua. He argued that the United States needed to get in front of events and assemble a coalition government. Otherwise, the situation would polarize even further, increasing the probability of a Marxist victory. Anthony Lake, who had directed Carter's foreign policy transition team and had been a close adviser to Vance, was the Director of Policy Planning in the State Department. He and I both agreed with Vaky's analysis, but not with his recommendation. We believed that the United States should not pursue a policy of overthrowing governments. Our current problems in the region stemmed in part from the history of U.S. interventionism, which, although almost always undertaken with good intentions, frequently had adverse effects on U.S. interests that outweighed any shorter-term benefits.

In frustration, and reminiscent of Pérez's conversation six months before with Carter, Vaky kept repeating that a failure to take control of events in Nicaragua would lead to a repetition of the Cuban crisis of 1957-58. I repeated to Vaky Carter's response to Pérez, and said that the President's policy could not be altered at this meeting. I suggested two preliminary steps before addressing the issue at a higher level: first, State should draft a paper defining the options for U.S. policy; and second, our ambassadors should seek advice on what should be done from the Presidents of Venezuela, Costa Rica, Panama, and Mexico. Vaky agreed and scheduled the next meeting on Labor Day, September 4, 1978.

By then, the situation in Nicaragua had deteriorated markedly, and Somoza had begun to arrest the leadership of the moderate opposition. Carter received messages from Pérez, Costa Rican President Rodrigo Carazo, and Mexican President José López Portillo. Brzezinski called me into his office on Labor Day at 9:00 A.M., and told me that Carter wanted a recommendation by the end of the day on how to respond to those messages. I told him that fortunately Vaky had scheduled a meeting that day at State; Brzezinski rescheduled it for the White House, to be chaired by his Deputy, David Aaron. Unhappy with the change in venue, Vaky nevertheless did not object since the meeting's purpose had changed; now, it was to present a recommendation to the President. From then on, U.S. policy toward Nicaragua would be hammered out in the National Security Council.

The National Security Decision-Making Process

The National Security Act of 1947 established the National Security Council (NSC) to coordinate and advise the President on national security matters. The statutory members are the President, the Vice President, the Secretaries of State and Defense, but all Presidents have added others, depending on the issue and the person.

Like any executive committee, the NSC has been adapted to serve the special needs of each President, but since President Kennedy, the NSC has consistently become known less as a Cabinet council and more as a part of the Presidential staff. The NSC staff reached its largest size under President Nixon when, with fifty professionals, it acted as almost a surrogate State Department. President Carter reduced the staff to thirty-five professionals and made it less hierarchical, but he soon discovered that his ability to be the premier foreign policy maker required a strong NSC staff. Its responsibilities are to coordinate policy, do long-term planning or propose initiatives, ensure that the President's decisions are implemented, and most importantly, to provide staff assistance for the National Security Adviser and President. What the NSC uniquely offers the President is a staff that views his problems from his perspective. That is why all Presidents interested in asserting control over foreign policy increasingly come to rely on their NSC staff more than on the personnel of the Cabinet departments, whose views often reflect their institution's interests more than those of the President.

Under Carter, the NSC was divided into two committees: a Policy Review Committee (PRC), charged with coordinating foreign, defense, and international economic policy, and chaired by the Secretary of a department, depending on the issue; and a Special Coordination Committee (SCC), chaired by the National Security Adviser and charged with coordinating intelligence policy, arms control, and crisis management. President Carter seldom chaired a formal NSC meeting, and he never chaired one on Latin American and Caribbean affairs.[4]

Instead, Carter made most of his decisions by reviewing a memorandum that summarized a PRC or SCC meeting, listed and analyzed the options, and described the recommendations of each of the departments. Carter generally would receive these memoranda the day of the meeting and return it to Brzezinski the next day. Other important modes of decision making were correspondence; meetings with other heads of state; and the Friday morning breakfasts, which were informal opportunities to meet with the Secretary of State, National Security Adviser, and others, such as the Vice President. Carter also invited new ideas and memoranda independent of the NSC meetings, but he required that all memoranda state clearly and fully the views of all related agencies. Carter organized the process to ensure that he made all the crucial policy decisions on Nicaragua and on most other issues as well.

As the crises proliferated in the second year of the Administration and the time available to Carter's senior advisers became scarce, the PRC and SCC meetings were increasingly chaired by deputies. David Aaron, who had left the Foreign Service in the early 1970s to work for Walter Mondale in the Senate, returned to the NSC on January 20, 1977, as Deputy Assistant to the President for National Security Affairs. He chaired the mini-SCC meeting about Nicaragua on September 4. These mini-SCC's proved to be very effective vehicles for refining options in order to make better use of the Cabinet's time.

When the action shifts to the White House, the power of the NSC to shape the agenda, select the participants, and interpret the results for the President naturally increases. However, the power to implement decisions remains in the Cabinet departments. Since almost all U.S. decisions on Nicaragua were diplomatic rather than military, economic, or covert, the State Department retained the principal position in policy making. The institutional tension between NSC and State derives in part from the former's control of the agenda and the latter's control of implementation. State Department officials tend to be anxious about the NSC usurping policy, and the NSC tends to be concerned that State either might not implement the President's decisions or might do so in a way that would make decisions State disapproved of appear ineffective or wrong.

Over time, U.S. policy toward Nicaragua became principally the product of the debate and dialogue between the NSC and the State Department. At the working level, Assistant Secretary Vaky and I would seek concurrence from our principals on decisions on which we agreed, and force decisions up to the NSC level when either we disagreed, or I thought the President would want to make the decision. The Assistant Secretary, as the head of a bureau and, in Vaky's case, as a senior person, was more inclined to make decisions independently or without clearing them. As a staff person, I viewed my principal responsibility as ensuring that the President made all "key" decisions, which I defined to mean any decision that would either substantially alter his previous policy or narrow his future options. My second responsibility was to monitor implementation of his decisions, and my third was to offer advice and ideas.

A representative of the CIA attended all SCC meetings to describe the current situation and to offer judgments about the likely consequences if a particular option were adopted, but in my experience, the career officers never proposed a policy themselves, even when they were asked. They were trained to believe that the preservation of their institution's integrity as an intelligence-gathering and analyzing operation required that they avoid policy making.

Representatives of the Defense Department and the Joint Chiefs of Staff also attended the SCC meetings. In 1975, the Bureau of International Security Affairs of the Department of Defense had combined the two Deputy Assistant Secretaries of Defense responsible for Asia and Latin America into a single position. Given the important U.S. military installations in the Pacific, the post was given to an Asian specialist, who lacked knowledge or interest in Latin America. The Defense Department therefore generally played a secondary role in policy toward Nicaragua during the Carter years.

As a rule, Vaky and I tried to reach some agreement before the meeting on minimal objectives. In the case of the mini-SCC meeting on September 4, we agreed to support a mediation effort led by Costa Rica and other nations in Central America.

Aaron called on Undersecretary of State David Newsom to offer his department's assessment. Where we came out, Newsom said, is that ultimately Somoza had to go. However, our ability to deal with the issue would become more difficult if that objective became clear initially. Therefore, State believed that we should stimulate Central American efforts to promote mediation as a first step. Vaky then developed his own position: no moderate solution will emerge by itself. Somoza has dug in. The Sandinistas are extremists with links to Cuba. We should avoid contact with them. Everyone is ready for a change in Nicaragua. Ultimately, Vaky said, the United States was the only actor capable of forcing the change. Tony Lake offered an alternative view, arguing that for reasons of principle, as well as politics, he would oppose going to a chief of state to ask him to step down. That was my position as well, and that was the main reason I had Lake invited to the meeting. Carazo had announced his willingness to mediate the conflict in Nicaragua, and the meeting concluded with a recommendation that President Carter send a letter to Carazo encouraging him to do that. Then, follow-up letters to the Presidents of Venezuela, Colombia, and Mexico would be sent by Carter encouraging them to support the Costa Rican effort. I drafted the letters with Vaky and Richard Feinberg, who was Lake's Latin American specialist, and summarized the meeting in a memorandum for the President.

Carter and his senior advisers had been as preoccupied by other matters as the "Latin Americanists" had been with Nicaragua. Impatient with the lack of progress on negotiations in the Middle East, Carter invited the Egyptian President and Israeli Prime Minister to discussions with him at Camp David on September 5. Carter had been warned of the risks of such an initiative, but he decided they were worth taking. Before the negotiations, he vacationed in the Grand Tetons with his family. There, on August 30, Carter was informed by Vice President Mondale that he would lose his natural gas bill, his highest domestic priority, if he did not return to Washington a few days early to lobby Congress.

Carter returned, and four days later, after instructing Brzezinski to obtain a recommendation on Nicaragua, flew to Camp David. From September 4 until his return to the White House at 10:00 P.M. on September 17, Carter, together with Vance, Brzezinski and his senior Middle East advisers, hardly slept as they tried to construct a framework for peace in the Middle East. The Israeli Prime Minister Menachem Begin later recounted: "President [Carter] worked. As far as my historic experience is concerned, I think that he worked harder than our forefathers did in Egypt building the pyramids."[5]

Behind the Mediation

September 5, before he began his talks, Carter reviewed the memorandum on Nicaragua and the letters to be sent to the Costa Rican President and others; and he approved the strategy. The fast pace of events in Nicaragua and Vaky's influence had caused a shift in U.S. policy from a position of strict neutrality in Nicaraguan politics to the acceptance, in principle, of mediation. The change was gradual and facilitated in three ways. First, the United States did not decide to mediate, but rather decided to support an initiative that had been proposed by Costa Rica. Second, the mediation was multilateral and thus would contribute to the goal of building a regional framework. Third, the United States had not yet defined what it meant by mediation, nor had it addressed questions of strategy or objectives for the mediation. Despite the pressures of the upcoming Camp David negotiations, Carter recalls that he was "able to focus on the issue and did view the shift as important."[6]

The decision came none too soon, because Carazo was having second thoughts. The letter from Carter bolstered him to continue to pursue the mediation, but he requested U.S. help to gain acceptance from the other Central Americans. Vaky thought this was a waste of time, and that only the United States could organize the mediation and make it work. In my view, even if the United States pressed the other Central American governments—all dominated by the military—there was at best a 50–50 chance of success; if we did nothing, however, the multilateral initiative would definitely die. Vaky agreed to send cables to our ambassadors in the region asking them to help the Costa Ricans. At the same time, the State Department made a public announcement indicating its support for the Central American initiative.

Another mini-SCC meeting was called for September 12. The participants were of a higher level and better prepared to discuss the issues. The Nicaraguan National Guard then had a force of 6,000; the FSLN had expanded their forces in the previous months to about 1,200. Although the Sandinistas had received training and some guidance from Cuba in the past, the CIA thought they were getting very little outside support at that time. Vaky explained that the Central American mediation was going nowhere because Somoza had persuaded most of the military governments not to participate.

Christopher outlined four options for U.S. policy: (1) neutrality, which he described as the status quo; (2) dissociation from Somoza; (3) support for Somoza; or (4) mediation. He quickly dismissed the idea of supporting Somoza for practical and moral reasons, and CIA Director Stansfield Turner agreed that such a strategy could only accelerate the polarization within Nicaragua. Dissociation was viewed as opting out of the crisis, and was discarded. The status quo option was a nonstarter, because the problem was worsening as we stood still. That left mediation, and the question was what kind.

Christopher proposed two options: (4a) keep Central America in front; or (4b) do it ourselves. Vaky and Newsom supported "4b," but Christopher defended "4a," saying we should try that first. He also opposed the idea of sending someone to speak with Somoza at this point, because that would be a shortcut to "4b." We might recommend that eventually, Christopher said, but we were not there yet, and the option had so many unattractive qualities that we didn't want to do it if we didn't have to. However, the group agreed to send William Jorden, former U.S. Ambassador to Panama, to several countries in the area, though not yet to Nicaragua, to consult. Christopher also proposed that we suggest to the moderate opposition that they issue an appeal for international mediation; that would provide a Nicaraguan handle for someone outside to grab. Christopher's recommendation carried the meeting by consensus. (Christopher set the position for State; Vaky had a voice, but no vote.) In effect the meeting agreed to try the same approach a little harder, but it also provided an opportunity to explore some new questions. For example, Aaron asked Vaky whether he felt the loyalty of the Guard was transferable, and Vaky said he thought it was.

But Vaky was frustrated by the meeting. He found himself caught between an Administration that was moving, in his mind, too slowly, and Carlos Andrés Pérez, who kept calling him, urging faster action. For two days, Vaky delayed sending cables to strengthen the Central American initiative or to encourage the moderate opposition to issue an international appeal for a mediation. He had opposed the former because he thought it a diversion and the latter because he felt the opposition was too weak and fragmented to make such an appeal. The day after the cables were sent, on September 15, the Broad Opposition Front (FAO) issued an international request for mediation. I then suggested we ask the FAO to direct the appeal to the Central Americans or another appropriate but specific audience; Vaky wanted it directed to the United States, but agreed to leave it up to the FAO to whom they would direct the appeal. The next day, the FAO directed the appeal to Latin America, not the United States! Nonetheless, the State Department immediately issued a statement supporting the opposition's call.

The United States was in front, in back, and on the side, pressing everyone, except itself, to mediate—to little effect. The Central American initiative was dying, partly because Costa Rica had found little interest among its neighbors and also because Carazo himself lost interest. The United States thought that Carazo was getting cold feet; in fact, he withdrew his proposal because his feet were getting warm. Instead of mediation, Carazo was preparing to offer his government's support to the Sandinistas. On September 12, just hours after the mini-SCC meeting ended, "a very important incident occurred," in Carazo's words. The Costa Rican frontier was strafed and bombed by the Nicaraguan Air Force, and students, who were celebrating independence day there, were injured. "That was the reason," Carazo later explained, "why I backed away from the mediation initiative. We were no longer completely neutral."[7] Prior to the incident, Pastora and the other Sandinistas had used Costa Rica, but without the permission of the government, which from time to time had harassed them. From September 12 until December 1978, Carazo allowed Edén Pastora to use Costa Rica freely to transport medicines and food for his forces, to organize and train his soldiers, and finally to receive armaments.

As the Central American initiative expired, the conflict grew more intense and more international. Costa Rica protested the Nicaraguan attack to the OAS, which sent a team to investigate, and Carazo requested help from Venezuela and Panama. Pérez and Torrijos sent planes and helicopters to Costa Rica on September 14. After our Chargé in Caracas reported a disturbing conversation he had with Pérez suggesting possible intervention, Vaky called him on September 18 and said that he hoped that Pérez would do nothing that would "inflame the situation or complicate it." In what Vaky recalls as a "volcanic" response, Pérez said: "I do not trust the U.S. now." After more conversation, Pérez agreed to channel his concerns through the OAS, but warned Vaky: "Do not defraud us."[8] Pérez also said that he thought the mediation would fail, but he would support it.

Venezuela had originally requested the convening of a Meeting of Foreign Ministers of the OAS on September 2, but it was postponed twice to permit the Central American initiative time and also to allow an OAS mission to investigate the border incidents. Finally, the day of Vaky's conversation, Venezuela called for an OAS vote to hold a meeting, and the vote was 23 in favor, with only Paraguay opposed. Nicaragua supported the vote in the surreal hope that the OAS would investigate Costa Rican support for the rebels.

In the afternoon of September 18, Aaron convened another meeting of the mini-SCC. It was clear to all that the Costa Rican mediation was dead, that the Sandinistas had much more support than anyone had suspected, and that the Guard was weaker. Christopher recommended that the United States try to use the OAS Meeting of Foreign Ministers to get a resolution to support a mediation effort, and that the United States indicate its willingness to be directly involved in such an effort, and, if necessary, to lead it. The mini-SCC still preferred a multilateral effort and recommended that Jorden be instructed to see Somoza in order to gain his agreement to a mediation and to make clear to him that the United States viewed the crisis as the result of his remaining in power. Aaron also suggested that the United States look into the idea of a peace-keeping force during a post-Somoza period to reassure the National Guard and to keep the situation from being dominated by the Sandinistas.

The representative of the Joint Chiefs of Staff for the first time expressed unease with the course of events and asked who was worse, Somoza or the Sandinistas. That question evoked silence; then Aaron and Christopher patiently explained the consensus of previous meetings: that the choice between Somoza and the Sandinistas was a false one; the longer Somoza stayed in power, the more likely it was that the Sandinistas would replace him.

That evening, President Carter addressed a joint session of Congress to describe the Middle East peace accords that he had just negotiated at Camp David. The next morning he reviewed the memoranda on the mini-SCC meeting and approved a more active strategy for the United States to participate in a mediation in Nicaragua. Again, the decision was facilitated by the multilateral character of the mediation, by the fact it remained undefined, and because the alternative had failed.

Bombing the Bunker

On September 19, the State Department issued an appeal for a truce, a human rights investigation, and mediation. That evening Somoza was interviewed on the McNeil-Lehrer television program, during which he insisted that he would not accept OAS mediation and would not step down before his term ended. Over the next two days preceding the OAS meeting, there were numerous reports of widespread atrocities in Nicaragua as the insurrection peaked.

The OAS meeting opened in Washington on September 21, and Christopher addressed the group. He called for a fact-finding mission to be sent to the Costa Rican border to reduce the potential of international conflict. To narrow the chasm separating Somoza from the Nicaragua opposition, Christopher announced: "We believe the good offices of concerned governments should be offered. The United States is prepared to participate in such an effort."[9]

After the session adjourned, I had dinner with the Panamanian Foreign Minister, an old friend. When we parted at about 1:00 A.M., we could not have guessed that within hours a bizarre chain of events would carry our two governments to the brink of war.

There had been warnings. Torrijos had met with Jorden on September 18 and had told him that he and Pérez wanted to take direct action to remove Somoza. Torrijos noted ominously that Venezuela's bombers were at the San José airport. Torrijos then flew to Caracas, and when he returned, his aide informed Jorden that Torrijos and Pérez had discussed a military solution. That day, as noted above, Vaky spoke with Pérez in an effort to calm him down. On September 21, Jorden met with Pérez in Caracas, and Pérez argued for more forceful action: "A Sandinista victory will open the door to Castro. . . . This will end in Cuban hands. The shame is this could be avoided, but the United States has not been decisive enough." Nonetheless, Pérez agreed to move his bombers from San José to David (in northern Panama) and Tocuman (Panama City's airport).[10]

Torrijos was discouraged that the United States had not been paying attention to the crisis, and he decided to use the presence of Venezuelan planes in Panama to force the pace of events. Late in the evening of September 21, Torrijos told Gabriel Lewis Galindo, former

Panamanian Ambassador to the United States, that he should inform the United States that Torrijos and Pérez would dispatch their planes to Managua the next morning to bomb "the bunker," Somoza's headquarters. Lewis told Jorden, who had just returned to Panama, and they conveyed the message to Washington in the early morning hours. Carter recalls that he was awakened at about 5:00 A.M. by Brzezinski with:

> word from Panama that they were launching an attack within an hour or so against Managua with their Air Force. I told him to send a message to Torrijos, to Pérez, and to notify our Ambassador in Nicaragua, and to place a call to Gabriel Lewis and also to Torrijos.
>
> Later, I joined in a conference call with them [Brzezinski and Harold Brown] on this. We decided to let General McAuliffe [U.S. Commander-in-Chief in Panama] alert his top officers and show some minimal sign of activity around our air bases in Panama, and for McAuliffe to visit Torrijos. . . .[11]

Brzezinski called me after talking with Harold Brown and President Carter. He asked me to rush to the White House to assist the President in placing a call to Torrijos.

In the meantime, Vaky called Pérez, who denied any knowledge of Torrijos' threat. Torrijos was at his remote retreat in Coclecito, a small poor village in the highlands of central Panama. By the time Washington was geared to respond, he had made himself unavailable ("he took a long walk to think," his aide said). Carter therefore called Gabriel Lewis, who had become a trusted friend during the Canal Treaty negotiations, and Lewis promised to convey Carter's deep concern to Torrijos. At 10:00 A.M., Lewis called back to tell us that the air strike would not occur that day, and that Torrijos had asked him to fly to Washington immediately.

At 11:00 A.M., Brzezinski called an urgent meeting in his office with Harold Brown, Air Force Chief of Staff General Lewis Allen, Warren Christopher, Stansfield Turner, Vaky, Aaron, and me. The issue was whether the United States should send F-4 interceptors to Panama to prevent the air strike. Aaron, Vaky, and I all argued strongly against doing this because the action would appear to Central America as if we were trying to rescue Somoza. The rather heated debate that ensued could have been avoided if anyone at the meeting had known that Panama did not have any fighters or bombers. Since Pérez had previously told Vaky that Venezuela's planes would not be used, the issue was moot. Nonetheless, under great tension, with little sleep and less information, the participants weighed several serious options, and Brzezinski decided to keep the interceptors on alert until the President reached Torrijos. Christopher would meet with the Costa Rican Foreign Minister and make sure that they were not going to encourage an attack against Nicaragua. The consensus was that the United States should contain the crisis in Nicaragua and not permit it to expand.

Both Brzezinski and Carter were scheduled to meet with a group of editors who were in Washington for a conference on Latin America. No one was aware that the Nicaraguan crisis was on the verge of becoming an international war, and Brzezinski therefore stunned the group when, at one point, he said that the President and he were up all night working on Nicaragua. The President then explained that: "We are trying through peaceful means to . . . put an end to the suffering. . . . We don't want to intervene in the affairs of a sovereign country. . . . [But] we are trying to work with our friends and well-meaning neighbors of Nicaragua to perhaps mediate the disputes . . . using . . . the OAS as a vehicle whenever possible."[12] Brzezinski further explained U.S. policy as neither a "hands-off policy" nor "engaging in interventionism." Rapid mediation was necessary to resolve the crisis and halt the polarization that could only lead to "extremism." But Brzezinski also vented his concern: "I would hope that there are forces in Nicaragua which are sufficiently committed to the democratic process and sufficiently strong in terms of their own vitality to make certain that any further changes in the nature of the Nicaraguan political system will not create a repetition of the Castro situation."[13]

At 3:00 P.M. Washington time, Torrijos came down from the mountain and returned Carter's call. The friendship and respect that had grown between Carter and Torrijos were unusual, given the extraordinary differences in personality and culture. Torrijos, a soldier and a populist, had a flair for pungent metaphors. The son of school teachers, he liked to confound his leftist friends by saying he believed in the classroom struggle, not the class struggle. And he confounded his conservative friends with his frequent use of leftist populist rhetoric.[14]

In that September 22 conversation, Carter and Torrijos tried to communicate in their own styles, leaving those who were also listening to the conversation bewildered. Torrijos first explained the problem in Nicaragua as he saw it: "[It is] a simple problem: a mentally deranged man with an army of criminals is attacking a defenseless population." Carter tried to pull Torrijos out of the world of García Márquez' metaphors into Carter's practical world of problems and solutions. Carter suggested that the way to address the problem was by mediation through the OAS, but Torrijos continued: "This is not a problem for the OAS; what we need is a psychiatrist." Carter persistently tried to obtain Torrijos' agreement to four points: (1) coordinated efforts among all peace-loving nations in the area, which meant no independent bomb attacks on Managua; (2) a strong mediation effort, in which Carter personally assured him the United States would participate; (3) helping the Red Cross to aid the victims of the violence; and (4) a commitment to nonintervention.

"Please confirm this," Carter said, calmly but firmly. He repeated the request a second time. Torrijos confirmed it in his way: "President Carter, you have a great deal of prestige on this continent; there is nothing you can't solve if you work on it."

Within an hour, Panama's Foreign Minister called me to convey a more direct message from Torrijos to Carter: Torrijos agreed to follow the U.S. line of nonintervention because of his respect for the President. I asked the Foreign Minister why Torrijos had threatened to attack in the first place, and he said that Torrijos had been receiving reports of unspeakable atrocities in Nicaragua and was advised that only something very dramatic would stop them. I suspected that was half of Torrijos' motive; the other half was to move the United States to displace Somoza. Carlos Andrés Pérez later said that Torrijos had dreamed up the entire idea, believing that it would scare Somoza into leaving.[15]

Saturday, September 23, was a day full of Nicaragua. It began at 9:00 A.M. with a stiff conversation between Brzezinski and the Panamanian Foreign Minister. Christopher, Gabriel Lewis, and I listened as Brzezinski omitted the routine cordialities and bluntly told him that Torrijos' threat was not appreciated. His tone and message surprised and upset the Panamanians, illustrating the gulf in perspective between the two governments even more vividly than the Carter–Torrijos conversation of the previous day. Having made his point about Panamanian military action, Brzezinski responded to their concerns on Nicaragua by saying that the United States was serious about getting rid of Somoza, but only through mediation and in a way that ensured the result was not a victory by the extreme left. The Panamanians were concerned about the possibility of intervention on behalf of Somoza from Guatemala and El Salvador, and Brzezinski said that we were concerned about intervention on behalf of either side. When the Panamanians pressed for a specific date for Somoza's departure, Brzezinski resisted. Christopher said that he didn't think Somoza would remain until 1981, but the precise date should be determined by the mediation. As he enjoyed doing, Brzezinski concluded the meeting by setting the crisis in a broader context. The issue was whether the United States, or Panama for that matter, should determine the composition of other governments. The United States was reluctant to consider such a role for itself, but it was prepared to consider such actions under extreme circumstances if there were "a genuine collective endeavor." The Panamanians, who were offended by Brzezinski's bluntness at the beginning of the meeting, were pleased and relieved by the clarity of his statement of U.S. policy at the end.[16]

Christopher and Vaky had been meeting with the foreign ministers at the OAS, and both concluded that OAS mediation was neither practical nor desirable. The prevalence of Latin American military governments whose claims to legitimacy were as tenuous as Somoza's made the OAS an unlikely organization to endorse an attempt to change the government in Nicaragua. The United States therefore sought an OAS resolution that would expedite a visit by the Inter-American Human Rights Commission and endorse the idea of a mediation.

Because of the many hands involved in drafting the resolution and the formidable conceptual task of reconciling the "principle of nonintervention" with international mediation of an internal political crisis, the resolution was a bit convoluted. The formula for providing an OAS "umbrella" over a mediation was that Nicaragua would be willing "in principle, to accept the friendly cooperation and conciliatory efforts that several member states of the Organization may offer toward establishing the conditions necessary for a peaceful settlement. . . ." With that, all that was needed was for the Nicaraguan government and the opposition to request a mediation, and for several governments to "volunteer." Experience had already convinced us that neither would happen without the United States.[17]

The same day, September 23, William Jorden met with Somoza. He read from instructions that had been carefully drafted within the Administration.[18] He had been instructed to say that Nicaragua's relations with the United States would be negatively affected if Somoza did not accept the mediation unconditionally. Jorden also told him that in the view of the Administration, Somoza was the cause of the polarization. The longer he stayed, the more likely it was that Nicaragua would go Communist. That was as close as the U.S. government would go at that time to suggest his resignation.

Prior to the meeting, Christopher had called William D. Rogers, then an attorney in Washington, to ask whether he would accept the role as U.S. mediator. Rogers said that he would accept, subject to four conditions: (1) he would travel to Managua only after a meeting with the President in order to show Somoza the President was committed to the effort; (2) the purpose of the mission was not to determine whether or even when Somoza would go, but how and under what terms; (3) Rogers would be authorized to negotiate with Somoza certain inducements—e.g., his exile and assets—to persuade him to leave; and (4) he would complete the mission before Christmas. After a short time, Christopher called Rogers back to inform him that the conditions were acceptable.[19]

Somoza responded sarcastically. After Jorden said that he did not want to be too specific about what the mediation would do since it was unique, Somoza snidely interjected: "The only one in America." When Jorden suggested Rogers as the U.S. mediator, Somoza rejected it out of hand: "He has stated biased opinions about the Somoza family." Jorden told Somoza that his "departure from office before 1981 [was] one of the possibilities that [had] to be considered" during the mediation.[20]

Somoza accepted the mediation on Monday, September 25, but he immediately began negotiating the membership of the mediation and its terms of reference. One of his demands was that the mediators include Argentina, Brazil, Guatemala, and El Salvador—four military governments. Christopher called a small meeting, including Vaky and me, in his office that evening, and we agreed Jorden should tell Somoza that the team would include Colombia, the Dominican Republic, the United States, Guatemala, and El Salvador.

The Colombian President then sent a letter to the President of the UN General Assembly condemning Somoza, who insisted in response that Colombia be excluded from the mediation. (U.S. officials were later told that the Colombian President sent the letter to avoid being involved in the mediation.) To retain balance between democracies and dictatorships, Jorden was instructed to tell Somoza that El Salvador would be excluded along with Colombia, leaving the mediation team to the United States, the Dominican Republic, and Guatemala. The Administration probably was mistaken in accepting Somoza's rejection of Rogers so quickly. Instead the Administration considered a number of people and, at Vaky's recommendation, decided on William Bowdler, who was Director of the Bureau of Intelligence and Research in the State Department.

Over 250 pounds and six and a half feet tall, Bowdler is physically imposing, but he speaks softly and with a gentle manner. He appears to move slowly and carefully in gait and speech, and the impression he leaves is one of directness, integrity, and solidity. Born in Buenos Aires, Bowdler had lived and served in Latin America longer than he had in the United States. He not only spoke Spanish like a native but possessed a sense of honor, respect, and "dignidad" that was more characteristic of Latin than North America. Like Vaky, he had served on the National Security Council (under President Johnson), and subsequently as Ambassador to El Salvador (1968-71) and Guatemala (1971-73). Like Solaun, Bowdler had a personal feeling for the Castro revolution in Cuba, having served in the U.S. Embassy in Havana from 1956 to its closing in 1961. Bowdler had the skill and strength of Rogers, but as a career official, he lacked the independence to go directly to the President rather than through the State Department. Bowdler was assisted by Malcolm Barnaby, a reliable veteran, and James Cheek, one of State's most capable middle-level officers. Cheek concealed behind his slow, deep Southern drawl an imagination and political savvy that were invaluable during the negotiations. He also knew many of the political actors, having served in the U.S. Embassy in Managua.

On September 30, the OAS Secretary General announced the commencement of the International Commission of Friendly Cooperation and Conciliation. The three governments then formally accepted the request from Somoza and the FAO to mediate, and the group traveled to Guatemala to define the terms of reference. Alfredo Obiols, former Guatemalan Vice Foreign Minister, Bowdler, and Dominican Admiral Ramon Emilio Jiménez agreed on a three-part strategy: (1) identify the positions of both sides; (2) promote direct negotiations; and (3) assist the negotiations. The instructions Bowdler had from Washington were more detailed, and included the objective of preserving the National Guard and indicating that if Somoza requested to come to the United States, that would be considered.[21]

The general strike had collapsed on September 25, and the next day the Guard regained control of the country, but the damage was extensive. The Red Cross estimated that 1,500 to 3,000 people had been killed during a month of civil war; a half-dozen cities had been devastated; and the homes of 30,000 people had been destroyed. The devastation was compared to the 1972 earthquake.[22] On October 3, the Inter-American Human Rights Commission arrived in Nicaragua to investigate. As a gesture to it, Somoza lifted press censorship on their arrival. The result was that the commission came face to face with the seething hatred people felt for Somoza.

Divergent Perspectives of the Mediation

GETTING NICARAGUANS ON BOARD.   The task of the three mediators was formidable. No one really wanted mediation. For Nicaraguans, as for the Carter Administration, "mediation" was the fall-back option, chosen because they felt they had no alternative.

Somoza probably accepted the mediation because he thought that he had no choice and that he could turn the mediation to his advantage. First, it would give him time to reinforce and reequip the Guard, and second, he could use the mediation to coopt, or if possible, divide the opposition and shift the terms of the debate from his resignation to the conditions for a free election in 1981. On October 4, he announced his plan to double the size of the National Guard to 15,000,[23] and he secretly began buying arms from whoever would sell.

Somoza welcomed the mediators with a sleight of hand: "In my opinion, the only thing wrong on the Nicaragua scene is the longevity of the name Somoza."[24] He admitted that this conclusion had emerged from his conversations with U.S. officials, but he then tried to explain why it was wrong. He made the familiar arguments that he was the head of a strong political party, a prestigious Cabinet, and the National Guard. He told the mediation team that a three-man delegation representing the Liberal Party would negotiate on his behalf.

The moderate opposition did not see any point to the mediation, and only accepted it because they felt they had no other alternative. Organized under the umbrella of the Broad Opposition Front (FAO), they also selected three representatives to negotiate on their behalf: Alfonso Robelo, the president of COSEP; Sergio Ramírez from the Group of Twelve; and Rafael Córdova Rivas, a lawyer who was the president of UDEL, the coalition created by the late Pedro Joaquín Chamorro.

On August 27, when Somoza first told the U.S. Ambassador he would negotiate, he also said that the problem was that the opposition would not. To a certain extent, he was right. The FAO did not want to have any direct contact with Somoza; they feared that he would divide them and coopt some as he and his family had done repeatedly in the past. Pastora later described their concerns most succinctly: "Somoza was a lost cause. Whoever dealt with him was diminished by the experience."[25] Moreover, the FAO did not understand why the United States was insisting on what it viewed as a charade. The solution to the crisis, in their view, was simple: Somoza should resign.[26]

Although Nicaraguans and most people in the region seemed fixated on Somoza's resignation, some in the U.S. government, notably Zbigniew Brzezinski, were more concerned about what would succeed Somoza. The political counselor of the U.S. Embassy in Managua provided a diagram of sixteen opposition groups that composed the FAO, and the heterogeneity and fragmentation of the opposition was not reassuring to those who agreed Somoza was the problem (see chart).

Clearly, part of the problem was also the endemic factionalism of Nicaragua's politics, which Somoza exploited and exacerbated, but which was indisputable. Chamorro, one opposition leader who might have been able to unite the groups, had been murdered a year before. Probably the only point on which all the representatives of the political groups associated with the FAO could agree was that Somoza had to go, although they disagreed on the mode of departure, with some insisting that he go in a box.

The Sandinistas initially were divided on the mediation. Like the National Guard, they had been battered in the fighting, and they welcomed the time afforded by the mediation to regroup, train new recruits, and obtain more arms and financing. Though Somoza may have thought that the Guard's repression intimidated the population, it had politicized the youth and dramatically expanded the FSLN base. As Humberto Ortega later explained: "Everybody had a relative or friend killed in the struggle [in September], and there was a great thirst for revenge."[27]

The Terceristas were skeptical of the mediation, but ever practical, they appointed Sergio Ramírez to the FAO negotiating committee while they prepared for "a second more successful assault."[28] Tomás Borge spoke for the other two factions in their opposition to the mediation: "We opposed the mediation because we didn't believe it would affect the structural basis of the repression."[29] In other words, he was afraid that the Guard would be unaffected.

THE MEDIATORS.　The Dominican Republic and Guatemala decided to participate in the mediation because the United States had requested their help. The new Dominican government under President Antonio Guzmán owed Carter a debt for its very survival. Carter's timely and strong message to the Dominican military as they were about to steal the election in May 1978 made possible the first peaceful change in government in one hundred years of Dominican history. Guzmán may also have thought that participation with the United States in the mediation would help him domestically and with the military. Guatemala's motives were less clear, although it appears that President Lucas volunteered more as a favor to Somoza than with the expectation of receiving some reward from the United States. Fortunately, both Presidents appointed as mediators people whom Bowdler knew well, and Lucas did not pay much attention to

The Political Opposition to Somoza, August 1978

Prepared by U.S. Embassy, Managua,
August 1978

LEGEND

FSLN – Sandinista
National Liberation
Front

GPP – Prolonged
Popular War
Faction of
FSLN

TP – Proletarian
Tendency,
Faction of
FSLN

UDEL – Union
of Democratic
Liberation

ANC – National Conservative
Action (PCN Faction)

MLC – Liberal Constitution-
alist Movement

PCN – Conservative Party

PSN – Socialist Party
(Communist)

PLI – Independent Liberal
Party

CGT – General Confederation
of Laborers

CTN – Central of
Nicaraguan Laborers

PSC – Social Christian Party

CUS – Confederation of
Labor Unification

MDN – Nicaraguan Democratic
Movement

_ _ _ _ Indicates Member of UDEL
= = =   Indicates Informal or Other Links
_____ Indicates Direct Links

RADICAL   LEFTIST   MODERATE   CONSERVATIVE the mediation until nearly the end, by which time it was difficult to alter the position of the Guatemalan mediator.

Although officially supporting the mediation as a gesture to Carter, both Pérez and Torrijos were pessimistic about what it would accomplish. This pessimism was shared by Vaky, who, like the moderate opposition, was worried that a multilateral mediation might deflect or divert the United States from the central issue: Somoza had to go.

Carter, Vance, and Christopher rejected two of Vaky's working assumptions: first, they did not want to be put in a position where they had to ask, let alone force, a head of state to resign; and second, they wanted to pursue a multilateral approach. These principles were not just moral abstractions but were grounded in a realistic calculation of the costs and benefits of intervention. To try to rearrange the politics of Nicaragua unilaterally would not only reinforce the protectorate mentality of Nicaraguans, it would saddle the United States with responsibility for ensuring that the outcome worked.

No one knew what would happen to the National Guard if Somoza left, or whether the opposition could cohere. If the Guard collapsed as a result of U.S. pressure, the United States would be responsible for eliminating the only barrier to a Sandinista military victory, or it would have to intervene militarily to prevent that. And this would occur at a time when most people believed that Nicaragua was reasonably stable by Latin American standards. The best approach seemed to be to work with other governments and to help Nicaraguans solve the problem themselves rather than try to solve it for them.

These were my views as well. In addition, I doubted that Somoza would step down just because the United States asked him. I suspected that he might be taping his official conversations (which he confirmed in his memoir), and that hours after our representative "talked turkey" to him, we would all be hearing it on the evening news. The President's Press Secretary would then be questioned the next day: "If President Carter is committed to the principle of nonintervention, why is he trying to overthrow Somoza?" If one juxtaposed the tape recording and the President's commitment to "never lie" to the American people, Carter would look foolish and impotent. Somoza would have a good laugh. In my mind, these were all powerful reasons for not being too explicit in seeking Somoza's departure. Vaky believed that if we were clear and tough enough with Somoza, he would not try something like that, and would simply leave. It was never clear how tough the United States would have had to be. Vaky also discounted the domestic political fallout, believing that could be managed.

The Administration returned to this issue several times, but the crucial point at this stage was that Vaky felt that Somoza had to be forced to resign as the key element of a negotiated transition. Bowdler shared Vaky's view, but the President and all his senior advisers disagreed. Both Vaky and Bowdler were dedicated professionals, who respected the President and would implement his decisions. Nonetheless, given all the pitfalls and roadblocks in the way of a successful mediation, the lack of enthusiasm on the part of the two key people implementing U.S. policy should have served as a warning signal, and would have, if the Administration had thought it had another alternative.

THE POLITICAL AMBIENCE IN THE UNITED STATES.   Carter's policy may have been hitched to certain moral principles, but it was not made in a political vacuum. From the beginning, the Administration was subject to stinging criticism from Somoza's friends and enemies. While trying to heal the divisions of Nicaragua, the United States found itself contracting the same dreaded disease of political polarization. The debate increasingly divided between those who saw Somoza as either a defender against Communism or a brutal dictator; both sides attacked the Carter Administration for supporting the other, but their real purpose was to try to influence the Administration to support their position.

On September 22, 1978, President Carter received a letter from seventy-eight members of Congress, led by Murphy and Wilson, urging Carter "to come publicly to the support of the Government of Nicaragua during this period of crisis." The letter reflected Somoza's view that the Communists' "goal is to make Nicaragua the new Cuba of the western hemisphere." The letter was published in the *New York Times* and the *Washington Post* on a full page with a graphic illustration of a hammer and a sickle carving up the Central American isthmus.

No one captured the extent to which Nicaragua was a metaphor for other concerns better than Senator Carl Curtis, a conservative Republican from Nebraska, in a remark to his former colleague, Gale McGee, the U.S. Ambassador to the OAS. Apparently confusing the Nicaraguan dictator with an Asian island, Curtis berated McGee: "Why are you guys [the Carter Administration] pushing around such a good friend of the U.S.? Why don't you leave Formosa alone?"[30]

Three weeks later, on October 13, eighty-six members of Congress sent a letter to Secretary of State Vance urging the Administration to "suspend all aid to the Nicaraguan government" on grounds that such aid sent "a misleading message of support" for Somoza. In fact, the Administration had suspended aid without ending the program in order to maintain a source of leverage to be used on Somoza if he rejected the mediation. Outside of Congress, some church groups and academics recommended that the United States support the Group of Twelve and the FSLN or incorporate them into a final settlement.[31]

What impact did the Congressional and interest group pressure have on the Administration? Some have suggested that Wilson and Murphy had a hammerlock on the Administration that prevented it from taking the steps necessary to secure Somoza's resignation.[32] Wilson forced the Administration to make decisions on foreign aid that the Administration would have preferred to avoid, but the decisions themselves reflected the Administration's judgment of the merits of the case. Moreover, when the issue came to be viewed in a political-security context, Congress's influence diminished.

The conservatives had less influence on the Administration than the liberal bloc, but neither shaped the White House approach. Generally, when Congress divides on an issue, it permits decision makers room to follow their own instincts. This was the case with Nicaragua, where the public and Congressional debate reinforced the Administration's feeling that its defense of its two principles of nonintervention and multilateralism was the right course, and that either defending Somoza or trying to overthrow him was a mistake. Political pressure neither constrained nor changed the Administration's policy; it reinforced the approach the Administration had already selected.

In the Middle

The Carter Administration's preference was to avoid unilateral interference in the internal affairs of countries like Nicaragua, but the crisis in that country and the demands made by democratic friends in the region forced a modification of that policy. The Administration discarded it with reluctance and in small steps. First, it accepted the importance of outside mediation as a way to resolve the crisis. Next, it supported an international mediation of neighboring countries; then it tried to organize that mediation. When that failed, the United States finally offered to take the lead, although it continued to insist on its multilateral character. When the OAS authorized its member states to help mediate the conflict in Nicaragua, the country that acted and negotiated the participation of the other members was the United States.

These were all procedural issues; the tough questions of objectives and strategies to achieve those objectives remained to be answered. The United States once again found itself in the middle of Nicaraguan politics.

Chapter 6

TRANSITIONS

To resign, which is what the opposition wants me to do,
would be to betray the aspirations of the people of Nicaragua
to live in a free society.
Anastasio Somoza, August 29, 1978

THE PERIOD between October 1978 and February 1979, when the mediation was bouncing back and forth between Somoza and the opposition, was a transitional one for Nicaragua. The question was whether the transition would lead to democracy, continued dictatorship, or civil war and revolution.

Building Bridges

It is hard to imagine a less propitious setting for negotiations to establish an "enduring democratic solution." No one was interested in negotiations except the White House and the two senior officials in the State Department. Fortunately for the United States, its mediator, William Bowdler, was a dedicated professional with the patience of Job.

When the mediators arrived, Somoza told a press conference that he would be prepared to discuss the 1981 election with them, but his resignation was out of the question. The Broad Opposition Front (FAO) publicly stated that Somoza's resignation was the only solution. In their first meeting, the FAO told the mediation team to obtain a date for Somoza's departure. Although sympathetic to their request, the team encouraged the FAO to draft a realistic plan for a transitional government that could be proposed to Somoza. The FAO had given no thought to a post-Somoza structure, and they first interpreted the advice to mean that the United States was not serious.

The FAO subsequently relented, drafted a plan, and submitted it to the team on October 25, 1978. The plan called for Somoza's immediate resignation along with that of his relatives in civil and military positions, the departure from the country of the Somoza family, a timetable for elections for a Constituent Assembly, the reorganization of the National Guard, and the installation of a new Government of National Unity composed of a Council of State and a three-man Junta. The Council itself would be composed of two represent-atives from each of the FAO's sixteen organizations and two from the Liberal Party. The Council would appoint the Junta that would im-plement the sixteen points of the FAO political program. The media-tion team then presented the plan to Somoza's negotiating team and waited for a response.

The psychological relationship between the FAO and the media-tors was delicate. Nervous about the outcome of the mediation, Al-fonso Robelo sought some assurance that its purpose was to "get rid of Somoza in the most peaceful and efficient way." Robelo claimed that he received such an assurance from the Dominican mediator, Ji-ménez, and later from Bowdler.[1] The mediation team, on the other hand, tried to lower expectations and focus the FAO on constructing a "silver bridge"—"puente de plata"—that would induce Somoza to leave.

The FAO was fragile not just because of decades of Nicaraguan fac-tionalism but because one of its members, Sergio Ramírez, was play-ing a double role, trying to lead the group and undermine it simulta-neously. Though technically representing the Group of Twelve, Ramírez was actually representing the FSLN, and although desig-nated by the Terceristas, he consulted regularly with leaders of the two other Sandinista factions.[2] The FSLN realized that if the media-tion succeeded, they would fail. On the day the FAO presented its plan to the mediation team, the FSLN directed Ramírez "to make a dramatic gesture—to resign and seek asylum" in the Mexican Em-bassy in a manner that would shock and fragment the FAO. He did as he was told on October 25, denouncing any outcome that left the Guard in existence as "Somocismo sin [without] Somoza."[3] The San-dinistas then delivered an ultimatum to the mediators that said they would begin fighting if no agreement was reached by November 21.

With the FSLN denouncing the mediation, Carlos Andrés Pérez be-came worried about a new round of violence. He suggested a standby peace-keeping force of troops from the United States, Venezuela, Co-lombia, and Panama to be sent to Nicaragua if fighting resumed. The United States began thinking about the idea too.

The departure of Ramírez did not destroy the FAO, but it increased the pressure on it to quit the mediation if Somoza did not resign. So-moza consulted with his colleagues on a response and at the same time tried to influence the United States. He asked Manolo Reboso, the Cuban-American Vice Mayor of Miami, to see me on October 30 in an effort to set up a secret meeting between Somoza and someone in the White House. I immediately informed both Brzezinski and

Vaky. I thought such a conversation might be useful as a way of reinforcing Bowdler and purging Somoza of the idea of a possible backchannel deal, but the Administration was still so sensitive about avoiding even the most remote resemblance to anything Henry Kissinger had done that both the State Department and Brzezinski rejected the idea.

Vance and Brzezinski's differences on SALT, China, and Iran were beginning to spill over in unusual ways to other areas, like Latin America, where differences either did not exist or were insignificant. When Vaky decided that the mediation had gone far enough and new instructions were needed to push Somoza into accepting the FAO proposal, Vance insisted that there should be a PRC meeting to be chaired by State, rather than an SCC meeting chaired by NSC. Brzezinski was not averse to trading off the chairmanship of a meeting on Nicaragua provided he retained the chairmanship on other issues of greater interest to him. Brzezinski also knew that his views on Nicaragua policy at that time coincided with those of Vance and Christopher.

Christopher therefore chaired a PRC meeting on October 31. Vaky had called it because Bowdler and he were worried that Somoza would use his press conference on November 3 to reject the FAO proposal and that this would fracture the opposition. On October 24, Bowdler cabled a proposal to the State Department to apply pressure to Somoza to get him to face his departure seriously, and this proposal was put before the PRC.

In my view, the timing of the Bowdler/Vaky proposal was premature. There would be a time for sanctions, but not before Somoza had even responded to the proposal and not on the eve of U.S. Congressional elections. A second reason for waiting was that the Inter-American Human Rights Commission had recently returned from a visit to Nicaragua appalled by the atrocities of the Guard. The publication of their report would improve the climate for such a step.

Brzezinski agreed with me, although for different reasons. He was more concerned about ensuring the solidity of the post-Somoza transition. He agreed that "Somoza had to go," but he threw Vaky's argument about the fragility of the moderate opposition back at him. If they were so fragmented and weak that they could not survive another round of negotiations or fighting, then what assurances did we have that they could take and hold power? He encouraged Vaky, as I had been doing, to work on post-Somoza leadership and on making contacts with the National Guard. Vaky's focus, like that of the FAO, Pérez, and Torrijos, was almost exclusively on Somoza's departure. Vaky recognized the importance of a post-Somoza plan, but, as he recalled, "it was very difficult to draw up plans and describe the scenario in the absence of Somoza's departure."[4]

General Smith of the Joint Chiefs of Staff shared Brzezinski's uneasiness about pushing Somoza, but Brzezinski made it clear that he thought Somoza would have to go; his preference was to press gradually in a way that ensured that the opposition would learn to organize themselves so that when they assumed power, they could govern. Christopher agreed with Brzezinski, and the two of them accepted a compromise proposal that Bowdler be instructed to speak with Somoza before the press conference to make two points. First, Somoza would be told that if he rejected the FAO proposal, that would signify that he had created a crisis to which the United States would have to respond appropriately. Second, to convey our seriousness, we would tell him that we were freezing aid and seeking a postponement of his government's request for a loan from the International Monetary Fund because approval at this time would be a political endorsement of his regime, which we would not make.[5] Christopher wanted the statement made by the entire team, if possible.

In addition, the PRC agreed to keep several democratic governments in the region fully briefed in order to be able to seek their support should the United States decide the time had come to pressure Somoza. In support of the objective of ensuring the continuity of the National Guard, the PRC decided that a U.S. official should communicate with a former General of the Guard, Julio Gutiérrez, who had distinguished himself as the commander of the battalion that had served in the Inter-American Peace Force in the Dominican Republic. Popular with his troops and known as so honest and incorruptible that even Pedro Joaquín Chamorro had singled him out for praise, Gutiérrez was exiled by Somoza—first as Defense Attaché in El Salvador and Guatemala, and subsequently as Ambassador to Japan.[6] The PRC decided to instruct U.S. Ambassador to Tokyo Mike Mansfield to meet with Gutiérrez.

Somoza sensed he had reached a crossroads. He wrote in his memoirs: "We went around and around in these negotiations, but were getting nowhere. However, one point was coming through loud and clear; the negotiating team had come to Nicaragua with instructions to get me out of office." He wrote that he then consulted with his Cabinet, the Liberal Party, and the General Staff of the Guard, and found that none of them could contemplate a future without him.[7]

On November 6, the Liberal Party—Somoza's mouthpiece—rejected the FAO proposal with a long and legalistic defense of the government and the constitution. The party insisted that Somoza could

not resign for constitutional reasons, but it offered instead a plebiscite to measure the popularity of the opposition and the Liberal
Party. If the opposition received a large share of the vote, Somoza
would allot them a proportional share of the power in the Congress.

The next day, the mediation team met privately with Somoza.
They noted the widespread sentiment in Nicaragua that peace would
not be possible while he remained in power, and they asked whether
he would resign to facilitate an arrangement between the Liberal
Party and the FAO. This went beyond Bowdler's instructions but represented the consensus of the mediation team. Somoza rejected the
idea, saying that he still enjoyed substantial support in the country,
and that a plebiscite to measure party strength would be the fairest
way to test his popularity.

Bowdler was feeling the pressure from the opposition and from the
burden of his task. To hold the opposition and the mediation team
together, he had to persuade them that the U.S. government would
be prepared to deliver Somoza when the time came, but he was not
at all certain his government would deliver, and he was uncertain
whether U.S. leverage would work. In a private meeting with Somoza
on November 10, Bowdler asked Somoza to reconsider, and felt Somoza might be wavering even though he said he would not resign.[8]
Afterward he called Vaky, whose patience had already been exhausted. Vaky then informed me that the time had come to move to
"step two"—full sanctions. We scheduled a PRC meeting on November 13, and Bowdler returned to Washington for it.

The Plebiscite

On Sunday evening, November 12, to review options for the PRC,
Vaky asked me to a meeting in his office with Bowdler, Brandon
Grove (one of Vaky's deputies), and Steven Oxman, Christopher's
special assistant. Bowdler informed us that the essence of Somoza's
counterproposal was a plebiscite; this was the first we had heard of
it. Oxman and I asked some questions, but both Vaky and Bowdler
abruptly dismissed the queries and the proposal. "It's a stalling tactic," Bowdler said. "He's throwing sand in our faces," Vaky added.
They believed Somoza would use the plebiscite proposal to drag on
negotiations, divide the FAO, and confuse the American people.

I agreed on Somoza's motive, but said that the purpose of the mediation was to negotiate a transitional government, and the United
States could not just dismiss an election as a method for accomplish-
ing that. We needed to respond in some way, and I asked whether we

could not turn the plebiscite proposal on its head: instead of voting on political parties, Nicaraguans would vote on Somoza. This would infuse the mission of the mediation—to have Somoza stand aside in favor of a new government—with legitimacy that would be impossible for Somoza to reject. The issue, I argued, was not whether to accept or dismiss a plebiscite, but whether negotiations could establish a free enough election to permit the Nicaraguan people to vote Somoza out. Negotiating those terms would be difficult, perhaps impossible, but we had to try. It would put us on a morally sound and defensible course, and if a plebiscite occurred, it would provide the FAO the opportunity to organize itself as a unified national party, which in turn would make it better prepared to govern. Whether or not negotiations succeeded, it seemed to me we had to call Somoza's bluff before he called ours. Both Vaky and Bowdler opposed the idea, but Oxman supported it.

The PRC meeting on November 13 started at 5:00 P.M. For nearly two hours, the Administration had its first high-level intense discussion on Nicaragua. Oxman and I suspected correctly that Vaky's two-page options paper would not mention the plebiscite, and we prepared another paper with the following three options for Vance, Christopher, and Brzezinski: (1) transform the plebiscite idea into a vote on Somoza's staying in power and negotiate terms that would ensure a free election; (2) dismiss the plebiscite and apply pressure (a full list of sanctions) on Somoza to negotiate his departure in accordance with the FAO plan; or (3) discontinue mediation and walk away from the problem.

The discussion of the three options reflected a sharp division. Vance, Christopher, and Brzezinski argued on behalf of option 1, Vaky and Bowdler for option 2. General Smith from the Joint Chiefs of Staff was predictably cautious, arguing against pulling out the U.S. military group—one of the sanctions—on bureaucratic grounds: "why us?" There were no advocates for option 3.

Bowdler explained that the FAO had already rejected the plebiscite proposal and felt exposed. He argued that they were capable of forming a government if Somoza stepped aside soon. Bowdler and Vaky argued that the plebiscite was diversionary; the opposition would never accept it and we would lose a crucial opportunity to resolve the crisis.

Brzezinski and Vance argued that we should tell the FAO that if they accepted the plebiscite idea, we would work to make it fair. If Somoza then rejected the plebiscite, we would back the FAO and impose sanctions against Somoza. If the FAO rejected it, however, Brzezinski said that the United States would be put in a bind. The meeting also emphasized the importance of implementing the previous decisions to meet with Julio Gutiérrez and consult with the Latin Americans—decisions that State had not pursued.

Brzezinski asked Bowdler whether Somoza would leave if we approved option 2 (sanctions). Bowdler said the odds were slightly better than 50–50. Following the logic of Bowdler's answer, Brzezinski hinted that if Somoza did not resign, the United States would be left without leverage, and the situation could become untenable very rapidly. International support for our position would be essential, but it did not exist at that time. That was Brzezinski's way of reminding State to consult with our Latin American friends, because it was believed that a strategy of isolating Somoza would be necessary and would elicit wide support. The PRC also emphasized again that the unity of the Guard was an important objective for U.S. policy. There was no disagreement on this latter point as everyone recognized that a post-Somoza government that lacked a firm military base could be overrun by the FSLN.

Vance said State would redo the memorandum for the President to reflect the three options. Vance permitted Vaky and Bowdler to make the strongest case for option 2 (sanctions) in the memorandum, and Christopher and his staff—with my help—made the case for option 1 (modified plebiscite). The next day Vance sent the memo to the NSC, which put a cover memorandum on top recommending option 1. Vance had deliberately chosen not to make a State Department recommendation, evidently because he did not want to undercut Vaky and Bowdler, his senior officers, even though he disagreed with them. Before making his decision, however, Carter called Vance, and he recommended option 1. Carter approved it.

The PRC debate showed that the major division within the U.S. government at that time was neither between bureaucracies—State versus NSC—nor between hawks and doves, but rather between the President's political appointees and career officials. The career officials—Vaky and Bowdler—were more attuned to the debate in Managua and more disposed to make the opposition's case for pushing Somoza out, whereas the President's appointees were more sensitive to developing a policy that was defensible in the United States and more inclined to advocate a North American approach to solving the problem—elections.[9] These alignments were neither unchanging nor predetermined, but the way the issue was then framed—plebiscite or overthrow Somoza—increased the likelihood of such an alignment. For a foreign policy to be effective, of course, it needs to weave together these two strands and sensitivities, and that is the purpose of the NSC process.[10]

Before returning to Managua, on November 15, Bowdler met with Carter for a brief conversation and a photograph. The purpose was to show that the President had confidence in him. Carter recalled that Bowdler and he "agreed to push a strict plebiscite." If Somoza did not accept the terms, then, in Carter's words, Somoza's "incumbency will be difficult to sustain." Carter also asked Bowdler for his impressions of Somoza and several other political leaders.[11]

Despite this opportunity to communicate directly with the President, or perhaps because of it, Bowdler returned to Managua discouraged, but he did not flinch. He did his utmost to prove wrong his previous prediction that the FAO would never accept a plebiscite. First, he had to persuade his fellow mediators, a challenge made more difficult by the publication of an article in the *Washington Post* on November 14 that described the other two members of the team as being directed by the United States. Nonetheless, he succeeded, and together, the three approached the FAO. Robelo's first reaction was negative, but he and his colleagues eventually realized, as the United States had, that opposing a free election was like opposing motherhood. In the end, the remaining organizations in the FAO voted 9 to 3 in favor of supporting a plebiscite on Somoza. (Four groups, including the Twelve, had left the FAO by this time.)

Bowdler worked with the mediation team and the FAO to draft a specific plebiscite proposal in which Nicaraguans could decide whether Somoza should remain in office. The plebiscite would be organized, administered, and supervised by an international authority of perhaps as many as 2,000 officials. To ensure the credibility and impartiality of the election, the FAO demanded the lifting of the state of siege (reimposed in September) and several other steps. If Somoza lost, the FAO plan for a transitional government would come into effect: (1) Somoza would resign and leave the country; (2) the Nicaraguan Congress would elect an interim President, and then be reconstituted to reflect the predominance of the FAO; (3) Congress would elect a new President, who would serve until free elections in May 1981.

Essentially, the mediators used the plebiscite as a bridge between two ostensibly irreconcilable positions. If Somoza won the plebiscite, his Liberal Party proposal would be implemented and opposition leaders would join the government. If Somoza lost, the FAO's proposal would be implemented. On November 21, the team presented the integrated proposal to both sides, and for the next two weeks, the details were negotiated. During this time, the Inter-American Human Rights Commission issued a devastating condemnation of the Somoza regime's actions during the insurrection, and that added to the pressure on both sides to reach agreement. On November 29, the FAO agreed to the general plebiscite proposal, and the next day, Somoza agreed.

In response to the FAO demands, which the United States supported, Somoza lifted the state of siege, declared a general amnesty, and revoked the "Black Code" censoring radio and television. On December 4, 1978, four days after he accepted the plebiscite idea, Somoza sent Luis Pallais, his cousin and leader of the Liberal Party, on a secret mission to Washington. For the first time, Pallais believed Somoza would accept a genuine plebiscite and would resign if he lost.

In anticipation of one possible outcome, Pallais sought answers to three questions: (1) Could Somoza and his entourage get asylum in the United States? (2) Would the United States extradite him? and (3) Would his assets be secure from seizure? Vaky checked with Christopher, but not with the NSC, and responded that under the right circumstances, the United States would grant asylum. Explicit guarantees on extradition and protection of assets, however, would depend on international law and treaties. It did not occur to Vaky to use the three questions as a bargaining lever to obtain Somoza's cooperation for the plebiscite proposal or for his resignation.[12] Pallais returned to Nicaragua to tell Somoza, who said the "answers were satisfactory."[13]

The clouds seemed to open for a moment. In a talk with newspaper editors on December 7, Carter explained how the United States "helped to shift the Nicaraguan circumstance from active and massive bloodshed and violence into a negotiation on the details of a democratic plebiscite. . . . We don't know that we will be successful, but I think that in itself is progress." The next day, for the first time during the mediation, both sides sat down across the table from one another to negotiate the specifics. Before this the mediators had been shuttling between both sides.

These events chilled the Sandinista leadership, who went to Havana to discuss strategy. On December 9, 1978, the leaders of the three factions of the FSLN issued a unity statement for reasons of fear and promises of help—the fear that the mediation might succeed combined with the personal influence of Castro and his promise of aid if they united. Their "communiqué," however, underscored their major concern:

> We have decided to unite our political and military forces in order to guarantee that the heroic struggle of our people not be stolen by the machinations of yankee imperialism and the trea-

sonous sectors of the local bourgeoisie. . . . We reject the imperialist mediation. . . .

A plebiscite . . . is no more than a trap that leads to compromise and to treason. The overthrow of the dictatorship through
revolutionary means and the dissolution of the National Guard
are the indispensable conditions for a true democracy.[14]

The leaders deliberately excluded Pastora from their meeting because they suspected his Social Democratic inclinations. However,
Pastora was the crucial link to Carlos Andrés Pérez and Omar Torrijos, and they therefore appointed him Chief of the Army—actually of
the southern front.[15]

On December 12, the *New York Times* published an editorial entitled "New Hope in Nicaragua," noting that "another round of civil
war may now be averted in Nicaragua, thanks mainly to an inter-
American team of mediators, led by the U.S." A *Washington Post* editorial on December 19 sang praises:

A month ago, Nicaragua seemed ready to resume a civil war that
could only have ended with the ravaging of the country and the
victory of an authoritarian regime either of the left or the right.
Today, it is just possible to hope Nicaragua is on the way to becoming a democratic society. . . . American diplomacy has
reached out to find and embolden and strengthen the democratic
moderates of a war-torn country.

Bowdler had managed, through herculean efforts, to maintain the
momentum of negotiations. On December 20, after more than eight
rounds of negotiations and numerous drafts, the mediation team put
forward a final detailed plebiscite proposal that reflected some of
both positions but was closer to the position of the FAO. The major
change from the November 21 proposal was that Somoza was permitted to stay in Nicaragua during the plebiscite campaign, although
his son and brother would still have to leave. If he lost the plebiscite,
Somoza would have to leave, but he could return if he so desired after
a suitable period. The mediation proposal compromised on the outcome if Somoza won the election. Somoza insisted that the opposition join to help stabilize the government, but the FAO refused to associate with Somoza under any circumstances. The mediators
proposed that the FAO become a "peaceful opposition" party in the
new proposal and suggested that the vote occur on February 25, 1979.

Partly because the proposal was much closer to their own than it
was to Somoza's, the FAO accepted it the next day. This was still a
difficult decision for the FAO because of the relentless pressure on

them from the FSLN and other groups to resign. Their acceptance reflected a greater degree of unity than anyone thought possible two months before. Since one of the purposes of the mediation was to encourage the unity of the moderate opposition, it was reassuring to know that this had occurred, even though the outcome was still in doubt.

Somoza's deviousness, however, tripped up the effort at its most promising point. His initial enthusiasm for a plebiscite had dissipated after it was turned back on him. Nevertheless, he sent Pallais to meet with Vaky again to discuss some of the details. Before leaving Managua Pallais satisfied himself that Somoza was still serious about a plebiscite, and when Vaky asked him the same question, Pallais answered confidently that Somoza was serious. However, by the time Pallais returned, Somoza had changed his mind. Before he had an opportunity to explore the reasons for the change, Pallais was called by Somoza into a Cabinet meeting discussion of the plebiscite. During the discussion, Somoza did not say a word. The debate went against the mediators' proposal, and the Cabinet voted "no." Pallais was shocked. "All Somoza had to do was say, 'yes,' and the vote would have changed." Pallais later discovered that a number of people in the Cabinet, led by Foreign Minister Julio Quintana, "had persuaded Somoza that he would lose a free election, and he wanted to stay in power." This was the decisive moment.[16]

The Cabinet and the Liberal Party negotiators, however, decided that it would be better to quibble over the proposal's constitutionality than to reject it. The United States, unaware of either Somoza's uncertainty or his final decision, was losing its patience nevertheless. General Dennis McAuliffe, head of the U.S. Southern Command in Panama, was authorized to accompany Bowdler on December 21. "The reason that I'm here," McAuliffe said, on behalf of the Pentagon, "is that we perceive that the cooperation you have given to the negotiating team is no longer evident."[17] McAuliffe continued: "We on the military side of the U.S. recognize . . . that peace will not come to Nicaragua until you have removed yourself from the presidency and the scene."

Somoza claimed his only objection was that the United States was demanding he permit an election "which would not be acceptable anywhere in the world." "If the plebiscite is organized along traditional lines, which the people of Nicaragua understand," Somoza said, "there will be no problem." Of course, this was the problem. The Somozas had never permitted a fair election, and he knew that better than anyone.

Somoza was left with no doubt about the intentions and objectives of the U.S. government, and acknowledged as much: "What [General McAuliffe] has actually outlined to me is that if I turn right, I hit the wall; if I go forward, I hit the wall; if I turn left, I hit the wall."

Anti-Climax

It was the day after Christmas that Cyrus Vance convened a PRC meeting with Harold Brown, David Aaron, General Smith, Bowdler, Vaky, McAuliffe, U.S. Ambassador to Managua Solaun, and myself. Bowdler explained that the mediation team had presented its revised plebiscite proposal on December 20. The FAO had accepted it, despite their doubts about their ability to contest Somoza's machine and the lack of support from *La Prensa* and the Archbishop.

Somoza's party had raised several objections, which Bowdler and McAuliffe interpreted as signs of Somoza's unwillingness to permit a fair election. The PRC meeting did not explore the details of Somoza's objections, but rather searched for a strategy that offered the best chance for getting Somoza to accept the plebiscite. The only debate was between those who wanted to apply the pressure in a phased approach (option 1: withdraw the entire military mission and one-half of the AID mission, all Peace Corps volunteers, reduce Embassy) and those who wanted to apply it all at once (option 2: total withdrawal of the entire military and AID mission, all Peace Corps, all significant Embassy staff, and the Ambassador).

Aaron, representing Brzezinski, argued for option 1 in order to leave something as an incentive and as future leverage in case Somoza did not move. Bowdler thought it would have a greater impact on Somoza if all the sanctions were implemented at once, and Vance agreed, though for a different reason: he did not want to endanger those who would be left behind. He was already worried about hostages, and the Shah had not even left Iran.

On December 27, Carter reviewed the PRC's recommendation and approved a phased approach of sanctions as a first step to persuade Somoza to accept the plebiscite. But Carter also wrote on the memo that we should wait for Somoza's counterproposal before implementing the sanctions. As it turned out, the United States received the counterproposal the same day as the President's decision, and once again, Somoza managed a reprieve.

The principal arguments in Somoza's counterproposal were not new to Bowdler, but they were to the President, who saw the cable describing the counterproposal before it was reviewed by his staff. Somoza thought the plebiscite should be run by a national rather than an international authority, because the latter would constitute an infringement on Nicaragua's sovereignty. Carter noted that this objection did not seem unreasonable in the light of the importance Latin Americans attached to sovereignty. Sensitized by the Canal treaties, Carter accepted Somoza's argument that the international "organization, control, and supervision of the entire plebiscite" was "interventionistic" and "an excessive demand." Carter's hand-written note on the cable also included questions about several other items in the counterproposal.

Everyone had thought the mediation was over. The two other mediators had left Nicaragua with no intention of returning. Vaky and Bowdler insisted that we ignore Somoza's counterproposal; they were convinced that the FAO would never accept any revisions to the original proposal.

The PRC had failed to explore the details of the differences between the mediation team's plebiscite proposal and Somoza's objections for several reasons. First, almost everyone distrusted Somoza and respected Bowdler, and at this late stage in the negotiations, after Bowdler had worked so hard on a proposal that he did not even support, no one wanted to second-guess him. Second, in the course of trying to hold the FAO together and to gain their agreement to the plebiscite, Bowdler felt compelled to accept many of their conditions, though these appeared excessive to people unfamiliar with Nicaragua's history. After forty-five years of Somoza's rigged elections, the FAO wanted air-tight guarantees that the election would be fair. Finally, the PRC was exhausted with the issue of when and how to "talk turkey" and recommended action.

On January 2, I stayed late to draft a memorandum offering three options to respond to Somoza's counterproposal and Carter's comment. I gave the memo to Brzezinski the next morning and recommended that the President discuss it at a small meeting with Vance, Bowdler, Vaky, Brzezinski, and me. Brzezinski did not have the time to pursue this and decided instead to give the memo directly to Carter, who then called Vance. They agreed with my compromise proposal to accept Somoza's request for a national plebiscitary authority, but to insist it should work alongside an international authority that would fully monitor, mediate, and arbitrate problems. I also recommended that we draw a circle around this last set of issues, and set a deadline and phase-in sanctions if Somoza tried to stall or renegotiate. Finally, I suggested we go to the FAO first and tell them our plan. If the FAO accepted it and Somoza rejected it, we would impose the sanctions. My proposal was approved on January 5.

The next day, Bowdler met with Robelo in Washington, and he ac-

cepted all of the points. Bowdler then persuaded the other two mediators, and together, the mediation team returned to Managua. Vaky
then asked me anxiously: "Are you people prepared to cross the Ru-
bicon?" I checked with Brzezinski, and responded affirmatively.

For the second time, the story was interrupted before its climax.
The three mediators delivered the final proposal on January 12, and
Bowdler remained after the others had left to encounter an assertive,
confident Somoza: "You [the Carter Administration] have been
threatening me since January 1977." He had had enough. He argued
that the FAO was weak and split, that he was strong, and that the
United States should support him. Bowdler told him this was out of
the question and insisted that Somoza accept the final plebiscite proposal. Bowdler now finally had authority to threaten sanctions, but
for some reason, he did not use it. The State Department spokesman
therefore said publicly that the mediators had presented the final proposal, and that Bowdler had stayed afterward to warn Somoza that if
he rejected the proposal, the situation in Nicaragua would rapidly de-
teriorate and U.S. relations would be negatively affected.

On January 18, the negotiating committee of Somoza's Liberal
Party accepted the proposal, but insisted on five changes: (1) they accepted the possibility of the OAS verifying the results of the plebiscite, but they opposed international arbitration of disputes; (2) they
rejected absentee balloting and (3) the involuntary departure of
Somoza's brother and son before the election; and (4) they insisted on
prior registration and (5) a change in the plebiscite question. The
change in the question was significant because it would have made it
both confusing and subject to manipulation.[18] In retrospect, the
other objections seem negotiable, but at the time, they just confirmed the Administration's suspicion that Somoza wanted to negotiate indefinitely. The Administration finally drew the line.

The next day, by coincidence, John Murphy and his wife had lunch
with President Carter and the First Lady. Carter wanted to discuss a
number of legislative issues, including legislation that would be reviewed by the House Merchant Marine and Fisheries Committee to
implement the Panama Canal treaties. Murphy was the influential
chairman of the committee.

Murphy tried to persuade Carter to support Somoza, but Carter refused outright, just as he refused to consider linking the Canal Treaty
legislation with Nicaragua.[19] Instead, Carter convinced Murphy he
was serious about Nicaragua, and as Carter recalled, he "made clear
to [Murphy] that Somoza could not go on as he was." According to
Carter, Murphy promised "to moderate Somoza's policies and bring
Somoza to the realization that there could be some peaceful resolu-

tion of the problem." Afterward, Vance reported that Murphy was "shaken" by Carter's arguments, and Somoza himself concedes in his book that Murphy told him he thought that "Carter's mind was set against Nicaragua, and that he simply could not get through" to Carter.[20]

Carter and Murphy also talked about working together on a compromise bill on the Panama Canal Treaty legislation, which they did. (The bill that Murphy shepherded through the Congress was not the one that the Administration initially wanted, but it was satisfactory, and in the end, Carter lobbied for it.)

On the same day, January 19, the FAO issued a communiqué condemning "the brutal intransigence of the dictator" and declaring the mediation closed. *La Prensa* headlines read: "Somoza Buries Mediation." The opposition almost seemed to breathe a sigh of relief that it was over, and they had survived. Bowdler left Nicaragua, stopping to tell Somoza that he would return only if Somoza accepted the proposal.[21]

The day before a PRC meeting to decide how to respond to the failure of the mediation, Henry Owen called to tell me of a conversation he had just had with Charles Wilson. Wilson had told him that as a graduate of Annapolis, he had originally joined the House Appropriations Committee to work on the Military Affairs Subcommittee, but he had to accept a position on the Foreign Operations Subcommittee until there was an opening on Military Affairs. He had just been offered the position he coveted on Military Affairs, but rejected it so he could continue to oversee the Administration's policy on Nicaragua. Wilson told Owen that the aid bill would encounter serious problems if the Administration reduced aid to Nicaragua any further. "He can single-handedly eliminate Latin America from the aid program this year," Owen said. A few hours later, Owen's Deputy Rutherford Poats called me to say that Vice President Mondale had received a similar call from Wilson.

Christopher convened the PRC meeting on January 26. In attendance were Brzezinski, Aaron, Harold Brown, Assistant Secretary of Defense David McGiffert, Chairman of the Joint Chiefs David Jones, Stansfield Turner, Bowdler, Deputy Assistant Secretary of State John Bushnell, AID Administrator John Gilligan, Henry Owen, and myself. As in Nicaragua, the United States appeared relieved to have reached the decision point. Bowdler summarized the mediation and concluded that the impasse could not be broken without making concessions to Somoza that were unacceptable to the FAO and to the other two mediators. There was a generalized desire to get past this issue, and no further discussion of the specific points of disagreement.

The discussion shifted to the probable consequences of the mediation's end. Harold Brown summarized the consensus: the longer Somoza stayed in power, the higher the chances were of a radical takeover. The only question was when the Sandinistas would assume power. Turner said that Somoza had built up the Guard during the mediation and that the FSLN had lost support and were refocusing on a longer-term armed struggle. The moderate opposition was also weak. Therefore, Turner judged that the chances of Somoza remaining in power until 1981 were better than even.

Bowdler said that the Sandinistas had organized a Patriotic Front, an umbrella organization to induce further defections from the FAO. Unless the United States quickly gave the moderates an alternative, they would ally with the left, shortening the timing of a Sandinista victory. Thus he and Harold Brown argued that even though sanctions might not affect Somoza, they were needed to bolster the moderate opposition and keep them from turning to the left.

There was agreement to impose sanctions against Somoza; the only question was which steps would communicate disapproval most effectively without generating significant extraneous costs, such as those related to Wilson's threats against the aid program. Brzezinski put the issue in a strategic framework that permitted a quick consensus. He said that the principal actions the United States should take against Somoza were symbolic and should be military and political. We should withdraw the U.S. military advisory group, terminate all military aid, and seek to ostracize Somoza in the OAS. Cutting off all economic aid at this time was not necessary or appropriate; some room should be left for the next stage. Bowdler agreed that the steps that would have the most impact on Somoza and on Nicaraguans were political and military; steps to terminate economic aid would only cause an uproar in Washington without adding significantly to our message in Managua. Bowdler suggested that the two suspended aid loans should remain suspended. The PRC also agreed that the United States would vote against all loans to Nicaragua in the international banks.

I returned to my office to write a summary of the meeting for the President and a decision memorandum. In addition, I wrote a memo for Brzezinski on a letter that John Murphy had sent the President after his luncheon. Murphy's letter read as if it were a legal brief for Somoza's counterproposal, making the case for each of Somoza's objections to the mediation team's proposal.[22] When I finished, I left the two items with Brzezinski's overnight secretary with instructions that part of the package was for the President and the other for Brzezinski.

This was an odd moment. Vaky and Bowdler had been advocating these actions for months, yet Bowdler acknowledged that the steps were unlikely to have an effect on Somoza. Although there was virtually no difference between the sanctions accepted on January 26 and those proposed earlier, Vaky and Bowdler feared that the sanctions might have less influence. And there was little discussion of what could be done after these steps. An unstated premise that hung over the discussion was that there was little more that could be done, even though all agreed that a serious crisis was looming.

It would have been logical to review the differences in the positions between the FAO and Somoza on the plebiscite more closely, because a plebiscite remained the only apparent method of moving Somoza out. But there was no discussion, probably because of bureaucratic fatigue and the psychological need to reach agreement and move to the next issue. This was especially true for the principals, who had spent the previous month arguing over SALT, China, and particularly over how to deal with the collapse of the Shah and the impending triumph of Khomeini.

The two revolutions in Iran and Nicaragua contained so many parallels that even the characters sometimes seemed interchangeable. During several discussions on the question of contacting General Gutiérrez as a possible head of a future National Guard, David Aaron and Harold Brown reminded each other that he was the Nicaraguan equivalent of General Fereidoun Jam, who had been considered a possible head of the Iranian armed forces, and therefore an alternative to both the Shah and the Ayatollah. Because the principals could not reach agreement on Iran, it was all the more refreshing for them to reach it on Nicaragua.

After the PRC meeting of January 26, attention shifted from Nicaragua so quickly that the decisions almost seemed to escape into a black hole and emerge in an altered state. On Saturday, January 27, I stopped by Brzezinski's office to see whether the decision memorandum had been sent to the President. I learned that Chinese Vice Premier Deng Xiaoping was coming soon for an official visit, and Brzezinski seemed more delightfully preoccupied than any time since he had worked on the President's schedule for his trip to Poland.

Proud of his role in what he considered the "historic" decision to normalize relations with China, Brzezinski was in the process of reviewing volumes of briefing books on China for the President. He suggested I speak to Aaron, who had the memorandum. Aaron had a penetrating intelligence, but organization was not his forte, and I

feared the memorandum might be stuck. On Monday, I checked
again, but by then the Chinese had arrived.

The memorandum finally went to the President on Wednesday,
January 31, but by mistake, it included the extra section (on Murphy's letter) I had reserved only for Brzezinski. Carter, like Brzezinski, read voraciously, quickly, and generally, with high levels of com-
prehension and recall. Memoranda were returned with comments
the same day they had been sent. Carter approved the recommendation of the PRC meeting to sanction Somoza.

But then Carter read through Murphy's point-by-point rebuttal of
the mediation team proposal and jotted in his neat script those
points, for example, on prior registration of voters, that struck Carter
as sensible. Indeed, on many of the differences, Carter's notes suggest
he found the Somoza/Murphy position better than the mediators'
proposal. No better illustration of Somoza's effectiveness in tran-
scribing Nicaraguan politics into the vocabulary of U.S. politics can
be found than in the President's handwritten notes. Murphy/Somo-
za's objection to the degree of international supervision and the
change of voting districts, for example, seemed reasonable if one
were thinking in terms of a democratic nation. However, exceptional
steps were necessary in Nicaragua to make an election credible.
Carter had not grasped that point, nor did the memo make it because
it was not supposed to be read by him.

I was rendered mute, and didn't know how to proceed. The impli-
cation of the President's notes was to reactivate negotiations. This
would have required a heroic, probably futile effort in Washington, in
the capitals of the other two mediators, and especially in Managua. I
was certain that the best response we could obtain from Vaky and
Bowdler was that the mission was impossible; at worst, they would
resign.

Vance and Brzezinski were trying to cope with Iran and SALT.
After obtaining his agreement to keep the information to himself until we figured out how to proceed, I informed Vaky over the phone of
Carter's comments. I heard silence and then a thud, the sound of a
forehead hitting a desk. If Carter's decision had leaked at that time,
the embarrassment would have made us look back nostalgically to
the leak of Carter's letter to Somoza. This was clearly the moment
for the President to sit down with his principal advisers and infuse a
new strategy with his own personal goals and commitment. But
there was no time for that.

I therefore decided to break the logjam by drafting a brief "reporting item" for Brzezinski to include in his routine morning memorandum to the President. The item informed the President that the State

Department would announce that the mediation had ended because of Somoza's intransigence, and the United States was responding with the sanctions he approved. I alerted Brzezinski to make sure that he understood the significance of the paragraph, and he sent it to the President on February 1. If the President wanted to change course, he would stop us. As it turned out, it was the same day that the Ayatollah flew to Teheran on a chartered 747, signaling the collapse of the Administration's Iran policy. The memorandum was returned the next day without comments. I told Vaky to go ahead.

Sanctions and Their Impact

Bowdler spoke to his counterparts from Guatemala and the Dominican Republic, and all agreed to sign a joint report announcing the end of the mediation. The United States then used the report as the basis for the State Department's announcement on February 8 that blamed the mediation's failure on "President Somoza's unwillingness to accept the essential elements of the mediators' most recent proposal. . . . Prospects for renewed violence and polarization, and the human rights situation . . . unavoidably affect the kind of relationship we can maintain with that government." The United States decided to take the following steps:

(1) the U.S. military group would be withdrawn and the military assistance program, which had been suspended, would be terminated;
(2) no new aid programs would be considered and the two loan projects would be held up, but those programs that were "well advanced" and aimed at "the basic human needs of the poor" would continue;
(3) all Peace Corps volunteers would be withdrawn; and
(4) the size of the Embassy would be reduced by more than half (from 82 to 37).

The statement concluded by urging other governments not to contribute to the violence and expressing the willingness of the United States to "resume the conciliation efforts should conditions and circumstances warrant."[23]

The next day, Carter received a letter from Senators Kennedy, Cranston, Javits, Sarbanes, and Hatfield supporting his decisions "to dissociate" the United States from Somoza. "They are a clear message that President Somoza can neither oppose democratic rule nor violate his citizens' human rights with impunity." They also urged him to take several additional steps if Somoza didn't reconsider his position, including enlisting other nations and the OAS; recalling our Ambassador; opposing all international loans; and reducing and possibly suspending meat and sugar import quotas.

La Prensa in Managua supported the Administration's decision, and the FAO breathed a sigh of relief that the United States had finally acted. The reaction in Latin America was generally favorable. But despite repeated decisions by the PRC, the State Department consulted but did not coordinate sanctions with the other interested Latin American countries.

The mediation—from October 6, 1978, to February 8, 1979—had accomplished more than anyone thought possible at the beginning even though it failed in the end. The mediation team found both the FAO and Somoza unwilling to negotiate, but by persisting and cajoling, the team succeeded in eliciting both a plan for a transitional government from the FAO and a proposal for a plebiscite from Somoza. The opposition was fragile at the beginning of the mediation, but over time, despite surreptitious attempts by the Sandinistas to undermine it, the FAO became stronger until they were prepared to sit across the table from Somoza's negotiators in December. There is credible evidence that Somoza seriously toyed with the idea of a plebiscite, but in the end, he decided not to risk a vote. There was nothing inevitable in the failure of the mediation, and considerable progress made on the road.

The United States insisted that the mediation be multilateral, but assumed the unquestioning lead. It debated objectives—whether to do what was necessary to push Somoza out of office or whether to insist on an election through which the people of Nicaragua could make the determination. Carter chose the latter option, and then the mediation team tried to develop the kinds of guarantees that would permit an election in Somoza's Nicaragua to be genuinely free. This proved extremely difficult and eventually impossible, because Somoza did not want a free election. The Carter Administration also debated tactics—when to apply pressure and in what ways. Vaky and Bowdler thought that pressure would be more effective during negotiations; Carter decided to threaten during negotiations and sanction only after negotiations failed.

In the end, the mediation failed. Instead of serving as a transition toward democracy, the mediation served as a resting place on the road to revolution. On that road, tragedy was wrapped in unintended irony: it was the very success of the mediation in almost achieving a plebiscite and a united moderate opposition that motivated the FSLN to bury their own differences and develop a winning strategy.

Chapter 7

MARCHING TO

DIFFERENT DRUMMERS

> "Our ability to maintain broad alliances. . . . succeeded
> in isolating the Somoza regime, achieving nation-wide anti-
> Somoza unity, neutralizing the reactionary elements in favor
> of intervention. . . .
>
> Our country is not an island like Cuba; we have to rely
> on neighboring countries. . . . We operated clandestinely in
> Costa Rica and Honduras. . . . The alliances . . . were of vital
> importance in our obtaining heavy weapons and sophis-
> ticated equipment. . . .
>
> The progressives [the bourgeoisie] realized that ours was
> a revolutionary movement and that we weren't totally in
> accord with their ideology, but they also realized that we had
> a political program that was, to a certain extent, of interest
> to them, and that we had military power."
> **Humberto Ortega[1]**

FROM THE IMPOSITION of sanctions in February to the Sandinistas'
"final offensive" in June 1979, the United States withdrew from the
crisis. Others, "marching to different drummers," moved to center
stage with the objective of overthrowing Somoza militarily.

Withdrawal Pains

On February 8, 1979, the Administration imposed most of the
sanctions that had been proposed by those inside and outside the
Administration as a means of forcing Somoza's resignation. But Somoza did not budge.

The Administration considered additional steps. Instead of closing
the Embassy, which would have precluded contact with the opposition as well as with Somoza should he decide to reconsider the plebiscite proposal, the Administration recalled Ambassador Solaun to
Washington in late February for "consultations," and he never re-

turned. He later resigned and returned to teaching. The Administration deliberately did not withdraw the mediation team's final plebiscite proposal in order to offer Somoza an exit if he should change his mind, though no one expected he would.

Sanctions are more effective as a threat than as a punishment. They were necessary in this instance in order to restore the Administration's credibility with the opposition and with other governments in the region. Having used most of the sanctions, however, the Administration found its options limited. Vaky recalled that the mediation had left him exhausted, and after the sanctions, he simply "didn't know what to do."[2] He had been the motor behind the Administration's policy review; when his motor stalled, the Administration's policy did as well.

The United States and Somoza both experienced withdrawal pains, albeit for different reasons. Somoza thought he would remain in power because of the Guard; he was not disappointed and worried enough about the loss of U.S. support to consider resigning. With the passing of the atmosphere of crisis, and no new ideas or options, the Administration turned its attention to other areas that had been neglected. For the Latin Americanists, this meant, among other things, completing the ambitious interagency policy review on Mexico in preparation for President Carter's trip there in February 1979. The next time that Vaky and I focused on Nicaragua was March 7. Although the United States had in effect given up on trying to influence Somoza, he had not given up trying to influence the United States. He sent a message expressing his interest in bilateral negotiations, but Vaky thought a cool and correct posture was the best approach to demonstrate that we were uninterested in his games, and I agreed. The President accepted that approach on March 14.

As predicted, the collapse of the mediation accelerated the polarization within Nicaragua. In the fall, the FSLN had established a united front, the United People's Movement, to compete with the FAO and also to absorb the organizations that broke from the FAO because of frustration in dealing with Somoza. After the collapse of the mediation, the FAO merged with this organization to form a new National Patriotic Front. Bowdler had feared this might occur if the United States failed to impose sanctions; it happened anyway.

Like the Administration, the Nicaraguan moderates did not know what to do after the mediation, but they had an additional cause for disillusionment: they had thought that the United States would remove Somoza. When Somoza remained, the Latin Americans were impelled either to believe that the United States was duplicitous or to reevaluate their assumption that it was omnipotent. Nicaraguans could not believe the latter, so they accepted the former.

Alfonso Robelo traveled to San José in January 1979 to meet with his old friend and schoolmate, Edén Pastora. As one of the principal moderate leaders, Robelo was looking for alternatives, and he queried Pastora about the Frente. He was surprised when Pastora warned: "We should make a strong alliance because the Communists are getting together. And we, the true Social Democrats, will be left aside."[3] Soon after that, Robelo gave an interview that indicated that he understood Pastora's point: "I have come to the conclusion that if there is a military victory of the Frente, and I think that improbable, we would end up under a totalitarian regime of the Communist type."[4] Although aware of the danger, both Pastora and Robelo then acted as if it did not exist. Indeed, Pastora gave the Sandinistas their most effective military operation, and Robelo later provided them the crucial seal of middle-class legitimacy.

Somoza was bothered by the sanctions, though he pretended not to be. When asked by the Voice of America for his reaction, he said: "Yeah, how about those jerks?" But then he insisted that "things [will] go on as before."[5] His supporters in the United States continued to try to reverse the Carter Administration. Charles Wilson, in particular, kept the pressure on Owen, Christopher, and myself, insisting that he would "wreck the train" of foreign aid if the Administration did not leave Somoza alone. The Administration had in fact concluded that more sanctions would not move Somoza but would leave the United States with fewer options in the next crisis, and so Wilson's influence appeared larger than it actually was.

Somoza himself continued to try to influence the American public. On his Easter vacation, Somoza was interviewed on "Face the Nation" and bragged that he had stood up to the Carter Administration: "I even had your Ambassador come and tell me that . . . President Carter and Secretary Vance wanted me to get off the Presidency, and I said no. . . ." Somoza said he was fighting Communism on behalf of the free world, yet the Administration imposed an arms embargo: "Back in 1947, that was enough to overthrow a country." Then, displaying confidence and bravado, he said that he would "neutralize the Sandinistas," who, he predicted, would "wither away."

His optimism was not without some basis. The National Guard had increased in size (from 7,500 in September 1978 to 11,000 in March 1979), and had received new shipments of arms from Israel, Argentina, and Guatemala. In an article entitled "Nicaraguan Rebels Losing Key Support," Charles Krause of the *Washington Post* wrote that Venezuela, Costa Rica, and Panama were reducing their support for the rebels, and he cited one source, whom he considered well informed, who concluded this "will probably mean that Somoza will remain in power until 1981—at least."[6] Several correspondents who had been prepared to give the FSLN the benefit of the doubt in October were more skeptical about their boasts to overthrow the Guard in April.[7]

The FSLN may have been relatively quiet, but they were not passive. They were preparing. On March 7, the FSLN organized a single nine-man National Directorate composed of three leaders from each of the three factions to coordinate military-political strategy. They continued small attacks, aimed as much at provoking the Guard—and gaining recruits—as in demonstrating they remained the only viable alternative to Somoza.

Robelo and his followers began organizing a general strike to overlap with an anticipated new round of fighting, but on April 30, Somoza jailed him and several of his colleagues. When he was released three weeks later, through repeated efforts by the U.S. Embassy, Robelo fled to Costa Rica to help the FSLN prepare a plan for a new government.[8] His imprisonment and subsequent departure was a significant first step in the transfer of legitimacy to the FSLN, although the United States failed to see that at the time.

Unfriendly Neighbors

Robelo found a sizable community of 60,000 Nicaraguan refugees in San José. One middle-class leader, Alfredo César, had left a comfortable job managing a sugar company to fight the Guard during the September insurrection. He had been captured and tortured, but he was not killed, in his view, because the jails were so crowded the Guard did not recognize him. When released due to the amnesty during the mediation, he fled to Costa Rica. Like César, some of those who fled Nicaragua also joined the Sandinistas, who maintained their headquarters in San José. The FSLN recruited not just Nicaraguans but Costa Ricans, Panamanians, and other Latin Americans. The sons of José Figueres and Omar Torrijos were already fighting with Pastora.

Since 1824, when Nicaragua's most southern province, Guanacaste, seceded to join Costa Rica, relations between the two nations have almost always been poor. Costa Ricans tend to be smug about their democratic institutions and condescending and not infrequently racist about the dictatorships that have ruled the Indian and mestizo populations in Nicaragua. The postwar feud between Figueres and the Somoza family brought all the underlying prejudices between the two nations to the surface, and the presence of 60,000 victims of Somoza's tyranny transformed the Nicaraguan rebellion into a Costa Rican national *cause célèbre*. Rodrigo Carazo Odío had been elected President of Costa Rica on February 5, 1978, and inaugurated on May 8.

In a retrospective interview, Carazo identified three stages in Costa Rica's policy toward Nicaragua during his Administration: (1) neutrality; (2) acquiescence; and (3) support for the Sandinistas. Each stage corresponded to an act of Nicaraguan aggression and to his perception of the nature of the threat his nation faced.[9]

From May until September 1978, Carazo claimed there was no official Costa Rican support of the Sandinistas, although ex-president Figueres was helping them independently. During this first stage, Costa Rican authorities preserved their neutrality by occasionally intercepting and arresting Sandinistas. The second stage of Costa Rican policy was provoked by the Nicaraguan Air Force attack on the border on September 12, 1978. Carazo then permitted Pastora autonomy to transport medicines and food and to organize within Costa Rica. Gradually, Costa Rica became less neutral and more supportive of the Sandinistas. On November 21, 1978, another incident on the border occurred, and there were Costa Rican casualties. Costa Rica broke relations with Nicaragua and undertook a diplomatic offensive in the OAS and UN to denounce and isolate Nicaragua and obtain observer teams to investigate the border incidents.[10]

Carazo, Torrijos, and Pérez all supported the mediation and reduced the flow of arms to the Sandinistas during this second period. But after another border incident in late December and the subsequent collapse of the mediation, Carazo concluded that "Somoza was a national security threat to Costa Rica." In this third stage, Costa Rica became what Humberto Ortega would characterize as the "excellent rearguard network that made it possible to . . . end the war quickly."[11] Carazo at this point sought help from Venezuela, Panama, and Cuba. His strategy was to "support Pastora 100 percent. We saw him as the only alternative."[12]

Costa Rica became the key link in an elaborate logistic system that began in Venezuela and Cuba and passed through Panama. According to a report issued in 1981 by a special commission established by the Costa Rican Congress, "approximately one million pounds of arms and munitions entered" Costa Rica between December 1978 and July 1979. The munitions flights were deliberately undocumented, but the commission estimated there might have been as many as sixty flights. "The entire operation," the commission concluded, "was expressly authorized by the President [Carazo] and the Minister [of Public Security Juan José Echeverría]."[13]

The first arms that the commission could verify arrived on February 22, 1979, in a Venezuelan Air Force plane. Four hundred M-14 rifles and about one million bullets were unloaded. An earlier shipment of one hundred M-14s had arrived from an unknown destination. Panama also provided one planeload directly and then transshipped arms from Cuba. Cuban flights would land in David in northern Panama. The arms would be unloaded and transferred to planes that flew to San José. From there, the arms would either be flown to Liberia, a Costa Rican town near the border with Nicaragua, or be driven by Ministry of Public Security officials in trucks. This system became too complicated and risky, and so by April, Panamanian DC-3s flew directly from David to Liberia.

Costa Rica was an essential component in the Sandinista strategy; it was the staging area for the war. But Costa Rica was unlikely to have played that role had it not been supported by Panama and initially by Venezuela. Torrijos of Panama and Pérez from Venezuela worked closely together, primarily to help Edén Pastora. Torrijos viewed Pastora as he did himself, a romantic, independent military figure in a profession that rejected both adjectives. Pérez began supporting Pastora in early 1978, although when Ambassador Vaky left Caracas in July, he still "had no inkling that Pérez was involved in helping the Sandinistas."[14] After the mediation failed, Pérez invited Luis Pallais to Caracas, and offered him a simple plan, which Pérez later recounted:

> It's real easy. You support Somoza; you are his relative; you are the president of the Congress. Try to convince your relative to leave Nicaragua. Ask Congress to name you President and then we can convene to negotiate with the guerrillas for a democratic solution. Pallais responded: "I wish I could do that, but I don't know what Somoza would do if I mentioned this possibility."[15]

Perez sent Pallais to Panama to have Torrijos work on him, which he did. Torrijos put Pallais on a plane to Managua and then leaked a story to the press that Pallais would be the newly elected President of Nicaragua. When Pallais arrived in Managua, Somoza confronted him with the news report. Pallais apologized and explained, and Somoza told him to clear the public record with a press conference, which he dutifully did.[16]

That was the extent of the mediation efforts of Pérez and Torrijos. After this, both pursued the path of war. In March 1979, Vice President Walter Mondale attended the inauguration of the new Venezuelan President, Luis Herrera Campíns. The next day, Mondale had breakfast with outgoing President Pérez. When Pérez asked how the United States would get rid of Somoza, Mondale told him that we shared Pérez's distaste for the Somoza regime and his fear of the consequences if Somoza stayed in power, but the United States did not intend to overthrow Somoza. Pérez became upset, stood up, and said: "In that case, blood will flow."[17]

Though Pérez left the Presidency, his concern for Nicaragua did not abate. He remained Vice President of the Socialist International, the international organization of Social Democratic parties, and at its regional meeting in San José on May 5, 1979, the International declared the Somoza dictatorship "the prime example of U.S. interventionism in the continent." It claimed Somoza was "still in power today thanks to U.S. support," and said the only road was "the armed struggle." This was an unusually belligerent statement from a group of democratic parties.

The new Venezuelan President had defeated the candidate of Pérez's party. Arístides Calvani, a former Venezuelan Foreign Minister and close adviser to Herrera at the beginning of his term, later estimated that Pérez might have spent as much as $100 million in support of the Sandinistas, but the newly elected President decided not to investigate what had been done, in part because the war against Somoza was very popular in Venezuela.[18] Herrera was more cautious, conservative, and concerned about domestic issues than his predecessor, but he continued to send arms secretly to the Sandinistas, although at a much reduced level. He used the same people and the same operation in the Venezuelan National Security Council that Pérez had used.[19]

The change from Pérez to Herrera and the consequent decline in Venezuela's influence with the Sandinistas was of great significance, because it occurred at the moment that the FSLN was preparing for its "final offensive" and when support for the Sandinistas in Costa Rica and Panama was reaching a fever pitch. According to Pérez, who only learned about it later, Carazo and Torrijos in late April "opened the door to Fidel Castro." Pérez said that both were frightened that Somoza might attack them, and they welcomed large shipments of arms from Cuba.[20]

In May, Pastora negotiated an arrangement with Cuban officials, Costa Rican Minister of Public Security Echeverría, and a commercial company called EXACO to fly arms directly to his troops in northern Costa Rica. At least 21 flights, each costing $8,000–10,000, went directly from Cuba to a small airstrip near the Nicaraguan border,

Llano Grande. These flights began in late May and continued through the Sandinista triumph in mid-July and carried about 31,000 pounds of arms. Echeverría supervised the arms shipments and their transfer to the FSLN.[21]

There were also unconfirmed reports of flights of 707s from West Germany with 60,000 pounds of arms and from Portugal with 90,000 pounds. Several other flights from Colombia, carrying boots, uniforms, and medicines, were confirmed as well as many flights from Panama.[22] The Sandinistas also imported some arms through Honduras, obtaining the acquiescence of its military by bribery, but the quantity of arms received in Honduras was quite small compared to the arsenal assembled in Costa Rica.

The United States received some information about arms smuggling, but until late June it never suspected that the arms flow was very large or that both the Cuban and Costa Rican governments were directly involved. Intelligence was weak because State and CIA gave the region low priority and thus reductions in overall levels of U.S. personnel abroad were felt immediately in Central America. Whenever information was received, however, the U.S. Ambassador was instructed to meet with Carazo and Echeverría to express U.S. concern. Both denied any involvement and insisted that the government was doing what it could to curtail the illicit smuggling. When I asked Carazo years later why they had struck a deal with Cuba, he said: "It was more important for Somoza to fall than to keep out the Cubans."[23]

The Calm and the Storm

Unaware of the buildup of military equipment in northern Costa Rica and the plans for a major offensive in early May, the Carter Administration continued its cool approach to the Somoza government. The Administration faced another awkward decision—a standby loan for Nicaragua in the International Monetary Fund (IMF). Many confuse the IMF with the World Bank and the Inter-American Development Bank, although the mission of these organizations is very different; the latter two are aid-granting development institutions. The IMF does not give aid; it maintains the international monetary system by lending money to member countries that have chronic balance-of-payments problems or budget deficits. All members have a legal right to borrow on their own contribution if they accept an austerity economic plan.

The Executive Branch has always tried to prevent efforts by Congress to introduce any political criteria—whether it be human rights, expropriation of property, or anti-Communism—into the Fund's decision making. There was therefore some concern that the Administration itself had introduced such criteria in November when it persuaded the IMF to postpone a loan to Nicaragua.

Although the Administration had tried to use that decision privately to communicate its seriousness to Somoza, publicly, it had continued to insist that the decision was nonpolitical and the result of the failure by the Nicaraguan government to accept an economic plan. The principal reason the Administration had sought the delay, however, was that it feared that approval would be interpreted as a demonstration of political support for the Somoza government.

By May 1979, however, the Nicaraguan government had not only negotiated an agreement to reduce its deficit by more than half in one year, it had already taken the most difficult step to implement it—a large devaluation. Because of the need to demonstrate consistency on its IMF position, the Treasury Department recommended voting in favor of the loan.

The issue represented a classic tradeoff between a global interest in maintaining "the rules of the game" for the international monetary system and a specific interest in avoiding any indication of support for a regime like Somoza's. The latter interest will prevail only when there is a compelling security crisis. In mid-May, there was a continuing security problem in Nicaragua, but it was difficult to argue that it was either compelling or a crisis at that time. The State Department decided to accept Treasury's position in exchange for a clarifying statement at the time of the vote: "The U.S. position on this request should not be interpreted as an act of political support for the Government of Nicaragua." That, of course, was nevertheless exactly the way both the supporters and the opponents of the Somoza regime interpreted the vote. At best, the Administration's position was viewed as inconsistent and inept.[24] It is worth noting that none of the Latin American democracies, including Venezuela and Costa Rica, voted against the loan.

May 16–18, 1979, the senior Latin American policy makers from Washington—from State, Defense, NSC, Joint Chiefs of Staff, CIA, Treasury, and Commerce—met in San José, Costa Rica, with all the U.S. ambassadors to Central America and the key neighboring countries for a Chiefs of Mission (Ambassadors) Conference. Such meetings permit the ambassadors and policy makers from Washington to review events and narrow whatever perceptual gaps may have emerged. Vaky and I also used the opportunity to meet with President Carazo, who hinted that the Sandinistas might be preparing for a new round of violence but denied any specific knowledge of arms flows to the FSLN.

On May 2, 1979, in advance of the meeting, the CIA prepared a secret intelligence assessment that indicated that Cuba saw "the prospects for revolutionary upheaval in Central America over the next decade or so markedly improved" but had adopted a selective, sophisticated "low-key approach" aimed at a war of attrition and avoiding any actions that could provoke a U.S. response. Since the fall of 1978, the CIA estimated that the Cubans had supplied two or three shipments of arms to the Sandinistas through the Panamanian government and had increased their on-island training. The report also cited two Cuban diplomats in Panama who told officials "that Cuba no longer believed that the FSLN would be able to topple Somoza before his term expires in 1981."[25]

Both the State Department and the CIA agreed that Somoza's Guard was stronger, larger, and had better trained and equipped recruits. The FAO had splintered after the mediation. As for the Sandinistas, they were recruiting about 150 new soldiers per month, bringing their numbers up to 2,000, but they had experienced substantial losses in the fighting. The U.S. participants in the Chiefs of Mission Conference sensed the political tremors in the region, but they had no geopolitical device to judge when those tremors would reshape the political landscape. No one guessed how soon it would be.

Within one week, the Mexican President met with Fidel Castro, broke relations with Nicaragua, and encouraged other nations to follow suit and isolate Somoza. On May 29, the Sandinistas then launched an offensive, that they called "final." It was not until mid-June that the United States recognized that it truly was.

Like most nations, including the United States, Mexico tends to project its own internal structure and historical experience internationally. It supports revolution in Central America, believing every nation ought to have one like Mexico's. Starting in the fall of 1978, the ruling party (PRI) and the Ministers of the Interior (Gobernación) and Foreign Affairs gave money to the Sandinistas,[26] much as the Mexican government funds and coopts local leftist groups. The Foreign Ministry also offered its Embassy in Managua as a sanctuary for Sandinistas who needed to escape the rigors of combat.

But the payments were a reflex; the Mexican government did not focus on the Nicaraguan revolution until two months before the triumph, nor did it know much about Central America. Neither President José López Portillo nor the two men who served him as Foreign Minister, Santiago Roel and Jorge Castañeda, had ever visited Central

America. These men were typical of the Mexican elite, which has historically looked to the United States and Europe, with almost no contact or interest in Central America, except Guatemala, since the 1930s.

Mexico's discovery of vast oil reserves in 1977 combined with oil price increases permitted López Portillo to pursue a more active foreign policy, and Nicaragua seemed an appropriate place to begin. Sandino was a hero in Mexico, where he had lived, and Somoza, a despicable North American client.

In late May 1979, López Portillo met for two days with Fidel Castro. Castro's visit was his first to Mexico since he came to power and his first to Latin America since the fall of Allende in 1973. The meeting presented an opportunity not only to praise each other but to criticize the United States. Castro also denied reports that Cuba was intervening in Nicaragua, suggesting that the United States was the guilty party through "the clearest product of U.S. intervention in Central America," Somoza.[27]

Two days later, Carazo arrived from Cost Rica with a message similar to Castro's. First, the Sandinistas were within a month of coming to power, but there was still time for Mexico to play an important role. And second, with Venezuela's role diminished under President Herrera, Mexico was needed to be the Latin American patron of the revolution. If the United States saw only Cuba as the major supporter of the revolution, it might intervene. López Portillo was convinced, and on May 20, he broke relations with Nicaragua.[28] He then sent two Foreign Ministry officials to Latin America to encourage others to break relations with Somoza, and he urged the United States to "modify its attitude" toward Nicaragua.

The Carter Administration was neither pleased nor surprised by the Mexican mode of consultation. Both Carter and Vance had previously sought advice from the Mexican government on Nicaragua, but they had not received much of a response. In September 1978, Vance had requested Mexican participation or support for the mediation. Santiago Roel later described his response: "I told Vance, you Americans created a monster, so you get rid of him. We don't want to be involved."[29] In February 1979, Carter explained U.S. policy toward Nicaragua in his visit with López Portillo and sought his advice. Once again, the Mexican leader rebuffed the request, responding with a discursive, conservative critique of Carter's human rights policy that implied that both Nicaragua's old and current troubles were wholly of U.S. manufacture.

The Mexican decision buoyed the hopes of the FSLN. One week later, on May 29, a Sandinista force of about three hundred crossed from Costa Rica into Nicaragua with the intention of reaching Rivas, about twenty miles from the border. The Nicaraguan government accused the Costa Ricans of harboring the FSLN, but the Costa Rican Deputy Public Security Minister, Enrique Montealegre, denied the guerrillas came from Costa Rica: "We do not understand what motivated the Nicaraguan government to come up with a such dangerous accusation."[30]

Sandinista radio announced the "hour for the overthrow" and urged Nicaraguans to participate in a general strike the next week. The attack received almost no press coverage in the United States, and the Administration viewed it in the context of the sporadic violence and repeated Sandinista threats of a major offensive that had been reported periodically since January.[31] Sniper fire was heard in León, Managua, and elsewhere, but the National Guard counterattacked and the offensive seemed to have been stopped.[32]

The CIA undertook a rapid assessment and concluded that the fighting could conceivably develop into a second insurrection on the level of the September crisis, but it would not be adequate to displace Somoza.

Secret Mission to Panama

At 1:00 A.M. on a Monday morning, June 4, I received a frantic phone call from Panama. Gabriel Lewis was calling at Torrijos' instructions. "General Torrijos," Lewis said, "is ready to move. He wants to speak to you right away." Ambler Moss, the U.S. Ambassador to Panama, was in Washington at the time, and at 11:00 A.M. that morning I was informed that President Carter wanted me to return with Moss to Panama on the noon flight. Moss reached the airplane first but had difficulty persuading the pilot that our mission was more important than his to leave on time. Fortunately, I arrived before the door closed.

During the flight, Moss and I discussed what we would like to be able to achieve, other than receive Torrijos' urgent appeal for Carter to rid the region of Somoza. We decided to try to calm Torrijos down in order to ensure passage of the Canal legislation, which was nearing a vote in the House of Representatives. Second, we would try to persuade Torrijos to stop sending arms to the Sandinistas. If at all feasible, we would try to obtain a pledge of noninterference in a letter from him to Carter. We thought there little chance he would send such a letter, but we prepared one anyway. We cleared these objectives with Vaky and Brzezinski during our stopover in Miami.

We arrived at 7:30 P.M. in Panama, and a helicopter flew us directly to Contadora Island off the Pacific coast. Torrijos greeted us with abrazos and an uncharacteristic Wall Street metaphor: "It's too bad the United States is always so slow to recognize new realities, and that you didn't have the foresight to buy a share of Sandinista stock when I was first offering it." "General," I said, "we have not come to buy Sandinista stock, but to try to get you to sell yours."

Torrijos explained that the Sandinista offensive was the final one, and would triumph in a few days. We told him that we thought this would be a second, serious round of violence, but Somoza would survive it. However, this crisis could shock Somoza sufficiently that he might finally realize that he could not survive. We suggested this would be a good time to discuss a moderate transitional government.

More important for U.S.–Panamanian relations, however, was the legislation to implement the Panama Canal treaties, which would either pass or fail in the next few weeks. Panama's activities would be crucial in Congressional deliberations. Torrijos wasn't interested in the legislation: "I am out of the Canal Treaty business," he said. We tried to get him to reconsider, but his thoughts were filled with Nicaragua.

We differed on our interpretations of the FSLN, with Torrijos believing, as many Latin Americans did at the time, that the Carter Administration's concerns were symptomatic of the U.S. obsession with Communism. We questioned him about reports of Panama's involvement in transferring arms to the Sandinistas, and he denied the charges. Since the implementing legislation would be at risk unless he could offer assurances that he was not interfering in Nicaragua's affairs, we asked whether he could convey his assurance to Carter in a letter. After the third request, and after he received our assurance that we would be just as diligent in preventing intervention from El Salvador, Guatemala, and Honduras to bolster Somoza, he agreed to send a letter, but suggested one should also come from Panama's newly elected President, Arístides Royo. We agreed. Although Torrijos retained the real power as Commander of the Guard, the Carter Administration had been encouraging him to transfer his powers to the new President. We flew back to Panama to negotiate the text of the two letters with Royo.

Moss and I first returned to the Embassy and tried to determine whether Torrijos could conceivably have been telling the truth. Torrijos insisted that the flights from Cuba were not carrying arms but were for cultural or sports exchanges. We were very skeptical, but we had no evidence at that time to contradict his statements.

Early the next morning, without sleep, Moss and I negotiated the text of the letters with President Royo and his advisers. When the time approached for the departure of my plane, I told Royo I would have to go, and he pointed his finger to the Foreign Minister and said: "Ozores, hold the plane!" The Foreign Minister called the airport, and that was that. Moss and I looked at one another, thought about his heated exchange with the U.S. pilot back in Washington, and silently pondered the differences between a big, powerful country and a small, weak one.

We finished the letters, accepting most of their language in order to retain one key sentence in both: "I am not intervening and will not intervene in the internal affairs of any country."[33]

I then returned to Washington, almost exactly twenty-four hours after I had left. I wrote the memoranda for the President on the plane. He saw them the next day and was pleased with the assurances from Torrijos and Royo, although none of us was quite sure what they meant, and the reports were unclear. Subsequently, there was some evidence that Torrijos took our concerns to heart, and that Panama may have suspended transshipments for a time.[34]

Fate would have it that on my first full day back, June 6, two Nicaraguan officials, Max Kelly and Luis Pallais, testified before the House Subcommittee on the Panama Canal of John Murphy's Merchant Marine and Fisheries Committee. The subject was Panamanian involvement in the arms traffic between Cuba and Nicaragua. They exhibited weapons and tried to use the hearing to defeat the legislation inplementing the Canal treaties.[35]

The same day Somoza declared a state of siege to permit him full powers to respond to the general strike and the widening guerrilla war. León, the second largest city, was now controlled by the FSLN, but the Guard was fighting back.

A New U.S. Plan

The Presidential Review Memorandum (PRM) on Central America that was begun in February 1979 was completed in early June. The purpose of the PRM—the highest level interagency review—was to examine in a systematic way the emerging challenges throughout Central America, not just in Nicaragua, and to propose new policies. Christopher chaired a Policy Review Committee meeting on June 11 to review the PRM. In attendance were Brzezinski, Aaron, Deputy Secretary of Defense Charles Duncan, General Smith of the Joint Chiefs, Deputy Director of the CIA Frank Carlucci, Vaky, Lawrence Pezzullo, the recently appointed U.S. Ambassador to Nicaragua, and me. The general assessment on Nicaragua was that the war was a standoff and the Guard would probably survive this round of violence, but that Somoza would not likely be able to serve out his term.

Brzezinski offered a three-point plan that followed from the discussion: (1) the United States should issue a clear statement calling for self-determination for Nicaragua and an end to the violence; (2) we should begin quietly exploring with other Latin American governments the idea of an inter-American peace force that would only act in conjunction with Somoza's departure; and (3) the United States should issue clear, forceful private and public warnings to cease the arms flow to both sides.

This would include a tough statement to the Israelis, who had been the source of some of Somoza's weapons. The Administration had agreed to do this several times before, but no one wanted to implement it. Vance had been devoting an increasing share of his time to the details of the Middle East peace negotiations and had thrown up his hands every time someone suggested that he put another demand on the table to the Israelis. This time he agreed to do it.

There was more discussion of the peace force idea, which had been first mentioned on September 18 and had even been proposed by the former Venezuelan President, Carlos Andrés Pérez. Vaky said he would not rule out the possibility of Latin American acceptance of such a force, provided that Somoza's departure was joined to it. Brzezinski acknowledged that he would be surprised if the Latin American governments accepted the idea at this time, but he thought that everyone ought to start thinking about it. Christopher asked the Pentagon to look into military contingencies, and Newsom made an implicit assumption explicit, that the United States would have to assume a major part of the responsibility for such a force, even though it would be a multilateral effort. "Yes," David Aaron quipped, "the peso stops here."

The proposal to link Somoza's resignation to a peace force seemed at that time to have some promise. Somoza might be persuaded to resign if he knew that the resulting vacuum would not be filled by the Sandinista military, and the Latin American democracies might support a peace force if that was required to obtain Somoza's departure and prevent a Sandinista victory. U.S. objectives were to gain support for a post-Somoza provisional government, the preservation of the Guard, and negotiations for free elections.

Although Nicaragua was the principal subject of discussion, the meeting also addressed the problems of the rest of Central America, and the outline of a policy was approved for providing aid to help Honduras make the journey toward democracy. El Salvador and Gua-

temala were much more difficult cases in which right-wing terrorism was more serious and ultimately the major factor in the growth
of the left-wing guerrilla movements. It was decided to press both
governments to stop the death squads and begin a dialogue with the
legitimate opposition.

That evening, June 11, Carter, with Ambassador Moss, Secretary of
the Army Clifford Alexander, and General McAuliffe of the Southern
Command in Panama, met with a group of one hundred members of
Congress. The principal purpose of the meeting was to persuade
them to vote for the legislation to implement the Panama Canal treaties, but inevitably, they asked about the reports of Panamanian arms
smuggling. In response to one such question, Carter said:

> First of all, I think the two issues [the implementing legislation
> and the Nicaraguan revolution] should be separated. . . . Panama
> has strong feelings that the Somoza government should not con-
> tinue in power. This is a feeling shared by many other countries
> like Colombia, Venezuela, Mexico. I think most of the OAS. The
> negotiating efforts [the mediation] on our part . . . were unfruit-
> ful.
>
> I have inquired to the Panamanian leaders as to whether or not
> they were interfering in the internal affairs of Nicaragua. They
> replied that they are not. I cannot deny, however, that Panama
> and Venezuela and other countries that I have already named
> might very well have given aid to the dissident groups opposing
> Somoza. . . . I think there is a general feeling down there among
> almost every nation that I know, and I have contacted almost
> all of them directly, that the Somoza government should be
> changed.
>
> But I can't comment on whether or not Panama has given aid
> to the opposition forces in Nicaragua. My guess is that they
> have. It is a common procedure, apparently, by many other gov-
> ernments that disavow any desire to become involved in the in-
> ternal affairs of Nicaragua.[36]

The next day Carter approved the recommendations of the PRC.
Cables were then sent to U.S. ambassadors in Latin America, instructing them to meet with the Foreign Minister or President and
seek support and advice on the idea of linking a peace force with Somoza's departure, and to stop the flow of arms. Ambassadors were
told to discuss the possibility of reconvening the OAS to "pass a resolution calling for a ceasefire, a halt to the flow of arms to Nicaragua,
and if possible, a high-level MFM [Foreign Ministers] mission to Somoza designed to urge and to help shape a peaceful transition to a rep-

resentative government."[37] On June 14, the day after the U.S. Ambassador in Israel delivered the démarche,* an Israeli ship with arms destined for Nicaragua turned around and returned to Israel.[38]

On June 12, the CIA revised its estimate of the situation. The Guard was weaker and the Sandinistas stronger than they had originally thought. The Agency judged that Somoza might be able to hold on to power for a short time. The next day, as the violence increased, the U.S. Embassy began evacuating Americans.

In Different Directions

To understand U.S. policy toward Nicaragua in the month prior to Somoza's departure on July 17, it is essential to realize the extent to which President Carter and his senior advisers were absorbed with many other matters, which they viewed, with justification, as of far greater importance to the United States. During the final month of the Somoza dynasty, Carter, Vance, Harold Brown, and Brzezinski flew to Vienna (June 15–18) for a summit with Soviet President Leonid Brezhnev and for the signing of the SALT II Treaty. From June 23 to July 1, they traveled to Japan and South Korea for state visits and also for a summit meeting of the industrialized democracies. Carter returned to the United States to find his popularity at its lowest level and gas lines longer than the United States had seen since World War II.[39] By July 3, the President retreated to Camp David to review a speech on energy, but he remained nearly two weeks for an intensive and pivotal reassessment of the state of the nation and of his Presidency. When he returned to Washington on July 14, five Cabinet Secretaries either were fired or resigned.

If the United States leadership was too distant from events in Nicaragua, Latin America may have been too close, concentrating on a gruesome, unforgiving war. The dominating questions were when and how Somoza would leave; few contemplated the implications of what would follow.

While Carter was flying to Vienna for a summit with the Soviets, the foreign ministers of the five countries of the Andean Pact—Venezuela, Colombia, Ecuador, Peru, and Bolivia—assembled to discuss Nicaragua. The Andean Pact had been originally established in 1969 as an economic organization, but it had assisted Torrijos on the Canal treaties and facilitated the transition toward democracy in Ec-

---

*A démarche is an official request to a foreign government to take a specific action.

uador, Peru, and Bolivia. By 1979, it had begun playing a political role that complemented its economic mission.

On May 28, 1979, on the eve of the "final offensive," the heads of state of the five countries met in Cartagena, Colombia, and issued a declaration that the situation in Nicaragua represented a threat to the peace of the Americas. After the meeting, the Venezuelan government sent a senior military adviser to Costa Rica, and the foreign ministers of Venezuela and Ecuador went to Managua to encourage Somoza to resign. Ambassador Bowdler met them before their journey, and asked what they expected would happen after Somoza left. They said they had not thought about it. They had no plan.

Somoza met with them, rejected the idea of a resignation, but expressed his interest in negotiating free elections in 1981. He had not grasped the new power of the Andean Pact or his own weakness. The Group of Twelve, representing the FSLN, did; they cultivated the Andean Pact countries, and when the foreign ministers met for a follow-up meeting on June 16, it was clear that the investment by the Twelve had paid off handsomely. The Andean countries declared the Sandinistas "legitimate combatants" in a "state of belligerency"; this implied that the FSLN and the Nicaraguan government were legally equivalent. The statement called on "all countries of the continent" to join in facilitating "the installation of a truly representative, democratic regime" in Nicaragua.

On the same date, from Costa Rica, Radio Sandino announced the names of a five-member Junta, which would serve as the head of the "Provisional Government." The members were Alfonso Robelo of the business community; Sergio Ramírez of the Group of Twelve; Violeta de Chamorro, the widow of Pedro Joaquín Chamorro; Moisés Hassán, a Sandinista leader of the National Patriotic Front with a Ph.D. in physics from North Carolina State; and Daniel Ortega Saavedra, one of the members of the FSLN Directorate. One week before the announcement, Robelo, Chamorro, and Ramírez met with the Ortega brothers and Borge in San José and discussed whether a member of the Directorate should be on the Junta. Robelo and Chamorro voted no, but the Directorate, which had designated them, also decided to put Daniel Ortega on the Junta. When Robelo and Chamorro insisted on the Junta's right to select the Cabinet, the Directorate accepted that point and told them: "We only want to set up a Sandinista Party, and we will organize the army." Robelo thought the moderates had won a victory.[40]

Also coinciding with the Andean statement and the announcement of the Junta was the invasion, led by Pastora, of a 400-man Sandinista force into Nicaragua to join with the 300-man force that had crossed on May 29. Pastora pledged to march to Rivas, twenty-five miles from the border, where he hoped to establish a Provisional Government. The next day, Ecuador broke relations with Nicaragua. It was rumored that the other Andean countries would soon follow, and that diplomatic relations would then be established with the new Junta.[41]

The United States had consulted with the Andean countries prior to their meeting and argued that such a decision would reduce the space for a moderate, democratic option, but U.S. views were evidently dismissed. Many still thought that the United States was looking to save its longtime client, Anastasio Somoza, though the Administration had never considered this an option.

These three events—the Andean Pact's recognition of a "state of belligerency," the establishment of a Provisional Government in San José, and the invasion from Costa Rica—transformed the crisis. The United States had received some word beforehand about each of these events, but still—coming together—they stunned the Administration, which had not fully grasped, and was not yet prepared to accept, just how different the Latin American view of the Sandinistas was from its own.

Chapter 8

THE RELUCTANT ARBITER

The art of statesmanship is foreseeing the inevitable and
expediting its occurrence.
Talleyrand

Destiny is not a matter of chance. It is a matter of choice.
William Jennings Bryan

It ain't over till it's over.
Yogi Berra

REVOLUTIONARIES, like politicians, are compelled to predict victory with regularity. Supporters repeat the predictions, but momentum occurs only when events convince skeptics that the predictions are credible. At that moment when minds are changed about the revolution's prospects, time is compressed: what was once an endless revolution suddenly is perceived to be within weeks of victory.

In the last month before Somoza's departure, the Sandinistas achieved momentum, and the Carter Administration's assessment of Somoza's tenure was squeezed from years into days. A combined CIA–State Department assessment in mid-May 1979 indicated that Somoza was likely to remain in power until 1981; on June 11, it was thought he would be forced to leave before 1981; on June 12, he was expected to last a short time; and on June 19, a week or more. The last assessment was repeated four times at approximately weekly intervals.

The Administration assumed that the Sandinistas were the most likely inheritors of Somoza's throne unless the United States could negotiate an alternative. A second judgment by the Administration was that a Sandinista military victory, as compared to a negotiated settlement, would significantly reduce the chances of democracy in Nicaragua and significantly increase the probability that a pro-Cuban/Soviet, anti-American regime would emerge.

For these reasons, and without internal disagreement, the United States returned to its more traditional role as the arbiter of Nicaraguan politics. In August 1978, ten months before, the Administration had rejected a request to mediate by Nicaragua's opposition for fear that would directly involve the United States in Nicaragua's internal affairs, violating its commitment to nonintervention. This commitment was eroded by the violence in Nicaragua, the fear that inaction could adversely affect U.S. interests, and the requests from friendly Nicaraguan and Latin American leaders. First, the United States mediated—bringing both sides together to try to negotiate a plebiscite. By mid-June, the United States was prepared to arbitrate—to try to help choose Nicaragua's leaders. The atmosphere of crisis and the perception of an imminent threat were so vivid that few noticed the fundamental change in U.S. policy or raised a question to stop it.

The OAS Meeting

On Monday, June 18, 1979, the State Department proposed that the OAS reconvene the Meeting of Foreign Ministers to address the Nicaraguan crisis. The decision to use the OAS was a sign that the department had not fully grasped the implications of the Andean Pact statement issued two days before; the Andean countries were moving in the opposite direction from that of the United States. To invite an OAS meeting was to invite an embarrassment at best, a collision at worst.

The United States was not alone in failing to understand "the change in the correlation of international forces." The Sandinistas were very fearful that the United States would use an OAS meeting to obtain support for a peace-keeping force, as it had done in 1965.[1]

The President and his senior advisers returned to Washington on the evening of June 18, and Carter immediately went to Capitol Hill to address a joint session of Congress on the SALT II Treaty. In the course of that speech, Carter connected his discussions in Vienna with events in the region: "I made it clear to President Brezhnev that Cuban military activities in Africa, sponsored by or supported by the Soviet Union, and also the growing Cuban involvement in the problems of Central America and the Caribbean can only have a negative impact on U.S.–Soviet relations."[2]

The stage was set for a decisive SCC meeting on June 19. The Sandinista offensive had stalled south of Rivas, and the FSLN appeared to be having resupply problems. However, the Sandinistas had demonstrated considerable power in several towns, especially León. Somoza was expected to survive at least a week. The Guard, although showing signs of strain, was holding together. There were no signs of a coup.

Brzezinski chaired the meeting that included Vance, Christopher, Harold Brown, Stansfield Turner, General Jones, Vaky, Ambassador Pezzullo, and me. Brzezinski said there was no interest in creating a crisis-like atmosphere after the summit, but events in Nicaragua would impact on U.S.–Soviet relations and on the President's domestic political standing, particularly in the South and the West. Then he crisply defined the objective for U.S. policy—to move Somoza out and create in his place a viable government of national reconciliation. The question was how to accomplish this goal.

Vance outlined a proposal that included (1) a cease-fire; (2) cessation of the flow of arms to both sides; (3) establishment of a government of national reconciliation; (4) humanitarian assistance; and (5) some basis for ensuring law and order during this period. Based on the initial consultations, Vance judged that the chances of gaining acceptance for a peace force were "slim." Brzezinski said that if the National Guard held together there would be no need for a peace force, but he feared a rapid process of disintegration after Somoza left, and steps should be taken to minimize that. He also pointed out that if we could assure Somoza that some portion of the Guard could be preserved, we would increase our chances of getting Somoza to resign.

Christopher and Vaky suggested that after Somoza's departure, a Government of National Reconciliation could invite help from the United States. Brzezinski questioned whether the government would hold together long enough. It was clear in the discussion that the major concern of the State Department was to ensure Somoza's departure while Brzezinski's was to ensure that the resulting government would be stable and capable of negotiating with the Sandinistas.

The SCC agreed to consult again with several Latin American governments on the five elements of a strategy, including the peace force idea. The peace force would not have to be an OAS force; like the OAS resolution the previous September, a regional blessing for a small ad hoc group would be sufficient. Vaky opposed mentioning either Cuba or the peace force idea in the speech Vance was to give to open the OAS meeting, because he feared it would be provocative. Everybody agreed to wait for feedback before making a decision. Stern messages would be sent to Torrijos and Carazo to get them to put a stop to the arms flow. Pezzullo would tell Somoza that the time had come to step down. Brown and Brzezinski both proposed that the President be informed that the discussion introduced two unattractive but possible alternatives: a Sandinista victory or U.S. intervention.

In the meantime, the fighting in Nicaragua grew worse. The destruction exceeded that of the earthquake; deaths were estimated in the tens of thousands. Since fighting had resumed in May, twenty thousand had fled the country, and many more were homeless. Virtually every city was under siege. Somoza warned the Guard that the Sandinistas would be savage if they came to power, and the Guard's fears made it merciless.

At the same time that reports of the brutality of the Guard were becoming almost commonplace, the Sandinistas were astutely reassuring the world about their democratic intentions. The announcement of the five Junta members was widely viewed as an important symbol of the moderation of the rebels. The Junta "stressed the need to maintain good relations with the United States, insisting that only two measures were not negotiable: expropriation of the Somoza family's business empire, and restructuring of the National Guard to eliminate officers directly responsible for repression."[3]

The FSLN receded from public view, letting Sergio Ramírez of the Junta be the main spokesman. He promised the new government "will take the route of representative democracy based on periodic elections, but with universal participation . . . within a multi-party system, of course. We have had too much of a one-party system."[4] Regarding the Sandinistas' ties to Cuba, Ramírez said that the United States had to "talk about Cuba to justify military intervention in Nicaragua," but he insisted, "the United States knows this [Cuban support for the FSLN] is not true, and the CIA also knows it is not true. If Cuba had given help, we would have already won the war because Cuba would not intervene to give just a few old rifles."[5]

In fact, at the moment of Ramírez's denial, the CIA reported that the Sandinistas had received 8 to 11 planeloads of arms from Cuba during the previous month. This proved a conservative estimate. Carlos Andrés Pérez later learned that Cuban advisers had also arrived in Costa Rica, and that "Cubans actually participated in the last segment of the war."[6] U.S. Ambassador to Costa Rica Marvin Weissman met with President Carazo and delivered a chilling démarche about the impact of his collaboration on U.S.–Costa Rican relations. Carazo reacted emotionally and said he would put a halt to it, but he did not.

On June 18, one hundred members of Congress and five Senators signed a letter to the President, which was reprinted as a full-page advertisement in the *New York Times*. Under the ominous headline "Congress Asks: Please, Mr. President, Not Another Cuba!" the letter urged Carter to support Somoza as a traditional ally, warning that his departure would lead to a Communist government.

Then, on the eve of the OAS session, an event occurred that transformed the Nicaraguan issue from a concern of specialists to one that evoked the deepest and angriest emotions in the American body politic. ABC news correspondent Bill Stewart was stopped by a Guard patrol and then executed in cold blood. This was no wild rumor; the event was filmed and shown on the evening news. The response by the public was unlike anything I had seen since I had been in the White House. The phone rang incessantly and telegrams to the President, which passed my desk, poured in by the thousands. These were not the product of an orchestrated letter-writing campaign, as would be seen after Secretary Vance's speech. The cables reflected the first installment on the national outrage that would reach its height and depth during the Iran hostage crisis. Here is a sample:

> If there is no military retaliation for the reporters [sic] murdered in Nicaragua, it will convince us that the Carter Administration is as I have thought, gutless.

> We feel it is about time the Presidency takes a firm stand against countries which commit such atrocities towards American citizens. . . . Why is the United States being so docile? It's no wonder we suffer from a loss of national pride.

> The United States should take some kind of stand. Send in the marines. Please protect us in foreign countries.

> I was shocked to see Bill Stewart murdered by Somoza's bandit troops. In sorrow and anger, I ask you to punish Somoza and to help the gorilla's [sic] bring him down.

The individual act of the Guardsman was obviously not authorized by Somoza, but by June 20, indiscriminate murder by the Guard was not unusual behavior. One consequence of the tragedy was that it quieted the thunder from the right in the United States.

On June 21, the United States opened the OAS meeting. Given the complexity and controversial nature of the U.S. proposal, there was not sufficient time to consult about all its elements. The preliminary soundings, however, were not all bad, and the Andean countries suggested that they might even take the lead. On the evening before the OAS meeting, the Venezuelan government expressed interest in negotiating a horse trade: Somoza would leave and an OAS mission would arrive to help with a transition government that would invite a peace force, if necessary. Venezuela promised to raise this idea with the other Andean countries.

The State Department drafted Vance's speech. It followed the decisions of the previous SCC meeting, except it omitted any reference to either the peace force or Cuban involvement, despite the President's mention of Cuba three days before. Carter asked to see the speech and, after consulting with Brzezinski, he wrote both points into the text, which Brzezinski showed me before sending it to State. I told him that neither point would be well received by the OAS, but the single reference to Cuba was needed, given the President's statement in Congress and the facts. I was very uneasy about mentioning the peace force publicly at this time, even though I was in favor of the strategy of linking Somoza's departure to such a force. We had not consulted adequately, and although Brzezinski viewed the 1965 intervention in the Dominican Republic by the inter-American peace force positively, I tried to explain that this was not the way many Latin American leaders remembered it.

Though Vaky had accepted the strategy at the previous SCC meeting, he now opposed both the strategy and the public statement; he tried to persuade Vance to speak to the President about omitting any reference in the speech. Vance called Brzezinski to see whether the President had inserted the lines himself and, having learned that he had, decided not to pursue it. Although leaving the President's single insertion that the OAS "consider on an urgent basis the need for a peace-keeping force to restore order" and permit elections, Vaky redrafted other portions of the speech to dilute the impact of the proposal by referring to an OAS "presence" or "appropriate elements" from OAS countries.[7]

Vance's speech tried to build on the Andean Pact's statement by proposing that the "solution [to the Nicaraguan crisis] must begin with the replacement of the present Government with a transition government of national reconciliation, which would be a clear break with the past." He called for a cessation of arms shipments, and in the single reference to Cuba, he noted that "there is mounting evidence of involvement by Cuba and others in the internal problems of Nicaragua." He also proposed a cease-fire and urged his colleagues to "immediately send a special delegation to Nicaragua . . . to facilitate the formation by the Nicaraguans of a transitional government." He warned, however, that "we must not leave a vacuum," and therefore the new government "must have at its disposal appropriate elements from OAS countries, acting within the inter-American system, to assist it to establish its authority and preserve the peace."

Vance stressed, however, that such an "OAS peace-keeping presence" should only be sent after the departure of Somoza as a way "to assist the interim government" bring peace and reconcile the forces that were fighting. At that time, everyone, including the FSLN, assumed that the National Guard would survive the fighting. The OAS "presence" would oversee the cease-fire between the two forces while assisting both sides to negotiate a merger. Finally, Vance called for "a major international relief and reconstruction effort," and assured the group that the United States was prepared "to contribute generously to that effort."[8]

At the same time that Vance was speaking before the OAS, the House of Representatives was completing its debate on the legislation to implement the Canal treaties. The day before, June 20, several conservative Republican members called for the first closed session of the House since 1830 in order to examine the evidence of Panama's involvement in arms trafficking to the Sandinistas. The evidence of some Panamanian involvement—as it turned out, a small proportion of what was sent—was persuasive, but the proponents of the implementing legislation insisted that the two issues should be kept separate. Majority Leader Jim Wright admitted that it was no "secret that General Torrijos . . . sympathized with the Sandinistas and had a vendetta against President Somoza." Wright continued: "Yes, many of those countries [Venezuela, Mexico, others] sympathize with the Sandinistas. I wish they did not, but they do, and they will do more so if we give to them the impression that we are looking for a way to welch on our word, and they cannot trust us."[9]

The initial reaction in the U.S. press to Vance's speech was not negative. Bernard Gwertzman in the *New York Times* described the speech as "an anguished turning point." He noted that the Carter Administration "does not intend to be too far out in front of the Latin Americans. It did not act until eight other countries . . . had either broken relations or signaled their unhappiness with the Somoza government."[10]

The U.S. press highlighted the demand by Vance for Somoza's resignation while the Latin American press concentrated on the peace force, almost to the exclusion of Vance's call for Somoza's departure. The gentlest criticism came from *La Nacion*, the Costa Rican newspaper, which wrote that Vance had "an incomplete understanding of the true political situation in Nicaragua" where "the ferocity with which the National Guard has acted brought things to such an extreme that it is extremely difficult to speak of reconciliation."

In San José, the FSLN immediately rejected Vance's proposal. They urged a continuation of the war "until we win or die." The Cuban government denied its involvement and called the peace force a pretext for intervention. The reaction in the OAS followed similar lines. The Panamanian government waited until the U.S. House passed the implementing legislation. It then broke relations with Somoza, recognized the Provisional Government, and offered a seat on its OAS delegation to Miguel D'Escoto, who spoke to the meeting on the Provisional Government's behalf.

Mexican Foreign Minister Jorge Castañeda was in Europe when the OAS meeting was called and only returned because he was told to do so by his President, whose instructions were simple: block U.S. interventionism.[11] In his remarks, Castañeda praised the Sandinistas for exercising "the sacred right of rebellion against tyranny, just as the Mexican people had done seventy years before." He opposed any plan for the OAS to negotiate with Somoza or any compromise that could lead to "Somocismo sin Somoza." Mexico, Panama, and the Andean nations not only did not share U.S. anxiety and reservations about a Sandinista military victory but had decided to run interference for the Sandinistas.

I returned from the OAS meeting to the White House to brief Brzezinski and found him in a very different world, contemplating military intervention. Since March 1979, Brzezinski had grown increasingly preoccupied with the "Soviets' creeping intervention in Afghanistan"; he felt that Carter's credibility with Brezhnev required a similar willingness to use force.[12] I countered that if we intervened unilaterally, we would justify Soviet action and provoke a strong reaction in Latin America. The OAS needed to speak before the United States considered any action.

The news coverage in Washington followed the OAS debate, and quickly shifted from the demand for Somoza's exit to the question of U.S. intervention. Jody Powell, the White House spokesman, was asked at the noon briefing on June 22 whether the President ruled out the use of American forces in Nicaragua. He responded with a prepared answer: "That particular question is one on which we are currently consulting with our friends in the OAS. We will be guided by those consultations and by the needs of the situation."

The Decision Not to Intervene

Carter used his "Friday morning breakfast" as one of his principal vehicles to discuss foreign policy issues, much as Lyndon Johnson had used his "Tuesday lunches." Originally intended to offer Vance a weekly opportunity to cover his agenda, the meeting, over time, came to include others, and on June 22, Harold Brown, Hamilton Jordan, and Vice President Walter Mondale joined the President, Vance, and Brzezinski. This presented Brzezinski with the opportunity to make the case for intervention, and he recalls he did so forcefully. He spoke "about the major domestic and international implications of a

Castroite take-over in Nicaragua. [The United States] would be considered as being incapable of dealing with problems in our own backyard and impotent in the face of Cuban intervention. This will have devastating domestic implications, including for SALT."[13]

After finishing his dark scenario, Brzezinski soon realized that his arguments were "not well received." According to Brzezinski, Vance reported that the OAS discussions were decidedly negative, particularly with regard to the peace force idea. Carter left no doubt that he had no intention of intervening unilaterally.

On Saturday morning, June 23, Brzezinski chaired an SCC meeting at 8:00 A.M. Harold Brown arrived in his jogging suit and greeted Vance, Christopher, General Lewis Allen, Stansfield Turner, Vaky, Bowdler, Pezzullo, Aaron, and me. The military situation in Nicaragua was viewed as a standoff. It appeared doubtful that Pastora could take or hold Rivas, and the fighting throughout the rest of the country reflected a rough balance.

Christopher briefed us on the discouraging debate at the OAS. Mexico, which had been the most antagonistic of the United States, was working with the Andean countries on a resolution that deleted the peace force and also omitted any reference to a cease-fire, a cessation of arms shipments, or any OAS involvement. Their objectives were to prevent any action by the United States and the OAS, force Somoza's resignation, and clear a way for the Sandinistas to take power. The Sandinistas had been successful in portraying the U.S. peace force proposal as a way to bolster Somoza, even though the first element of the proposal was his departure. Incredibly, this view took hold.

The U.S. proposal was dead; the issue for the SCC was whether to try to negotiate a modification of the Andean–Mexican proposal that would permit the United States some authority to negotiate a transition in Nicaragua. The SCC agreed to pursue that route.

After the Friday breakfast, the talk of unilateral intervention had ended, except that both Brown and Vance put themselves clearly on record as opposing it. Both said that they would prefer to pursue multilateral mediation, but if necessary, the United States should pursue its own diplomatic-political strategy. The SCC discarded the peace force idea and accepted the State Department's "sequencing strategy"—after a new government was installed, the United States could help to support it while it opened negotiations with the Junta. Christopher and Vaky were authorized to explore this idea for a post-Somoza government with the Venezuelan Foreign Minister.

Brzezinski said that Jack Murphy had called the President the night before to tell him that Somoza was prepared to step down if he could receive assurances that the National Guard would be supported and the Liberal Party would be included in any post-Somoza government. The SCC discussed ways to keep the Guard from collapsing after Somoza left and agreed that a new Commander would have to be appointed and put in charge soon. When the subject had been discussed in the fall, the person who was recommended by many in and outside Nicaragua was Julio Gutiérrez, the former Guard General, who was now Nicaragua's Ambassador to Japan. Ambassador Mansfield had spoken with him then. Vance agreed to meet with him when he arrived in Tokyo for the summit. The objective was to try to persuade Gutiérrez to return to the area, perhaps to Honduras or Venezuela.

The SCC also agreed that Somoza and Gutiérrez should be told that if Somoza stepped down, the United States would provide sufficient support to the National Guard to guarantee its stability during the transition period. (There was no discussion about either the magnitude or the kind of support that would be needed.) Bowdler would communicate that to Somoza. Finally, the SCC recommended that the President should again send messages demanding they stop their arms shipments to both Carazo, who it appeared was not fully in control, and to Torrijos, who appeared totally out of control. The President's clear decision to rule out a peace force had forced his advisers to focus on an alternative strategy, and the meeting was remarkable for the degree of consensus.

Christopher, Vaky, and I then went to the OAS to try to negotiate a satisfactory resolution. The Andean countries seemed initially eager to exclude the United States from the resolution, but they soon realized that their resolution was unlikely to pass without U.S. support. Christopher therefore worked with them and was able to insert several key passages in the resolution, including one that urged "member states to take steps that are within their reach to facilitate an enduring and peaceful solution of the Nicaraguan problem." The resolution did much else. It was unprecedented in calling for the "immediate and definitive replacement of the Somoza regime," which it declared "the fundamental cause" of the crisis. The resolution called for the "installation . . . of a democratic government . . . [and] the holding of free elections as soon as possible."[14]

The resolution passed on June 23, 1979, by a vote of 17 for, 2 against (Paraguay and Nicaragua), and 5 abstentions. The resolution was far from what Vance had proposed, but considering the reaction by Mexico and the Andean countries, it at least did "permit constructive actions by the member countries"; this was sufficient to permit the United States to negotiate a transition in Nicaragua legitimately.

After the OAS meeting ended and Carter had departed for the Far East, I completed a summary of the SCC meeting and the decision memorandum, and we cabled them to the President in Tokyo. On Sunday, June 24, we received a message that Carter approved all the recommendations of the meeting except that he was unwilling to offer support unconditionally to a post-Somoza National Guard. He decided that he would only offer such support if he determined that the transition government was legitimate, and he would judge that by whether it obtained support from other Latin American governments and from the Nicaraguan people. This June 24 decision by the President to make aid to a post-Somoza Guard conditional would be a crucial one.

The OAS resolution frightened Somoza. At 10:30 P.M. on the night of the passage of the resolution, several correspondents overheard Somoza on shortwave radio personally poll each of his military commanders in the field on their loyalty. Somoza condemned the OAS action as a "flagrant intervention into the internal affairs of Nicaragua," and asked his commanders if they were willing to fight with him to defeat the enemy. "I ask each of you to acknowledge," Somoza said, and then one at a time, each of the nineteen said: "Yes, sir, understood sir."[15] In a nationwide address that Sunday evening, he vowed to keep fighting, but in his memoirs, Somoza recalls his reaction differently. The defiance at the time was replaced in retrospect by sadness and the claim that he realized the OAS vote symbolized his end. He therefore wrote his resignation at that time and put it in his pocket for the appropriate moment.[16]

In Tokyo, Vance met with Gutiérrez and found him ready to return, but only after Somoza left and only by invitation. Gutiérrez said he would consider returning earlier only if invited to join the Junta.

While Washington policy makers were preoccupied with the OAS, the Chargé of the U.S. Embassy in Managua had a pivotal meeting on June 24 with the leadership of the FAO—Rafael Córdova Rivas, Luis Sanchez Sancho, and Jaime Chamorro. They expressed disappointment that the OAS resolution had given legitimacy to the FSLN. They had asked Alfonso Robelo to be the FAO's representative on the Junta, but as an organization, the FAO was still debating "whether to maintain its independent identity or to support the Provisional Government" in San José. Córdova and Sanchez were frank in their preference to maintain the FAO's independence, but they were seeking guidance and support from the United States. Although trying to imply that he thought independence from the Provisional Government was preferable, the Chargé admitted that the United States did not have a position. This was an important opportunity that was lost because communications between the Embassy and Washington were poor, and the Embassy did not understand the debate in Washington well enough to know how to plug into it.[17]

Two Pillars

In order to hammer out a policy on Nicaragua, Brzezinski had been asked by the President to remain in Washington for a few days after Carter departed. He convened an SCC meeting on Monday morning, June 25. Mondale attended along with Harold Brown, David Mc-Giffert from Defense, Gen. David Jones and Gen. John Pustay from the Joint Chiefs, Christopher, Turner, Bowdler, Pezzullo, Vaky, Aaron, and me.

The Administration supported a strategy of trying to establish a second pillar of power that would be independent of Somoza and could then negotiate with the Sandinista Junta. Prior to the meeting, I briefed Brzezinski on my fears that State was slowly moving to a different strategy of accepting the Sandinista Junta as inevitable and trying to broaden and moderate it. To me, the question was not the breadth of the Junta but who controlled the military. If the Sandinistas were left with a monopoly on military power, the moderates in the Junta would be at the mercy of the Directorate.

First, the CIA updated us on the situation in Nicaragua, repeating their prediction of the previous week that Somoza had at least one more week. There was some discussion about whether there were Cuban advisers in Costa Rica, but the evidence was still uncertain. Brzezinski then posed the central question for the meeting: do we seek to widen and moderate the Junta, or create an alternative governing structure with an independent power base that would negotiate with the Junta? If the first option were chosen, the United States should encourage moderates to join the Junta and other governments to negotiate with the Junta; if the latter were chosen, we ought to try to discourage moderates from joining or endorsing the Junta and encourage governments to withhold recognition.

Christopher advocated pursuing both strategies simultaneously. We should begin talks with the Junta to moderate them and, at the same time, quietly try to negotiate the establishment of an Executive Committee, which could become an alternative source of power when Somoza left. This committee could ask General Gutiérrez to return and reform the National Guard. The United States could then call for a cease-fire, an arms embargo, and humanitarian assistance and urge both sides to negotiate with each other. If the United States could effectively work both strategies simultaneously, we would be well positioned to assist in the reconciliation process between the Sandinista Junta and the Executive Committee. Everyone agreed with this two-pronged strategy, even while accepting the chances for its success as about 50–50. David Aaron and I were concerned that the only way to encourage an Executive Committee at this time would be to offer some explicit assurances of help; otherwise, moderates would be vulnerable and fearful of joining. This issue was not addressed then.

The analogies with Iran were obvious to those who had experienced similar agonies several months before when the Shah fled. Harold Brown said that the people who negotiated the departure of the Shah were the first ones shot by the revolutionaries. Mondale asked who would try to stabilize the Nicaraguan military as U.S. General Robert Huyser had done in Iran.

Brzezinski summarized the consensus of the meeting to pursue both strategies—moderate the Junta while attempting to establish an Executive Committee—simultaneously. He said he would talk to Gutiérrez again when he reached Tokyo. Pezzullo would go to Managua to speak with Somoza and obtain his resignation, put together an Executive Committee, and work on ways to ensure the survival of the Guard. Bowdler would go to San José to talk to the Junta. At one point in the meeting, Mondale, who was attending his first SCC meeting on Nicaragua, asked where Somoza would go when he resigned. Brzezinski answered playfully: "We have a spot for him in Minnesota."

The main card the United States had to play was Somoza's resignation. Pallais and Murphy indicated that Somoza was prepared to resign under certain conditions, but the time had come to receive the answer directly from Somoza. Pezzullo met with Somoza and John Murphy soon after his arrival at 4:30 p.m. on June 27. Somoza introduced himself as "a Latin from Manhattan," and Murphy as "a witness."[18] Pezzullo went straight to the point: "We don't see the beginning of a solution without your departure." Somoza said he was prepared to accommodate the United States, although he wanted guarantees that his country would not go Communist. Somoza said he had called the Nicaraguan Congress into session and was prepared to step down the next day, but Pezzullo asked him to put it off for a couple of days while he got "organized a little bit." Pezzullo assured him that one U.S. objective was to preserve the Guard in some form.

In my conversations that day with Vaky, I sensed a shift in his thinking toward a single strategy of trying to influence and broaden the Junta. I informed David Aaron, and he called a mini-SCC meeting the next day, June 28, at 8:00 A.M. Brzezinski had spoken with Julio Gutiérrez in Tokyo and had found his views unchanged since his conversation with Vance: he would only return to Nicaragua if invited by a new government. Those at the mini-SCC meeting understood the importance of someone of independent stature taking charge of the Guard soon. Therefore the group tried to think of how to encourage Gutiérrez to return before Somoza departed, without letting it appear that the United States was orchestrating his return. Somoza, who hated Gutiérrez, had learned of our interest in him and had already called him twice, letting him know that he could expose and undermine him if he wished.[19] One suggestion was to try to encourage Torrijos to invite Gutiérrez. Moss mentioned this to Torrijos, who said he liked the idea, but Moss does not know if Torrijos ever pursued it.[20] Another very serious problem was that as the war became more ferocious, the idea of permitting the survival of any part of the Guard became increasingly problematic.

A serious gap had opened between U.S. policy makers in Washington and policy implementers in Managua, though no one in Washington was aware of its breadth.

Pezzullo had a formidable task—obtaining Somoza's resignation, establishing an Executive Committee, preserving the Guard—but everyone had confidence in the new Ambassador. Larry Pezzullo was an unusual foreign service officer. The best officers, as a rule, are superb observers and reporters of politics in foreign countries; but few are political operators, and of these, fewer understand or appreciate the parameters of American politics as well as those of foreign governments. Pezzullo, who concealed his subtlety behind a blunt-sounding New York City accent, was one of those few. The Administration was so anxious for him to succeed and so confident in him that no one thought to ask whether he knew enough about the key actors in Nicaragua or whether the Embassy had enough capable staff to achieve these objectives.

The answers to these unasked questions were negative. When he arrived in Managua on June 27, he found an Embassy in "complete disarray." Since the sanctions had been imposed in February, the Embassy had been reduced to a very small size, and the officers were, with good reason, deeply concerned with the country's security as well as their own. The State Department had not informed them about the Administration's thinking or even its decisions. Their principal responsibility had been to organize evacuation flights for thousands of Americans and diplomats of other nations.[21] C-130s would fly to Montelimar, Somoza's small airfield on the Pacific coast, and the Embassy staff would organize convoys to drive the evacuees there.

Managua, to Pezzullo, was "like a war zone," with fighting in the streets. People were scared, tired, and uncertain of what would happen. Before his meeting with Somoza, Pezzullo decided to brief his staff quickly. They did not even know that Washington was focusing on Nicaragua. He assured them of Washington's attention but he was careful and selective in conveying information. A quick judge of people, Pezzullo sized up the principal members of the mission as either "nonsubstantive" or "unreliable." Many on the staff correctly perceived that Pezzullo did not trust them. Lt. Col. James McCoy, the Defense Attaché, recalls that many of the staff were uncertain or suspicious of Pezzullo.[22]

Until a new Deputy Chief of Mission arrived in two weeks, Pezzullo functioned as a one-man operator. Although he had had some brief contact with Nicaraguan affairs as Deputy Director of the Office of Central American Affairs from 1972 to 1974, he was unfamiliar with most of the leading political actors. There was obviously no time or opportunity to travel through the city or the country; indeed, the war made any travel perilous. He found himself negotiating more and more with Somoza in part because it was difficult and dangerous to arrange other meetings.

After meeting with Somoza on June 27, Pezzullo turned his attention to contacting people for the proposed Executive Committee. Had he arrived one or two days earlier, his prospects would have been much better. Since their conversation with the Chargé on June 24, the FAO had been meeting regularly to decide whether to retain their independent status, which would have made them the ideal vehicle for the Executive Committee, or to offer their complete support and endorsement to the Provisional Government in San José. It was the same dilemma preoccupying the Carter Administration yet, tragically, there was little communication at this crucial moment because the embassy was weak and the State Department was concentrating on the OAS and other issues.

The FAO was bitter about the failure of the mediation and even more upset that the United States had hardly contacted them since the imposition of sanctions in February. On the day that Pezzullo met with Somoza, June 27, the FAO finally decided—after not hearing from the Embassy—to issue a communiqué: "The Junta, on which the FAO is represented, and which the FAO has supported and continues to support, constitutes the beginning of that democratic and pluralistic regime which must accede to power upon the fall of the Somocista government."[23] The Embassy staff had briefed Pezzullo on the moderates' mistrust, and the FAO statement implied that the space for a moderate alternative was closing rapidly. On June 28, after reading the FAO statement but before having had much opportunity to talk with moderates, Pezzullo cabled his quick assessment of the Executive Committee (ExCom) proposal: "After less than one day here, it is apparent that we have little if any chance of putting together an Executive Committee of any size." He recommended instead that Somoza turn power over to a member of Congress who would call for a cease-fire and form a Government of National Reconciliation.[24]

And yet this quick conclusion about the nonviability of the Executive Committee did not seem to be supported by the reports of his and others' conversations. On June 28, Pezzullo met with the Archbishop, who said that he would "convene his Presbyterian Council to come up with some names and ideas" for a transitional government. The Archbishop said that he doubted the FSLN would accept the idea, but according to Pezzullo, he "did not assert it would not work."[25]

The next day Pezzullo met with Ismael Reyes, the president of the Red Cross, who "appeared fascinated by the idea and viewed it [the Executive Committee] as a noble effort." Reyes said the proposal "would benefit from Andean or Central American sponsorship," but he would not commit himself to participating because there were "too many unknowns." Because he thought Somoza would leave before July 4, Pezzullo guessed that the committee could not be put together in time.[26]

The same day, the Director of Central American Affairs in the State Department met with Arturo Cruz, a member of the Group of Twelve, who had just arrived in Washington after a trip to San José. Cruz said that a broadened Junta was not the answer since the question was who had the guns? He supported the idea of a "neutral force [to] stand temporarily between the National Guard and the Sandinistas." Cruz said that the FSLN, with whom he had just met in Costa Rica, wanted to replace the National Guard with its popular militia, but he believed "that a compromise can possibly be found providing a role for the less-tainted elements of the present Guard."[27]

Although State was persuaded by Pezzullo's conclusion that an ExCom was not viable, the NSC gave more credence to the reports from his conversations as well as the one with Cruz that it was still possible, provided the United States offered clear assurances. Anxiety and urgency underlay both perceptions: State felt that the momentum was shifting toward the Junta in San José, and valuable time was being lost to influence it. NSC agreed that time was running short, and that this was all the more reason to do what was necessary to implement the ExCom idea. NSC feared that the lack of commitment by State to the ExCom idea would doom it, while State did not want to commit itself to a strategy that it judged would fail.

As in the fall, the issue was not seen this clearly at the time; indeed, it was perceived largely through interacting suspicions. Both sides felt the other was wasting valuable time pursuing a chimera. The issue that divided the government—really State from NSC—in the spring was whether to accept an FSLN victory as inevitable and adjust to that, or to believe that nothing is inevitable until it happens, that important opportunities remained to shape Nicaragua's political future up until the moment that power was transferred and, to a lesser degree, after that. When the inevitable is desirable, it is a pleasure to expedite its occurrence. When the inevitable—or rather the increasingly probable—is undesirable, then either one modifies objectives, as the State Department was doing, or one accelerates the search for alternatives, however unlikely, as the NSC was doing.

The mini-SCC meeting on June 28 decided not to decide; Pezzullo should continue to pursue the two tracks. Aaron and I agreed that the Administration had reached a crossroads; if we failed to make a clear decision, we would have to acquiesce to an inevitable Sandinista victory. We therefore wrote a memorandum describing the choice that the United States faced for Brzezinski to give to the President in Tokyo. We felt that the State Department's strategy of broadening the Junta missed the point. If Nicaraguan history contained any lessons, the key issue would be who had the guns. A strategy that offered the government to the Sandinistas would leave the democrats with no alternative source of power. The Executive Committee idea, though still a long shot, was the only viable option for preventing a total Sandinista victory. To induce moderate leaders to join such a committee and give it any hope for success, the United States would have to provide some assurances—physical, financial, and political. That was the choice.

State also sent a cable to Vance. Their main argument was that the momentum was shifting to the Junta, and the Executive Committee was not viable. State wanted to avoid any action that could antagonize the San José Junta, which knew of U.S. efforts to set up an alternative government and did not like it. If the United States demonstrated a sincere interest in working with the Junta, it would reap the benefits when the Junta came to power.

Brzezinski agreed with his staff, and Vance with his, and the two debated the issue in Tokyo. Aaron's cables and phone calls had made Brzezinski feel that the situation was "fast deteriorating." He met the President at the U.S. Embassy residence in Tokyo. Carter was preoccupied with "a very ugly confrontation [with] the Europeans." "This was not a time," Carter recalled, "when I wanted to forget about economic summit matters and spend a lot of time on Central America." Carter decided he wanted "to talk with Torrijos and see how the Central American leaders size up the situation," before making a decision. He recalled that he "wanted the Junta and/or Executive Committee to be representative of all democratic factions and friendly to the other democracies (Costa Rica, Venezuela, and Colombia) and Panama." He also thought Torrijos might be helpful in implementing any new decisions.[28]

In the afternoon of June 29, Aaron chaired a mini-SCC meeting to preserve as well as to develop some options for the President to consider in advance of his meeting with Torrijos. Aaron criticized a cable that State had circulated to U.S. embassies summarizing policy in a way that made it appear that the United States was pursuing a single track—to negotiate with the Junta—rather than the two tracks approved by the President. Pezzullo had been pursuing the Executive Committee strategy for only twenty-four hours, and had found some interest. It was too soon to abandon the strategy.

Vaky tried to turn the issue around and insisted that the question had become how to stop the fighting. This was the first time in a year of NSC meetings that anyone had suggested the central U.S. objective was something other than preventing a Sandinista victory. Christopher agreed with Vaky, and said we would be missing an important opportunity to moderate the FSLN if we didn't try to work with them now. His opinion was that economic aid after the revolution would be the main source of U.S. influence. Vaky said the Executive Committee idea was not viable; the time had come to choose which side of the street we wanted to work.

Aaron restated the Administration's initial objective, but sidestepped a debate by saying that the SCC had a responsibility not to reduce the President's options before his meeting with Torrijos. Christopher agreed to ask Pezzullo to continue looking for leadership in the Guard and for an Executive Committee or, if necessary, a single transition figure.

On June 30, Pezzullo responded to the questions the mini-SCC posed for him with two critical analyses. First, with regard to the military situation, he concluded that "the National Guard remains a strong fighting force, though somewhat enfeebled by shortages of essential material." He wrote that there was a "better than even chance" that "we can preserve a reorganized and reconstituted National Guard."[29] On the Executive Committee, he wrote that the key people would not join it "without greater assurances, one of the most important [of which] would be some tangible evidence that a reconstituted National Guard would stand firm and support them."[30]

At this time, the FSLN was working overtime to project an image of moderation. Alfonso Robelo and Alfredo César wrote the "Program of the Government of National Reconstruction," which, to their surprise and delight, the FSLN embraced.[31] The program described all the human rights that would be enjoyed by the people of the new Nicaragua. Two items omitted in the plan were who would control the military and who would guarantee respect for human rights. After forty-five years of the Somozas, the moderate leadership still had not discerned the sources of Somoza's power; the Sandinistas had.

The moderate members of the Junta never discussed who would lead the new army, or whether or how the Junta would command it. "We were totally blind to anything other than overthrowing Somoza," recalled Robelo. This was confirmed by César, who became Secretary of the Junta. They also paid little attention to the United States when it proposed the Executive Committee idea or the appointment of a new Guard Commander. Robelo said he "never focused on military power." He admits that Bowdler "tried to get me to do that, but I was too wary of being called a friend of the gringos, and so didn't do it."

On June 28, the *New York Times* disclosed the four parts of the U.S. plan: (1) the resignation of Somoza; (2) the appointment of a constitutional Junta (distinct from the FSLN Junta) by the Nicaraguan Congress; (3) the immediate appointment by that Junta of a broadly based provisional government made up of distinguished Nicaraguans (the Executive Committee); and (4) immediate contact between the provisional government and the FSLN Junta to form "the most widely based provisional regime possible." Public disclosure sabotaged this plan and strengthened the FSLN's defenses against a U.S.-sponsored government. The next day, the Junta, FAO, and COSEP all publicly rejected "the U.S. plan." They reiterated support for the FSLN Junta and said they would not participate in any competing administration.[32] From then on, the Junta, and of course the FSLN, insisted on eliminating the middle steps and transferring power from the Congress directly to itself.

Vaky called me several times on June 30 and tried to convince me to abandon the Executive Committee idea and move to a single track. There was no doubt that the *New York Times* story had hurt the prospects for an ExCom, perhaps fatally, but I questioned whether one could realistically expect to win over the military leaders of the Sandinistas in the last days of their revolution after they had been fighting U.S. imperialism for two decades. As long as there was any possibility of placing a buffer between them and exclusive power, should we not reach for it? Expanding the Junta seemed like an exercise in absurdity because the FSLN would decide what, if anything, the Junta would do. Moreover, that same day we received Pezzullo's cable that the Guard and the ExCom were viable if the United States provided assurances. Vaky argued that the Executive Committee was not feasible, and we were losing time.

After a conversation with Somoza on June 29, Pezzullo gave visas to his entire entourage. Murphy called Christopher to tell him that Somoza was ready to hear from the United States about when the plan should be set in motion. Unfortunately, there was not much of a plan left.

The Torrijos Conspiracy

When he was informed that President Carter had asked to see him secretly in Washington, Torrijos said he felt like a schoolboy being called to the principal's office for a scolding. And yet Carter, who had kept his word and paid a heavy political price for new and just Canal treaties, was one of the few people Torrijos trusted.[33] Torrijos had always wanted to work with Carter in Central America, but never knew how. This visit, he thought, might present such an opportunity.[34]

On the flight from Central America to Florida, Torrijos drank pink champagne as if it were water and he had been in the desert for weeks without liquid. As it turned out, he crashed minutes before the plane landed. Flat on his back and filling the small aisle in the jet, Torrijos' companions decided to create a diplomatic incident to keep the Customs and Immigration authorities from boarding the plane and seeing Panama's Maximum Leader in such a state. Gabriel Lewis bounded off the plane, and angrily insisted on calling the White House to protest the insulting behavior of the officials. He demanded an apology. Unaware of the specific circumstances, the White House quickly apologized and asked local officials to expedite the trip.[35]

On July 2, the eve of Torrijos' trip, Bowdler, Pezzullo, and Moss returned from Central America for a long, sober SCC meeting followed by a meeting with the President to prepare for the discussions with Torrijos. The SCC, and the subsequent meeting with Carter, resolved the debate over the two tracks that had begun at the Deputy level. The State Department position prevailed, although not completely.

The major thrust of U.S. policy would be to moderate the Junta rather than to try to establish an Executive Committee.

At this SCC meeting, everyone was first brought up to date on events and the evolving views in the region. Turner explained that morale was beginning to slip in the National Guard as ammunition was running out. Bowdler said that both Torrijos and Carazo supported a cease-fire with both sides standing in place. Both wanted Somoza to leave but, according to Bowdler, neither wanted a Sandinista takeover. Their deeds impugned, if not belied, their words, but Moss confirmed that Torrijos believed anything was negotiable with the FSLN, even a possible fusion with the Guard.

Pezzullo said that Somoza was ready to go and was only waiting to hear of the date and the details. Pezzullo laid to rest the Executive Committee idea, calling it impractical because there was only a handful of moderate leaders in Managua, and none of them had any confidence in the United States, nor did they want to be associated with a U.S. plan. Without clear support from the United States, all believed they would become victims. Pezzullo insisted there would not be a power vacuum after Somoza's departure, because the Guard would be turned over to a new individual. Some confidence-building measures would be necessary, however. Bowdler also tried to reassure the SCC and described the Sandinistas as an undisciplined fighting force. If the new Guard Commander had assurances of U.S. support, and if the foreign ministers of several Andean countries flew to Managua when Somoza departed in order to lend stability to the arrangement and give the Guard time to cohere, then a stable transition was possible.

Harold Brown, Brzezinski, and Aaron were skeptical that a transition could be managed or that the Sandinistas would hold to a bargain. As the discussion evolved, Vaky and Christopher advocated that the United States try to influence the Junta, and avoid becoming associated with the Guard for fear this would prolong the civil war. In response to a question from Brown about what would keep the new government from falling victim to the leftists, Vaky suggested that their desire for economic assistance was a great source of leverage.

Brzezinski, Brown, and Aaron feared that such a strategy might very well leave the Guard decapitated and demoralized. They thought that U.S. interests in a stable post-Somoza environment would be better served by focusing on ways to support the Guard. After more than two hours of debate, Brzezinski summarized the discussion in terms of four points of consensus: (1) the United States would actively seek a candidate for Guard Commander and gain Torrijos' acceptance as a first step toward gaining wider support for the new leader in the region; (2) the United States would seek to replace the Junta with a different one that included: Sergio Ramírez, Alfonso Robelo, Ismael Reyes, Mariano Fiallos (the Rector of the National University), and the new Guard Commander; (3) the President would insist that Torrijos halt the arms flow or the United States would reserve the right to resupply the Guard; and (4) after Somoza's departure, the United States would provide humanitarian aid to contribute to the stability of the new government.

These four points concealed the sharp division between the two strategies that were debated at the meeting. During the discussion, State appeared to be on the defensive, but the opposite was the case. Brzezinski suspected that their position was closer to that of the President's, and when he failed to persuade Christopher, he decided to concede the fundamental point—that we would aim to influence the Junta of the Provisional Government rather than try to establish a separate pole of power. However, Brzezinski conceded that point at the cost of proposing a plan that was unrealistic, and State did not object because they knew they had won their point.[36] The President was not well served by this compromise, and he was the first one to realize it.

In the afternoon, Harold Brown and the representatives from State and NSC met with the President to discuss the SCC's recommendations and propose a strategy for the meeting with Torrijos. Brzezinski was generally very effective in summarizing a complex meeting concisely and in a way that highlighted the critical issue even when it had not been obvious to its participants. This was not the case that afternoon, however. His summary of the SCC was abbreviated and unhelpful to the President, who began interrupting and questioning him.

Carter quickly grasped the unreality of the plan, and was impatient and sharp in his questions. How can you expect to negotiate with the Sandinistas a total revision of the Junta that virtually excluded them, he asked? State accepted his point, and suggested as an alternative adding the names to an expanded Junta, which would also include the Commander of the Guard. Brzezinski tried to focus the discussion on the connection between the Junta and the armed forces. Carter understood the importance of having a moderate on the Junta, which would have effective control over the army. "We don't want Ortega to be Minister of Defense," Carter said.

Brzezinski realized that he failed to persuade the President and so he retreated to his apocalyptic scenario, warning Carter that what was at stake is not just the formula for Nicaragua, but a more basic matter, namely whether in the wake of our own decision not to intervene in Latin American politics, there will not develop a vacuum, which would be filled by Castro and others. In other words, we have to demonstrate that we are still the decisive force in determining the political outcomes in Central America and that we will not permit others to intervene.[37]

Brzezinski's anxiety had caused him to abandon his forward-looking vision of the region in favor of a traditional "spheres of influence" approach. He knew the President was unsympathetic to his definition of the crisis or of the U.S. role and noted in his diary that "the State Department types were absolutely delighted by this exchange. One of them even grinned openly. My own judgment is that we are about to produce for ourselves another Iran but close to home."

Pezzullo was impressed by Carter. As he later recalled:

What struck me was the realism of the man. Carter seemed to sense just natively that the amount of things open to us was very limited. We didn't have a wide array of options. We couldn't demand anything; we couldn't really drive things in any direction. The most we could do was play a role and hopefully with deftness . . . of positive influence. That struck me because I think the tendency of policy planners in Washington is to assume that the United States can do more than it really can. . . . Carter instinctively realized that we had a marginal role to play, but we can play an intelligent one.[38]

Carter had both a different picture of the crisis and a different strategy than Brzezinski's. He wanted to preserve the Guard and secure a base for the moderates in the new government, but he believed the Guard would only survive if it were viewed as legitimate in Nicaragua and among a few of the democratic governments in the area. The President was the first person in his Administration to raise the issue of the legitimacy of the Guard as a key factor in its viability and in determining U.S. policy. Carter said that if Torrijos, Pérez, Carazo, or the Andean leaders were willing to accept Gutiérrez or Guerrero (two names of Guard Commanders that were being considered), then Carter would be willing to send help to the Guard. His purpose in bringing Torrijos to Washington was to try to capture international legitimacy for a reconstituted Guard. Turner suggested that the United States could support them indirectly through Israel, but Carter said that he would have no objection to doing it directly and overtly, provided it was legitimized by some of these countries.

Carter wanted to avoid a repetition of the defeat of the peace-keeping proposal at the OAS. As far as tactics, Carter said that he would try to make his plan appear as if it were just an endorsement of elements suggested by Pérez and Carazo. He understood that if the plan looked as if it had been made in the United States, that would be, in his words, "the kiss of death."

In effect, Carter adhered to his multilateral strategy—at this point, for practical reasons as much as for principle's sake. If other countries chose to help the Provisional Government rather than try to preserve the Guard, then U.S. support for the Guard would guarantee a prolongation of the war, while allying the United States to an indefensible organization. Carter's motives were somewhat different from that of the State Department: he believed in a multilateral approach or at least one in which the United States would not confront the Latin Americans, whereas State wanted to try to influence the Junta of what it perceived would be the new government. Nonetheless, Carter, as Brzezinski suspected, ended up closer to the recommendations of the State Department. He was unwilling to provide prior and unconditional assurances to the Guard or to an Executive Committee. Without such assurances, the ExCom was a dead letter. Carter preferred to try to influence the Provisional Government by expanding the Junta to include the leader of the Guard rather than to establish a separate political-military pole of power. He wanted to put the United States alongside its Latin American friends rather than in a position where it might confront them.

Overnight, several of us refined the specific plan, and at 9:00 A.M. on July 3, Carter presented it to Torrijos in the Oval Office. Carter was relaxed but firm with Torrijos. He explained that the reason for the invitation was because he knew Torrijos better than others in the region and the two of them had worked together well on another exceptionally difficult task—the Canal treaties. He then described a seven-part plan as if it were really developed by Pérez and Carazo, and just endorsed by Carter. (This was not entirely disingenuous, as the Administration had incorporated their views and those of others as it drafted the plan.) The seven parts were:

(1) Agreement between Panama, United States, Costa Rica, and Venezuela on the specific names that should be suggested to expand the San José Junta.

(2) Agreement on who would direct the Guard in Nicaragua during the transition. Two suggestions were Gutiérrez and Guerrero. The Commander should be on the Junta and perhaps serve as Minister of Defense.

(3) The Junta would agree to a ceasefire, a standstill for the two military forces, no reprisal, and a merger of military forces when peace is restored.

(4) No arms would be transferred to the FSLN or to the Nicaraguan government during this period.

(5) The United States would ensure Somoza's departure and would organize a humanitarian aid program.

(6) On Somoza's departure, the Nicaraguan Congress would name a President who would serve "for a brief time" (1–2 days; although Brzezinski later said "no more than 10 days"). The President would be someone independent like Fiallos or Reyes, and he would call for a cease-fire and would name the Commander of the Guard.

(7) The new President would then resign and transfer power to the Junta, which in turn would organize elections.

After describing this plan, Carter tried to lighten the conversation for a moment by asking Torrijos whether it was satisfactory to him for Somoza to leave. Torrijos became animated, calling it the best thing that could happen to the world. He compared the plan, which he described as good, to taking a screw out of a DC-10 while the plane was flying. "The trick," he pointed out, "is to keep the plane flying." Torrijos insisted that it was very important that the plan not fail.

Both agreed that Torrijos would be the main exponent of the plan, and the United States would take a back seat, supporting and endorsing the proposals put forth by others at the appropriate time. However, though Carter agreed to a low public profile, he told Torrijos that the United States would remain involved in the transition. The United States, however, would try to influence events in Nicaragua, as it had many times since withdrawing troops in the 1930s, without using its hands.

Carter asked Torrijos if the Sandinistas would accept the plan. Torrijos said that he thought they would, but "I'll need a few hours to sell the list to them." He also gave Carter "a high percentage of assurance" of stopping the arms flow. Though Carter pressed him to confirm the details, Torrijos avoided them, saying that what mattered was the "attitude" and the flexibility of those who were negotiating. Carter stressed the importance of agreeing on a new Guard Commander, saying that he understood that Pérez and Carazo thought Gutiérrez would be the best. Torrijos was vaguely agreeable. Carter concluded the hour-long meeting by telling his staff to answer any additional questions Torrijos might have about the plan, and by asking Torrijos to offer advice on the content and timing of Carter's future public statements.

Torrijos was unfamiliar with either the names or the details involved in a possible transition. It appeared that he had not thought about anything beyond Somoza, and it was questionable whether he was doing this even after his conversation with Carter. As Torrijos thought out loud about the plan, his ideas coalesced around the emotions and the feelings of the Nicaraguan and Central American people. He became excited, calling the plan spectacular, indicating that it could transform the feelings of Nicaraguans overnight from hatred of the United States to love. He also spoke genuinely and with great warmth of his own relationship with Carter. It was clear that Torrijos wanted the Carter plan to succeed; what was less clear was whether he would remember the plan by the time he returned to Panama. He took no notes.

After his meeting with Carter, Torrijos spent the rest of the day with Brzezinski, Christopher, members of the State Department, and myself to work out the details of the proposal. But he continued to avoid details. Occasionally, one of his advisers, Marcel Salamín, a shrewd Panamanian leftist whose sympathies with the Sandinistas were more transparent than his motives, would mention that the Guard was totally discredited. It might be possible to integrate some Guard officers into a Sandinista army, but the idea of fusing the two armies was impractical. In discussing names of possible Guard leaders, Salamín mentioned the names of people who had defected from the Guard to join the Sandinistas. Torrijos did not comment on this point, but at other times his remarks suggested that he viewed the preservation of the Guard as of great importance.

Salamín's comments presaged the second crucial issue the Administration would address in Somoza's final month. The first issue—the Executive Committee or the Junta—was decided in favor of the latter. The second issue—whether to work for a fusion between two separate armies or a merger *under* the umbrella of the Sandinista Army—was never debated as openly or clearly as the first, but a similar dynamic—fed by the momentum of events in Nicaragua—led again to the latter option.

Torrijos returned to Central America exuberantly optimistic that he could sell the plan. Bowdler stopped in Guatemala to try to persuade Col. Inocente Mojíca, who was the Nicaraguan Defense Attaché there, to return to Managua to start to rebuild his contacts. Bowdler was unsuccessful. Vaky flew to Venezuela, Colombia, and the Dominican Republic. This was the beginning of the last attempt by the United States to piece together a more moderate Nicaraguan government.

Through June to early July, the position of the U.S. government toward Nicaragua was transformed and driven by events and fears as the possibility of a Sandinista takeover increased. The United States searched desperately for a "third force," an Executive Committee to serve as a buffer between the National Guard and the Sandinistas, but few moderates were left in Managua to consider it, and they would only do so if the United States provided the kind of unconditional assurances that Carter was unwilling to give in the absence of some international support. The moderates in Nicaragua finally abandoned hope of an alternative to the Sandinistas just when the United States was really prepared to develop one.

Though the United States thought it had stepped into the role of arbiter, it had not. Decisions on the future government of Nicaragua were being made in Washington, but they were not being implemented anywhere. Other decisions would matter more.

Chapter 9

DENOUEMENT

Things which you do not hope,
Happen more frequently
Than things which you do hope.
Titus Maccius Plautus

DURING the early morning hours of July 4, after what seemed like only one hour of sleep, I was awakened by a telephone call from the White House Situation Room. The Duty Officer informed me that two letters had just arrived at the White House for President Carter from the Embassy of Nicaragua. I asked for an update on the fighting in Nicaragua, and was informed that the National Guard was being beaten badly. Another report indicated that Somoza would call the Nicaraguan Congress into session that day.

The Duty Officer told me that Brzezinski wanted an immediate analysis of the letters and a recommendation to bring to the President during his intelligence briefing that morning. Exhausted, but moving on spurts of adrenalin, my mind raced through hundreds of permutations of what the two letters might contain. I dressed and drove to the office. When I arrived, the Duty Officer handed me the letters as if they were heavy with the weight of history. I opened them anxiously and read them. They were two "July 4th Birthday Greetings" from Anastasio Somoza and the Nicaraguan Ambassador, Guillermo Sevilla-Sacasa. The Ambassador was famous for littering the White House with this kind of missive, and I wondered whether these reflected a machine that didn't turn off, a grotesque joke, or a metaphor heralding the last act of a Pirandellian play.

Translating the Plan into Panamanian

The first report that Torrijos sent us on his negotiations was upbeat. He indicated that he was moving on several fronts simultaneously, and that Carazo and Andrés Pérez liked the plan. This was the last such report we received from Torrijos, though his efforts continued. Needless to say, he did not complete his mission in a few hours.

The issue that became the biggest obstacle was in many ways the least important, the expansion of the Junta. The two moderates on the Junta—Violeta de Chamorro and Alfonso Robelo—were the most vigorous in their opposition to expanding it, for fear their own power would be diluted. Moreover, to compensate for their bourgeois background, they tried to sound more defiant and revolutionary than the Sandinistas.

The FSLN Directorate consulted with Castro, who indicated that he saw no problem with expanding the Junta.[1] (It is interesting that the FSLN felt the need to consult with Castro on this issue; it is more interesting that he had to tell them that the Junta did not matter.) The Sandinistas repeatedly showed their willingness to compromise on the issue of the Junta's composition, while the moderates were intransigent.

The public persona of the moderates and the Marxists therefore reversed. The Directorate tried to sound as moderate as it could, privately reassuring everyone while remaining in the background of a Provisional Government, which issued a "Plan of Government" and position papers as if it were a think tank or a Presidential commission. The combined impact of these two sounds—of militant moderates and moderate Marxists—was of a Nicaraguan government-in-exile, demonstrating its pluralistic character to the world.

By July 8, the United States had obtained ostensible support for the plan from the Latin American governments, but the Junta (by then called the Provisional Government) still blocked it. That evening the Junta spokesman Miguel D'Escoto called an aide to a member of Congress and asked that a letter be conveyed from the Provisional Government (PG) requesting a meeting with President Carter.

The *New York Times* reported the next day that the "fundamental obstacle to a negotiated settlement is still disagreement over the future role of the National Guard." In fact, despite herculean efforts by many, there seemed to be little progress on anything.

Brzezinski convened an SCC meeting at 5:00 P.M. on July 9 to review the negotiations. There was no progress on either the expansion of the Junta or the naming of a new Guard Commander. Gutiérrez had been ruled out since he would not return to the region and Somoza rejected him. Panama continued to put forward names suggested by the FSLN, notably Bernardino Larios, the Guard officer who had been jailed after an abortive coup in August 1978. When he escaped, he joined the FSLN. The Defense Department thought he was a good man, but he lacked command experience and any real following in the Guard. It suggested several other names, including Col. Inocente Mojíca, whom Bowdler and Pezzullo had met briefly in

Guatemala. Brzezinski urged State and Defense to agree on a new Commander, but resolution of that question was connected with the issue of what assurances, if any, the United States could give a post-Somoza Guard.

State opposed any aid to the Guard while the war continued, but it agreed to permit the Defense Attaché in Managua to inform possible candidates for Guard Commander that the United States envisaged a possible role for a purged Guard and would try to undertake rapid humanitarian assistance in a manner that it hoped would stabilize the situation. The SCC also discussed the letter from the Junta and agreed to hold out a possible meeting with the Secretary of State as an incentive for the Provisional Government to accept the nominations for the Guard Commander and the expanded Junta.

The Directorate and the Junta rejected the conditions for the meeting with the Secretary of State; their tactics increasingly resembled those of Somoza's during the mediation. They appeared to be playing for time. Ramírez later confirmed this: "When the Yankees pushed for two more members on the Junta, I judged they realized that the Guard was defeated [and this] was the only way that remained for them to influence events."[2] The underlying reason for the Sandinistas' momentum and the systematic weakening of the U.S. negotiating position was the rather sudden shift in the balance of military power. The Embassy was aware of this shift. On July 7, Pezzullo sent a telegram to the State Department indicating that "the GN [Guard] supply lines have been severely restricted whereas the FSLN has an open supply line." He estimated that the Guard would run out of ammunition "within less than two weeks." Since their only effective instrument for fighting was air power, Pezzullo wrote that "it would be ill-advised to go to Somoza and ask for a bombing halt," as the FSLN was advocating, unless the FSLN agreed to a cease-fire, which, he assumed, they would not do.[3]

Since the United States could not stop the flow of arms to the FSLN and would not send arms to the Guard, U.S. negotiators were playing poker against a stacked deck. Their "ace in the hole," the resignation of Somoza, had become a liability. After nearly a week of negotiations, Torrijos, Carazo, and Peréz had failed to achieve agreement on anything, even a cease-fire. As the negotiations bogged down, Torrijos backed away, and as Bowdler filled the vacuum, Torrijos let it be known that the plan was "American," not Panamanian.[4]

The issue that the FSLN watched most carefully was the National Guard. They argued that the Guard was unsalvageable as an institution and sought to discredit and subvert any proposal that would leave it intact. Costa Rican President Carazo agreed,[5] but Torrijos disagreed. According to Gabriel Lewis and Ambler Moss, Torrijos believed right up until the end—July 19—"that the Guard would be saved."[6] But it is not clear what Torrijos did to preserve the Guard, and the person who often represented him in the various discussions in the region, Marcel Salamín, believed the Guard would have to be dismantled.

In their meeting with Bowdler on July 10, the members of the Junta indicated that they expected power to be transferred directly to them; to assuage United States concerns about the Guard, they expressed a willingness to incorporate some reformed elements in a Sandinista army. Brzezinski and Aaron recognized this as a turning point—perhaps the last before a Sandinista victory—and called an SCC meeting at 5:00 P.M. on the same day. Before the meeting, Vaky called to tell me that he thought the Guard would not hold together, and that we should discard the illusion that it would.

Brzezinski opened the SCC meeting on July 10 by asking sarcastically whether, in the light of Bowdler's conversation with the Junta, the United States should be a willing or an unwilling tool for dismantling the Guard. The war appeared to be wearing down the Carter Administration as much as the Nicaraguans.

The United States decided to force the pace of events for two reasons: first, the killing in Nicaragua was weighing on the Administration. As Somoza let it be known that he was only staying until the United States indicated the circumstances of his departure, the weight grew heavier.[7] Second, as the Guard's arsenal and petroleum stocks shrank and the Sandinistas' stockpile continued to seem inexhaustible, the Administration began to fear a complete collapse of the National Guard, which would leave the FSLN beholden to no one and restrained by no one.

The SCC meeting on July 10 therefore decided to bring the crisis to a head. First, the United States would seek the support of Torrijos, Carazo, and Peréz in asking the Junta one last time to expand its membership to be more representative of the Nicaraguan population and to call publicly for a cease-fire, standstill of military forces, and free elections. In the absence of such steps, the United States would consider alternative approaches to facilitate a transition. The Administration had no idea what alternatives were available, but threats made in desperation are not generally inhibited by the absence of rational alternatives. Second, the United States, with, it hoped, Torrijos, Carazo, and Pérez, would press for a new Guard Commander. The United States would also pledge to supply humanitarian assistance through him and a group of prominent civilians as well as through the FSLN. Third, the United States would inform Somoza that it saw no reason for him to postpone his departure.

Because the limits on the ability of the United States to influence the post-Somoza period were apparent, there was a discussion about whether the United States should walk away from Nicaragua. As he had in a previous meeting, David Aaron argued that the United States should not play the role of midwife to a Sandinista military regime; let the others sort it out. Like Mondale, his mentor, Aaron had an acute sense of the political dimension of foreign policy issues. His concern anticipated the criticism leveled against the Carter Administration by Richard Nixon. At a press conference in Mexico City, after visiting the Shah of Iran, Nixon said that Carter shouldn't "grease the skids for our friends." Nixon also repeated Somoza's refrain, which Somoza's actions had almost made true, that the alternative to Somoza was a "Castro-type government." The choice, Nixon said, was "not between Somoza and somebody better, but between Somoza and somebody much worse."[8] But except for Aaron, those at the SCC, including Brzezinski, felt that the United States was already in so deeply that it had a responsibility to see the project through and try, in the post-revolutionary period, to reduce the chances of vindictive violence, and increase the chances of democracy.

Bowdler presented the July 10 SCC ultimatum to the Junta on July 11 at 6:30 P.M. in Puntarenas, Costa Rica, where the Junta had been meeting with Carazo, Peréz, José Figueres, and a number of other leaders from the region. The Junta responded, though not in the way the United States had hoped. The Junta's "Plan to Achieve Peace" would transfer power from Somoza through the Nicaraguan Congress directly to the Government of National Reconstruction, which would be led by the Junta and which would then dissolve the Congress and the National Guard. All those in the Guard who had not committed crimes and wanted to leave would be permitted to do so; others who wanted to be incorporated into the Sandinista Army would be considered. The Junta also announced a Cabinet, which included appointments of Bernardino Larios, the National Guard defector, as Defense Minister; Tomás Borge, as Minister of the Interior; Arturo Cruz, as head of the Central Bank; and Miguel D'Escoto as Foreign Minister.

At the same time, D'Escoto told the press that the Junta's new proposal "appears to move them closer to American notions of proper terms for settling the civil war." Although the Junta's proposal demanded power to be handed to them in a single step, a *Washington Post* reporter described it as "the most conciliatory [decision] made by the prospective junta government to date," and the State Department, viewing the outcome as inevitable, called it "positive."[9]

With regard to concerns about human rights, pluralism, and an end to the violence, Peréz suggested the Government of National Reconstruction respond to the OAS resolution of June 23 to replace Somoza with a letter affirming its commitment to free elections and other human rights.[10] On July 12, the Junta sent a letter to the OAS Secretary General with a copy of the plan and a request that the Secretary General forward both to the foreign ministers of the governments of the OAS. In the letter, the Junta sought support from the OAS by referring to the "historic" OAS resolution of June 23. The letter pledged "full respect for human rights" and invited the Inter-American Human Rights Commission to visit Nicaragua as soon as the new government was installed. The Junta promised to ensure an orderly and peaceful transition and avoid a "bloodbath." It invited the foreign ministers of OAS countries to participate in the transfer of power to the new government as a way of lending stability to the process. Finally, it committed the new government to "the first free elections that our country will have in this century," although it omitted the resolution's recommendation that these be "as soon as possible."[11] The human rights pledges were important as a baseline from which democrats could measure the direction of a future government.

Bureaucratic defeats affect people differently. Vaky had been worn down in the early fall by bureaucratic losses, but until the failure of the mediation, his response had been to repeat the same recommendation—"talk turkey" and impose sanctions. Brzezinski responded differently to his repeated failure to persuade the President to his views in June and July. Rather than repeat the same option, Brzezinski chose instead to start and end almost every meeting with an impassioned statement that the United States was sitting passively as a historical change was occurring in Central America. He convened an SCC meeting on July 13 and spoke "of the baton being passed from the United States to Cuba." "It fills me with unease," Brzezinski said. "We must lean harder on the Latin Americans to recognize that their security is involved."

Of course this was where the Administration, including Brzezinski, had begun, and it was fitting that was where it ended up. Brzezinski himself had written of the need for change in Central America, for social justice and greater national autonomy, but when the change came, it took a form and followed leaders that were hostile to the United States. It was especially discouraging to the Administration that many friendly Latin American governments appeared to view the United States as a more serious security problem than the Sandinistas. The gap in security perceptions was symbolized by the decision of the Costa Rican Congress on July 11 to demand the withdrawal of U.S. aircraft sent to Costa Rica for purposes of evacuating U.S. citizens in case of emergency. Carazo had approved the request on July 8, but the Congress rescinded his decision three days later. At the time, it appeared that the Costa Rican Congress was trying to embarrass Carazo as much, if not more, than the United States. In retrospect, there were probably many in Costa Rica who feared that the U.S. personnel stationed in the region might learn the full extent of Costa Rican arms trafficking.

Brzezinski believed that the National Guard was going to collapse unless there was outside intervention, and he knew the United States would not intervene. The basic problem, he said, was that the President will not intervene alone, and the Latin Americans will not join. The United States would not support the Guard, because Latin Americans would be on the other side. There was no choice. The conclusion was that a left-of-center government would emerge; the question was whether it would be "Castro-ite." When Christopher asked for a definition, Brzezinski said that a Castro-ite government would be one that supported Cuban and Soviet foreign policy and insurgencies abroad—for example, in El Salvador. The SCC meeting on July 13 ended with a consensus that Somoza must go, but disquiet as to what would follow. Vaky, trying to facilitate a decision to bring the war to an end, reassured his colleagues that the Guard might not collapse, and even if it did, many democratic governments had a stake in helping Nicaraguan democrats.

By force of habit, the SCC usually made recommendations, and on July 13 it made five, which the President approved. First, Pezzullo was instructed to give a list of potential Guard Commanders to Somoza and to talk to him about it. Second, Vance would send a letter to various foreign ministers in Latin America urging them to play a more assertive role to ensure that Nicaragua would have a pluralistic future. Third, to counter a statement of the Junta that negotiations had broken down with the United States, we would reiterate our interest in talks and Bowdler would continue to press for assurances that the transition would be smooth and as bloodless as possible. Fourth, Pezzullo was to ask Somoza to depart soon. And fifth, because Pastora was considered more independent than the Directorate, a meeting with him was authorized to explore future possibilities for cooperation. The Administration had already done considerable work on developing a humanitarian assistance strategy to help Nicaragua in a postwar period. These were the first decisions taken in preparation for a Sandinista Nicaragua.

For about eight months, Carazo and Torrijos had been trying to arrange a meeting between Pastora and U.S. government officials, and each time the Administration, after much soul-searching, rejected the idea. U.S. officials wanted to learn more about the Sandinistas, and especially about some of the leaders, but feared that if the meeting became known, as it suspected it would, this would unwittingly discourage the moderate opposition in Nicaragua and shower legitimacy on the Sandinistas. Because this was contrary to U.S. objectives, the U.S. government postponed the decision. By late June, however, it was clear that the Sandinistas would be a major—perhaps the major actor in a post-Somoza government, and U.S. officials finally met with several Sandinistas, beginning with those perceived to be more independent. What the United States discovered was that Pastora was much more suspicious of the United States than the United States was of him. The initial discussions were difficult and not satisfactory.[12]

Preserving the Guard: The Formaldehyde Solution

Since the crisis began, one of the central issues had been the composition of the military in a post-Somoza Nicaragua. Given the history of the country, one would have expected this to be the pivotal issue for everyone, yet the only group that defined and doggedly pursued a strategy on it was the FSLN. The U.S. government considered the problem, but its decisions were never formulated into a clear and coherent strategy and almost no decisions were implemented.

Beginning on September 12, 1978, at one of the first mini-SCC meetings, Aaron had asked Vaky whether he thought the loyalty of the Guard was transferrable, and Vaky responded that he did. The next week there was some discussion about what was needed to assist the Guard in an interregnum, but only at a PRC meeting on October 31, 1978, did the United States clearly define the preservation of the Guard as a central objective. After that, there was some discussion about ways to achieve this objective at almost every meeting.

The Administration recognized the moral problems and risks associated with helping a Guard that was corrupt and tied to Somoza. But so too did the FAO, and it included a restructured Guard as part of its proposal in October 1978 for a post-Somoza government. The Guard's atrocities during the insurrection were mostly committed by the "special forces" of Tacho III, Somoza's son, and one sign that the population did not identify all of the Guard with these excesses was that the Sandinista Army accepted some Guardsmen into their forces after the triumph.[13] The Carter Administration also understood that when the civil war ended, the side that controlled most of the arms would be the one that shaped the political future of the country. For that reason, the Administration looked for ways to build a military base under a moderate civilian leadership.

When the NSC began again in June 1979 to discuss policy in the light of the "final offensive" of the Sandinistas, the SCC declared as one of its highest priorities that a post-Somoza government should not have to rely exclusively on the military power of the FSLN. Vance and Brzezinski both met with Julio Gutiérrez, and many believed these contacts were just the tip of a much larger effort by the U.S. Embassy in Managua and by the Pentagon in Washington.

When one sought explanations for the failure to implement the key goal of appointing a new Guard Commander as the first step toward preserving the institution in some form, many were offered: "there is, after all, a war under way in Nicaragua"; "no candidate is willing to come forward"; "Somoza doesn't like that particular candidate." The source of the possible candidates was never clear to the White House. The State Department accepted the importance of this objective, and as late as July 13, Vaky assured the SCC that the "objective was not unattainable," yet it evidently attached low priority to it. The Defense Department was distraught about the direction of events but, inexplicably, did not pursue it. Most of those who attended the SCC meetings, including myself, were unaware of the Embassy's personnel problems and assumed that a wide range of contact was maintained with Guard officers at all levels, and that plans were well advanced to ensure the continuity of the Guard after Somoza.

The assumptions were totally false. Ever since Anastasio Somoza García had first secured control of the Guard in 1933, the Somoza family had sought advice, assistance, and identification with the U.S. military, but they were always careful to make sure that U.S. advisers worked through them—or through designated officers—and not directly with the Guard. Somoza made sure all Guard officers reported to him any and all contacts with U.S. officials. Much of the information that the United States obtained on the Guard was therefore provided by Somoza. After the sharp reduction in U.S. Embassy staff in February 1979, the amount of information on the Guard and much else declined even further.

State Department political officers infrequently surveyed the

Guard because they were careful not to tread on the bureaucratic turf of the Defense Attaché. The principal mission of the Attaché was to obtain information on military capabilities and requirements—"order of battle" information. They had a "trained incapacity," in Robert Merton's phrase, to think about, let alone pursue, questions related to the Latin American military as a political institution.[14]

By and large, the U.S. government knew less about the Guard than Somoza knew about the U.S. government. Indeed, as U.S. Ambassador to Managua, Pezzullo suspected that Somoza used his longstanding contacts with the Pentagon to keep track of what the Embassy and the U.S. government were doing.[15] Pezzullo was therefore selective in what he permitted the Defense Attaché, James McCoy, to know about U.S. policy. He was so selective that McCoy never learned of the crucial June 24 decision by President Carter to support the Guard after Somoza's departure *only if* it could demonstrate some domestic or international legitimacy.

From at least 1976 to July 1979, there were no independent, unauthorized contacts between U.S. government officials and Guard officers. McCoy said he would never arrange a meeting on his own. The Embassy would have to make a recommendation as a "country team" to Washington, and that was unlikely, in his view, while Mauricio Solaun was Ambassador. After Solaun left, there were no initiatives from the Embassy. Moreover, McCoy opposed such contacts because in his view, "it would have looked like we were trying to replace Somoza. This would have upset Somoza." Besides, Tacho III had already warned McCoy that he might have an "accident" if he contacted a Guard officer without clearing it with him first.[16]

After numerous decisions by the SCC to expand contacts with Guard officers, McCoy finally received instructions. He arranged a meeting on July 10 with four or five lieutenant colonels and asked them what they thought a post-Somoza Guard would look like. The officers appeared dumbfounded at such a question; none had contemplated such a future. After the meeting, the officers immediately informed Tacho III, who called his father. Somoza, who was meeting with Congressman John Murphy at the time, placed a direct call to General Edward Meyer, Army Chief of Staff, and denounced McCoy in the strongest terms. Meyer then cabled the Embassy to inquire what McCoy was doing. The cable arrived even before McCoy had returned to the Embassy from his meeting.[17]

At the same time, Somoza called Pezzullo and asked him to meet immediately in the back room of a small restaurant. This was the first time that Pezzullo had met with Somoza alone, and Pezzullo was struck by how nervous and angry he was.[18]

"He let me have it as soon as he came into the restaurant," Pezzullo later recalled.

"You're going to get me killed," Somoza barked at him.

"What are you talking about?" Pezzullo asked.

"McCoy was going around talking to people in the Guard about what it would be like after I'm gone," said Somoza.

Pezzullo recalled that Somoza's "point was that if the Guard knew he was leaving, they would kill him." Pezzullo failed to grasp the significance of Somoza's indiscretion, but he responded in kind, saying that Somoza could only blame himself for his interview with the *Washington Post*, in which he suggested he was about to leave.[19]

Somoza admitted he had been drunk and that the interview was a mistake, but Pezzullo then conceded: "O.K., I take your point. We shouldn't get too far out in front until we get everything decided." He then returned to the Embassy to tell McCoy not to talk to any people in the Guard without his prior authorization. Pezzullo did this because he didn't trust McCoy, who he thought was trying to figure out a way to resupply the Guard, and because he thought Somoza and his son were the keys to preserving the Guard. McCoy felt betrayed by this single encounter with the Guard, and reciprocated Pezzullo's distrust. In McCoy's view, Pezzullo's "objective was to put the Sandinistas in power," and McCoy could not understand that.[20]

Both Somoza and Tacho III agreed with Pezzullo that the Guard's senior officers—the "Somocistas"—would depart with them. The son was helpful in describing traits of the junior officers. Both suggested candidates for Guard Commander, and Pezzullo forwarded these to Washington or directly to Bowdler in San José to clear with the Junta. Because Washington was unfamiliar with most of the officers, Pezzullo and Bowdler were left to swing back and forth between the outgoing Somoza government that sought through this appointment to maintain its influence in Nicaragua and the incoming revolutionary government that wanted a figurehead to preside over the collapse of the Guard.

Because Pezzullo did not use the Defense Attaché and had no one else to rely on, the U.S. government had no independent channel to the Guard in the final month. In addition, this problem was not addressed simply because Pezzullo did not consider the maintenance of the Guard a high priority. He had begun to focus his greatest attention on making sure that "the countdown for the plan" would work.[21] He also thought that the "plan" was the most effective way to ensure the preservation of the Guard. Once a cease-fire and a stand-down occurred, the Guard would win the time and space to redress its wounds. After Somoza left, the FSLN forces, which were mostly brave young people with no training or military experience whatsoever, were likely to disintegrate more quickly than the Guard.

The first irony was that the strategy relied on Somoza when his interests were clearly at odds with those of the United States. Second, the strategy depended on Somoza's judgment of people and Nicaragua's future—two subjects in which his previous track record was something less than stellar. Somoza had personally conveyed his fears about what his officers would do if they knew he was leaving to Pezzullo, but Pezzullo did not see this for what it was—an admission that Somoza's most important interest was to keep the Guard completely uninformed and unprepared for his departure. It is true that Somoza's long-term interests would have benefited from a Guard that remained strong after his departure, but Somoza's own political demise was the result, in part, of his chronic myopia. To the last minute, Somoza kept the Guard completely dependent on him, and under these circumstances, the Guard could not have been expected to cohere. In retrospect, Pezzullo believed: "If Somoza had told [the Guard] to tough it out, they could have, but he lied to them because he feared he would be killed."[22] To have relied on Somoza was a serious mistake.

Even if the United States had developed and implemented a sound strategy to preserve some portion of the Guard, it is by no means certain that it would have succeeded. Not only had the corruption and atrocities of the Guard transformed some of the nation's youth into Sandinistas, it had embittered many Nicaraguans. Moreover, the incestuousness of the Guard and the Somoza family led to the question whether one could survive in Nicaragua without the other. For these reasons, a good strategy might not have succeeded; a non-strategy, however, was guaranteed to fail.

The Last Days

At 6:15 P.M. on July 13, Anastasio Somoza placed a telephone call to Jimmy Carter. Jim Wright, the House Majority Leader and a friend of John Murphy, had spoken with Vance, who assured him that the President would talk with Somoza. But after consulting with the President, Christopher, Somoza's nemesis, and I received the call. Somoza said that he wanted to come to Washington to explain to the President how he could contribute to the national security of the United States. He informed us that the Andean Pact was intervening in Nicaragua's internal affairs. Christopher promised to convey the message to the President, but at the same time he urged Somoza to meet with Ambassador Pezzullo.

Wright called Christopher the next day to complain that Vance had broken his word in not permitting Somoza to speak to the President. At Christopher's suggestion, Brzezinski spoke with Wright and explained the situation in Nicaragua and U.S. policy. When informed that the United States had asked Somoza to resign, Wright protested that asking a head of state to step down was extreme. Brzezinski explained that the circumstances were extreme, and the longer Somoza stayed in power the more ominous the outcome. He said that even staunch anti-Communist governments like Brazil had broken relations with Somoza. Like Brzezinski, Wright was uneasy about the change that was coming, but he agreed that the American people would not support intervention to preclude it. Wright was essentially playing back to the Administration the arguments for not overthrowing Somoza that it had found persuasive in the fall. Circumstances had indeed changed since then.

In San José, Bowdler and U.S. Ambassador to Costa Rica Marvin Weissman were preoccupied with the possibility of a "paredon"—lining people up against the wall for executions as Bowdler had seen in Cuba after Castro came to power. They encouraged the Junta to be explicit about how they would implement guarantees of safe haven for those who wanted to leave the country, and they succeeded in reaching an agreement that involved the Church and the Red Cross. This may have been the one most important and tangible achievement of the United States in the final month of negotiations.

Suspicious of U.S. intentions, the Junta turned to an old Somoza trick of trying to make it appear that the United States supported them. Their purpose was to reassure the international community and advertise their legitimacy. After a meeting with Bowdler, Sergio Ramírez told the *New York Times* that "there is no point of disagreement between us." Miguel D'Escoto said that Bowdler had told them: "You are the government of Nicaragua."[23] Neither statement was accurate, but at this late stage there was no incentive for the United States to deny them. This was not the only tactic that D'Escoto and Ramírez had learned from Somoza.

Somoza was still worried about the Guard. He had assured his officers that military aid would arrive after he left, despite repeated statements to the contrary by Pezzullo.[24] The night of July 13, he decided to make one last effort to marshal support for the Guard, and flew to Guatemala. President Romeo Lucas García had been an important source of his arms, via transshipment, but that had stopped. Somoza asked Lucas to bring together the other military leaders of Central America for two purposes: to discuss the possibility of intervention to help the Guard at the last moment; or to obtain a pledge of a planeload of supplies for the Guard to arrive after Somoza left. At a minimum, he hoped to obtain a statement of political solidarity that could reassure the Guard.[25] In the middle of the night, the U.S. government learned of Somoza's trip and of the possibility of Central American intervention under CONDECA (the Central American Defense Organization). The governments were not inclined to intervene on behalf of Somoza, but the United States was asked its view. The United States indicated that it would oppose such intervention.[26]

In frequent conversations with Somoza, Pezzullo had meticulously developed a plan that he thought would work for the transition. Simultaneously, Bowdler had negotiated the same points with the Junta. The script went as follows. Somoza would resign from the Presidency and the Guard. He and his entourage—family, all the generals, and most of the colonels—would then fly to the United States. A new Chief of Staff, whose name would be approved by the Junta, would be appointed. The Nicaraguan Congress would accept Somoza's resignation and appoint a new President, who would meet at 8:00 A.M. at the Camino Real Hotel at the airport with a delegation of representatives from the Junta, the Directorate, Ambassador Bowdler, and Archbishop Obando y Bravo. The delegation would have arrived by plane from Costa Rica. The President would announce an immediate cease-fire and a standing-in-place of the two armies.

The Archbishop would then deliver a speech, declaring an end to the war. He would also seek to reassure Nicaraguans that both sides had pledged not to undertake any reprisals and to respect sanctuary in the churches and in Red Cross facilities. The Junta would discuss the political issues and the formal transfer of power with the President, and the new Commander of the National Guard would discuss the details of the cease-fire and a fusion of forces with the Directorate. Within 72 hours, power would be transferred formally from the new President to the Junta.

On July 12, Somoza decided that Francisco Urcuyo Maliaños, the speaker of the lower house of the Nicaraguan Congress, would be the next President. Urcuyo was a physician in his mid-60s, and, according to Pallais, was chosen because of his loyalty. Pezzullo, in his words, "didn't know Urcuyo from a hole in the wall." On July 14 and 15, Pezzullo discussed the scenario step by step with Somoza and Urcuyo. After the second meeting, Pezzullo asked his new Deputy Chief of Mission, Thomas O'Donnell, to meet again with Urcuyo to make sure that he understood the plan. Urcuyo was silent in these meetings. When asked whether he accepted the plan, he was evasive, saying that he could not commit himself since he was not yet President.[27]

Urcuyo recalls his meetings with Pezzullo and Somoza, but says that the plan called for him to stay in power for "a reasonable amount of time, six or seven months." Then he would hand power to a democratic junta, which would call elections. He did not consider the Junta in San José "democratic." After his second meeting with O'Donnell at the Hotel Intercontinental on July 15 at 6:00 P.M., Urcuyo was called across the street to "the Bunker," Somoza's office in the military compound. Somoza asked Urcuyo about his Cabinet, and Urcuyo said that it included representatives of the Conservative, Liberal, and Social Christian parties, "and even a Sandinista."[28]

On July 15, Bowdler told Pezzullo that the Junta was sending two representatives to Managua to discuss the transition with Urcuyo. Pezzullo met with them when they arrived, and learned that they wanted to compress the transition to about five minutes—an immediate transfer from the Congress to the President to the Junta, as they had told Bowdler on July 10. Pezzullo told the delegation that he thought the revised plan was "unrealistic," but he also said that he didn't want to get in the middle of their negotiations with Urcuyo. He gave them Urcuyo's number and told him that they would be calling.[29]

One of the Sandinista representatives, Noel Rivas, a former leader of the Nicaraguan Chamber of Commerce, called Urcuyo to congratulate him and tell him the plan called for an immediate transfer of power to the Junta. Urcuyo was very upset and told Rivas "it couldn't be." Urcuyo then called Somoza, who after speaking with Pezzullo, informed Urcuyo that Rivas had fabricated the story.[30] Urcuyo therefore ignored the statement.

Although the SCC meeting on July 13 decided that Pezzullo should identify a Guard Commander, it was two days before Pezzullo gave Somoza a list of six names from which to select one. The list had been developed by McCoy and others in the Embassy. Somoza rejected Col. Mojíca and chose Col. Federico Mejía, a National Guard engineer in his mid-40s. "You know your onions," Somoza said, approving of the list.[31]

Pezzullo recalls sending a flash cable about the new Guard Commander to Washington and San José on July 15, and Bowdler indicated that the Junta approved of the choice. The plan, according to Pezzullo, was that Mejía would be Chief of Staff rather than Commander, and Humberto Ortega would also be Chief of Staff of the FSLN. The third member of the triumvirate responsible for negotiating a cease-fire and fusion of forces would be Bernardino Larios. Pallais insists that the final arrangement involved Mejía being promoted to General and designated National Guard Director and Army Chief of Staff.

A decision was then made that Somoza would leave early in the morning of July 17. The night before, Somoza phoned Pezzullo and warned him about allowing the Sandinista military to arrive at the airport the next day. "After all, we're in the middle of a war, and somebody [could] get trigger happy." "That sounded reasonable to me," Pezzullo recalls thinking. "I hadn't thought of it; I don't think anybody had."[32] Pezzullo then called Bowdler, who spoke with the Sandinista leadership, and all agreed that the United States would provide an Army plane for the new Guard Chief of Staff, Col. Federico Mejía, to fly with McCoy to Costa Rica to meet with the new Sandinista leadership to discuss the terms of a cease-fire. The purpose of sending McCoy was to assure Mejía that he wouldn't be taken hostage. Pezzullo tried to reach Somoza and Urcuyo to confirm this, but could not.

Pezzullo then called Mejía directly at 10:00 P.M., July 16. It was the first time that he or anyone from the U.S. Embassy had ever spoken with the new Guard leader, and Mejía knew nothing of this plan. Pezzullo, assuming Mejía did know, did not bother describing it; he just told Mejía that McCoy would meet him at the airport at 7:00 A.M. the next morning. A U.S. Army plane would fly them to Costa Rica for the meeting. Mejía listened quietly, and Pezzullo became uneasy. At 1 A.M., he sent McCoy to the bunker to make sure that Mejía was going to the airport in the morning. This was also McCoy's first meeting with the new Guard leader. After a brief conversation, McCoy called Pezzullo and told him that Mejía could not go because the President had ordered him to stay to discuss the military situation at a meeting at 10:00 A.M. Pezzullo shouted: "Which President?" McCoy wasn't sure. Pezzullo then called Mejía repeatedly, but Mejía refused to receive the phone call. The next morning, he did not go to the airport.[33]

Washington was even more bewildered about what was happening. Brzezinski chaired an SCC meeting on July 16, with Brown, Christopher, David Jones, Vaky and his senior deputy, John Bushnell, John White from the Office of Management and Budget, and me attending. Most of the SCC members did not know that Somoza was leaving the next day, that Mejía had been selected as Chief of Staff, or the complex arrangement that had been worked out with Larios and Ortega. The meeting actually discussed for the fourth consecutive time Col. Mojíca, the Nicaraguan Attaché in Guatemala, as a possible head of the Guard. In the last week, events were moving rapidly in Central America as well as in Washington. There were so few people doing so many things that there was hardly enough time to read cables let alone write them. Communications broke down.

The major issue for the SCC was how to distribute food and medicines after Somoza left. The SCC decided to distribute aid in two ways that would strengthen moderates—through the Red Cross and the Provisional Government. Aid in Managua would be dispensed mostly through the Red Cross, but the United States would ask the president of the Red Cross, Ismael Reyes, to broaden the leadership of the organization and to consider using the National Guard. At the same time, the special AID representative, David Lazar, who had been sent to San José, would tell the Junta that the United States was prepared to be helpful if they broadened their capability to provide aid. The SCC also recommended a large airlift to Managua to begin immediately after Somoza's departure and the request by the new government.

The Andean Pact ministers were considering flying to Managua to lend their support to the new regime, and the United States encouraged them. Torrijos noted that he wanted to train the Nicaraguan military, lest the Sandinistas become a "hippy military force." The SCC decided to try to encourage Panama and the Andean countries to take the lead in dealing with the Sandinista government, and the United States would support them.

Exit

At 1:00 A.M., July 17, the Nicaraguan Congress convened in the Hotel Intercontinental and quickly accepted Somoza's resignation. Somoza then traveled in a convoy to the airport and left at about 4:00 A.M. The Congress elected Urcuyo President. In a nation-wide address, Urcuyo declared that Somoza's departure marked "an era which is definitively canceled." He urged his fellow Nicaraguans "to forget the past in the name of the present, with our eyes on the future." Instead of calling for a cease-fire, however, he asked "all of the irregular forces [to] lay down their weapons." Instead of transferring power to the Provisional Government in San José, he invited the Inter-American Human Rights Commission to visit and called "fervently for dialogue" with "all the democratic groups of the nation."[34] Though he did not actually say that he would complete Somoza's term, as the press and Ambassador Pezzullo reported, he did not sound like a man who would be leaving in 48 or 72 hours.

Urcuyo then walked to the bunker—his new office—and Pezzullo phoned him there at 4:00 A.M. The Ambassador reminded Urcuyo of the plan, which required Mejía's departure at 7:00 A.M. for Costa Rica and Urcuyo's welcome to the Archbishop and the Junta at 9:00 A.M. (It had been postponed one hour.) Urcuyo rejected both requests, insisting that Mejía was needed in Managua for a meeting at 10:00 A.M. with the Guard commanders "to discuss military strategy."

Tired and strung out, Pezzullo called Vaky and told him "the whole thing is coming apart." Vaky suggested he try again. Bowdler told the Junta to wait. Pezzullo and McCoy then went to the Presidential House and woke up Urcuyo. Urcuyo later wrote that he told Pezzullo that he would turn over power in a constitutional process to a democratic junta, but not a Communist one. He claimed he did not know anything about Pezzullo's plan. The two traded insults, and then Pezzullo returned to the Embassy and called Washington. Vaky told him to try yet again. In the meantime, there was an SCC meeting scheduled that afternoon to decide what the United States should do.[35]

Beginning at 3:30 P.M., the SCC met for one hour. Because of the rapidity of events, few outside of the State Department knew the details of the elaborate plan that had been negotiated during the previous week. State—Vaky and Christopher—thought the plan was workable, but feared that Urcuyo was destroying it. Their comments reflected the anger of Pezzullo, who judged that Somoza was responsible for Urcuyo's decision to stay; and they also were sensitive to the Junta's suspicions, which were being conveyed in colorful language to Bowdler in San José. The Junta was convinced that the latest turn of events was part of a U.S. plot. State therefore wanted to try to force Urcuyo out.

Brzezinski and David Jones suggested that the Latin Americans should be encouraged to play a larger role, and that the United States should issue a statement that Urcuyo was acting on his own. Although the SCC was uncertain of Urcuyo's intentions, there was a certain irony in his scheme, which was essentially the Executive Committee idea that State had declared a nonstarter three weeks before. Urcuyo did not want to hand over power to the FSLN in one step; he claimed he would transfer power to a broadly based group of democratic opposition leaders, some of whom he wanted for his Cabinet. But the situation was much more fragile than Urcuyo realized.

Bushnell said that several C-141s filled with food were prepared to fly to Managua, and Gen. John Pustay noted that Torrijos had suggested that our "silhouette loom large" with such planes. But the Sandinistas were very anxious that these planes might be carrying something other than food, and asked us to wait. State agreed. Pezzullo was instructed to try to get the plan back on track, and Bowdler to reassure the Junta. Pezzullo called Mejía, and explained the entire plan to him for the first time. Pezzullo warned him that Urcuyo was "going to destroy the National Guard" but "he wouldn't hear of it."[36]

Early in the morning of July 17, after hearing of Somoza's resignation but before hearing Urcuyo's speech, Carlos Núñez, a Sandinista leader, recalled that "the Frente made a rapid evaluation of the state of their forces and ordered a mass advance on Managua, calculating that they would need three days to take the capital and wipe out the last of the Guard." During the day and into the night, some of the "heaviest" fighting occurred.[37] Humberto Ortega later told Pezzullo that the FSLN never intended to negotiate with the Guard or accept a cease-fire or standstill. They intended to march into Managua and destroy the Guard.[38]

Urcuyo met with the new High Command of the Guard and told them of Pezzullo's proposal that Mejía meet with the Sandinista commanders to plan a cease-fire and unification of forces. Mejía then phoned Humberto Ortega, who demanded unconditional surrender, attributing this change to the fact that Urcuyo violated the first understanding.[39]

The senior officers of the Guard met in the evening of July 17 to assess their military supply problems. They were aware that the Sandinistas had redoubled their efforts and controlled León, Granada, Chinandega, Estelí, and Puerto Somoza. Some units of the Guard had deserted during the day. After the meeting, about 8:00 P.M., Nicaraguan Lt. Col. Alberto Smith called McCoy and then Pezzullo to ask whether U.S. military aid would be coming. Pezzullo encouraged Smith to keep the Guard united, but said they could not expect aid from the United States. Smith then accused Pezzullo of destroying the National Guard. "Weapons were promised," Smith said. "Somoza told us he had an understanding with the United States that they would rush in and help us." Pezzullo asked about the morale in the Guard, and Smith told him the Air Force had already fled and that Tacho III's elite force was breaking up. Pezzullo encouraged Smith to preserve what he could of the Guard and call for a cease-fire.[40]

McCoy was called again by the Guard commanders at 2:30 A.M. "They said that the National Guard commanders had decided it was all over without U.S. support, and they were getting on planes to Honduras and so forth." He had an assistant check, and by 6:00 A.M., July 18, he concluded that the Guard no longer existed and informed Washington.

To dissociate the United States from Urcuyo's actions, the State

Department announced that Pezzullo was leaving with most of his Embassy staff on July 18. Pezzullo described the airport as pure pandemonium. Guard officers and enlisted men tried desperately to get out. Based on Pezzullo's judgment that Urcuyo was responding to Somoza's instructions, Christopher called Somoza in Miami to try to get him to persuade Urcuyo to keep his agreement. Somoza turned on the amplifier on the telephone for everyone to hear. Murphy, who was present, recalled that Christopher began the conversation: " 'You're not welcome here because you haven't lived up to our arrangement.' Somoza said: 'What's the matter?' He [Christopher] said, Urcuyo refuses to leave. Somoza says: 'Tell him to leave. You told me to leave, and I left.' "[41]

But Somoza called Urcuyo anyway and, according to Pallais, said: "Look, Chico, you are in a very difficult situation because they just told me that all the promises of safe haven in this country will be taken away from me and my family. . . . You must do something." Somoza suggested that he resign and transfer power to the military, and Urcuyo agreed.[42] Somoza, fearful the United States might carry out its threat and extradite him, decided to move that same day to the Bahamas.

In the afternoon, Urcuyo asked the Guatemalan President, Lucas, to send a plane to evacuate him and his government. Prior to his departure, Urcuyo tried to transfer power to Mejía, as Somoza had suggested. Two hours later Mejía called back and said: "Mr. President, leave with your presidency because we are not going to share power with these Communists. We are also leaving."[43] Forty-three hours after assuming the Presidency, Urcuyo left.

When the plans for the transition ceremony in Managua fell apart, Costa Rican President Carazo asked the Mexican government to provide a plane to fly several Junta members into León in the early morning of July 18. Having waited and waited for the denouement, Robelo, a member of the Junta, and Alfredo César, the Secretary to the Junta, were startled by the rapidity of events. Both had expected that the Guard would survive through the stand-in-place formula, even though the Directorate had told them the Guard would collapse. Neither had thought about how military power would be organized after Somoza's exit. Bowdler had tried to get them to focus on the need for a "counterweight," but in Robelo's words, "I didn't see it then."[44]

Costa Rica immediately recognized the Junta as the Government of Nicaragua. The next day, the Junta and all the Sandinista leaders arrived in Managua amid much cheering and rejoicing. The Archbishop, Bowdler, and numerous foreign diplomats witnessed their swearing in. At the suggestion of the United States, Costa Rica, Mexico, and the Andean Pact all pledged an active role in Nicaragua, to prevent it from becoming "another Cuba."[45]

At dawn on July 19, soon after Urcuyo's departure, Mejía also left, leaving Lt. Col. Fulgencio Largaespada, the head of the traffic police, to be the last Director of the National Guard and negotiate the surrender with the Sandinistas. In Nicaragua—a nation, but also a metaphor—the man who presided over the final collision between the Guard and the Sandinistas was, appropriately, a traffic cop.

From the U.S. government's perspective, the Somoza dynasty ended in much the same way it had begun. In 1934-36, the United States was displeased by the gradual accretion of power by Anastasio Somoza García, but it decided that stopping Somoza would be costly and would reinvolve the United States in Nicaragua's internal affairs. President Roosevelt was so determined to avoid reinvolvement that the United States did not even raise its voice in protest.

In 1978-79, the United States raised its voice and reduced its aid and support to demonstrate its displeasure with the Somozas, but that was insufficient. To most Nicaraguans and Latin Americans, Anastasio Somoza Debayle was anathema, and if the United States would not overthrow him, then the Sandinistas—with wide support—would, and did. In the fall of 1978, the United States was motivated to deepen its role in the conflict in order to keep the Sandinistas from taking power, but by June 1979, after the Sandinistas had won broad support from the middle in Nicaragua, the Andean countries, and the OAS, the United States judged that the moderate "third force" alternative had evaporated. Both times—in October 1978 and June 1979—President Carter chose to support the Latin American democracies and not intervene.

In 1934-36 and 1978-79, Nicaraguans were certain the United States was in the middle of its politics, but in both periods, that was an illusion. A Nicaraguan—Anastasio Somoza García—took power in 1936 and his son was replaced as a result of a violent revolution in 1979. On both occasions, the United States was a witness to events it did not like.

Part III

RELATING

TO THE REVOLUTION

In that new world which is the old . . .
Alfred, Lord Tennyson, *The Departure*

Chapter 10

CARTER: MUTUAL RESPECT

AND SUSPICION

> If you don't hold me responsible for everything that occurred
> under my predecessors, I will not hold you responsible for
> everything that occurred under your predecessors.
> **Jimmy Carter's advice to the FSLN**[1]

> Avoid the early mistakes we made in Cuba, the political
> rejection by the West, premature frontal attacks on the
> bourgeoisie, economic isolation.
> **Fidel Castro's advice to the FSLN**[2]

SINCE the Sandinista triumph in July 1979, United States policy toward Nicaragua has changed from open and ample support for the revolution to indirect war. At the beginning, the United States government deliberately suspended its suspicions about the Sandinistas; seven years later, the United States wanted to believe and publicize the worst accusations against the Sandinistas. In comparison, Nicaraguan policy toward the United States has undergone no comparable transmutation. In 1979, the Sandinistas were prepared to believe the worst about the United States, and seven years later, their beliefs were confirmed.

Despite the initial mutual suspicions, or rather because of them, both governments sought to construct a nonhostile relationship. Such a relationship was motivated more by fear than respect, but it represented a genuine and reciprocal effort nonetheless.

U.S. policy is not so neatly divided between the Carter and the Reagan Administrations as some might think. There was some continuity, and indeed some irony. Both Administrations sought to moderate and contain the revolution. Neither was very successful. Ironically, the Carter Administration was on the verge of terminating its aid program to Nicaragua when it left office, while its successor entered with a mandate to end aid but did not do so for nearly ten weeks.

Despite a few connecting threads, the differences between the two

Administrations in both the perception of the revolution and the strategy to relate to it dwarfed the similarities. The next four chapters will describe how and why two U.S. Administrations tried to relate to the Nicaraguan revolution and how and why their best efforts were stymied.

The Carter Administration's Lessons

The ghost of Cuba past, which had haunted U.S. policy makers as Somoza was falling, continued to taunt them after the Sandinistas marched into Managua. The question was what lesson should be drawn from the U.S. relationship with revolutionary Cuba that would be useful as the United States approached revolutionary Nicaragua. Some writers concluded from the earlier experience that the United States pushes revolutions to the left and to the Soviet Union by a kind of self-fulfilling prophecy. By calling Castro a Communist and acting as if he were one, according to this argument, the United States eventually contributed to his becoming a Communist and his revolution becoming anti-American.[3]

Others have suggested that Castro deliberately provoked the United States to gain nationalistic support, consolidate and centralize his control, implement a thorough revolution, and justify a closer relationship with the Soviet Union and Cuba.[4]

The principal lesson that the Carter Administration drew from the previous experience was that Castro's slide toward Communism and the Soviet Union was partly the result of confrontation with the United States in 1959 and 1960. The United States had not "pushed" Castro to the left, but the tough response to Castro's decisions to gain control of Cuba's politics and economy had accelerated its revolution and hardened its anti-Yankee posture.[5] With each U.S. reaction to each Cuban provocation, the relationship worsened and the United States moved further from its interests in a moderate, non-Communist regime. Cole Blasier described the essence of the action–reaction cycle that led to the destruction of the U.S.–Cuban relationship: "Almost from the beginning, Castro and the United States expected the worst from each other, and neither was disappointed." Philip Bonsal, who was U.S. Ambassador to Cuba during this period, reflected on the mistakes that the United States had made and concluded that a less hostile response by the United States to Cuban nationalizations might have deprived Castro's revolution of its nationalistic fervor and offered more space for internal criticism.[6]

Different members of the Carter Administration drew different conclusions, but overall, the Administration's policy was premised on this lesson. The Administration tended to believe that hostile policies by the United States had been counterproductive, giving revolutionary regimes the excuse or the reason for radicalization. Having failed to prevent the Sandinistas from coming to power, the Administration wanted to avoid repeating the rest of the Cuban experience in Nicaragua.

The Benefit of the Doubt

On the first full day of the new Nicaraguan government, July 20, the United States government convened a meeting of the SCC to define its policy. Nicaragua, however, was not the only subject of debate. Attention had shifted to the rest of Central America. Having failed to manage political change in Nicaragua, the issue before the SCC was whether to try a different approach toward the other countries. The question was fundamental, and therefore hardly debated by the Administration.

The choice was whether to bolster the military governments in the region or to try to pressure them to open up to the new social and political groups that were demanding important reforms. Henry Kissinger would argue that the "moderate, democratic alternative" that the Carter Administration sought did not exist. Many at the other end of the political spectrum made the same argument, only with the opposite prescription: instead of defending the status quo, the left argued that the United States should ally itself with the forces of the future.[7] The Carter Administration had, of course, made its choice: it was both philosophically and temperamentally incapable of supporting either military dictators or leftist guerrillas. Carter himself sketched the outlines of the policy at a Friday morning breakfast before the SCC meeting.

Brzezinski opened the meeting on July 20 by elaborating on Carter's outline. He said that a historic change had occurred in Central America. The United States could not and did not want to support a mindless bolstering of the status quo. The Carter Administration would continue to support moderate change as the only alternative to violent revolution. No one disagreed, and the discussion shifted to Nicaragua.

Once the Sandinistas entered Managua, the Administration unified in its prescription for U.S. policy. No one argued for either dissociation or hostility toward the new regime. People had questions and doubts, but few had illusions about the Sandinista Directorate's preferences for Cuba and Marxism, and its visceral hatred of the United States. Still, the governing coalition was broad, and even within the Directorate, there were likely to be some important differences, say, between a Tomás Borge, who had been a member of the Communist Party, and the rest of the leadership, which was young, much less educated, and unlikely to have his deep doctrinal convictions. Some Sandinistas might be social democrats; others might only be superficial leftists or Marxists without being Leninists. The question was who would prevail, and whether ideology could be moderated by a tolerant U.S. policy.

These issues were not debated at any length because no one saw any other viable option other than to seek a good relationship with the new government. Having decided against intervention before the Sandinistas marched into Managua, the Carter Administration naturally viewed intervention afterward as out of the question, particularly given the warmth with which the revolution was greeted among its democratic neighbors.

Some thought that perhaps the United States could turn the self-fulfilling prophecy to its advantage. Whether the Sandinistas were Communists or not, perhaps it would be better to treat them like democrats, and maybe the Sandinistas—or rather some of the key leaders—might even begin to behave like democrats. As they dealt with the hard realities of governing and trying to meet the needs of their people, the new Nicaraguan leadership might come to realize that the United States and the Nicaraguan private sector had more to offer than Cuba or ideology. This thesis was first proposed by a Venezuelan leader, who suggested that instead of trying to lift the "mask of democracy" from the faces of the Sandinistas to show they were really Communists, it would be better to try to take the mask seriously—at face value, so to speak—and by doing so, try to graft the mask to their faces.

Because of the consensus on goals and tactics, the SCC discussion of Nicaragua concluded rapidly and with no important disagreements. U.S. objectives were:

(1) *internal*: to assist the revolution to fulfill its stated promises of political pluralism, elections, and a vigorous private sector, and conversely, to reduce the chances that the revolution would become Communist;

(2) *strategic*: to deny the Sandinistas an enemy and thus a reason for relying on Cuban and Soviet military assistance; and

(3) *regional*: to make clear that a good relationship with the United States was contingent on Nicaraguan non-interference in the internal affairs of its neighbors.

To achieve these objectives, the United States would: (1) rapidly seek to establish good relations with the regime; (2) provide emergency food and relief supplies and develop a long-term aid program; (3) work with friendly democratic governments in the area and Europe to encourage them to be helpful as well; and (4) find ways to help the moderates in and outside the government, who were more likely to favor a democratic Nicaragua. The political premise underlying this strategy was that the majority of the national coalition that was taking power in Nicaragua was interested in democracy and was not hostile to the United States, and that a strategy of patience, assistance, and restraint was more likely to produce a friendly, non-Communist regime than a strategy that ignored, threatened, or attacked the new government. In fact, the converse more nearly reflected U.S. policy: the Administration believed that a Communist regime was more likely to emerge if the United States adopted a confrontational approach.

The United States decided to play for the long term. To implement the policy, Carter, like Eisenhower twenty years before with Castro's new government, sent as his representatives people who were liberal, active, and potentially sympathetic. Lawrence Pezzullo, who had deliberately not presented his credentials to Somoza, became the Ambassador to the new government, and Lawrence Harrison, who had more than twenty years experience in Latin America and the Caribbean, was made the AID mission director. The new government passed the United States a note on July 23, 1979, indicating that it wished to uphold its international agreements and continue good relations with the United States. The United States confirmed the request and affirmed its interest in good relations.

As the Junta paraded through Managua, it felt the euphoria of a people both relieved to have removed the Somoza dynasty and excited with the prospect of creating a "new Nicaragua." The Junta would need all the nation's exuberance and unity to cope with the formidable task of reconstruction. Managua had not recovered from the earthquake of 1972 when it was wracked by insurrection in 1978 and 1979. Using his Air Force to try to regain control of the country, Somoza had leveled many towns. As many as 500,000 people—about one-fifth of the nation—had become refugees.

Two studies by the United Nations and the Inter-American Human Rights Commission estimated that during the war against Somoza as many as 45,000 people had been killed (80 percent civilians), up to 160,000 were wounded, and 40,000 orphaned. About one million Nicaraguans were in dire need of food, and 250,000 of shelter. To pay for the war, Somoza had increased his country's debt to $1.5 billion—most of it in short-term loans and at high interest rates—and had looted the Central Bank. Economic losses due to the war were estimated at $2 billion.[8]

President Carter approved a generous relief package. In less than two weeks, the United States sent 732 metric tons of food by air and another 1,000 tons by ship. It purchased 9,600 pounds of medical supplies and funded other international relief efforts as well. Carter sought a symbol to demonstrate his sincerity and considered sending his son Chip on a special flight. Instead, on July 28, Ambassador Pezzullo returned to Managua with a message that the "President is sending this special plane [Air Force One] as an expression of his personal good will to the people of Nicaragua and to the new government."[9]

Though the Administration was united in its approach to Nicaragua, there was no consensus in the country. During a press conference on July 25, Carter therefore welcomed the chance to respond to the conservative critique that Nicaragua was a victory for Cuba and a loss for the United States:

> It's a mistake for Americans to assume or to claim that every time an evolutionary change takes place or even an abrupt change takes place in this hemisphere, that somehow it's a result of secret, massive Cuban intervention. The fact in Nicaragua is that the incumbent Government, the Somoza regime, lost the confidence of the Nicaraguan people. There was a broad range of forces assembled to replace Somoza and his regime. . . .
> We worked as closely as we could without intervening in the internal affairs of Nicaragua with the neighboring countries and the so-called Andean Group. . . .
> We have a good relationship with the new government. We hope to improve it. I do not attribute all the change in Nicaragua to Cuba. I think the people of Nicaragua have got enough judgment to make their own decisions, and we will use our efforts in a proper fashion without interventionism to let the Nicaraguans let their voice be heard in shaping their own affairs.[10]

With the policy toward Nicaragua established, and the problems of the rest of Central America worsening, the Latin Americanists turned to the rest of the region. Because of the Administration's confidence in its new Ambassador and his AID mission director, the details of Nicaragua policy were left to them. The Embassy was encouraged to continue doing what it had been instructed to do during the Somoza regime—seek out moderate and independent elements and encourage and assist them to play an active role in defining the structures and policies of the new regime.

One of those independent leaders was Edén Pastora. U.S. officials had met with Pastora as the insurrection was reaching a climax in late June and again after Somoza left. They listened to him and informed him that the United States was prepared to support social democracy in Nicaragua, if that was his objective. He listened, but nothing in his previous experience led him to trust or even believe the United States. Senior Panamanian and Venezuelan officials also approached Pastora and urged him to keep his supporters together with the arms they had used or captured. He was "euphoric" at the time, and in his words, "didn't pay attention" to such advice. Later, he would acknowledge that "it was a mistake."[11] Pastora was excluded from the Directorate, but he remained the most well known and attractive of the Sandinista leaders. Moreover, he also led the bulk of the Sandinista Army—over 2,000 soldiers on the date of the Junta's arrival in Managua out of a total of about 5,000 Sandinista soldiers.[12]

The Distribution and Purposes of Power

On July 20, 1979, a coalition representing the complete spectrum of non-Somocista political and economic groups took power in Nicaragua. There were many predictions about who or which group would prevail, but these predictions were founded less on analysis than on fears or hopes. American conservatives saw the Sandinistas as committed Marxist-Leninists who served the Soviet Union. On the other hand, several well-known Marxists visited Nicaragua in the months after the revolution and returned distressed that the more pragmatic elements of the Sandinistas appeared to have mortgaged the future of the revolution to cope with the immediate needs of the people.[13]

At the time, no one knew how deep the divisions were between the three factions of the Sandinistas. Their unification appeared "tactical," much like their alliance with the bourgeoisie. Nor was it clear who would control the military, because Pastora had the most cadre. Technically, the five-member Junta headed the Government of National Reconstruction. Two were moderates; two, Sandinistas; and the alignment of the fifth, Sergio Ramírez, was unclear. A poet who had lived and worked in Costa Rica and Europe, Ramírez had been the Group of Twelve's representative on the mediation, before resigning on October 25. Many viewed him as a moderate social democrat. According to the "Plan of Government" of June 18, 1979, that Robelo had written, the Junta would function as the executive branch of the new government and would share legislative functions with the Council of State, which would be created later with representatives of 33 organizations. The FSLN would only control 12 of 33 seats.[14] The 18-member Cabinet included Bernardino Larios, the former Guardsman, now Minister of Defense, and a number of other moderates, particularly in the economic ministries.

Like most everyone in Nicaragua, the members of the Junta celebrated, and paid little attention to how power was being divided. According to Alfonso Robelo, it took several months before he realized that "someone in olive green," a representative of the 9-member Directorate (the Comandantes), was present at every Junta meeting. Before any important decision, the Junta heard from the Comandantes, and their views always seemed to prevail.[15]

On July 20, the day the U.S. National Security Council was meeting to decide on a new approach to Nicaragua, the Directorate was meeting in the bunker that Somoza had used as his war room. The Directorate had fought with guns so long that it was quite natural that they—alone of all the Nicaraguans—considered first how to organize military power in Nicaragua to ensure that they could make the last, if not the first decisions. The Guard had disintegrated, and one issue they discussed was the manner in which Guardsmen should be arrested and treated. The views of the United States and friendly governments in the region reinforced those who wanted to be fair with those members of the Guard who would not pose a threat to the revolution.

The main issue, however, was how the Directorate could take power from Edén Pastora. Some argued for an open fight; others, opposed that, insisting that unity was imperative. At that moment, Pastora burst through the door. Part of him noticed that the noise in the room he had heard outside a moment before had ceased as he entered. It was the kind of incriminating, embarrassing silence that suggested he was the subject of the discussion. Another part of Pastora, spontaneous and flushed with the joy of victory, prevailed, and he greeted the others with abrazos. Then, without knowing the question the Directorate had been debating, Pastora turned to Humberto Ortega, the Commander of the Sandinista Army, and answered it, probably to their disbelief, most assuredly to their satisfaction. He told them that he had brought his entire 2,000-man army to the outskirts of the city of Managua and left them there because he did not know where to put them. "What do I do with these people? Whom do

I turn them over to? Where do I take them? Do I disarm them? What do I do?"[16]

Pastora was told that the Directorate would be sending people to take command of his force, and they asked him to be the Vice Minister of Interior. He accepted, even while recognizing that he would be junior to his old rival, Tomás Borge. With Cuban advisers, the Directorate focused its efforts at organizing the army, establishing the police and internal security, and organizing "popular," mass organizations, including the Sandinista Defense Committees, which were based on the Cuban block Committees for the Defense of the Revolution. The Directorate postponed the establishment of the Council of State until the new mass organizations were established and could be represented.

In the beginning, of course, there was considerable chaos in Managua. The "muchachos," the boys who did most of the fighting and dying during the insurrection, still had guns and felt powerful; but they were young and unemployed. The FSLN had important positions, but as Borge put it, they "didn't even have offices."[17] On July 28, the members of the Directorate held a press conference at their newly established military barracks in Managua. Their purpose was, as the first speaker put it, "to make one thing clear. . . The only official spokesman for the Sandinista Front are the members of the National Directorate." Then, Borge introduced himself as "organizing the national police force [and] . . . the state security organizations," and Humberto Ortega said that he was "organizing our Popular Sandinista Army."[18] Larios, the moderate Defense Minister, was not present.

The moderates in the Nicaraguan government had learned from Somoza the need for an apolitical armed force; the FSLN had learned the opposite lesson. In Borge's view, there was no such thing as neutral education or an apolitical army; education and the armed forces either served the revolution (government) or they undermined it.

By September 21, 1979, the Directorate had consolidated its power and organized a three-day conference with the cadre of the Sandinista Party to review how they took power, how they would keep it, and what they would do with it. At the end of their meetings, the Directorate wrote a summary of conclusions—the 72-Hour Document— and then circulated it widely in order to permit all "militants, both within the country and abroad" to understand the "political guidelines" of the revolution.[19] It confirmed the main interpretations of the Carter Administration.

The Directorate identified four enemies of the revolution: the "traitorous bourgeoisie, vestiges of Somocismo, the ultra-left sectors, and American imperialism, the rabid enemy of all peoples who are struggling to achieve their definitive liberation." The Directorate had designed the government as "a special class alliance . . . to neutralize Yankee intervention." The Marxist jargon is thick, but if one focuses on substance, the document reveals a realistic leadership that understood that its success stemmed from "political pragmatism." "We should avoid unnecessary theoretical arguments," the Directorate warned, because the "most serious internal danger" is factionalism. Unity is key. Their principal objective: "develop bold social plans in the fields of education, health, and housing in order to bring the revolution to the masses. Give priority to the peasant population, particularly on the northern border and the Atlantic coast." This represented a joining of their idealism (social programs), their constituency (peasants), and the two strategic regions where they expected U.S. intervention to occur.

Because of the power of U.S. imperialism, they recommended "an instinctively defensive posture." Their revolution should spread by example rather than by being exported. They should be "conservative" domestically and internationally.

From the beginning, there was a debate among the moderates and within the FSLN about whether the latter's commitment to political pluralism, a mixed economy, and nonalignment was genuine or merely "tactical"—whether the Sandinistas would implement these objectives or postpone them indefinitely.[20] Although some Sandinistas wanted a "socialist revolution" immediately, the 72-Hour Document accepted that the country was not ready for it, and it implied that a more cautious strategy prevailed. As the moderate groups deepened their understanding of the Sandinistas, they began to accept the Carter strategy—that the most likely way to transform "tactical" decisions into permanent ones was to prove to the FSLN that friendship with the local middle class and foreign democracies was so beneficial that it would be too costly to sever such ties.

Although the ideological rhetoric was thick, the document and the policies that emerged from the government suggested a genuine and continuing commitment to the revolution's three objectives—pluralism, a mixed economy, and nonalignment—albeit with reservations. While the FSLN concentrated on the military, internal security, and its mass organizations, there was ample space in the Nicaraguan political scene for groups and organizations that were independent of the Frente. The new government issued a comprehensive bill of rights, ended the death penalty, lifted press and broadcast censorship, and took great care that the National Guardsmen arrested after the victory would be treated with due process.[21]

Somoza's National Guard had burned the offices of *La Prensa* as an act of vengeance in the closing days of the revolution. Soon after the triumph, the newspaper's owners quickly reestablished its voice, and it did not suffer serious censorship until after the declaration of the state of emergency in March 1982. COSEP, the business association, played an important role articulating the private sector's interests and concerns. The Sandinista leadership repeatedly approached COSEP to negotiate a wide range of issues. Finally, the independent labor unions that had struggled with the Somoza dynasty found room to organize and grow in the aftermath of the revolution even though they would soon face stiff and unfair competition from Sandinista-sponsored unions.

In time, the FSLN would try to bring each independent group under its umbrella, much as the Mexican ruling party had done. If a group resisted, the Frente would test its mettle with a combination of inducements and harassment, but if the group—including the Church—still resisted, the FSLN often retreated.

In terms of foreign policy, the new government immediately joined the non-aligned movement and established close relations with Cuba. Relations with the Soviet Union were established later, and a Soviet Ambassador only arrived in early 1980. On the UN votes to condemn the Soviet invasion of Afghanistan, Nicaragua abstained, while Cuba and Grenada supported the Soviet Union. Nicaragua also devoted considerable efforts to cultivating relations with its Latin American neighbors and with Western European governments.

Economically, the government brought Nicaragua into the modern era, albeit by Central American standards. It initiated a number of health and welfare services for the poor in the rural and urban areas and announced a national literacy program. Like its neighbor Costa Rica, Nicaragua nationalized the banking industry, trade in agricultural products, and mineral companies. As promised in its program, the revolutionary government also nationalized all of Somoza's properties. As a result, the public share of Nicaragua's gross domestic product increased from 15 percent in 1978 to 41 percent in 1980.[22]

Although some of the government's early decisions seemed directed to reassuring the middle class in Nicaragua and democratic governments abroad, there remained a deep residue of suspicion among all parties. The Sandinistas did try to negotiate differences with business and the Church, but their rhetoric emphasizing the class struggle impugned those efforts and reinforced suspicions. In October 1980, Borge explained the essence of the problem, without appearing to be aware of why he was a part of it. Regretting that "we have a backward capitalist class" in Nicaragua, he proceeded to divide the country into the masses, who were insecure before the revolution but were now secure, and the "social groups that ruled the country":

> Those who before caused insecurity to the big majority of the population now feel insecure themselves—even though this revolution has been extremely flexible and has given everyone an opportunity. They feel insecure even though we have seriously proposed—and this is not just a tactical or short-term thing—that we maintain a mixed economy and political pluralism. We mean it when we talk about political pluralism and a mixed economy.
>
> But what happens is that a thief thinks everyone else is like him. And these people think we are tricking them, when in fact we are going to great pains to show them that we are not lying, that in fact they are the ones who historically have been the liars. They can't concede the possibility that there might be people who aren't liars, and therefore they feel nervous. Obviously, this is a vicious circle, because this insecurity causes them to decapitalize their businesses. But when they do that . . . the revolutionary government becomes concerned."[23]

Borge was incapable of understanding how people on the other end of his class rhetoric—the "liars" and "thieves"—would interpret his remarks. Some were prepared to discount it and try to solve problems one at a time. Others believed that a relationship with Marxists was not possible.

Relating to the United States

Deciding on a policy toward the United States could not have been easy. The Sandinistas, including Pastora, had felt that they had been fighting the United States for as long as they had been fighting Somoza. They knew, and expected, the Carter Administration to try to prevent them from coming to power, and indeed, were surprised that they succeeded. Their ideology was publicly anti-imperialist when it wasn't more candidly anti-American. Tomás Borge asked a composer to write an FSLN anthem to be sung with the Nicaraguan national anthem. Borge told me that he asked that a phrase, "Yankees—enemy of humanity," be included to remind Nicaragua's youth of the danger from the north.[24]

The Sandinistas reciprocated the suspicions that U.S. policy makers had of them, but their mistrust was related to the asymmetry in power: the Sandinistas had to be much more suspicious because the capacity of the United States to undermine their revolution was infinitely greater than their capacity to affect U.S. interests. Moreover, a chasm of differences in personal experiences separated the two sets of leaders. North Americans engaged in the bureaucratic intrigue of leaking memoranda; Sandinista intrigues were literally matters of life and death. With a median age in the mid-50s and a global perspective in which Nicaragua was of marginal importance, U.S. decision makers could rationally step back and decide not to call the Sandinistas "Communists" for fear they could become them if they weren't already.

One could not expect a comparable detachment from the Directorate, whose median age was about 30 and whose principal experience was fighting the National Guard. To survive in such a world, one had to develop an acute sense of paranoia and trust only a very few people or none at all. In a democratic system, the people who rise to the top generally have the most friends; the Sandinistas, who lived to govern, rose because they treated the world as their enemies. Compromise, essential to a democratic system, was alien to the guerrilla. Given their temperament and experience and the emotions of the moment, it is hardly surprising that few of the Sandinistas could restrain themselves from repeated references to the United States as an imperialistic enemy of humanity. Just as Borge was unaware how his comments that all businessmen were "thieves" might affect their views of him, the Sandinistas appeared unaware or disinterested that their charges of U.S. imperialism evoked resentment and confirmed suspicions in the United States.

Without knowing the specifics of the Directorate's debate, one can imagine that there might have been three views on what to do about the United States. The practical view argued that U.S. aid and friendship were essential to Nicaragua's development. The more cynical, or perhaps realistic, view would be that the United States would use its aid to strengthen the bourgeoisie and try to divide the left; it would be safer to insist on an arm's length approach and not accept aid. A third view would insist that the FSLN have no illusions about U.S. imperialism, but that the Sandinistas were intelligent enough to know how to use the aid to serve their purposes rather than the Americans.' It would appear that the third view prevailed.

How did the Sandinistas justify to themselves the aid they received from the enemy? Undoubtedly, a few sniggered at the ingenuousness of the colossus, confirming their belief that the "correlation of forces" was indeed changing. Perhaps others felt that the United

States needed to give aid to atone for its guilt in supporting Somoza. A few others postured defiantly against U.S. imperialism even while they accepted aid. For example, on August 5, the Junta complained to the press that U.S. aid was inadequate, even though it then exceeded that of all other countries.

In the same spirit, high officials from both the United States and Nicaragua met on August 10, 1979—the occasion being the inauguration of the new Ecuadorean President, Jaime Roldos. Attending the meeting were Rosalynn Carter, Secretary of State Cyrus Vance, Pete Vaky, and I on the U.S. side, with Edén Pastora, Violeta de Chamorro, and Miguel D'Escoto representing Nicaragua. Pastora warned that Nicaragua would turn to the "Socialist bloc" for weapons if the United States did not provide them. When asked why Nicaragua needed more arms if it had enough for two armies, Pastora admitted: "We have enough arms to equip the Sandinista Army from the Israeli Ghalils and American M-16s captured from the National Guard, but these weapons represent the suppression of the Nicaraguan people, and we would like to exchange them for other arms." I then queried why he thought another shipment of M-16s would be different from those. The discussion drifted inconclusively. To ensure that his colleagues knew of his resolute defense of Nicaragua, D'Escoto, in a condescending style that mimicked the way some Nicaraguans felt they had been treated by the Yankees, informed the *New York Times* what "he" had told Vance:

> The Nicaraguans are fully aware of the role the United States has played in Nicaragua and that the resentment against the American government is very deep. I [D'Escoto] told him [Vance] the United States should keep a low profile when making suggestions to us, and he said he understood. At no point did he try to contradict me, and he was very correct.[25]

Some photographers had learned of the meeting, and as the group assembled for a picture, Pastora whispered impishly to Vance: "I wonder who will be hurt more because of this picture?" Vance laughed, and judged that he would.

He was wrong. The next day in Managua, Borge held a press conference to criticize his subordinate for speaking out of turn. Borge said that Nicaragua would not buy arms from Communist nations because it did not want to leave the impression that it was aligning with Communism.[26] Borge enjoyed confounding the public perception of him as the "hard-line Communist" and Pastora as the independent. At the same time, he could not resist the opportunity to embarrass Pastora.

Whether wittingly or not, Borge's contradiction of Pastora did the Carter Administration a favor. A request by Nicaragua for military aid raised questions that the Administration preferred to avoid. One does not want to arm a potentially unfriendly nation, nor does one want to offer it an excuse to request aid from the Soviet Union or Cuba. Nonetheless, the issue did not go away, and the United States resolved the dilemma by offering "nonlethal" military equipment—trucks, medical supplies, communications equipment—and military training.

When Torrijos informed the U.S. Ambassador to Panama that he was sending several of his officers to advise the Sandinistas on the organization of a police force, the United States encouraged him, particularly because the United States was prohibited by law from helping foreign police forces. Torrijos said he wanted to "try to beat Fidel at his own game of conspiracy" and give the Sandinistas an alternative to Cuba. He told one senior U.S. military officer: "The coloration of the new government will be neither Castro nor Iran. It would change colors depending on who's looking." But he also said that he thought it would be "moderate," a word he had learned had great significance to North Americans.[27] By the time the Panamanian officers arrived in Managua, hundreds of Cubans were already advising the Nicaraguans. Torrijos began to suspect that he was more interested in alternatives than the Sandinistas were. Instead of training the police, the Panamanians were assigned the demeaning task of training Nicaragua's traffic police.[28] Just as he seemed to buy stock in the Sandinistas before others in the region, Torrijos appeared to be among the earliest to become "disillusioned" with them.[29]

The United States decided to offer military advice and aid to the Sandinistas for much the same reasons as Torrijos: to offer an alternative, to begin to build military relationships with the Sandinistas, and to learn more about their officers and their organization. Three U.S. military officers stationed in Panama were sent to Nicaragua to discuss military training with the Sandinistas. This, in turn, posed a difficult question for the Sandinistas, and the slowness and the ambiguity of their reply suggests that Borge's comment in August may have had an additional purpose other than to embarrass Pastora. Borge did not want a military relationship with the United States for all the reasons that the United States wanted one. In the end, the Directorate never formally requested or formally rejected military aid and training from the United States, which for similar reasons was neither generous nor negative. However, the FSLN restricted access by the U.S. Defense Attaché in much the same ways that Somoza had.[30]

On August 1, 1979, before Pastora's conversation with Vance, Venezuela privately put the Sandinistas to the test. Foreign Minister José Alberto Zambrano and General José Antonio Olavarría, Deputy Director of his country's National Security Council, visited Managua and met first with the Minister of Defense, Bernardino Larios. The Venezuelans offered military aid and advice, and Larios accepted it enthusiastically. However, Larios suggested they also speak with Humberto Ortega, the Chief of Staff of the Armed Forces. Ortega was just as clear as Larios, except that he rejected the aid, saying that they had already received enough arms from Cuba. The Venezuelans were stunned, but chose not to publicize the response or to inform the United States.[31]

The Sandinistas preferred the United States to help rebuild the economy. To discuss this issue as well as the overall relationship, three members of the Junta and the Foreign Minister requested a meeting with President Carter in advance of a speech that Daniel Ortega would be delivering to the United Nations. The Administration recognized the political delicacy of such a meeting, and also its parallel with the visit of Fidel Castro in April 1959, when President Eisenhower did not meet with him. Commentators asked later whether such a meeting could have prevented the subsequent confrontation between the United States and Cuba.

On September 24, 1979, Daniel Ortega, Sergio Ramírez, and Alfonso Robelo from the Junta and Foreign Minister Miguel D'Escoto were escorted into the Cabinet Room of the White House, where they met with Carter, Mondale, Christopher, Vaky, Pezzullo, Henry Owen, and me. Carter welcomed them and reiterated his desire for friendship. Then Carter emphasized the importance he attached to three U.S. concerns: nonintervention by Nicaragua in the affairs of its neighbors, a truly nonaligned status, and human rights and democracy. The United States planned to aid and support Nicaragua, but Carter wanted to make sure that Nicaragua understood that these items "do concern us."

Ortega was equally direct, though considerably less diplomatic: "We are interested in obtaining frank and unconditional support from the United States. We know you can provide a lot." Responding to Carter's principal concern about Central America, Ortega insisted that Nicaragua's principal task was reconstruction. "Nicaragua is not a factor in the radicalization of El Salvador—now, in the past, and it will not be in the future. Nor in Guatemala." Although clearly an overstatement, Ortega's comment reflected the Sandinistas' decision at that time not to aid their Salvadoran and Guatemalan comrades.

The Somoza Dynasty: from left, Anastasio Somoza, Jr., his mother, Anastasio Somoza, Sr., and Luis Somoza in 1956. AP/Wide World Photos

"BY GOLLY, YOU'RE RIGHT, MR. SOMOZA—COMMUNISTS EVERYWHERE! I HOPE YOU GOT 'EM ALL"

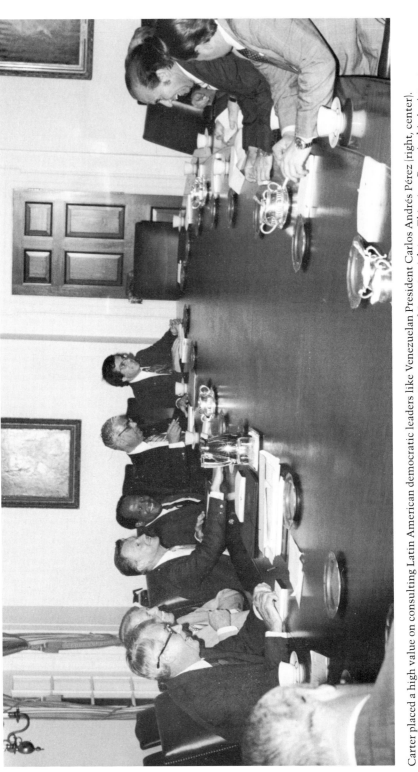

Carter placed a high value on consulting Latin American democratic leaders like Venezuelan President Carlos Andrés Pérez (right, center). Participants on the U.S. side were (from left) Secretary of State Cyrus Vance, Carter, National Security Adviser Zbigniew Brzezinski, Assistant Secretary of State Terence Todman, then U.S. Ambassador to Venezuela Viron Peter Vaky, and the author. White House photo

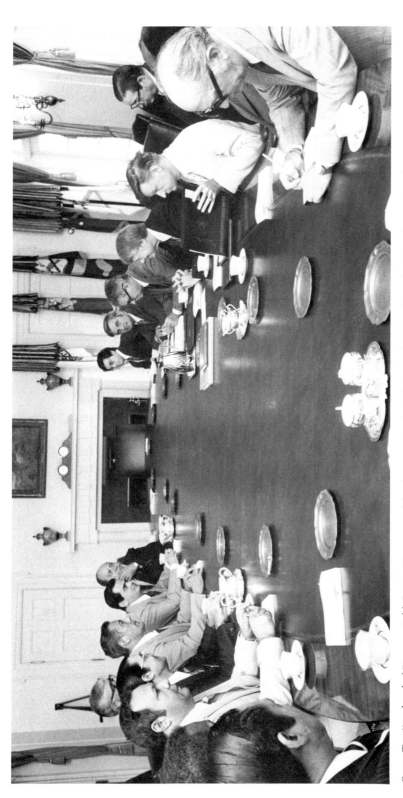

Omar Torrijos, head of Panama, told Carter: "Somoza is like the screw in a DC-10. The trick is to keep the plane flying after the screw comes out." Participants in this meeting on the U.S. side were (from top) the author; Vice President Walter Mondale, Vance, Carter, Brzezinski, Todman, and U.S. Ambassador to Panama William Jorden. On the Panamanian side, Panama's Ambassador to the U.S. Gabriel Lewis is at the top; Torrijos is third from the top. White House photo

Carter's meeting with William Bowdler, U.S. representative to the OAS mediation, on November 15, 1978. White House photo

In August 1979, Rosalynn Carter and Cyrus Vance met with the new Nicaraguan leaders at the inauguration of Ecuador's President. From left, Miguel D'Escoto, Mrs. Carter, Violeta de Chamorro, Vance, Edén Pastora, and Christina Chamorro. At far right is U.S. Ambassador Raymond E. Gonzalez. After the meeting, Pastora impishly asked Vance which of them would be hurt more by the photograph.

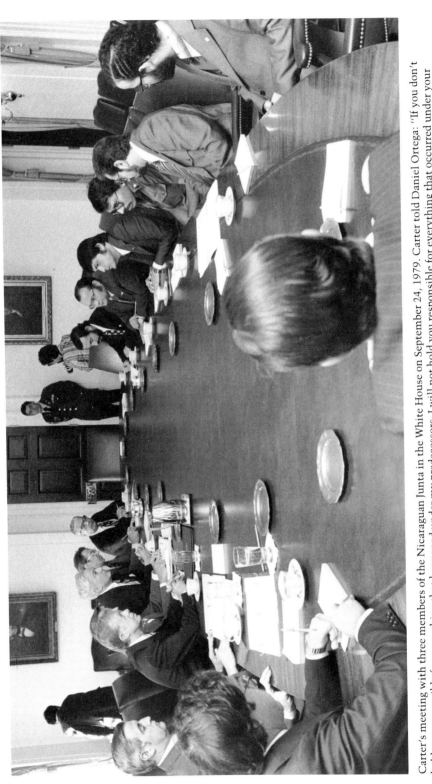

Carter's meeting with three members of the Nicaraguan Junta in the White House on September 24, 1979. Carter told Daniel Ortega: "If you don't hold me responsible for everything that happened under my predecessors, I will not hold you responsible for everything that occurred under your predecessors." On the U.S. side, from top: Vaky, U.S. Ambassador to Nicaragua Lawrence Pezzullo, Henry Owen of the NSC, Brzezinski, Carter, Mondale, and the author. On the Nicaraguan side, from the top: Embassy staff member; Foreign Minister Miguel D'Escoto; Sergio Ramírez, Daniel Ortega, and Alfonso Robelo of the Junta; and Rafael Solís, Nicaragua's Ambassador to the U.S. White House photo

Bill Mauldin

"Omnipotence was fun."

By permission of Bill Mauldin and Wil-Jo Associates, Inc.

Ronald Reagan, giving a speech on the need to support the Nicaraguan Resistance. White House photo, Pete Souza

Reagan meets with the civilian leaders of the Nicaraguan Resistance, April 4, 1985: contras Alfonso Robelo, Arturo Cruz, and Adolfo Calero. All three had opposed Somoza, and the first two had held important positions in the Sandinista government. White House photo, Pete Souza

Carter concluded by referring to the anti-American statements that Ortega and other leaders had made, and said that good relations are difficult to establish in the light of such statements. With his tongue in cheek, Carter said: "If you don't hold me responsible for everything that occurred under my predecessors, I will not hold you responsible for everything that occurred under your predecessors." There were smiles around the table, and Ortega mentioned to Carter as he was leaving that "we will not link you with the past."

Carter then excused himself but asked the other U.S. participants to remain and discuss in greater detail with the Nicaraguans their economic needs and U.S. concerns. Christopher explained, to Ortega's apparent surprise, Carter's goal to reduce the budget deficit and its implications for aid to Nicaragua. Nonetheless, through reprogramming, the United States had already provided $8 million of disaster aid and had approved another $39 million for projects. The Nicaraguans said that their priority was to reschedule their debt, and asked the United States to pressure the banks. Owen responded that the best first step toward obtaining bank compliance was to reach agreement with the International Monetary Fund. Significantly, there was no discussion of military aid.

Christopher explained that the concern the Administration felt about human rights in Nicaragua under Somoza would remain as important under the new government. Ramírez said that a similar motive propelled the revolution, and the new government was determined to make human rights a reality in Nicaragua. Ortega complained of former Somocistas, who were organizing with "agents of the CIA" to attack the country. He mentioned "Comandante Bravo," Somoza's most famous colonel, who had fought Pastora to a standstill in the south. Christopher assured him that the United States opposed any such efforts and that the CIA was not involved.

Four days after his meeting with Carter, on September 28, 1979, Daniel Ortega addressed the UN General Assembly and asked the international community to assume the Nicaraguan debt. (He later withdrew this proposal.) He then announced that Nicaragua was still "a target for imperialist policy. The most aggressive circles of the United States and of Central America dream of restoring Somozaism to our country. A macabre alliance . . . is trying to develop the idea that Sandinoism is a threat to the government of El Salvador." The speech sounded as if the meeting with Carter had little if any impact on Ortega, but *Barricada*, the Sandinista newspaper, reported the next day that Ortega had denounced CIA maneuvers in Central America, though he had not. Possibly, that deletion was a concession to the meeting.

The American People Debate Nicaragua

When the Sandinistas requested aid from the United States, they were most probably unaware of George Washington's warning that "it is folly in one nation to look for disinterested favors from another; ... it must pay with a portion of its independence for whatever it may accept." The price paid to the Soviet bloc for aid is large, but privately contracted; the United States generally demands less and gives more, but its demands are public and thus more embarrassing to a recipient acutely sensitive to infringements on its sense of dignity.

The need to obtain Congressional approval for new aid to Nicaragua opened a national debate in the United States. Though the aid might have brought the two governments together, the debate inevitably separated them. The Sandinistas had not yet even adjusted to the State Department, whose modus operandi was private diplomacy, when it found itself the subject of Congress's abrasive scrutiny. For their blasts at U.S. imperialism, the Sandinistas received from Congress the American equivalent of rhetorical retaliation.

On September 11, 1979, after a month of interagency reviews on Central America, Assistant Secretary of State Vaky and Ambassador Pezzullo presented the Administration's policy on Nicaragua and Central America before the House Subcommittee on Inter-American Affairs. Their main purpose was to begin building support for future requests for aid to Nicaragua. Vaky's approach was frank and direct. He stressed the importance of the economic dimension in shaping the future course of the Nicaraguan revolution:

> While it is true that Marxist elements are well-positioned to exert power, they do not yet dominate the situation. Moderate democratic elements capable of exerting influence and power of their own also exist in key places in the Government and in society. . . . Nicaragua's future internal policies and relationships with the outside world will, in fact, be determined by those Nicaraguans who best define and meet the country's needs during the reconstruction period. . . . The course of the Nicaraguan revolution can thus be affected in no small way by how the United States perceives it and relates to it.[32]

He and Pezzullo encountered some stiff questions from friends as well as foes of the Administration. Democratic Chairman Gus Yatron asked whether the Sandinistas were "Marxist ideologues." Pezzullo responded that there were many "who have been weaned on Marxist philosophy," but "the practicality of running a government with economic difficulties of monumental proportions forces them to be pragmatic." Rep. Dante Fascell sought explanations for the Sandinistas' anti-American statements, their treatment of the press, and the arms they were receiving from the Soviet Union. Fascell, however, conceded that the only sensible policy was to compete with the Soviets by providing aid.[33]

As soon as AID's program was ready in November, President Carter sent it to Congress, requesting $80 million as a supplemental in Economic Support Funds for Central America and the Caribbean. The message announced that the region was in a "crisis" and U.S. national interests required a quick response. But althugh the region was in crisis, the Administration's budget limitations and its perception that the threat was not immediate resulted in a relatively meager request. Moreover, almost all of the money was requested for one country—Nicaragua—and of that, $70 million would be a loan (60 percent of that to the private sector) and $5 million a grant for private organizations working in the country.[34]

The debate on aid to Nicaragua tested the patience and tolerance of an American people who had grown impatient. The issue was whether the United States should help a group of young revolutionaries who, at best, disliked the United States, and were very fond of Cuba. The Administration, of course, did not frame the issue that way, nor did the Sandinistas see the issue in those terms. The Administration's basic argument was summarized by Clement Zablocki, then Chairman of the House Foreign Affairs Committee: "I cannot give my colleagues any assurances that if we approve this assistance that Nicaragua will not fall within the Marxist orbit. But . . . if we do not, we will be abandoning the field to Castro and his Soviet bosses—with adverse consequences for our own national security."[35]

That argument and Administration muscle ultimately carried the bill through an extremely grueling debate. Conservative Republican Rep. Robert Bauman insisted that Nicaragua was already lost, and the United States was foolish to give money to Communists. Rep. Edward J. Derwinski, who would join the Reagan Administration as Counselor to the State Department, opposed the bill because of the "major presence of Cubans and to a lesser degree, East Germans in Nicaragua."[36]

Rep. Lee Hamilton, a supporter of the aid, was aware of the Sandinistas' "hyperbolic, bombastic condemnation of 'Yankee intervention,' [and found it] very disturbing. It has not been explained to my satisfaction. Moreover, if it is taken seriously, then it must be seen as inconsistent with the claim that Nicaragua desires cordial relations with the United States." Still, Hamilton noted a recent article in *La*

Prensa headlined "U.S. Had Helped More Than During the Earth-quake." He argued that as long as *La Prensa* was free to publish such articles, the United States would be making a serious mistake to abandon the revolution.[37]

On February 25, 1980, the House held its third secret session in history in order to examine classified data on Soviet-bloc involvement in Nicaragua. At its close, Rep. Jim Wright concluded that the information did not convince him Nicaragua was Communist-controlled. Congress then passed the aid, but only after adding numerous amendments, requiring the President to take into account the Sandinistas' commitment to human rights, labor union rights, free press, and much else. Most important, before disbursing the aid, the President would have to submit a certification to Congress that Nicaragua was not supporting insurgents abroad.

Though the Senate passed the bill in January and the House in February, a delaying maneuver impeded final passage of the authorization act until May 19, 1980. Several private groups, including the Council of the Americas, which represented 80 percent of U.S. businesses with investments in Latin America, lobbied hard for the aid. On May 9, 1980, the Council sent a telegram to all members of Congress, acknowledging that the aid had some risk, but: "We believe . . . that the risk is worth taking." The economic aid survived the battle, but Robert Bauman succeeded in defeating the military aid portion, arguing: "We have given them more than $60 million in the last fifteen months. All we have gotten back, in every international forum . . . was vile, consummate attacks on the people who have paid the bill."[38] The decision by conservatives in the United States not to offer any more military aid appropriately matched Sandinista reluctance to accept such help.

The President signed the bill into law on May 31, but the appropriations process provided the opponents another opportunity to delay its passage until July 2, 1980, and a last-minute amendment prevented the President from disbursing the funds until October 1, 1980. By that time, Ronald Reagan was the nominee of the Republican Party, whose platform deplored "the Marxist Sandinista takeover of Nicaragua" and recommended the end of the aid program.[39] The Republican Convention was only one of many harbingers that the mood of the country had changed. The nation and the world would have to wait until November 1980 to learn just how definitive was the transformation.

Symptomatic of this change was the number of articles by conservative columnists during the summer of 1980 about Nicaraguan collaboration with Cuba and support for leftist guerrillas. In fact, as we shall see, the Sandinistas were still trying to deflect or divert internal and external pressures to help the Salvadoran rebels. To compensate for their lack of real solidarity, the Sandinistas sought other means to prove their radical credentials. In March 1980, Daniel Ortega attacked the United States for "trying to drown Jamaica and Grenada, and threatening to intervene in El Salvador."[40] At the same time, Hugo Torres, the Deputy Minister for State Security, accused the CIA of "trying to promote unrest . . . [and] divide the Nicaraguans even with regard to religion. It is promoting the failure of the economic reactivation."[41] The charges were without any basis, but each accusation made it more difficult for U.S. supporters of the aid to defend it.

The Sandinistas became much more open in their Cuban and Soviet relationships and less tolerant of the moderate elements in their coalition. Robelo found himself engaged in a losing struggle with the FSLN to implement the Council of State as originally envisaged. On April 16, 1980, the Junta met to consider the Frente's proposal to expand the Council of State to 47 members in order to include the new mass organizations created by the FSLN; this would give the FSLN an absolute and fixed majority. Robelo and Violeta de Chamorro voted against the proposal, and Ramírez and Moisés Hassán voted in favor. Daniel Ortega was out of the country at the time. Three days later, Chamorro resigned in protest, though she concealed her real concerns by citing health reasons. On April 21, the proposal was published as a decree with all five names at the bottom.[42]

The next day, Alfonso Robelo resigned from the Junta and held a press conference to criticize the FSLN for imposing changes on the Plan of Government without obtaining a consensus. The Council of State was only one issue for Robelo; he had also been pressing for an electoral timetable and greater access to the news media by political parties. He said that he resigned to force the FSLN to "reflect on what it is doing. We hope they will reconsider." The Directorate responded by calling Robelo a wealthy capitalist who could not identify with the people or their revolution.[43]

Events within both countries were becoming linked and entangled. The resignations in Managua impeded the Congressional effort to approve the aid to Nicaragua, which in turn exacerbated divisions within Nicaragua. Ambassador Pezzullo decided that both the U.S.–Nicaraguan relationship and the future of pluralism in Nicaragua depended on whether the moderates and the FSLN could refashion a compromise. Two years before, the Carter Administration agonized over whether to mediate the Nicaraguan crisis, but no one raised any objection in April 1980.[44] The Frente wanted COSEP, the business as-

sociation that had gradually become the center of the political opposition, to participate in the opening of the Council of State on May 4,
1979. COSEP viewed the Frente imposition of a permanent majority
on the Council of State as a typical Somoza maneuver.

Pezzullo mediated an arrangement whereby COSEP agreed to accept the Council of State, participate in its inauguration, and support
two new moderates for the Junta, Arturo Cruz, the president of the
Central Bank, and Rafael Córdova Rivas. In exchange, the FSLN
agreed to announce a timetable for elections by July 19, 1980, the
first anniversary of the revolution.

Robelo decided to test the limits of the new political bargain. In a
speech on May 10, 1980, to gain support for his party, the Nicaraguan
Democratic Movement, he openly criticized the Sandinista ideology
for the first time, but he did so carefully and indirectly. He chose to
respond to the Sandinista attacks against capitalism and imperialism
by attacking Communism and the concept of the class struggle: "We
are openly against the reign of terror which Communism implants in
the nations which it oppresses. . . . We reject class hatred. . . . We
must not forget that only work produces wealth and that without
production, we can only divide poverty."[45]

The resignations of the moderates in Managua and the changing
mood in the United States affected Congressional perceptions of Nicaragua. Many North Americans were beginning to feel as if radicals
were taking advantage of U.S. patience and generosity. The Sandinistas did not understand this any better than North Americans could
understand or accept the anti-American rhetoric of the Sandinistas.

Chapter 11

CARTER: MUTUAL

TEMPTATIONS

The only way to get rid of a temptation is to yield to it.
Oscar Wilde

THE FIRST ANNIVERSARY of the Nicaraguan revolution—July 19, 1980—occurred, appropriately, between the Republican and Democratic Party conventions. Both nations were sitting on the proverbial fence trying to decide how to view the other. The American people were about to choose between two profoundly different perspectives, one that saw the Sandinistas as a direct threat to U.S. interests and another that saw them as a difficult problem. The first, Republican vision pledged to cut aid and stop the Marxist-Leninists, and the second, Democratic vision counseled patience and perseverance.

The Nicaraguan government was also uncertain about the United States. One faction demanded confrontation with the United States and support for revolutions throughout Central America; the other counseled caution.

These two visions competed to define each nation's policy, but the competition did not occur in a political vacuum. On the contrary, changes within Nicaragua and in its international relationships as well as changes in the world strengthened the credibility of the narrower, more bellicose vision in both countries. From mid-1980 to the inauguration of Ronald Reagan in January 1981, both governments communicated their fundamental concerns to the other and both were tested by high-risk, but also potentially high-yield, temptations to resolve the ambiguity in the relationship with a lightening change.

Changing Internal and International Relationships

By July 1980, the revolution had not mellowed, but neither had it hardened. International observers could still draw on diverse phenomena to confirm their fears or their hopes. Alan Riding described the ambiguity, albeit with a positive spin:

Rather than adopting a Cuban or other revolutionary model, the Sandinistas have been feeling their way along a narrow path between their dreams and their capabilities, with realism generally winning. Their rhetoric, above all in foreign policy, remains leftist, but their policies are pragmatic and, at times, even conservative.[1]

The regime was still willing to negotiate in order to maintain a relationship with Nicaraguan moderates and international democrats. At the same time, the FSLN was ready to take some risks to proclaim its special relationship with Cuba. For the first anniversary celebration Fidel Castro was invited to be the principal foreign speaker, even though that cost Nicaragua the attendance of both Omar Torrijos and Rodrigo Carazo.

But revolutionary Nicaragua still wanted good relations with democracies in Latin America and Europe, and although it asserted its identity by criticizing the United States, it also wanted "normal" relations with it. Recognizing the regime's need to be recognized, the Carter Administration sent to the anniversary ceremony a senior delegation led by U.S. Ambassador to the UN Donald McHenry and William Bowdler, who had become Assistant Secretary of State for Inter-American Affairs when Vaky resigned in December 1979. The delegation included a banker, a Senator, and the National Commander of the Veterans of Foreign Wars.

Castro, who had been told by me and others that the Carter Administration would interpret any criticism of Reagan or praise of Carter as unfriendly and unhelpful, gave a forty-minute speech in which he blasted Reagan and the Republican Party platform and complimented Carter for adopting "a more intelligent and constructive policy" toward Nicaragua than previous Administrations had adopted toward Cuba. But he couldn't resist a chance to poke the United States: "We welcome the aid that the United States has given, but our only sincere regret is that it is so little, so little for the richest country in the world that spends $160 billion on defense."[2]

Daniel Ortega delivered the main speech for the Nicaraguan government and devoted most of it to criticizing past U.S. interventions. His only allusion to elections was to say that they would be held "appropriate to the spirit of democracy."

The Sandinistas tried to placate Carazo, who had declined to come, by inviting him to speak at the closing ceremony of the Literacy Crusade on August 23, 1980. The Nicaraguans were justifiably proud of the success of their first major project, which involved one-fifth of the population over a five-month period and reduced adult illiteracy from 50 percent to 12 percent. With considerable Cuban assistance, the regime viewed the crusade as an opportunity to reduce illiteracy, show the poor that the new government was pursuing their interests, and indoctrinate the people to the revolution. Costa Rica had also offered its teachers, but the FSLN preferred to use Cubans.[3] As a result, 1,200 teachers from Cuba participated, along with 40 from Costa Rica, 70 from Spain, and 39 from the Dominican Republic. The FSLN would not accept Peace Corps Volunteers, because they viewed them incorrectly as CIA agents.

Carazo's visit in August 1980 served as an important marker, both for pluralism in Nicaragua and for Nicaragua's relationships with those democratic countries that had been crucial for the Sandinista victory. The visit also had an interesting parallel with an event twenty-one years earlier. Carazo made a plea for elections. A similar plea had been made by José Figueres in Havana on March 22, 1959, on a platform shared with Fidel Castro. When Figueres, who had sent arms to Castro during the revolution, completed his speech, Castro openly insulted him for having "been influenced by the campaigns in the international press attacking the Cuban revolution."[4] Humberto Ortega did the same to Carazo, calling the demand for elections part of an international counterrevolutionary conspiracy. Ortega then read an FSLN communiqué that defined "democracy" as "participation [that] does not begin and end with elections." He said the electoral process would begin in 1984, leading to elections the next year. Their purpose would be to "improve the power of the revolution, not a raffle to see who has power, because the people have the power through their vanguard, the FSLN and its National Directorate."[5]

Ortega's speech infuriated COSEP, which felt that the Frente had betrayed its promise of May 4 to announce a timetable for elections. Of course Ortega did announce a timetable, but it was considerably different and more distant than what COSEP wanted. The speech also embarrassed Carazo, who was already in serious political trouble because of the Costa Rican legislative commission that had been established in June 1980 to investigate charges of arms trafficking by his Administration. Carazo therefore decided to cool relations with Nicaragua, and by 1981 and 1982, the relationship had chilled.[6]

The Costa Rican trajectory symbolized the changing character of Nicaragua's international relations in the year since the revolution. After the Sandinistas triumphed, Venezuela decided to help the moderates play a role in assisting the revolution to fulfill its pledges. On February 27, 1980, Venezuela pledged to guarantee Nicaragua's oil supply, and in July, Mexico agreed to sell Nicaragua one-half of its oil needs. Although Venezuela and Mexico used the same instrument to

help and influence Nicaragua, the two governments pursued different ends. Venezuela, especially under Herrera Campíns, was vigor-
ously anti-Marxist and determined to help Nicaraguan moderates
build a democracy, like Venezuela's. Mexico saw its interests served
by helping a Marxist, anti-American government in Central America
as it built a hegemonic political party like the PRI of Mexico.[7]

Compañeros and Contras

Although Nicaragua wanted aid from the United States, and the
United States wanted democracy for Nicaragua, these issues were
secondary to their security interests: the FSLN wanted to prevent the
United States from helping the counterrevolution, and the United
States wanted to prevent Nicaragua from supporting revolutions in
other countries.

Shortly after the Sandinistas marched into Managua, former National Guardsmen began to plot their return. In September 1979,
when Ortega complained that Comandante Bravo was conspiring
with "agents of the CIA" to overthrow the Sandinista government,
the U.S. government was unaware of any such activities. However,
one month before, on August 1, 1979, Enrique Bermúdez, who was
the Defense Attaché in the Nicaraguan Embassy during the revolution, "Bravo," and several other former Guard officers had met with
Rep. John Murphy in Washington and had then held a press conference in which they tried to warn of the threat of Communism. They
received almost no press attention. They met afterward to talk about
plans to overthrow the Sandinistas. Two months later, Bravo went to
Honduras to meet with some of his men. The Sandinistas were waiting for him. On October 10, 1979, he was tortured, mutilated, and
murdered.[8]

Guardsmen in Honduras sought help from other governments,
though not from the United States. They distrusted the Carter
Administration almost as much as they hated the Sandinistas. Later
reports hinted that the contra war in Nicaragua was actually begun
by the Carter Administration, but these reports are false.[9] Indeed, the
Carter Administration did not believe there were any significant efforts by ex-Guardsmen to attack the Nicaraguan government, and interpreted Nicaraguan charges as an excuse for militarization or as
evidence of the regime's paranoia. Testimony to the World Court by
the Nicaraguan government later confirmed the Carter Administration's interpretation. Luis Carrión Cruz, Vice Minister of Interior,
told the Court that "organized military and para-military activities"

began in December 1981. Prior to that date, Carrión said, there were "a few small bands very poorly armed, scattered along the northern border. . . . They did not have any military effectiveness."[10]

The United States, however, took seriously reports about possible Nicaraguan support for leftist guerrillas in Central America, and the Sandinista government was sensitive to these concerns. In their first press conference on July 28, 1979, the Directorate specifically denied

> that we are organizing internationalist brigades in Nicaragua to fight in Guatemala and El Salvador. Nothing could be more false and absurd than this. At this time, and ever since we started our struggle, the Sandinista Front's primary concern has been the fate of the Nicaraguan people. Today, our task is reconstruction. . . . We are not going looking for conflicts elsewhere.[11]

The 72-Hour Document confirmed that the Directorate was saying this privately as well as publicly. According to Pastora, however, the debate within the Directorate about whether to help their Salvadoran and Guatemalan compañeros began almost immediately after the triumph; it was not resolved for more than a year.[12] The U.S. Congress remained skeptical, and had amended the aid bill for Nicaragua to prevent disbursement of aid to Nicaragua until the President consulted with the intelligence community and certified to Congress that the Nicaraguan government was not helping foreign insurgents.

Given the deluge of intelligence reported in the newspapers on Sandinista support for the Salvadoran rebels, few expected Carter would certify. In mid-September 1980, for example, *Time* magazine predicted that Carter would "put off signing the bill until after the November elections. To sign it now might give the Republicans a campaign issue that the President scarcely needs."[13] The politics of the issue did not deter Carter, who signed the certification. It concluded: "On the basis of an evaluation of the available evidence, the Government of Nicaragua 'has not cooperated with or harbors any international terrorist organization or is abiding, abetting, or supporting acts of violence or terrorism in other countries.' "[14]

Conservatives were upset by the certification, particularly because Anastasio Somoza was murdered in Paraguay five days later. Though many suspected the Sandinistas were ultimately responsible, the only evidence pointed to South American terrorists.[15] Rep. Robert Bauman insisted on a Congressional hearing, but it was inconclusive, like the evidence.[16]

The certification was a short statement at the end of a long review. The Administration had received reports of arms smuggling through

Nicaragua to the Salvadoran rebels, and there were analysts—particularly in the Defense Intelligence Agency but also in the CIA—who judged that the reports were probably accurate. However, the State Department interpreted the law as setting two minimal criteria for judging the reports. First, was the Nicaraguan government involved in the arms trafficking? Reports suggesting that some in Nicaragua might be aiding the Salvadoran insurgency would not meet this test, unless there was proof of government involvement. Second, was the proof conclusive? This required a judgment by the intelligence community on the reliability of the reports.

In September 1980, Carter's senior advisers—Secretary of State Edmund Muskie, Brown, Brzezinski, and Turner—found cause for concern that the Nicaraguans *might* be involved, but the evidence was not conclusive. However, before recommending that the President sign a certification, they instructed Ambassador Pezzullo to meet with Nicaraguan officials. The Nicaraguans denied any "governmental" involvement, but asserted that the government of Nicaragua could not be held responsible for the activities of individual Nicaraguans. Pezzullo warned them that U.S. concerns extended to all activities within their borders.[17]

After examining the evidence, the Secretaries of State and Defense, the Director of the Central Intelligence Agency, and the National Security Adviser all agreed that the proof was not conclusive that the Nicaraguan government was directing the arms smuggling. Carter signed the determination, but the Administration decided to send Deputy Assistant Secretary of State James Cheek to Managua to underscore the Administration's concern. Cheek told Daniel Ortega and other members of the Junta that if the United States found that Nicaragua was cooperating with or aiding rebels in other countries, it would terminate the aid program. The argument that the Sandinistas could not control all activities in Nicaragua was not acceptable. The Nicaraguan leadership said that they understood the message, and they promised that all steps would be taken to ensure that such activities not occur.[18]

According to documents captured later from the Salvadoran guerrillas, Cheek's démarche achieved its purpose. On September 27, the Nicaraguans told the Salvadorans that the United States had sensitive information, and therefore the Nicaraguans would not permit any arms shipments. The Salvadoran in charge of organizing the arms shipments wrote: "It seems very strange to us that a gringo official would come to them [the FSLN] to practically warn [them]. . . . If they have detected something concrete, it is logical that they would hit us and they would arm the great propaganda machine and not that they would warn us."[19]

U.S. information was not "concrete," but the Sandinistas told the Salvadorans it was in order to justify a halt to the arms shipments. That left the guerrillas bewildered, and the Sandinistas with more time. Since the Sandinista victory, the Salvadoran guerrillas, who had provided money (through kidnappings) and cadre to the Sandinistas during their revolution, had sought FSLN help.[20] The FSLN felt a camaraderie and supported the Salvadoran revolution morally, but it was reluctant to translate that abstract support into arms or training, which could endanger the Nicaraguan revolution.

During the first anniversary celebration, a senior delegation of Salvadorans arrived in Managua and, by their own account, "were told to keep ourselves locked up and not to go out" for nearly two weeks. Their report on the trip is revealing: "The Frente undervalued them and ignored them. . . . There was not a relationship of mutual respect but rather one of imposition. The Frente was very conservative, and it had a tendency to look down on the situation [in El Salvador] and to protect the Nicaraguan revolution."[21]

The FSLN promised their support, but continued to attach conditions that infuriated the Salvadorans. First, Nicaragua insisted on Salvadoran unity, on the grounds that aid could not be used effectively until that occurred. In 1979 and 1980, with Cuban help, the Salvadoran guerrilla groups united to form the military Farabundo Martí National Liberation Front (FMLN). At that point, the Sandinistas offered the Salvadorans the names of arms smugglers from Costa Rica and Panama who had helped ferry arms during the Nicaraguan revolution. However, that was halted in June 1980 when a small Panamanian plane crashed in El Salvador with arms that had been stockpiled in Costa Rica during the Nicaraguan revolution.[22] In July 1980, the FSLN criticized the Salvadorans for inflating the number of their forces, having bad propaganda, and lacking concrete plans. Nicaragua postponed its assistance again by suggesting the Salvadoran guerrillas develop direct relationships with Cuba and other Communist governments. Jorge Shafik Handal, the leader of the Salvadoran Communist Party, and others traveled throughout the Communist bloc. Vietnam, with the largest stock of surplus U.S. arms, was the most forthcoming. Several other governments promised to provide token support, and Cuba promised to transship the weapons to the guerrillas.

The FSLN therefore successfully diverted the Salvadorans for fifteen months. However, by September 1980, the Sandinistas could no longer avoid the Salvadorans' supplications. About 120 tons of weapons from Vietnam had been stockpiled in Nicaragua. On September 26, the Salvadorans complained that they had received less than four tons; the next day, they were told of Cheek's démarche and of the suspension of all shipments.[23]

The Sandinistas continued to stall through October. The FSLN decided not to host a meeting of Communist parties of Central America in mid-October because they wanted to keep their distance from the Salvadoran conflict. Cuba hosted the meeting instead. However, to compensate, the Sandinistas agreed to permit the Salvadoran guerrillas to operate a clandestine radio station in Nicaragua.[24] It appears that the goal of avoiding a hostile relationship with the United States continued to inhibit, though not completely to preclude, the FSLN's revolutionary inclinations.

On October 10, 1980, Tomás Borge was probably partly truthful when he said:

> We have promised in all seriousness not to send arms or troops to help the Salvadorans, and we have kept our promise. Mr. Carter can rest assured that we are keeping our promise. . . . There is not the slightest danger that someday it will be revealed that we sent arms because we haven't.[25]

Beginning in the fall of 1980 and lasting until April 1981, the United States and Nicaraguan governments passed through exceptionally awkward transitions—within each country and between the two. The Iranian revolution had asserted its national purpose by taking the United States "hostage," and this provoked a nationalistic surge in the United States, which contributed to Ronald Reagan's landslide victory on November 4, 1980. Governing during the "lame duck" period was especially difficult with regard to an area like Central America, where the views of the incumbent and the incoming President appeared most different. The Carter Administration continued its policies, but the region began to respond to a different President who had not yet taken office.

The Nicaraguan government also was under stress. The Directorate saw the beginning of a militant internal and external opposition, and it feared that the Reagan Administration might exploit any division within Nicaragua to undermine the revolution. Some believed that the new Administration would undertake the "imperialistic intervention" that they had long expected but nevertheless hoped would not occur. The challenge for the Sandinistas was how to defend themselves and their revolution.

Both the United States and the new Nicaraguan government had been struggling for sixteen months to overcome deep-seated suspicions and construct a new relationship. In the United States, there were some who had never thought the United States could deal with "Communists"; others had reluctantly come to that conclusion. And Nicaragua had its counterparts, declaring the futility of dealing with "imperialists." In both nations, these people became stronger.

During this uncertain period, both governments were tested by temptation—the possibility of attaining the "perfect" solution. In this case, as in many others, the "perfect was the enemy of the good." For the Sandinistas, the temptation was disguised as a successful revolution in El Salvador. For the United States, the temptation was a coup that would eliminate the Marxists from the Nicaraguan government. Biting this tempting apple poisoned the relationship each had been trying to nurture.

Salazar and the Counterrevolutionary Temptation

Humberto Ortega's speech in August 1980 postponing elections and distorting their purpose provided the spark that ignited Jorge Salazar, the young and dynamic president of the Union of Nicaraguan Agricultural Producers. Salazar had a reputation of integrity, and many viewed him as a natural leader of the opposition. In October 1980, the U.S. Embassy was told that a group of moderate civilians, led by Salazar, and non-Marxist Sandinistas in the Nicaraguan military were conspiring to overthrow the Directorate. The Ambassador was informed; he was not asked for help.[26] Less than one month before the U.S. Presidential elections, Pezzullo passed this time bomb to the senior levels of the Carter Administration. If an attempted coup in Nicaragua occurred, it would undoubtedly affect the campaign, but the precise nature of its effect was difficult to assess because so much depended on how it would occur and whether it would succeed.

The conspiracy posed the same difficult question for the Nicaraguan moderates who were contacted by Salazar as it did for the United States. Most moderates within and outside Nicaragua hoped for a change in government or at least a change in leadership that would be less attached to the Soviet Union and Cuba and more interested in democracy. Some were coming to believe that the only way change could occur was by force. Some Americans shared this view. Both sets of actors felt the moment had arrived when Salazar, a popular and charismatic leader, informed them that there existed such a group in the military and they had already contacted him.

The question for the United States was what, if anything, it should do. If the United States remained passive while the moderates rose up to overthrow the Directorate and then were eliminated by the Sandinistas, not only would that extinguish any remaining hope for moderation, but the United States would appear once again several steps behind events, or worse, irrelevant (at a moment when the President needed desperately to look assertive).

If the plot was genuine and stood some chance of success, should the United State help? Some in the Administration were prepared to pay the price of again being labeled "interventionistic" if the coup succeeded, but if it failed, not only would the Carter Administration be blamed for ineptness, but its strategy of trying to moderate the Sandinistas would be finished. On the other hand, if this conspiracy was actually just a sophisticated way to entrap moderates, then the United States should discourage them, or alternatively, keep its distance.

The conspiracy, in short, was a high-risk temptation. It could be the last chance to depose the Communists in the Nicaraguan government. Or it could erase the non-Marxists from the Nicaraguan government in a single stroke. Some of the suspicions that the Carter Administration had about the Directorate had been confirmed in the past year. Those who were most pessimistic and suspicious of the Sandinistas tended to be in favor of supporting a coup, and those who were less pessimistic both about what had happened in Nicaragua and what could be expected in the future were more inclined to resist the temptation.

Pezzullo, in the latter camp, believed the conspiracy was an entrapment. Another senior official with considerable experience with Cuba explained that Castro started entrapping his enemies in Cuba shortly after taking power. Using agent provocateurs, Castro would raise the hopes of his enemies, and when a critical number of the opposition had committed themselves, he would arrest them all. Castro and his government had improved this skill since then. The kind of conspiracy that Pezzullo described looked to this individual as if it had been made in Havana. There was a second tough question that the Administration would need to address: if it were genuine, how should the United States anticipate or respond to any effort by Cuban military forces to defend the Sandinistas?

All of the agony of trying to forge answers to these tough questions as the Presidential election approached was preempted by Pezzullo's growing conviction that the conspiracy was an entrapment. He warned Salazar. Edén Pastora, who learned that the Directorate knew of the plot and had condemned Salazar to death, also warned his friend, but to no avail. Salazar restricted his contacts. The election passed in the United States. On November 16, the security police confronted Salazar in a gas station and shot him. It is not known whether the conspiracy was a government entrapment from the beginning, or whether the Sandinistas only learned about it later and then turned it to their own ends. It is also not known whether there was any support within the military for a more moderate approach to domestic and international problems.

El Salvador and the Revolutionary Temptation

Just as the Carter Administration was grappling with what to do about the Sandinistas, the Directorate was probably addressing the mirror question: How should Nicaragua respond to the election of Ronald Reagan? No doubt there were some who said that Reagan's election confirmed the Sandinistas' expectations about U.S. imperialism; the Directorate should accelerate the building of its defenses. Others may have argued that a new Administration should be given the benefit of the doubt and time to adjust its preconceptions to international realities.

The two arguments were not necessarily incompatible. The FSLN strengthened its armed forces and stepped up its harassment of internal moderate groups. The police arrested Robelo on November 9, 1980, and censored press coverage of his political party's upcoming rally at Nandaime. Salazar was killed one week later, and the government began to harass and restrict the access to the radio by the Church and especially Archbishop Obando y Bravo.[27]

Central Americans followed the U.S. election as if their future depended on it, and in a sense, it did.[28] With Reagan's victory, right-wing leaders danced in the streets of Guatemala City. In El Salvador, the right unleashed a wave of repression, killing six opposition leaders, four American nuns and religious workers, and two American labor organizers.

The Salvadoran left, believing Reagan would intervene in El Salvador, decided to try to complete the revolution before he could stop them. The guerrillas therefore posed for the Sandinistas almost the same question that Salazar posed to the United States: should Nicaragua support the Salvadoran guerrillas' "final offensive" to seize power? The probability of success was low, but the outcome was optimal. On the other hand, if the Sandinistas did not help the Salvadoran guerrillas and they were defeated, that might set back irrevocably the chances of revolution in El Salvador. If the FSLN failed to help in the hour of need, what effect would that have on its image among leftists in the world? If the Sandinistas provided strong support to the Salvadorans to achieve victory, the United States would almost certainly discover it, and that could permanently affect relations with the United States, particularly with the new Administration.

There were two major differences between the two questions the two governments faced. First, the Salvadoran guerrillas (and the Cubans) posed the question of aid directly to the FSLN; Salazar had not asked for help from the United States. Second, the Salvadorans were determined to launch the "offensive" on a specific date, so the Sandinistas may have believed that they would not have a second chance: either support the Salvadorans in the hope they can win, or passively watch the revolution die in El Salvador.

Though the questions were similar, the differences might explain why the two governments answered differently. The United States was not really asked for aid, and available evidence seemed to suggest that the coup was not genuine. The United States therefore did not have to make a decision, and it did not. The FSLN was asked, and there was no doubt that the bus was leaving; as Ken Kesey wrote in another context: you either had to get on the bus, or get off. The Directorate chose to get on, but the available evidence suggests it was not an easy decision.

Several years later, after exploring this issue with a number of Sandinista leaders, Pezzullo concluded: "They were torn in this. They were pressured by their so-called friends or colleagues in Salvador, and yet there was a desire to have a relationship with the United States, even though they found us to be a little difficult to comprehend or to trust."[29]

On November 1, 1980, the Salvadoran logistics coordinator in Managua informed the guerrilla general staff in El Salvador that the Frente had finally approved their plans and had scheduled the first shipment of arms to begin on November 4. But the Sandinistas were nervous—"it is such a hot potato for them"—and they wanted to expedite the shipment of 109 tons of arms in November. Apparently, they were feeling pressure from Cuba, which expected to send 400 tons to Nicaraguan warehouses ready for transshipment. The Nicaraguans had "taken a firm step," and suddenly, the Salvadorans had more equipment than they could handle.[30]

Why did the FSLN make the decision to help their Salvadoran compañeros so massively? A senior Nicaraguan government official told me that the Directorate made the decision because they thought the rebels would win in El Salvador. Like the Mexicans coming to the support of the Sandinistas two weeks before the final offensive, the

Nicaraguans thought they could gain influence with the Salvadorans if they helped at this critical juncture. (They apparently failed to remember how limited and illusory the Mexican influence on them proved to be after the victory.)

Perhaps some Sandinistas thought that their relationship with the United States would come to an end when Reagan was inaugurated regardless of what they did. They had read his speeches and the Republican Party platform, and it appeared that a Reagan Administration would not accept their revolution. One cryptic reference in a Salvadoran guerrilla letter of November 1, 1980 ("K"), suggests a more sophisticated analysis. The Salvadoran wrote: "The United States elections no longer pose any problems; the results do not matter." This implies a sensitivity to the volatility of American politics in the last months before an election, but from their perspective no matter who was elected, the United States would attack their revolution.

Perhaps the FSLN thought a revolution in El Salvador might divert Reagan from Nicaragua whether the "final offensive" succeeded or not. (In the short term, they were right.) Or perhaps the "United States" was not such an important factor in their calculations; more important might have been the internal political debate within the Directorate, or the pressures of a logistical structure that awaited only their decision, or perhaps their long-term commitment to revolution abroad. Whatever the reasons for the Directorate's decision to help the Salvadoran guerrillas, the long-term consequences were grave for both.

On January 2, 1981, CIA aerial photography revealed a C-47 on a small airstrip at Papalonal, 25 miles northwest of Managua and just a short hop across the Gulf of Fonseca to El Salvador. The CIA had been watching the field change from a small dirt airstrip of 800 meters used for agricultural purposes in July 1980 to a 1,200-meter graded strip with turnarounds, hard dispersal areas, and storage buildings by late December. The pattern and speed of construction convinced the experts of its military function. The CIA analyzed the pictures from the aerial photography together with a vast quantity of new intelligence from many different sources that had been collected during the previous month and sent a report to the White House on January 6, 1981.

That report for the first time, in my opinion, provided conclusive proof that the Nicaraguan government was providing significant amounts of aid to the insurgency in El Salvador. Such an airstrip could not have been built or operated without a decision by the Nicaraguan Directorate or its Military Commission.[31] The law on Nicaraguan aid did not leave the Executive Branch with any option but to terminate aid. I called Assistant Secretary of State William Bowdler and then David Aaron, who scheduled a mini-SCC meeting the next day to review the intelligence and develop options for U.S. policy toward El Salvador and Nicaragua. Carter, Brzezinski, Christopher, and numerous others were working almost without stop to try to obtain the release of the American hostages in Iran, and it was decided to seek the President's decision only after the options were fully developed.

The intelligence community had developed four separate sources that confirmed Sandinista arms shipments by boat, land (through Honduras), and most recently, by air. In November, a Costa Rican arms trafficker had sold several planes to a Honduran aviation company that was a Sandinista front. The company took possession of the planes and sent them to Papalonal for flights to Lempa and Santa Teresa airstrips in El Salvador. On November 25, one of the planes crashed at Santa Teresa, and because of that, the FSLN suspended flights. They began again on January 2, and plans called for four flights per week until the offensive when daily flights would begin. Cuban and Nicaraguan officials were directing the operation.[32]

Those at the January 7 meeting decided to instruct Ambassador Pezzullo to deliver a stiff démarche to Sandinista officials. There was much discussion about how to use the evidence at international forums to both condemn the Nicaraguan intervention and forge an international response. The intelligence community was asked to develop options on how to capture planes or encourage people to defect and testify on the actions. A debate, which continued and deepened during the Reagan Administration, ensued between the political appointees and the officials of the intelligence community. The political appointees argued that the intelligence should be declassified and offered as proof in international forums; the intelligence community was naturally more sensitive to protecting its sources and methods. It was also decided to send a foreign service officer, Jon Glassman, to El Salvador to help that government prepare a case for the OAS against Nicaraguan intervention based on the reports captured from the guerrillas.

Pezzullo received the instructions, and on January 9, he "reminded Borge of the government's promises not to become involved in the Salvadoran conflict, warning that the first casualty of any such action would be U.S.–Nicaraguan relations." He was assured that Nicaragua's policy had not changed. Borge "acknowledged the possibility that some arms might have passed through Nicaragua and some people connected with the government might have assisted in some way, but insisted that Nicaragua was acting responsibly and had even recently intercepted a truckload of arms passing from Costa Rica to El Salvador." Borge was slow to realize that this cover story had been blown away. Pezzullo alluded to some of the specific reports and demanded that the Frente stop using the Papalonal airstrip and close down Radio Liberación, the Salvadoran guerrilla radio station.[33]

The timing of the démarche was perfect, but the Sandinistas evidently decided that they could not hold back the momentum of the revolution. The next day, January 10, 1981, Radio Liberación broadcast to guerrillas in El Salvador that "the decisive hour has come to initiate the . . . battles for the seizure of power." Shortly after that, Radio Managua, the FSLN station, reported: "A few hours after the FMLN General Command ordered a final offensive to defeat the [Salvadoran] regime, . . . the first victories in the combat waged by our [sic] forces began being reported."[34]

The "final offensive" was a fiasco. The guerrillas expected a popular insurrection and the assassination of Napoleón Duarte and other leaders. They struck at about forty locations throughout El Salvador and destroyed a major army arsenal, but the army remained united and the population was unresponsive to the rebels' rhetoric. The guerrillas proved they were much weaker than they had thought. By Monday, January 12, the final offensive apparently peaked.

On January 14, a mini-SCC meeting was held to review the situation. Because the Salvadoran military had taken most of the steps that Duarte and the United States had demanded[35] and because of the urgent need to replace the arsenal, the group recommended to the President a modest supply of $5.9 million of arms and ammunition to the Salvadoran government. The President approved the proposal, and the decision to send lethal military aid was announced on Monday, January 19, after members of Congress were briefed over the weekend. This was the only military aid the Carter Administration sent to El Salvador, and the statement described two reasons for the release of funds: the positive recent decisions by the Salvadoran government, and the evidence of outside support for the guerrillas.

On Friday afternoon, January 16, Aaron chaired a mini-SCC to develop a ten-day strategy that would give the new Administration time to decide what it would do. It was recommended that Pezzullo meet with the Nicaraguans that weekend to inform them that aid was suspended and that their continued support of the Salvadoran rebels could lead to a rupture in relations. The President approved the recommendation, and Pezzullo informed the Sandinistas that aid was suspended. They then promised to close Radio Liberación, which they did on January 20, and to take "strong measures" to prevent the "funny business" at the airfields and other "unofficial activities."[36]

Carter later had an opportunity to explain to the Sandinista leadership in person his decision on aid:

> I had no alternative but to cut off aid to the Sandinistas before I
> left office, because there was evidence that was clear to me that
> the Sandinistas were giving assistance to the revolutionaries in
> El Salvador, and the law required me to stop the aid. I was very
> eager to give the people of Nicaragua economic aid after the revolution, but it was not possible under those circumstances.[37]

On Monday night, January 19, 1981, the General Services Administration shipped the last files—the historical record of the Carter Administration—to Atlanta. As I was cleaning out my desk, I received a draft memo from the State Department for Carter to give to Reagan the next day on whether to terminate aid to Nicaragua. The next day was the inauguration. Both Carter and Reagan had other things on their minds.

The State of Relations

As Carter left office, the relationship between the United States and the revolutionary government of Nicaragua had been tested over an eighteen-month period. Neither side scored very well, but both sides passed.

Neither the internal situation in Nicaragua nor its relationship to the United States had met the hopes of the optimists or the fears of the pessimists. By the standards of most revolutions, Nicaragua's was reasonably moderate. There were no executions or "bloodbaths," as occurred in Cuba and Iran. In fact, Nicaragua outlawed the death penalty, and there were few reports of human rights violations in the first two years.

There were signs of moderation and signs of Marxism-Leninism. There was space for political parties and groups, but the FSLN began to build powerful internal security and armed forces. The government negotiated to reschedule rather than repudiate its international debt, and there were few expropriations beyond Somoza's estates. Eighteen months after Castro took power, he shut down or seized all the independent press and media and limited the role of the Church, but in Nicaragua, La Prensa remained a vigorous voice of opposition and the political influence of the Church steadily increased. Although many Cuban opposition leaders, including some early supporters of the revolution, had left or been imprisoned within Castro's first eighteen months, almost no moderate Nicaraguan leaders had left by January 1981. Though business leaders were reluctant to make significant new investments, they did make some investments, and the economy began to recover. Businessmen also became important political as well as economic actors.

But there were also ominous signs. The Marxist optic of the FSLN prompted them to find enemies where there were only people who disagreed; it prompted them to treat adversaries as if they were "criminals" or "thieves." These attitudes mortgaged the future of the revolution, though few realized it then. The deeply rooted anti-Americanism of the revolution would also bear bitter fruit, but at the beginning, the United States was Nicaragua's most generous donor, providing $118 million in direct aid and encouraging the World Bank and the Inter-American Development Bank to loan $262 million.

The Nicaraguan government successfully cultivated good relations with Latin America and Europe, but from the start, it was clear that its closest relationships would be reserved for Cuba and Soviet-bloc countries. Viewing others with some suspicion, Nicaragua particularly did not want a military relationship with the West. The United States remained at the center of Nicaragua's consciousness, but it had become "the enemy" with limited direct influence.

The decision by the Directorate to aid the Salvadoran insurgents was a major miscalculation, which, in effect, ended the era of support by the United States. It also occurred at a moment when a new Administration was coming into office with a very different perception of the revolution. Under the best of circumstances, it would have been difficult to persuade the Reagan Administration to be patient and forge a long-term relationship with Nicaragua. Unfortunately, it was not the best of circumstances, and the Sandinista support for the Salvadorans was a major contributing factor.

Even without conclusive evidence, the new Administration believed the Sandinistas would try to overthrow its neighbors; the Sandinistas provided the evidence that confirmed their worst suspicions. This new Administration, as we will see, drew very different lessons than its predecessor had from the experience of the Cuban revolution.

Chapter 12

REAGAN: MUTUAL

RESENTMENT

We are always reacting [to the Soviet Union]. . . .
Next time we might have a few spots of our own in their
backyard picked out.
Ronald Reagan, 1967[1]

We know that our essential responsibility is to work for
the building of the Nicaraguan economy, but it is still more
essential to defend ourselves, to mobilize our people, to
prepare an army capable of dealing blows to any other army.
It is more essential that our mass organizations are armed to
the teeth.
Jaime Wheelock, January 1981[2]

BY THE 1980 Presidential election, according to two public opinion
analysts, North Americans "felt bullied by OPEC, humiliated by the
Ayatollah Khomeini, tricked by Castro, out-traded by Japan, and out-
gunned by the Russians. . . . Fearing that America was losing control
over its foreign affairs, voters were more than ready to exorcise the
ghost of Vietnam and replace it with a new posture of American as-
sertiveness."[3] As Carter had reflected America's need in 1976 to restore honesty and integrity in government, in 1980, Ronald Reagan
reflected America's need to take control of its destiny and the
world's.

The Reagan Administration's Lessons

Reagan offered a vision of the world that was uncluttered with the
complexities that had distracted previous Presidents. To him, the
problem was Soviet expansion and the solution was American
power. "The inescapable truth," Reagan stated, "is that we are at war,
and we are losing that war simply because we don't or won't realize
we are in it . . . [and] there can only be one end to the war. . . . War
ends in victory or defeat."[4]

Central America, so close to home and seemingly so threatened, became a central part of his campaign. To Reagan, the Panama Canal treaties were not only a "surrender" of vital interests, they were a dangerous invitation to the enemies of the United States. Although some saw the threat to U.S. interests in 1979 as distant or insignificant, Reagan viewed the Communist threat in the region as pervasive, immediate, and dire. He therefore sounded the alarm that "the Caribbean is rapidly becoming a Communist lake in what should be an American pond and the United States resembles a giant, afraid to move."[5]

Reagan carried this perspective into the White House in January 1981.[6] The lesson he learned from Cuba was different from that learned by Carter. Reagan blamed President Kennedy for not saving Cuba when he had the chance: "We have seen an American President walk all the way to the barricade in the Cuban Missile Crisis and lack the will to take the final step to make it successful."[7] Presumably, the "final step" would have been an invasion to remove Fidel Castro. Whereas Carter believed that the best way to prevent Nicaragua from becoming another Cuba was to avoid confronting the new revolutionary regime, Reagan had learned the opposite lesson. Reagan felt the United States must not give Nicaragua time to consolidate its revolution. The time to confront a radical regime was at the beginning.

The Carter Administration had tried to paste "the mask of democracy" on the Sandinistas' face; the Reagan Administration tried to remove the mask and show the world they were really Communists. That is why the Carter Administration hesitated to call the Nicaraguan government Marxist, and why the Reagan Administration relished the use of the term, daring the FSLN to deny it. The Carter Administration offered aid as a first step toward a new, respectful relationship; the Republican Party platform demanded the termination of aid to Nicaragua as a first step toward supporting "the efforts of the Nicaraguan people to establish a true and independent government."[8]

Despite the bellicose rhetoric, the Reagan Administration gave the Sandinistas nearly three months and a second chance before cutting aid. This occurred because the Administration focused on a limited agenda and was slow to place its people in key staff positions and to establish an interagency decision process.[9]

Into the new Administration bounded Alexander Haig as Secretary of State. In his memoirs, Haig said that he wanted to send just two signals abroad at the beginning: first, a warning to the Soviets "that their time of unresisted adventuring in the Third World was over," and second, that U.S. relations would be conditioned not by a government's respect for human rights but by its friendship with the U.S. government.[10] He chose to draw the line against the Soviets in El Salvador, describing the Administration's approach succinctly: "It is our view that this is an externally managed and orchestrated interventionism, and we are going to deal with it *at the source*."[11]

Haig addressed the problem of Nicaraguan subversion unilaterally and in an East–West framework rather than regionally and as a violation of the Rio Pact. Instead of helping El Salvador use the evidence of Nicaraguan support for the Salvadoran rebels to make its case to the OAS, Haig released the evidence of Soviet–Cuban involvement in a White Paper in February 1981.

Haig asked Pezzullo to return to Washington in early February for a policy review. The Acting Assistant Secretary of State, John Bushnell, a career foreign service officer, proposed three options for U.S. policy toward Nicaragua; all of them recommended a new certification that would end aid to the Sandinistas. Nicaragua had closed Radio Liberación after Pezzullo's initial démarches in mid-January and had interrupted the flow of arms to the Salvadorans. However, during the first week of the Reagan Administration, the FSLN began moving supplies to El Salvador again. Ironically, the Carter Administration probably would have selected one of Bushnell's options, had it had time. Haig asked for Pezzullo's judgment, and he said that none of the options was any good, which Bushnell called the "zero option."

Pezzullo explained that the aid served as essential leverage to negotiate an end to the arms trafficking. Haig listened, and then said that he chose the "zero option." He asked Pezzullo to return to Managua and tell the Sandinistas that there had been a change in Washington, and the new Administration would no longer tolerate their adventurism.[12] In mid-February, Pezzullo met Daniel Ortega and Sergio Ramírez. Given previous pledges that had been made to him by the FSLN and then broken, Pezzullo specifically identified a number of actions that the Sandinistas would need to take to demonstrate their good faith. He said that in the meantime, the United States would withhold aid. Within one month, the United States would assess the Sandinistas' response and judge whether to renew or terminate aid.[13]

Ortega and Ramírez responded officially on behalf of the Directorate that they understood U.S. concerns about El Salvador, and they would not "risk our revolution for an uncertain victory in El Salvador," although that was precisely what they had done. The Nicaraguans told Pezzullo they had taken a firm decision not to permit Nicaraguan territory to be used for transshipping arms to El Salvador.

Ortega admitted that they had been "very permissive in allowing the FMLN [the Salvadoran guerrillas] to mount operations in Nicaragua," but promised that "not a single round" would pass through Nicaragua again.[14]

According to Pezzullo, U.S. intelligence soon found that arms traffic from Nicaragua had stopped, but some Reagan Administration officials claimed that the Nicaraguans had closed "established routes" but were already seeking new ones. Pezzullo felt that the Sandinistas had responded to U.S. concerns and that aid should not be terminated. He acknowledged that Nicaragua might support the Salvadorans again, but to have effective influence in the future, it was necessary for the Administration to demonstrate that it would adhere to its part of the understanding.[15]

Pezzullo was surprised therefore, when the President decided to terminate aid on April 1, 1981. The State Department's announcement was strangely contradictory. It confirmed that Nicaragua had ceased military support for the Salvadoran guerrillas, and because of this "favorable trend," the United States held out the possibility of resuming aid in the future. But aid was ended because "evidence continued to mount that the FSLN was engaged in continuing supply efforts as well as accumulating in Nicaragua arms for the FMLN." Pezzullo was not aware of any reliable evidence of such efforts continuing.[16]

Pezzullo was perplexed that the United States had thrown away its only leverage. He had come up against the limits of the new Administration: given Reagan's campaign rhetoric and the Republican Party platform, there was simply no way that the Administration could have renewed aid to Nicaragua. Indeed, compared to the President's campaign rhetoric, the statement was remarkably conciliatory.

Pezzullo had told Haig that he intended to resign and leave Managua in August, but before leaving, he encouraged the new Assistant Secretary of State, Thomas Enders, to meet with the Sandinista leaders and explore whether a bargain was possible.

The Fork in the Road

Beginning with a blunt exchange of views with Nicaraguan leaders on August 12 and continuing through five more meetings ending in October, Enders tried to negotiate an agreement. In response to Enders's principal concern, Daniel Ortega said:

As for the flow of arms to El Salvador, what must be stated is that as far as we have been informed by you, efforts have been made to stop it. However, I want to make clear that there is a great desire here to collaborate with the Salvadorean people, and also among members of our armed forces, although our Junta and the Directorate have [made] a decision that activities of this kind should not be permitted. We would ask you to give us reports about that flow to help us control it.[17]

Enders was unwilling to provide any additional intelligence, which he feared would compromise U.S. sources and only cause the Nicaraguans to choose alternative routes. Nonetheless, during this period, he developed a proposal composed of five points: (1) Nicaragua would end its support for foreign insurgencies; (2) Nicaragua would cease its military buildup and reduce its armed forces to a level of about 15,000 (down from the existing level of 23,000); (3) the United States would pledge not to intervene in Nicaragua's internal affairs and to enforce U.S. neutrality laws; (4) the United States would renew economic aid; and (5) the United States and Nicaragua would expand cultural relations. Enders also communicated U.S. concerns about political pluralism, a mixed economy, and Nicaraguan relations with the Soviet Union and Cuba, though the proposal did not explicitly cover these points.

As the Nicaraguans considered the proposal, the Administration began the first of a series of large military exercises in the area; this one was off the Caribbean coast of Honduras. The maneuvers and parts of the proposals confirmed the Sandinistas' suspicions of the Reagan Administration. From their perspective, the United States was "merely promising to do what it should be doing already—enforce its laws to stop the paramilitary training of exile groups openly preparing to 'oust the Communists' from Nicaragua."[18] While the United States promised nonintervention, it began military maneuvers. While it promised aid, it publicly canceled $7 million of the economic support funds that the Administration had said it would hold in suspension.

For parallel reasons, Enders was having difficulty gaining Administration-wide agreement on the proposals. Hardliners asked how the Sandinistas could be trusted to stop supporting the Salvadoran guerrillas if they would not even admit to supporting them in the first place. In September, the U.S. Embassy in Managua obtained the text of a speech by Humberto Ortega in which he declared that "we are anti-Yankee, we are against the bourgeoisie. . . . Sandinism without Marxism-Leninism cannot be revolutionary." Another diplomat in

Managua overheard Bayardo Arce, one of the most radical leaders, saying "we will never give up supporting our brothers in El Salvador." On October 7, Daniel Ortega again denounced U.S. imperialism at the United Nations. All these events were used to confirm the point that the Sandinistas were not serious about negotiating.

Instead of redrafting the proposal, on October 31, the Nicaraguan government delivered to the Administration complaints about the military exercises, the aid cancellation, and the lack of action against the exile groups. The Administration interpreted this as a rejection of its proposal and the end of negotiations.[19]

The problem was that both governments were constrained by officials who used the events to prove that the other side was untrustworthy. The Sandinistas thus failed to respond specifically to the proposal from Washington, and the Reagan Administration was unable to return to Managua to explore the nature and the depth of the Sandinistas' concerns or to try to negotiate an alternative formulation. Instead of negotiating seriously, each side, for its own reason, preferred to rest on its preconception that the other was not serious.

This failure to negotiate seriously was a significant, missed opportunity that some on both sides, but especially the Sandinistas, would regret. In their first meeting, Enders told the Nicaraguans: "There is a fork in the road [in our relationship]. One way leads to accommodation; the other to separation."[20] In fact, the other path led to confrontation.

Ortega responded with his own threat:

> We too have seen the crossroads. We have decided to defend our revolution by force of arms, even if we are crushed, and to take the war to the whole of Central America if that is the consequence . . . We have an historical prejudice towards the United States, because of that country['s] . . . attitudes which makes us fear attack from it, and look for all possible means of defense. We are interested in seeing the guerrillas in El Salvador and Guatemala triumph, when we see that there is no good will in the United States towards us.[21]

The Administration considered that it had "tried" negotiations and found the Sandinistas uninterested. In the future, both sides chose to strike postures rather than negotiate; there is no evidence of any progress in subsequent talks between the two governments. After the fall of 1981, the covert and overt warriors replaced the diplomats.

A sign of the Reagan Administration's predilection to posture rather than communicate can be seen in its choice of ambassadors.

Neither of Pezzullo's two successors had experience in Central America. By good fortune, both were intelligent and talented individuals, but that was not the reason they were chosen. The Administration chose individuals whose most recent assignment reflected its picture of Nicaragua. Anthony Quainton, who arrived in Managua in March 1982, had most recently been Director of the Office for Combatting Terrorism in the State Department. By the time Quainton was replaced in 1984, the Administration viewed Nicaragua as a Soviet satellite, and it appointed Harry Bergold, then U.S. Ambassador to Hungary. To the disappointment of the ideologues in the Administration, both soon found that their previous experience was of marginal relevance to Nicaragua.

Haig was serious when he recommended going "to the source." In June 1981, Haig first submitted a specific proposal to the National Security Council to bring "the overwhelming economic strength and political influence of the United States, together with the reality of its military power, to bear on Cuba" by a blockade and other military actions. The proposal was rejected for four reasons. First, Secretary of Defense Caspar Weinberger feared another Vietnam, and the Joint Chiefs feared that the Soviets might respond with actions in another part of the world. Second, the rest of the Administration doubted that Congress or the public would accept such action without some provocation by Cuba. Third, some in the State Department doubted that a blockade would affect Castro's support for revolutions in Central America. And fourth, the White House political advisers wanted to keep the President and the public focused on a tax cut. Haig, by his own admission, was "virtually alone."[22]

In a National Security Council meeting on November 16, 1981, two weeks after negotiations with Nicaragua ended, Haig tried again with slightly different proposals, and finally achieved some results, although not what he wanted. The NSC made two pivotal decisions, which were formalized in National Security Decision Document no. 17 signed the next day by President Reagan.[23] First, rather than reject Haig's blockade outright, Reagan ordered contingency planning for the use of U.S. military forces, including "a petroleum quarantine and/or retaliatory air reaction against Cuban forces and installations," but this would only be taken in response to "unacceptable military actions by Cuba" rather than as part of a U.S.-initiated pressure campaign.[24]

The second decision—for the CIA to fund and direct a secret anti-Sandinista guerrilla force—was of greater consequence for the future course of the Administration's policy. The President authorized $19 million for a 500-man Nicaraguan force aimed primarily at the "Cuban infrastructure in Nicaragua that was training and supplying arms to the Salvadoran guerrillas." Ironically, Haig opposed that decision too, but in his words, "was overruled." Haig's reasons for opposing it were, first, that "covert action was a contradiction in terms. There were no secrets." Second, the problem—Cuban–Soviet intervention—was much larger than Nicaragua, and needed a broader response. Third, the contras were a "cop-out," providing the illusion of solving the problem while escalating the level of violence. Finally, Haig felt strongly that the United States ought to address Nicaragua's external behavior rather than "tell others what form of government they must have." He correctly judged that the contra strategy would tempt the Administration to slide toward the objective of trying to change the Nicaraguan government, which he foresaw as unlikely and as a source of problems for the United States in Latin America.[25]

The groundwork for the Presidential finding to support the Nicaraguan resistance had been set earlier in 1981 when the Reagan Administration decided not to enforce the neutrality laws against the Nicaraguan and Cuban exiles who were training in Florida and California to overthrow the Nicaraguan government. The Administration initially saw these camps as bargaining chips in negotiations with the Nicaraguan government.[26] The FSLN saw Reagan's lack of interest in enforcing the neutrality laws as a sign that he supported the exile groups, and although that was not true then, Nicaragua's disinterest in serious negotiations soon made it true.

On March 9, 1981, Reagan signed a "Presidential Finding" authorizing the CIA to undertake covert actions in Central America to interdict arms trafficking to Marxist guerrillas.[27] Using the authority provided by that finding, CIA agents began to organize disaffected Nicaraguans. Edgar Chamorro, who later became a leader of the contras, was first asked in August 1981 to participate in "an important meeting in Guatemala with U.S. officials, the National Guardsmen [the core of the contras at that time], and their Argentine military advisers." As a result of the meeting, those Nicaraguans who had grown disenchanted with the revolution reluctantly decided to unite with the Guardsmen and form the Nicaraguan Democratic Force (FDN).[28]

Although the contras were still small bands of ex-Guardsmen, they had obtained some support from the Argentine military government, which sent military advisers to Honduras in December 1980 to help train them. The U.S. government was unaware of these activities at the time. The reason for Argentine military involvement, according to former Argentine Foreign Minister Oscar Camilión, was that Argentine military intelligence had discovered some Montoneros (Argentine guerrillas) in Managua, and "the Argentine military saw their mission as to fight Montoneros wherever they were."[29] If the FSLN was an ally of Argentina's enemy, then Argentina would help the FSLN's enemy; it is a simple political rule that has led to the grafting of other rivalries—Israel vs. the PLO, West vs. East Germany, and of course, the United States vs. Cuba and the Soviet Union—onto Nicaragua.

By November 1981, when the National Security Council decided to support the contras, William Casey, the Director of the Central Intelligence Agency, could argue that the United States was just supporting a program assisted by the Argentines that was already under way.[30] Within a month, Enrique Bermúdez, the former Nicaraguan Defense Attaché in Washington, moved to Honduras and became the most important exile military leader. He remarked that he soon felt the Americans supplant the Argentines, although no real fighting had begun yet.[31] On February 14, 1982, the *Washington Post* disclosed the $19 million covert action program and indicated that the money had been used to support about 1,000 fighters and to help middle-class leaders in Managua.[32] The next month, Enders traveled to Argentina to coordinate policy toward Central America with the military government. There, he announced that the Argentine military government had an important role to play in Central America.[33]

Soon after the meeting in Argentina, on March 14, a group of former National Guardsmen, trained in demolition by CIA agents, destroyed two bridges in northern Nicaragua. The attack—the first major assault in Nicaragua—represented a watershed both for the Administration and for the Sandinistas. The Administration had committed itself to the FDN; it had trained and supplied them. Henceforth, abandoning the contras would be perceived as a sign of weakness by the Sandinistas and Moscow, and in the Reagan Administration, no charge was more fatal. After March 1982, according to a senior Administration official, the U.S. strategy came to rely more and more on armed struggle, and U.S. objectives expanded, as Haig had warned, from a desire to interdict arms to El Salvador to a demand for internal changes in Nicaragua.[34]

The Sandinistas responded to the news reports and the bombings by declaring a state of national emergency. They imposed direct censorship, increased surveillance, and arrested a number of moderate leaders, including Alfonso Robelo, accusing them of complicity with the contras. At the request of several governments, the Sandinistas released Robelo, who then fled to San José, just as he had done after being released from Somoza's prison three years before. In Costa Rica he met with other Nicaraguans and discussed what to do about the revolution. None wanted to associate with the Guardsmen, but all had lost hope in civil means of influencing the regime.

Edén Pastora had left Nicaragua on July 7, 1981, claiming at the time that like Che Guevara, he wanted to make more revolutions. In fact, he was disillusioned with the revolution, but was uncertain what to do. He went to Panama to consult with his old friend Omar Torrijos, but days later, on July 31, Torrijos was killed in a plane crash. Soon after that, Tomás Borge visited Pastora in Panama and persuaded him to go to Cuba to speak with Castro. The Sandinistas and the Cubans were afraid that Pastora might divide the revolution. When Castro could not persuade Pastora to return to Nicaragua, the Cubans kept him in Havana as a virtual hostage. Only after Martin Torrijos, the General's son who had fought with Pastora during the revolution, invoked his father's memory did Castro permit Pastora to leave.[35]

After meeting with Robelo and Arturo Cruz, who had resigned as Nicaragua's Ambassador to the United States on November 14, 1981, Pastora held a news conference in San José on April 15, 1982. In his colorful style, reminiscent of Torrijos, Pastora castigated the Sandinistas for betraying the revolution to the Cubans: "Fifteen days after the triumph in 1979, I saw Sandinista commanders returning home in Cuban uniforms, and I realized at that moment that our revolution was beginning to lose its originality." He demanded the Directorate return to its pledges of political pluralism, a mixed economy, and freedom of religion and the press, or "I'm going to take them out of those Mercedes [Benzes] at gunpoint." But he also said that he was only "opening fire politically." He hoped the Directorate would change, but he had no intention of associating with the contras.[36]

Two months later, on June 16, 1982, after many of the leaders of his political party (the Nicaraguan Democratic Movement) had left Managua, Alfonso Robelo and Pastora jointly announced in San José the creation of a political-military alliance (ARDE) to fight the Sandinistas. Pastora did not begin armed attacks in Nicaragua until April 1983. Although he resisted CIA pressure to join forces with the FDN and claimed independence from the CIA, he received money from the agency through intermediaries.[37]

The bombings on March 14, 1982, were a crucial turning point not only for U.S. policy and the contras but also for politics in Nicaragua. The Nicaraguan government intensified its repression of suspected sympathizers in the north and drove many apolitical Nicaraguans out of the country to join forces with the FDN. Moderate leaders were tempted to believe that the Directorate's days were numbered, and the future was with those outside the country. The strategy to support the contras in 1982, therefore, had the effect of hastening the polarization in Nicaragua and diminishing the possibilities for peaceful change.

The Sandinistas shared the credit for polarizing the country, even before the March bombings. Their heavy-handed attempts to integrate the culturally different Caribbean coast—composed of blacks and Indians who spoke mostly English and disliked the Latins in the west—provoked a bloody clash. The Sandinistas knew that the United States had used the Atlantic coast as its base for intervention in the past. Fearful that the Indian groups could be used for counterrevolutionary activities by the United States again, the Sandinistas' suspicions and arrogance turned a relatively apolitical people into counterrevolutionaries.

In February 1981, the Nicaraguan government jailed Steadman Fagoth Muller, the most important leader of the MISURASATA (the organization of Indian groups), and released him in May on condition that he go to a socialist country to study. Instead, he fled to Honduras and joined the contras. By the end of the year, the Sandinistas undertook a brutal, forced resettlement scheme to move about 8,500 Indians away from their native homes on the Honduras border. The Sandinistas later acknowledged the terrible human rights abuses that occurred during the evacuation. The result was that the FDN incorporated a potent indigenous group of rebels from the strategically vulnerable east coast of Nicaragua.[38]

In the third year of the revolution, the Sandinista government began to feel the pressure of internal criticism and external aggression, and it moved more rapidly to give the "masses" a greater stake in the revolution. Confiscations of farms increased in order to provide more land for peasants' cooperatives. To solidify Nicaragua's external support, Daniel Ortega flew to Moscow six weeks after the bombings of the bridges to discuss increased aid.

Constraints: Congress and Contadora

The Reagan Administration's proclivity for unilateralism did not mean that it could pursue its objectives without restraint. Actually, the Administration had more difficulty obtaining Congressional and public support for the contra program than the Carter Administration had obtaining aid for the Nicaraguan government in 1980. Internationally, many of the governments in the area that had helped the Sandinistas to overthrow Somoza and recover economically had become disenchanted by late 1982, but none was prepared to defend the contras. The Administration, therefore, had to cope with two sets of constraints—internal and international—simultaneously.

From the first briefing on the program, both Democratic and Republican members of the House Permanent Select Intelligence Committee expressed concern about the objectives of the contras, the degree of control the Administration could exercise, and whether the strategy could lead to war between Honduras and Nicaragua.[39] Because "neither El Salvador nor its close neighbors possessed the capability to interdict arms," the Committee decided that the United States was justified in undertaking covert actions as long as that was the objective. In April 1982, the Committee adopted an amendment in the classified annex to the bill that affirmed this point.

News reports, which included statements by contra leaders that their goal was to overthrow the Sandinista government, prompted Congress in December 1982 expressly to prohibit the use of U.S. funds for that purpose.[40] Sponsored by Rep. Edward Boland, the Chairman of the House Intelligence Committee, the amendment was adopted unanimously, 411–0, by the House of Representatives.

At the same time, several of Nicaragua's neighbors, led by Mexico and Venezuela, were becoming concerned about the direction of both the Nicaraguan revolution and U.S. policy. As the covert war became a "public secret," Venezuelan President Luis Herrera Campíns criticized Reagan's policy and said that Venezuela would continue its ties to Nicaragua "while there is a possibility that they will realize their pluralistic projects."[41]

Like Venezuela, Mexico had lost some of its enthusiasm for the Nicaraguan revolution, but it was hardly prepared to abandon it. In an important speech in Managua in February 1982, Mexican President José López Portillo offered to try to mediate between the United States and Nicaragua. His proposal resembled Enders', but he tried to make it palatable to the Nicaraguans by putting it in terms of a warning to the United States:

> I can assure my good friends in the United States that what is taking place here in Nicaragua . . . does not constitute an intolerable danger to the basic interests and the national security of the United States. What does constitute a danger for the United States is the risk of history's condemnation as a result of suppressing by force the rights of other nations.[42]

None of these warnings or proposals bore fruit, and the war in the region worsened. In January 1983, the foreign ministers of Mexico,

Venezuela, Colombia, and Panama met on the Panamanian island of
Contadora to begin a unique negotiating effort. For the first time in
history, Latin American governments seized the initiative to super-
vise peace negotiations in Central America. For the first time in the
twentieth century, the United States was not only not involved in
the negotiations; it was excluded.

Neither the United States nor Nicaragua had much faith in Contadora's ability to achieve peace. Nevertheless, both governments
tried to steer Contadora to serve its interest while trying to make it
appear that the other was the obstacle to peace. The Sandinistas decided to try to use the Contadora Initiative to preclude U.S. intervention; the United States viewed the initiative with a combination of
hope and fear—hope that it would either demilitarize Nicaragua or
isolate it, fear that it would allow Nicaragua the time and space to
consolidate its revolution.

In early 1983, the war in El Salvador reached its most dangerous
phase, and the Reagan Administration sought much larger amounts
of economic and military aid in order to shore up the government.
Congress pressed the Administration to give more attention to negotiating in Nicaragua and to the human rights abuses of El Salvador's military. Opposition to the contras was also growing in Congress. Warnings by retiring generals confirmed the fears of those who
thought the Administration was slipping down the slope toward intervention, and public opinion polls reinforced these views.[43]

To mobilize public support for aid to El Salvador and to preclude
efforts to stop funding the contras, Reagan addressed a joint session
of Congress on April 27, 1983. In the speech, he identified Nicaragua
as the principal threat to the region and to U.S. interests:

> The government of Nicaragua has treated us as an enemy. It has
> rejected our repeated peace efforts. It has broken its promises to
> the Organization of American States, and most important of all,
> to the people of Nicaragua. . . . Nicaragua's government threat-
> ens Honduras. . . . The national security of all the Americas is at
> stake in Central America.[44]

Independent of Congress, the President raised the costs to Nicaragua of its policies. In May 1983, Reagan sharply reduced Nicaragua's
sugar quota, valued at about $18.5 million. Although sugar was not
nearly as important to Nicaragua as it had been to Cuba twenty-five
years before when the United States cut its quota, the act was widely
perceived as a repetition of that decision and another step toward
breaking trade relations.

The Fruit of Resentment

While Nicaragua's neighbors were still trying to subdue their suspicions of the Sandinistas, the Reagan Administration entered office wearing its distrust on its sleeve. Like its predecessor, the Reagan Administration had a global agenda that had important implications for Nicaragua. The Carter Administration's human rights focus opened Nicaragua to new political forces. The Reagan Administration looked beyond the longstanding policy of containment to a more revolutionary strategy of seeking "targets of opportunity," vulnerable areas where U.S. support for guerrilla movements could overthrow Marxist governments.

The Nicaraguan regime shared with the Reagan Administration a Manichaean view of the world—a world of allies and enemies. The Sandinistas had fought a war, and they had less patience for peace. Their ideology was better suited to mobilizing the masses against a national enemy than providing incentives to increase production of goods and services. Each action by the Reagan Administration prompted the Sandinistas toward a higher level of vituperation against U.S. imperialism, thus justifying and reinforcing the Reagan Administration's strategy.

Both sides were ideologically committed to defeating the other: the Sandinistas sought revolution against imperialism, and the Reagan Administration sought a victory against Communism. Both found it hard, if not morally indefensible, to compromise such objectives.

Chapter 13

REAGAN: MUTUAL

OBSESSIONS

Reagan has become an obsession for us, and we've become
an obsession for him.
Tomás Borge[1]

Curses are like young chickens;
They always come home to roost.
Robert Southey

BY 1983, the resentment that the Nicaraguan and U.S. governments
felt toward each other had changed into an obsession. A sign of this
was that the more determined each side became, the further it moved
from its goal and national purpose. Yet neither was deterred or diverted, because both had long stopped measuring the effectiveness of
their policy by whether they achieved their objectives. The United
States seemed to evaluate its policy in terms of the damage inflicted
on Nicaragua; and Nicaragua, in terms of the embarrassment caused
to the United States. In the end, however, each government seemed
to harm itself more than it did the other.

Threats maintained the cycle of mutual obsession. The United
States threatened Nicaragua if it did not stop helping Salvadoran
guerrillas, and Nicaragua threatened revolution throughout Central
America if the United States did not stop helping the contras. Nicaragua's threat served to justify the contras, which in turn justified Nicaragua's threat, and so on.

Deepening the Commitment

In September 1983, to allow it more flexibility and to concede the
point Congress had made that the contras were not interdicting
arms, the Reagan Administration submitted a second Presidential
Finding. The finding authorized "material support and guidance to
the Nicaraguan resistance groups" for two purposes: inducing the

Nicaraguan government "to enter into negotiations with its neighbors, and putting pressure on the Sandinistas and their allies to cease provision of arms, training, command and control facilities and sanctuary to leftist guerrillas in El Salvador."[2]

The new finding not only circumvented the first Boland amendment, which prohibited aid to overthrow the government, but also replaced a specific goal—interdicting arms—with an open-ended, unattainable objective—"putting pressure." The finding symbolized the Administration's deepening commitment to the contras and its growing belief that the only way to stop the Sandinistas from helping other revolutionaries was to change their government or overthrow them. In line with this broader objective, the Administration expanded its military aid, training, and military exercises with Nicaragua's neighbors.

At about the same time, two U.S. aircraft carrier battle groups held naval exercises off each coast of Nicaragua. U.S. forces constructed several airfields in the south of Honduras to support the contras and provide a contingency option for the United States to attack Nicaragua if provoked. Reagan's speeches and his personal involvement emboldened some in his Administration, who began talking openly about military victories in Central America.[3] Sandinista prophecies appeared fulfilled. The imperialists were on their doorstep, and as the House Intelligence Committee concluded, the contras provided an additional reason for Nicaragua to fight back:

> Inflicting a bloody nose on nations achieves a purpose no different with nations than with individuals. It tends to instill a deep desire to return the favor. The Sandinistas are no different. Their policies have not softened; they have hardened.[4]

The Sandinistas were better prepared to deal with the war than with the peace that preceded it. Nicaragua's economy had failed to attain its prerevolution level by 1983. Investment had stagnated or declined, depending on the sector. The external debt, which was high at $1.5 billion in 1979, reached $3.8 billion in 1983. Agriculture—the dynamic center of the economy before the revolution—declined markedly. In 1982, cotton exports were about half the 1978 level, and meat exports fell from 57 million pounds (1976-77 average) to 32 million pounds.[5] As the war intensified, the economy sank even further.

Tomás Borge acknowledged: "To make war is relatively simple. But to carry on after victory, to make war against poverty and backwardness and egotism and bureaucracy is something else."[6] Nicaragua increased the size of its armed forces from about 5,000 on the date of the Sandinista victory to 15,000 in 1980, 31,000 in 1981,

88,000 in 1983, and 119,000 in 1985; from 3 tanks in 1979 to 50 tanks in 1983; from 2 antiaircraft guns and no missile launchers in 1979 to 150 antiaircraft guns and 30 missile launchers in 1983. With Cuban and Soviet help, the Sandinistas built the most powerful military force in Central American history in a relatively short time .[7]

The contras were estimated to have 5,000 to 12,000 fighters in late 1983, and 10,000 to 20,000 by 1985.[8] The Sandinista military buildup preceded the war against the contras, but accelerated as a result of it.[9] The buildup occurred for several reasons: to raise the costs to the United States of an invasion, to defend against counterrevolutionary activity, and to discipline and indoctrinate the youth to be loyal to the revolution. Anti-Americanism is a major element of the nationalism of the Nicaraguan revolution. The contras have made the threat from the United States credible, and they have motivated the young and the government to a higher level of dedication and hard work than can be found anywhere else in Central America.

The invasion of Grenada in October 1983 enhanced the credibility of U.S. threats and had an immediate impact on the Sandinistas. Borge, the Minister of Interior, assured U.S. Ambassador Quainton that the United States need not worry about protecting U.S. citizens—the alleged reason for the Grenadian invasion. In case of emergency, Nicaragua had a well-organized plan, which designated three hotels and several airplanes for evacuating U.S. citizens. There would be no need for the United States to use any of its own forces to help, Borge told Quainton.[10]

Roger Fontaine, the Latin Americanist on the NSC at that time, subsequently wrote of the invasion's impact on Nicaragua: "In a virtual panic, Managua, among other things, closed down the Salvadoran guerrilla command and control center in Nicaragua and sent most of the FMLN/FDR leadership packing."[11] The Administration was delighted to see the Sandinistas squirm, but it was either unable or unwilling to translate that pressure into effective influence in negotiations. One week after the invasion, President Reagan himself hinted at the reason when he was asked about a recent Nicaraguan proposal. He said: "I haven't believed anything they've been saying since they got in charge."[12] John Horton, a retired senior CIA official, explained that the Administration had stopped seeking a negotiated solution:

This [Reagan] administration considers agreements with Marxist-Leninists to be risky—as indeed they are—but it also finds them too distasteful and inconsistent with its own tough posturing to be a serious option. The administration did not simply

fail to give sufficient hearing to a diplomatic strategy; it ideologically shackled its imagination and so was not free to use the informed pragmatism that enables a skilled diplomat to probe for
solutions.[13]

As the United States disengaged from negotiations, Nicaragua became interested. This may have been a ploy; it appeared that Nicaragua's interest in negotiating only waxed when U.S. interest waned
(and vice versa). Or Nicaragua's flexibility might have been a response either to U.S. threats and contra activities, or to new pressures coming from previously friendly sources. The leaders of the Socialist International had defended Nicaragua, but they were
concerned that the Sandinistas were not fulfilling their promises of
political pluralism. The Contadora Group also began negotiating a
treaty that included many of the points on security first mentioned
by Thomas Enders, as well as other points on democratization. By
the fall of 1983, Daniel Ortega publicly accepted a "regional declaration of objectives to foster elections and democratic institutions, to
remove outside military advisers, and to halt outside military aid to
the region."[14]

The Administration was less interested in using its success in
Grenada to obtain an agreement with Nicaragua than to gain approval by Congress of $24 million in aid to the contras. In a nation-
ally televised speech, the President called Sandinista rule "a Communist reign of terror," and then said: "Communist subversion is
not an irreversible tide. We have seen it rolled back . . . in Grenada.
And there democracy flourishes. . . . All it takes is the will and resources to get the job done."[15]

However, Congressional support for the contras, always tenuous,
collapsed in the spring of 1984 after a series of disclosures of CIA supervision and involvement in the mining of Nicaragua's harbors and
the destruction of the oil storage facility in Corinto.[16] In speeches on
radio and television, Reagan appealed for more funding for the contras, but he failed to persuade either Congress or public opinion. Aid
to the contras, which had amounted to $72–$100 million, ended on
October 1, 1984. As an acknowledgment of the unpopularity of the
program, President Reagan stopped campaigning for the contras and
began campaigning for reelection on a peace platform.

A Pause for Elections

On June 1, 1984, Secretary of State George Shultz visited Managua
to begin talks with the Nicaraguan government that continued until

January 1985. These negotiations proved an effective rebuttal to the argument of Democratic Presidential candidate Walter Mondale that Reagan's reelection would mean U.S. involvement in war in Central America. In the end, Central America played a small part in the voters' calculations, and President Reagan won by a landslide.

Like Somoza, the Sandinistas often looked for opportunities to outsmart the U.S. government. In that spirit, on February 21, 1984, the Nicaraguan government advanced its national elections from 1985 to November 4, 1984—just two days before the U.S. elections. Bayardo Arce candidly explained the reason:

> One by one, we've been eliminating the pretexts used by Washington. The only argument they had left is that we are . . . governing without a popular mandate. By moving the elections date up, we brought a political element into the defense of the revolution. Perhaps if it were not for the aggressions and the possibility of Reagan's re-election, we would have waited until 1985.[17]

In 1984, the opposition, led by the Coordinadora Democrática Nicaraguense, a coalition of moderate political parties, a labor union, and a business association, was divided, although most members agreed to participate if the FSLN permitted a free election. When informed of Nicaragua's announcement to hold elections, Reagan dismissed it as "the kind of rubber stamp that we see in any totalitarian government."[18] A senior Administration official later explained to the *New York Times* that "the Administration wanted the opposition candidate, Arturo Cruz, either not to enter the race, or, if he did, to withdraw before the election, claiming the conditions were unfair." This official said that the Administration feared that if Cruz ran, "the Sandinistas could justifiably claim that the elections were legitimate, making it much harder for the United States to oppose the Nicaraguan government."[19]

Cruz was selected in early July by the Coordinadora to be the united opposition's candidate for the Presidency, but he insisted that the FSLN accept a number of conditions related to the elections as well as a future dialogue with contra leaders before he would participate. Rallies held by Cruz and his supporters were harassed by "turbas," Sandinista mobs, reinforcing the opposition's insistence on certain minimal conditions.

Leaders from the Socialist International (SI) tried to mediate between the two sides on September 30 in Rio de Janeiro at an SI meeting that both Cruz and Bayardo Arce attended. These discussions as well as the elections themselves have been subject to varying interpretations, but it appears that there were elements in the FSLN, notably Arce, and in the Coordinadora, probably in the business community, who did not want the Coordinadora to participate in the elections. When Cruz accepted the SI's proposal, Arce was surprised and rejected it.[20] Cruz nonetheless kept trying to negotiate, but to no avail. Part of the problem was that the opposition conditioned their participation on a number of demands. Some were unrelated to the elections, and all were difficult for the Sandinistas to accept without appearing to be weak. For example, the opposition insisted on the separation of the state and the army from the party. Though an important objective, it was unrealistic to expect this to be negotiated before the election.

On October 19, the U.S. Ambassador was instructed to meet with Virgilio Godoy, the leader of the Independent Liberal Party (PLI) and a Presidential candidate with no direct tie to the Coordinadora. The Ambassador and other groups and governments encouraged Godoy to withdraw, and he did.[21] As had happened six years before and many times before that, the Nicaraguan government and the opposition could not reach agreement on the terms that would permit a free election. One difference was that in 1978, the United States tried to bridge the gap between the two positions; in 1984, it tried to destroy any bridges.

According to the official results of the elections, nearly 1.1 million Nicaraguans voted, representing 75 percent of the eligible voters. Of those who voted, 63 percent voted for Daniel Ortega as President, and 64 percent for Sandinista National Assembly candidates. The opposition parties won 35 of 96 seats in the Assembly. The State Department spokesman dismissed the election as "just a piece of theater for the Sandinistas."[22] The Latin American Studies Association delegation complimented the Sandinistas for a heavy voter turnout and an election that was an "impressive beginning."

Perhaps the best assessment of the elections was made in a letter to Daniel Ortega from Carlos Andrés Pérez, who had participated in the Socialist International negotiations. Pérez opposed the "shameless intervention" of the contras, but he declined to participate in the inauguration, offering the following reasons:

Without attempting to play down the importance of the electoral process of November 4, 1984, in which you were elected President, those of us who believe we have done so much for the Sandinista revolution feel cheated, because sufficient guarantees were not provided to assure the participation of all political forces. Sadly, the limiting in this way of true political pluralism weakened the credibility of the elections.[23]

The elections, in short, were another lost opportunity for the Nicaraguan government, its opposition, and the United States to bridge the ever-widening chasm. Arturo Cruz later expressed great regret that he did not participate.[24] Within one month of the election, the FSLN rejected the national dialogue that it had promised the opposition during the campaign.

The Reagan Doctrine on National Liberation

In his second term, President Reagan probably devoted more time and gave more major speeches on Nicaragua than on any other single issue. He did this because he believed in the contras, but two-thirds of the American people did not. Incredibly, U.S. policy toward Nicaragua became central to the Administration's overall approach to the world.

Those who were uncertain whether Reagan's reelection would mean pursuing peace initiatives or confrontation had their answer on election night. Moments before Reagan's acceptance statement, White House sources told CBS news that the Soviet Union was sending MIG-23 jets to Nicaragua, and that this might provoke an air strike by the United States or even an invasion. A few days later, the Soviet ship docked in Nicaragua, and helicopters—not MIGs—were unloaded. That crisis passed. The Administration sent two other signals. To reassure the contras and the Hondurans of its continued determination, the Administration ended talks with the Sandinistas begun by Shultz the previous June, and withdrew from the World Court's case on Nicaragua.[25]

In his 1985 State of the Union address, President Reagan transformed his contra program into a policy on national liberation movements: "We must not break faith with those who are risking their lives on every continent from Afghanistan to Nicaragua to defy Soviet-supported aggression and secure rights which have been ours from birth. . . . Support for freedom-fighters is self-defense." At a press conference on February 21, 1985, Reagan described his goal as seeing the Sandinista government "removed in the sense of its present structure," and he said his support for the contras would stop when the Sandinistas "say uncle."

Because of strong Congressional opposition, the Administration decided to request humanitarian rather than military aid for the contras, and to put the request in the form of a proposal: the United States would suspend the aid if the Sandinistas engaged in a dialogue with the contras under the auspices of the Nicaraguan Bishop's Conference.[26] The Sandinistas rejected the proposal, and so did Congress.

One of the arguments made in the Senate for opposing aid to the contras was that the United States ought to consider other steps—like economic sanctions—before trying to overthrow a government. The Administration accepted the point. On May 1, Reagan decreed a trade embargo by declaring a national emergency and describing the Nicaraguan government as "an unusual and extraordinary threat to the national security and foreign policy of the United States."[27]

Daniel Ortega, Nicaragua's President, left for a visit to Moscow only days after Congress's vote and unwittingly strengthened the Administration's argument. By June, the Administration found the votes to pass $27 million in humanitarian aid to the contras. This was the first time both branches of the U.S. government openly debated and approved support for a movement whose aim was to overthrow a government with which the United States had diplomatic relations. Congress included an amendment urging the President to use the funds in a way that would advance peace negotiations between Nicaragua and its opposition.

The Sandinistas had received sophisticated military equipment and, by the end of 1985, were beginning to use it effectively against the contras. In February, 1986, President Reagan—saying "you can't fight attack helicopters piloted by Cubans with band-aids and mosquito nets"[28]—formally asked Congress to approve $100 million in aid for the contras—75 percent of it military aid. Once again, he combined strident attacks against the Sandinistas and Congressional opponents with a willingness to make symbolic concessions, such as appointing Philip Habib as his Special Envoy for Central America and resuming funding of Edén Pastora.[29] But it was only after vigorous lobbying by the President and a significant Nicaraguan incursion into southern Honduras that the Administration was able to win Congressional approval of $70 million in military aid and $30 million in nonmilitary aid. The law permitted the delivery of the first weapons to the contras on October 1, 1986.

Contadora and Its Offspring

The conflict spurred other initiatives in the region. The foreign ministers of the Contadora Group (Mexico, Venezuela, Colombia, and Panama) and a four-nation support group (Argentina, Brazil, Uruguay, and Peru) met with Secretary of State George Shultz on February 10, 1986, to request that the United States open talks with the Sandinistas and stop funding the contras. Reagan refused to meet them and ignored their request.

Nonetheless, by June 1986, the Contadora Group had navigated the Central American states through four drafts of a treaty. The one submitted to the Central Americans on June 6, 1986, was the product of considerable compromise on all sides. That treaty mandated an end to support for "irregular forces" (the contras) and "insurrectional movements" (guerrilla groups); a freeze on new arms purchases; the gradual reduction of armaments, foreign military advisers, and foreign military bases; and steps toward national reconciliation. Procedures on implementation and verification were refined and sharpened with each draft.[30]

As the June 6 deadline for signing the treaty approached, both Nicaragua and the United States displayed signs of nervousness born of suspicion that the other might obtain the better part of the agreement. Nicaragua first indicated it would not sign the agreement unless the United States began direct negotiations and stopped supporting the contras. This relieved the United States of making a decision on what it would do if Nicaragua signed.

The Peruvian government then proposed a face-saving way for the Nicaraguans to sign the agreement but not to ratify it until the United States accepted its terms as well.[31] The United States learned of this arrangement, and a fight within and between the State and Defense Departments began on what to do if Nicaragua signed. Philip Habib wrote a letter to Rep. James Slattery on April 11, 1986, pledging that the United States would cease its support for the contras "from the date of signature" of the treaty. But many in the Defense Department and some in State were not prepared to abandon the contras for what they believed would be an ineffective treaty. The Pentagon released a report predicting a "big war," involving over 100,000 U.S. troops and costing more than $9 billion in the first year, if the Contadora Pact were signed. Their argument was that Contadora would delay the day of reckoning with the Communist regime of Nicaragua, and this would be more costly to the United States. The State Department immediately attacked the report as "an internal Department of Defense study written under contract and released without authorization." Defense rejected State's claim, and the White House denied there were any differences. Finally, Assistant Secretary of State Elliott Abrams declared that Habib's letter was mistaken; it should have said that the U.S. would cease support of the contras when the treaty was implemented, not just signed.[32]

The Nicaraguan government saved the Reagan Administration from tearing itself apart. Nicaragua continued to insist that the contras be disbanded *before* they would sign, and they criticized the treaty for trying to force Nicaragua to disarm. "We are not going to disarm the revolution," Daniel Ortega said. Deputy Foreign Minister Victor Hugo Tinoco criticized the treaty for being "close to the U.S. position" and for adopting the U.S. "strategy to isolate Nicaragua."[33]

Costa Rica, Honduras, and El Salvador were also not yet ready to sign. They asked for further negotiations on verification, arms control (how much and how to reduce each country's defense establishment), democratization, and reconciliation. On June 7, 1986, the Contadora Group withdrew the deadline for achieving agreement. On June 20, after it was clear that the treaty needed more work and five days before the U.S. House of Representatives voted on aid to the contras, the Nicaraguan government announced that it would sign the June 6th treaty.[34]

To resuscitate a nearly comatose Initiative, the two Secretaries General of the United Nations and the OAS offered their organizations' aid to implement the treaty, and then joined the foreign ministers of Contadora and the support group for a quick tour of Central America in January 1987. But instead of trying to narrow differences between the governments, the impressive delegation just listened to each government for a few hours before flying to the next country.

A second set of initiatives emerged from the newly elected democrats in Central America. Guatemalan Christian Democratic President Vinicio Cerezo invited his Central American colleagues to a summit meeting on May 25, 1986, to discuss peace in the region and the possible establishment of a Central American Parliament. The discussion among the Presidents was frank and wide-ranging. Costa Rican President Oscar Arias confronted Daniel Ortega, as he later related: "The difference between you and the rest of us is that we are prepared to become leaders of the opposition, while you are not. You are not prepared to risk political power. And his answer was yes, this is true—our democracy is different."[35] Nonetheless, the Presidents judged the meeting useful and scheduled a second summit for later in 1987.

Like the rest of his countrymen, Arias disliked the Sandinistas, but he also opposed the contra program and enforced his nation's neutrality by closing a contra airbase in the north of his country.[36] On February 15, 1987, he offered a ten-point peace plan to develop the democratization elements of the Contadora Treaty. His plan would begin with an amnesty, cease-fire, and dialogue between the governments of Nicaragua and El Salvador and the internal opposition. Support for all insurgencies would end, and a "monitoring committee" would help implement the agreement. Nicaragua initially condemned the plan until it learned that the United States had reservations about it; then Nicaragua expressed some interest.[37]

Both the Contadora Treaty and the Arias Plan contain significant innovations for constructing a peace, but they also have flaws, similar to the treaties of 1907 and 1923. Neither has enforcement provisions, and both permit important issues to be negotiated after the treaties are signed rather than before. The Contadora Group has been unable to complete the final 20 percent of the treaty because it believes that either the United States or Nicaragua would not accept it.

In June 1979, Latin America effectively blocked a U.S. proposal for replacing Somoza with a transitional government. Since then efforts to achieve peace have been made outside the OAS. Latin America and the United States have discovered that they can block each other; neither has yet discovered how to cooperate.

Consequences of the Contras: Nicaragua

Since 1981, the United States has significantly increased its military involvement in Central America, using new military bases in Honduras and conducting fourteen major military exercises by 1987. Neither Nicaragua nor Cuba has been intimidated. Instead, they have received increasing quantities of military equipment from the Soviet Union. Both governments were more militarized and tied to the Soviets in 1987 than in 1981. Since 1981, Nicaragua's armed forces have increased fourfold. In 1980, Nicaragua received 850 tons of armaments from the Soviet bloc; in 1985 Nicaragua received 18,000 tons, and according to President Reagan, a total of over $1 billion of Soviet-bloc aid.[38] Nicaragua had military advisers from the Soviet Union and East Germany and at least 800 from Cuba.[39]

Central America also became more militarized. While suffering the worst economic depression in fifty years, the region increased military spending by 50 percent in real terms from 1979 to 1983.[40]

Nicaraguan economic dependence on the Soviet Union also deepened as the Central American Common Market fragmented, Mexico stopped exporting oil, and the United States halted trade.[41] The moderate opposition within Nicaragua opposed the embargo, fearing that it would reduce their ties to the United States. By the end of 1986, the economy was in desperate straits with acute shortages of food and other products, a currency almost without value, inflation at more than 700 percent, and a debt that had more than tripled to $5.3 billion since the revolution. Real average wages had declined 40 percent since 1981, and defense and administrative expenditures as a percentage of the total government budget had increased from less than one-third in 1983 to more than one-half in 1985.[42] The human cost of the war grew as well, with over 18,000 Nicaraguans killed since 1982.[43]

The continuing war polarized politics in Nicaragua. Some, like Jaime Chamorro, a *La Prensa* editor, believed that "if the contras did not exist, the Sandinistas would have no need to maintain a facade of democracy, and *La Prensa* and the other [independent] institutions would be finished."[44] Others, like Roberto Cardenal, another editor of *La Prensa*, believed that the contras weakened the internal opposition and reduced the chances of a nonviolent solution: "We are losing strength as our leaders leave. The feeling is that the game is outside, that the possibility of exerting pressure exists only outside the country." Luis Rivas Leiva, a leader of the Social Democratic Party in Nicaragua, criticized the Reagan Administration's strategy: "When they think of the opposition in Nicaragua, they think only of the military opposition."[45]

Jaime Chamorro was proven wrong. After the House approved aid to the contras in June 1986, the Sandinistas closed *La Prensa* and prevented Bishop Pablo Antonio Vega and Rev. Bismarck Caballo, a spokesman for Cardinal Obando, from reentering the country. Daniel Ortega said: "War will be met by war. . . . Those who are against the people and in favor of Reagan have the option of going to Miami. There will be no more tolerance."[46] Rivas Leiva and other moderate leaders went to Miami. To President Reagan's proposal that the Sandinistas begin a dialogue with the Nicaraguan opposition, Daniel Ortega said: "They want dialogue in order to destroy the revolution, and those Nicaraguans who repeat those words are either stupid or, more likely, are being paid by the CIA."[47] The Sandinistas readied for more war, acquiring 40-60 advanced helicopters from the Soviet Union in three shipments between 1984 and 1987.[48]

Nicaragua is not another Cuba, although many of its political and military organizations resemble those of Cuba. The Sandinistas harassed an independent press for seven years, but only closed *La Prensa* in 1986 after Congress passed $100 million aid to the contras. Nicaragua curbs the power of the Church, but the Church is a vivid symbol of opposition in the country. The FSLN is the dominant party, but it permits other parties to criticize the government openly.

By calling their opponents class enemies and mercenaries, the Sandinistas have precluded a dialogue that could permit them to negotiate an exit from their war and their national predicament. Instead, the harder they fight, the further they move from their original aims. The Sandinistas sought independence, but they have been forced to become more dependent on the Soviet Union. They sought to build a new nation, but they have turned their nation into an army. They sought to improve the quality of life for the poor, but it is the poor who are fighting and dying. The important advances made at the beginning of the revolution in health care and literacy and their commendable efforts at land reform have been jeopardized by the militarization of the country and the diversion of scarce resources to the war.[49]

Home to Roost

The original goals of the Reagan Administration's policy toward Nicaragua were to end Nicaraguan support for Salvadoran guerrillas, reduce Nicaragua's dependence on the Soviet Union and Cuba, and increase the prospects for democracy. Like the Sandinistas, the harder the Administration has tried to achieve its goals, the more elusive they have become. Democracy's prospects are lower and Nicaragua's dependence on the Soviet Union is greater in 1987 than in 1981.

The picture of Nicaraguan support for Salvadoran insurgents is less clear. David MacMichael, an analyst who worked at the CIA from 1981 to 1983 and testified before the International Court of Justice, said that the evidence was convincing that Nicaragua had helped the Salvadoran insurgents in 1980 and early 1981, but after that period, neither the United States, El Salvador, nor Honduras apprehended any significant shipments of arms from Nicaragua to Central American rebels. Most of the evidence that the Administration used to show Nicaraguan support for subversion came from the earlier period, but there were a few later examples. The Intelligence Committees reported in 1983 and 1984 that they continued to see some evidence of arms transfers by Nicaragua, but these have not been regular or major. The International Court weighed all of the published documentation, including reports by Sandinista defectors, and concluded much as MacMichael did—that Nicaragua did transfer large amounts until early 1981, but after that, the evidence was less certain and, if it occurred, the amounts were small.[50] Unfortunately, Nicaraguan denials of any support have impugned their credibility.

The Reagan Administration's support for the contras is unprecedented in its scale, duration, and openness. In comparison, the "big stick" of Theodore Roosevelt was more civil and subtle. Roosevelt did not take Panama as he himself boasted, but rather signaled very indirectly to the principal conspirator that he would not be unhappy to see a change in government there. Roosevelt also pressed for international treaties on Central America rather than covert wars. In comparison, from 1982 to 1987, the Reagan Administration provided more military aid to the contras to overthrow the Nicaraguan government than the United States had provided to all five Central American countries from 1962 to 1980.[51] The Administration, by foreclosing negotiations, came to rely on the contras as its only instrument for pursuing U.S. interests.

Of greater consequence, the Administration became so obsessed with Nicaragua that it violated the nation's core precept—respect for the rule of law internationally and at home. Instead of the United States taking Nicaragua to the International Court on charges of subverting its neighbors, Nicaragua took the United States on April 9, 1984. Not only was the Administration not embarrassed by its subsequent withdrawal from the case, but in meetings with its Central American allies, Administration officials proudly pointed to the withdrawal as evidence of the strength of the U.S. commitment to the contras.

The World Court, nonetheless, heard the case, and on June 27, 1986, in a judgment of 546 pages, it found the United States in breach of international law for "training, arming, equipping, financing, and supplying the contra forces" as well as for mining the harbors and attacking various facilities in Nicaragua. The U.S. judge, who tried to defend the United States as acting in "collective self-defense," admitted he was troubled that the United States had not previously sought a collective judgment from either the UN or the OAS.[52]

It was probable, if not logical, that an Administration that showed so little regard for international law would eventually be charged with bending, and perhaps breaking, U.S. law. When Congress prohibited government funding for the contras in October 1984, the CIA sent instructions to its field stations to cease all support for the contras, except for "intelligence-gathering purposes," which was permitted by the law.[53] However, officials in the National Security Council secretly continued and expanded the operation.

Two years later, on October 5, 1986, the Nicaraguan government shot down a C-123 cargo plane. One of the crew members, Eugene Hasenfus, parachuted to safety, and subsequently told the press that the plane had dropped arms and supplies to the contras and that U.S. officials in Honduras and El Salvador were involved in the operation. Assistant Secretary of State Elliott Abrams insisted that the flight was a "private initiative" and that there was "no U.S. government involvement direct or indirect" in supplying arms to the contras.[54]

In fact, the U.S. government was intimately involved, and as the story unfolded, the Reagan Administration faced its most serious crisis. Administration officials had diverted profits from arms sales to Iran to provide arms to the contras at a time when that was prohibited by law. After receiving a report from the Attorney General, on November 25, 1986, President Reagan admitted that he was "not fully informed" of this activity. Two individuals who did know, National Security Adviser John Poindexter and NSC staff member Lt. Col. Oliver North, were dismissed. A special prosecutor, two Select Congressional Committees, and a Special Review Board, chaired by former Senator John Tower, were appointed to investigate the operation and possible violations of laws.

The Senate Intelligence Committee's preliminary investigation and the Tower Commission's report confirmed that Oliver North had organized and directed a vast covert operation outside the government that involved retired military officers, former intelligence agents, and arms smugglers; one of their jobs was to assist the contras during the period when Congress prohibited it. Several individuals in the government assisted their efforts.[55]

The Congressional hearings, which began on May 5, 1987, investigated the details and tracked the money that had passed through fourteen corporations and thirteen bank accounts. Congress established that North solicited funds, and President Reagan helped by meeting with several potential donors. Senior U.S. officials also requested money from the Saudi royal family ($32 million), the Sultan of Brunei ($10 million), Taiwan ($2 million), and possibly Israel. Between 1984 and 1986, when the contras were complaining of a lack of funds, their own records indicated that they received over $100 million.[56] When asked about why the feudal kingdoms of Saudi Arabia and Brunei and the Taiwanese dictatorship provided money for the contras, President Reagan said it was because they "share our feeling about democracy."[57] Although President Reagan denied he knew that the profits from the arms sales were diverted to the contras, after less than three weeks of hearings, only 24 percent of the American people believed him.[58]

North had begun to establish his private network in 1984 and was involved in planning individual operations. For example, on September 1, 1984, North and a CIA official discussed a specific operation with Adolfo Calero, one of the leaders of the contras, and advised him to postpone it or risk losing a helicopter. Six months later, North recommended to his superiors that the U.S. help the contras seize or sink a Nicaraguan ship.[59] By July 1986, North's operation had acquired more than $4.5 million of assets, including six aircraft, warehouses, and an airfield in Costa Rica.[60]

The motive for the overall operation was a combination of the President's commitment to the contras and Congress' ambivalence. President Reagan, according to former National Security Adviser McFarlane, "repeatedly made it clear in public and in private that he did not intend to break faith with the contras. . . . People turned to covert action because they thought they could not get Congressional support for more overt activities." Since the CIA and State and Defense Departments would not circumvent the law, which required a Presidential Finding and notification of Congress, the NSC, the President's staff, became, in McFarlane's words, "the agency of last resort."[61]

On November 25, the day he was relieved of his duties by the President for possible violations of the law, North was in the hotel room of Richard Secord, a retired Air Force General who had helped manage the operation. The telephone rang. North picked it up and snapped to attention. President Reagan was calling to congratulate North on a job well done. The President called North a "national hero," and then offered the ultimate compliment: "Your work," he told North, "will make a great movie one day."[62]

The issue was no longer whether any senior Reagan Administration official had broken the law, but how many officials and how many laws were broken. The chickens, who had gone out and broken international law, had come to roost.

An Assessment of the Politics and the Policy

In a speech on Nicaragua, President Reagan confided that he felt "ashamed" when he read the remarks of a Nicaraguan contra:

> You Americans have the strength, the opportunity, but not the will. We want to struggle, but it is dangerous to have friends like you—to be left stranded on the landing beaches of the Bay of Pigs. Either help us or leave us alone.[63]

In many ways, the contra effort has resembled the Bay of Pigs operation, in which the United States organized, trained, and armed Cuban exiles to overthrow Castro. That operation was an embarrassing failure, but different lessons have been drawn from it. Some have suggested it should not have been done; others, that the United States should have followed through with direct military support.

In his speech, President Reagan left no doubt which of the two lessons he drew from the Bay of Pigs. After citing the remarks of the contra, he asked Congress "to send a message to this brave Nicaraguan and thousands like them. Tell them America stands with those who stand in defense of freedom."

But America did not stand united on the contras. Most Americans, preoccupied by other matters, did not even know which side the U.S. supported in Nicaragua. In April 1986, after three years of considerable press coverage and numerous Presidential speeches, only 38 percent of the American people knew that the United States supported the contras. As to whether the U.S. should support them, there was relatively little change in public opinion from June 1983 to May 1986: 23 to 31 percent supported aid to the contras, and about 53 to 66 percent opposed it.[64] The 2:1 public opinion ratio against aid to the contras was the Sisyphean rock that Reagan had to push up Capitol Hill for each vote.

To understand the politics of the issue, however, one needs to look below the surface of these surveys and examine the differential impact of the issue on the two political parties. A May 1986 poll showed that only 16 percent of the Democrats supported aid to the contras while 75 percent opposed it; 36 percent of the Republicans supported aid, while 51 percent opposed it.[65] A more revealing poll focused only on the 38 percent of the American people who knew the U.S. supported the contras. Among this better informed group, which is more likely to vote in primaries, 67 percent of the Republicans supported aid, and 64 percent of the Democrats opposed aid.[66] As both parties became more ideological and different from each other, the contra issue became one of the litmus tests of loyalty.

The contra issue contains an internal contradiction, which explains why a consensus has been elusive in the United States and why both parties enjoy raising the issue among their "converted" but are more careful about using it among independents. Simply, Republicans revel in the patriotic rhetoric of fighting Communists and supporting "freedom fighters," but fear looking too bellicose; and Democrats like to invoke "Vietnam," but fear looking soft on "national security" issues. These fears are legitimate both politically and from the standpoint of national interest. Americans do not want war, nor do they want their enemies to increase or expand. If the American people fear U.S. involvement in an unnecessary war, Democrats benefit. If the American people fear the Democrats would be ineffective in containing our enemies, Republicans benefit. American interest in Central America heightens not because of what people want but because of what they fear. Therefore, Republicans warn of "another Cuba," while Democrats warn of "another Vietnam."

In brief, the issue divided the United States, although, of course, not as much as the United States polarized Nicaragua. The two nations' politics remained entangled and stalemated.

In an assessment of the Reagan Administration's strategy, former NSC staff member under Reagan Roger Fontaine described it as a "qualified failure." He doubted that the Sandinistas could "be dislodged by a guerrilla army" or that they would offer "any convenient casus belli" for U.S. intervention. He implied that the United States should but probably would not overthrow the Sandinistas.[67] Therefore, from the perspective of U.S. interests, supporting the contras has not been the realistic strategy, which would have been to contain the revolution. But the Administration has been more concerned with increasing the costs to the Sandinistas than in pursuing U.S. interests.

The ultimate mark of a mutual obsession is that it evokes parallel behavior. Thus, the Reagan Doctrine on national liberation came to resemble the Sandinistas' "revolution without borders." The difference, according to the Reagan Administration, was that the United States was right, and Nicaragua was not. The Sandinistas, as Borge noted, have also become obsessed with Reagan. They are more interested in scoring propaganda points against the United States than in talking with their own people.

The resulting relationship of counterproductive policies and strident name-calling has served neither nation. Ramiro Gurdian, a Nicaraguan businessman, tired of listening to the ricochet of rhetoric, said in despair: "There is Sandinista rhetoric; there is Reagan's rhetoric; and then there is reality. They are three different things."[68]

Part IV

LOOKING BACK AND AHEAD

In few maladies are the pathogenic factors so
darkly hidden as the neuroses, and many modes
of treatment (e.g. persuasion) can only be
described as a blind fight with unseen foes. When
the morbid factors are appreciated and precisely
defined, our power of managing them is
considerably increased.

Ernest Jones, *Papers on Psychoanalysis*

Chapter 14

NIGHTMARES COME TRUE:

AN EXPLANATION

The past is never dead; it's not even past.
William Faulkner

IN THE LONG and sad relationship between the United States and
Nicaragua, the two nations and their neighbors have had their share
of hopes and fears, dreams and nightmares.

In September 1978, the Carter Administration hoped that Nicaragua would make a peaceful transit toward democracy in which the
United States would play a minimal role. Its nightmare was a Sandinista military victory.

Anastasio Somoza, Jr., first dreamed that eventually he would pass
his Presidency to his son; he feared that if he resigned, his country
would be wracked by war and captured by Marxist Sandinistas. If he
had to leave Nicaragua, Somoza wanted to live in Miami. His worst
nightmare would not have placed him as the victim of a bazooka attack in Paraguay.

The Sandinistas dreamed that they would be the vanguard of a revolution that would be an inspiration for Latin America. In the "new
Nicaragua," there would be jobs, health care, and education for all.
Their nightmare was that U.S. imperialism would make war against
them, the economy would fail, and they would become dependent on
the Soviet Union and eternally vulnerable.

The Reagan Administration hoped that support for a rebel movement would promote democracy in Nicaragua. And it feared that
Nicaragua might look more like Cuba after the civil war than it did
before.

Fidel Castro hoped that revolutionary Nicaragua would be the
model for Latin America that Cuba had failed to be; he feared that
Nicaragua would repeat all of Cuba's mistakes. The Soviet Union
shared Cuba's hope, and also feared that Nicaragua would become
another economically dependent client, like Cuba.[1]

The friends of the United States—Venezuela, Costa Rica, Panama,
the moderate opposition in Nicaragua—had an obsessive dream that

Somoza would fall. This dream so filled their thoughts that they gave little thought to their nightmare—that Marxists would capture the revolution and Castro would be its patron.

The friends of the United States enjoyed the dream for a moment and suffered the nightmare for years. For everyone else, only the nightmares came true. The history of U.S. policy toward Nicaragua since 1978 lends itself to a familiar if unfortunate question, who lost Nicaragua? However, with respect to Nicaragua, everyone lost. The question whether the nightmares could have been avoided is the subject of the next chapter. In this chapter, we will try to understand why the nightmares came true.

Repeating U.S. Policy: Seven Stages

With almost uncanny precision, U.S. policy toward Nicaragua passed through each of the seven stages of U.S.-Cuban relations twenty years before: from identification with the regime in 1974 to indirect war in 1982.

1. IDENTIFICATION. The power of Anastasio Somoza García and his two sons rested first on their control of the Guard, second on a united Liberal Party, and third on their identification with the United States. The United States sometimes protested or rejected that identification, and in 1945, 1947-48, 1963, and 1978-79, tried to encourage Somoza to step down or not to seek reelection. Nevertheless, at critical periods during the Cold War and during the tenure of two U.S. Ambassadors, Thomas Whelan and Turner Shelton, the United States identified its interests with those of the Somoza family. It was a short-sighted policy in which the United States paid a heavy price.

2. DISTANCE AND DISSOCIATION. In 1975, after the resignation of Richard Nixon and his Ambassador, the United States began to distance itself from Somoza. The Carter Administration withdrew U.S. support from Somoza, but it initially rejected the opposition's request to mediate because it wanted to separate itself from a past in which it had been the pivotal political actor in Nicaragua. It altered this preferred policy in September 1978, when it appeared that Somoza was trying to eliminate the moderate option and leave Nicaraguans and Americans with a simple but unacceptable choice between Somoza and the Communists. There was a consensus in the Administration that the longer Somoza remained in power the more

likely it was that the Sandinistas would win a violent revolution. The issue became how to prevent that worst-case scenario without harming other interests.

The United States reluctantly decided to mediate, but it did so in small steps that permitted policy makers to think that the change did not weaken the Administration's commitment to nonintervention and that it reinforced other principles, like regional cooperation. Carter's first decision was to support a Central American mediation effort, and when that failed, he insisted that U.S. mediation be undertaken within a multilateral framework under the auspices of the OAS.

To those inside and outside the Administration who had a different view of the appropriate U.S. role, each decision by the Administration was frustrating and inadequate. A more pragmatic perspective recommended that the United States force Somoza's departure. Although President Carter's aversion to mediation was overcome, he was reluctant to accept a unilateral strategy because he believed a multilateral approach was in the best long-term interests of the United States, and he would not approve overthrowing Somoza. Instead of forcing Somoza's resignation, the Carter Administration tried to negotiate the terms that would permit a free plebiscite. That effort failed, and the U.S. imposed sanctions against Somoza in February 1979.

3. THE LEFT LEGITIMIZED BY THE MIDDLE. Between February and July, the middle drifted toward the Sandinistas, as the United States had feared they would. Having failed to secure Somoza's resignation, the moderates in Nicaragua despaired. They did not have the patience or the organization to wait; they thought the Sandinistas were more moderate than they actually were; and they ignored the United States and listened to Costa Rica, Panama, and Venezuela, all of whom had decided that the only way to displace Somoza was by helping the Sandinistas. Alfonso Robelo later explained that he joined the Junta of the Revolutionary Government "because the support of Torrijos, Carlos Andrés Pérez, and Carazo gave me confidence that it was the right thing to do."[2]

The intrinsic weakness of a policy of distance and dissociation is that it ultimately depends on the blind man seeing the light. Having decided not to overthrow Somoza and having been unable to encourage his departure through sanctions, the United States lacked a policy during this period. All it could do was hope that the blind man, Somoza, would see. Instead, the blind man was struck by lightning. In the month of June, as the Sandinistas' "final offensive" gathered military equipment and assembled political support, the United States came to recognize that its nightmare was coming true.

4. THE SEARCH FOR A THIRD FORCE. The United States searched desperately for an Executive Committee of credible moderate leaders that would assume power after Somoza's departure and call for a cease-fire. That would have allowed time for the Guard to stabilize and for the Committee to negotiate a modus vivendi with the San José Junta.

The strategy failed. After the sanctions, the U.S. Embassy in Managua had few officers to maintain contacts with the opposition. By the time that Ambassador Pezzullo arrived, the moderate opposition was embittered, and many had gone to San José and allied with the Junta. When the moderates were ready, Somoza was intransigent, and the United States did not move him; when Somoza was ready to go, and the United States was ready to facilitate a new government, most of the moderates were not. Those few who were prepared to consider an Executive Committee wanted unequivocal assurances from the United States.

Because of Latin America's growing support for the Junta, the widening insurrection in the country, and the atrocities committed by the Guard, Carter made his support conditional on multilateral cooperation, which did not materialize. The Executive Committee idea died. Working with other leaders in the region, the Administration negotiated a final arrangement that both precluded a bloodbath and permitted a relationship to be developed with the incoming Junta.

5. RELATING TO THE REVOLUTION. After the Sandinistas' victory, the Administration sought good relations. The United States tried to help the revolution, deny it an enemy, and hope the new government would become more pragmatic and less ideological. The relationship was awkward, but the Nicaraguan government showed it was not impervious to internal or to outside Western influence. There were signs of arbitrariness and tyranny but also of political space; independent institutions were harassed, but permitted to exist and criticize; the government seemed willing to share some power, but not all of it; the Sandinistas were interested in diversifying their relations with Europeans and Latin Americans, but reserved their principal relationships with Cuba and the Soviet Union; there was enthusiastic support for health and education, but these services were delivered in a Marxist, anti-American package; and there was moral solidarity with other revolutionaries, but the FSLN restrained their impulse to provide material support.

6. DISTANCE AND NEGOTIATION.   In mid-November 1980, despite promises, the Nicaraguan government decided to provide massive aid to the Salvadoran rebels. On receiving the evidence in its last days, the Carter Administration suspended its aid to Nicaragua. The Reagan Administration entered office with a pledge to end aid and a perception that Nicaragua and Cuba were major threats to U.S. interests. Nonetheless, the Administration negotiated with the Nicaraguan government, which halted its arms transfers to the Salvadorans. For political and ideological reasons, the Reagan Administration did not resume aid.

A second round of negotiations tested the ability of two extremely resentful governments to reach an agreement on security issues. Neither side passed the test. The Reagan Administration then walked away from the bargaining table, convinced the Sandinistas were not serious. The Sandinistas did not read the United States any better; they were unaware that this was their last chance to negotiate peacefully with the Administration.

7. CONFRONTATION.   President Reagan's decision to support exiles whose goal was to overthrow the Nicaraguan regime was a fateful one, which led to a gradually deepening American commitment to the rebels and an escalation of the war. The watershed occurred on March 15, 1982, when the Sandinistas declared a state of emergency in response to military attacks by the contras and the disclosure of the U.S. covert program. Prior to that date, no important Nicaraguan leader, except Pastora, had left the country for exile. Subsequently, there was a steady stream of moderate leaders joining the violent opposition.[3] With the intensification of the war, the political space in Nicaragua grew smaller and the dependence on Cuba and the Soviet Union increased.

Explaining U.S. Policy

From identifying with a dictator to confronting a revolutionary government: How can we explain the evolution of U.S. policy toward Nicaragua?

REPETITION.   U.S. objectives toward Nicaragua in the twentieth century can be described succinctly as seeking to: (a) preclude the emergence of a regime that might be hostile to the United States and friendly to its adversary; (b) prevent instability from being exploited by a rival power;[4] and (c) deter or preclude Nicaragua from interfering in its neighbors' affairs.[5] These, of course, are classic security interests and explain the continuity of U.S. concern. U.S. policy makers focus on Nicaragua when they perceive a threat to one of these interests. Then, they pursue a fourth interest: (d) to promote peaceful change by economic and political development.

The cycle in U.S. policy between neglect of Nicaragua and panic when events seem to veer in an adverse direction, an often-described cycle,[6] is merely a restatement of the security motive that drives or stalls U.S. policy. Primary U.S. interests in Nicaragua and the region do not stem from a desire to extract resources or to implant a political philosophy, although the history of U.S. policy in Central America is replete with examples of both, but from fear, a rather unseemly fear for such a large nation facing such a small one, but a fear nevertheless that a hostile group could come to power and ally with a rival of the United States. Some U.S. policy makers have exaggerated the threat; others have underestimated it; but few have denied it.

The security motive helps to explain why and when the United States became exercised about developments in Nicaragua, and it partially explains why the United States identified with Batista and Somoza and confronted the Cuban and Nicaraguan revolutionary governments. But it does not adequately explain why the United States dissociated itself from Batista and Somoza and why it initially respected the two revolutionary governments. Nor does it explain the repetitive pattern of U.S. policy.

The U.S. government draws its specific policies from a reservoir of national experiences, a kind of collective political subconscious. "Foreign policy," Arthur Schlesinger, Jr., wrote, "is the face a nation wears to the world."[7] All nations project their style, political culture or character, and interpretations of recent history onto the international landscape. The less a nation knows about the world, the more its policy resembles its character rather than that of the nation that is the target of the policy. This is true of all countries. For example, Mexico's policy toward Nicaragua is more easily understood as a projection of its history than as a coherent strategy for addressing Nicaragua's predicament.

Because each national experience is unique, one would expect that different nations, even those with similar interests, would pursue different policies toward the same crisis. The United States, for example, repeatedly proposed elections as the strategy for resolving conflict in Central America; Mexico never did. Mexico supported revolutions; the United States opposed them.

"Political culture," as one element of the national experience, may also help to explain why a nation's decisions that are separated by a generation may be so similar—for example, the similarities between the Bowdler Mission to Nicaragua in 1978 and the Stimson Mission fifty years before. But in implying an immutable, predetermined inheritance, the term "political culture" unnecessarily constrains.[8] For that reason, "political character" or "style" might be better for referring to the political attitudes and beliefs that North Americans use to understand and approach local and international politics.[9] In citing "national experience" as a source of U.S. foreign policy, I want to draw a concept broad enough to include style and character; my purpose is to visualize the source of U.S. foreign policy as relatively stable but also capable of adapting as the nation's perception of itself and the world changes.

In the case of Nicaragua, the question of why the United States "so often supports dictators"[10] is easily answered: it mostly didn't. Most U.S. administrations were uncomfortable with the Somoza regime and particularly with its attempts to identify with the United States. When did the United States support him? President Nixon shared Somoza's fervently anti-Communist view of the world, and others thought the Somozas hardly the worst dictators in an area that appeared to have no aptitude for democracy. When the United States needed Nicaragua's support either for specific actions in Guatemala or Cuba or for a global objective, the United States subsumed its dislike for the regime. This, of course, is the tradition in international relations.

Given this tradition, what is most surprising in U.S. policy toward Nicaragua is not the moments when it has treated Somoza well but the historically longer-lasting periods of detachment from and distaste for the regime. Since Somoza took power in 1936, the United States has spent much less time debating whether to support him than it has trying to decide what to do about him. The explanation for this resides in the political character, values, and experience of the United States, which has always given more attention to the character and internal behavior of regimes than have most other nations.

North Americans identify with the "middle" abroad, meaning not just the middle class or businessmen but rather all people and groups in favor of gradual and peaceful change. In a 1974 poll, nearly three-fourths of the American people agreed that it was "morally wrong" to support military dictatorships even if that government provided military bases for the United States.[11] Because North Americans dislike dictators, U.S. policy makers are generally defensive about charges of supporting them. For example, when Luis Somoza visited the United States in 1959 as Nicaragua's President, he was surprised and upset that the Administration "shied away" from him. The State Department was worried, according to an internal memorandum, that official contact with Somoza would confirm "accusations that the U.S. favors dictatorships."[12]

When the "middle" delegitimizes a dictator, U.S. officials are compelled to follow the "middle." Even a conservative Administration cannot sustain a policy of supporting a dictator if the middle groups in that country have rejected him. That explains the distancing from both Batista and Somoza. It also explains why the Reagan Administration, which had originally embraced Philippine President Ferdinand Marcos and Haitian President Jean-Claude Duvalier, kept its distance when the middle openly opposed both leaders.

The United States is uncomfortable about supporting dictators but also about overthrowing them. In response to the question whether the United States should ever consider overthrowing a Latin American government, 63 percent of the American public said no; 24 percent said yes.[13] For an American, elections are the natural "middle path" between dictators and revolutionaries. An election is often the last idea considered by people trying to remove a dictator, but it is generally the first thought of U.S. policy makers.

Some in Latin America believe that revolution is the only way to overcome the structural barriers that prevent social justice, but almost no North Americans believe that. U.S. views are shaped by an eighteenth-century constitution that encourages incrementalism. Because class mobility is the norm in the United States, North Americans reject the Marxist premise that the class struggle is permanent.

Rather than accept permanent divisions, U.S. policy generally aims to bring groups together for dialogue. Typically, the U.S. government referred to the Junta in San José as the head of the Government of National *Reconciliation* while the Junta called it the Government of National *Reconstruction*. U.S. policy makers tend to reject the idea that there are no middle options. As long as there are two views, there has to be a middle option; the only question is whether the two sides can be moved to accept a compromise. U.S. policy consistently projected this aspect of its national experience onto Nicaragua. Even the Reagan Administration repeatedly pledged to suspend support for the contras if the Sandinistas agreed to a dialogue with the contras.

An important element in the U.S. political character is the tendency to mix principle, a vision of what the United States should do, and pragmatism, what it can do.[14] The dislike for the Somoza regime reflected the principle; the occasional compromises, pragmatism. The President pronounces the principles: for Carter, it was nonintervention, human rights, and regional consultation; for Reagan, anti-Communism and democracy. The President's advisers try to apply the principle to solve problems or crises, but sometimes a principle impedes a solution to the problem. In that case, the President maintains the principle until a stronger case can be made for modifying or discarding it. Those who do not share the vision or who see an easier way to solve a problem are frustrated. But the distinction between these two points should not obscure the facts that principle rests partly on a pragmatic cost-and-benefit calculation and that the pragmatic argument often has a strong moral basis.

An important debate during the Nicaragua crisis that illustrates this tension in the national style was whether to force Somoza's resignation. The pragmatic argument was very powerful: no one could force out Somoza but the United States; failure to do so would lead to a Sandinista victory. The analysis was accepted, and it proved correct. Yet the Administration did not follow the analysis to its logical conclusion. Why? There were five reasons: the threat, the principle, the consequences, the uncertainty, and the precedent.

First, Somoza was an indirect, not a direct threat to U.S. interests. The Administration disliked Somoza's regime, but the only threat that it posed was that its continuing in power increased the chance of a Sandinista military victory, which, it was believed, was more likely to threaten U.S. interests.

Second, the principle of nonintervention was a fundamental element of Carter's approach toward Latin America, but it was not sacrosanct. As Carter stated: "We have no inclination to interfere in the internal affairs of other nations *unless* our direct security interests are threatened." Because Somoza did not directly threaten those interests, the United States would not intervene. "Intervention" has been defined and interpreted in many different ways. The Carter Administration defined it narrowly to mean that the United States would not unilaterally overthrow a standing government. A collective effort was viewed differently.

A third reason for not overthrowing Somoza stemmed from a concern with the consequences of the action. If the United States had forced Somoza out, it would have had to assume responsibility for the consequences, which would almost certainly have been a period of great instability. It was also possible that the National Guard, which was so closely tied to Somoza, might collapse on his departure, leaving a clear path for the Sandinistas to come to power. In short, deposing Somoza could produce the very outcome the United States wanted to avoid. Moreover, the United States would probably have had to deepen its involvement in Nicaragua to keep the opposition from fragmenting and the Guard from either disintegrating or taking power.

A fourth reason was uncertainty and a lack of information. A nation, like an individual, infrequently takes undesirable actions unless it has no other choice. As late as one month before Somoza fled Nicaragua, the United States thought a "third force" could assume power because it was unaware that the Sandinistas had accumulated an arsenal and logistics network sufficient to defeat Somoza. Nor did the United States know that the FSLN's political support from Latin American democratic governments was so deep that it could preclude a third option. Even Daniel Ortega, who knew that, later admitted he was uncertain that Somoza's end was near. Alfonso Robelo later said he was surprised when the Guard collapsed.

Fifth, the decision to force the resignation of a foreign head of state is, as Jim Wright said, "extreme." Somoza was despised with good reason, but compared to several other military dictators in Latin America, like Pinochet of Chile, Videla of Argentina, Stroessner of Paraguay, or Castro of Cuba, he would hardly qualify as the most ruthless. If one started by overthrowing Somoza, then where would one stop?

In sum, the United States chose not to overthrow Somoza because of a national experience that seeks "middle options" abroad as well as at home and because of a mixture of principle and pragmatism, a tension that has long shaped U.S. foreign policy. What is most illuminating is how this reluctance to overthrow a right-wing dictator in the midst of a succession crisis also characterized the policies of Eisenhower and Kennedy in the Dominican Republic (1960-61), Kennedy (1961-63) and Reagan (1985-86) in Haiti, and Reagan (1985-86) in the Philippines. In every case, the President rejected the option of pushing out a rightist dictator. In the one case where an Administration did force out a dictator—Diem of South Vietnam—the Kennedy Administration soon regretted it.[15]

The U.S. predilection for the "middle" explains both the desperate search for a "third force" as the succession crisis in Nicaragua reached a climax and the decision not to intervene when the United States finally recognized the strength of the rebels' support among moderates within the country and among legitimate democratic governments in the region. From the beginning to the end of the crisis, the "middle" unknowingly stimulated, guided, and defined the parameters of U.S. policy.

In relating to the Cuban and Nicaraguan revolutionary governments, the United States was initially sympathetic, but this changed as it began to realize that the revolutionaries viewed the United

States as its enemy and acted on that perception. Judging by the statements of Congressional supporters as well as opponents of aid to the Sandinista government, the American people had a low threshhold of tolerance for virulent criticism by leaders of small, neighboring nations like Nicaragua who were at the same time requesting aid. The United States slid toward confrontation because of a visceral reaction, but it confronted Nicaragua, as it had Cuba, only when it perceived that its security interests were affected.

The role of Congress in shaping foreign policy increases when the Administration's policy shifts from diplomacy to the use of resources—for example, foreign aid. Then, Congress plays the role of a balancer of U.S. national interests. It compels liberal Presidents to give greater emphasis to security concerns and conservative Presidents to give greater weight to humanitarian concerns. Congress reluctantly approved aid to revolutionary Nicaragua during the Carter Administration, and only with the condition that aid would be ended if Nicaragua supported insurgencies abroad. And it reluctantly approved aid to the contras because of President Reagan's lobbying, and only after insisting that his Administration give more attention to negotiations and to stopping the human rights violations of the contras.

Although individual legislators tend to assault Administrations from one side or another, Congress as an institution tends to constrain and balance the President's activism. By compelling Presidents to give attention to interests that Congress thinks are being neglected, Congress reflects and reinforces the centrist tendency of the U.S. national experience on foreign policy.

As the United States repeated the seven stages in its relationship with Nicaragua, it was guided by its national experience through a polarized terrain of unattractive options. It began its journey by dissociating itself from the dictator, then searched futilely for a middle option, then stumbled through a half-hearted attempt to relate to the revolution, and finally was drawn into an unproductive confrontation. At each step, the U.S. government sought a "middle path."

EXPLAINING CHANGE. In addition to the continuity and the repetition in U.S. policy toward Nicaragua, one can also see important policy changes over time. Choices were made from a wide range of options and instruments, from trying to stabilize a dictator to trying to destabilize him, from aiding the military to assisting economic development. When faced with the prospect of Somoza taking power or being reelected, the administration of Franklin Roosevelt remained silent, that of Harry Truman broke diplomatic relations, and that of Richard Nixon helped him secure another term. When faced with a leftist Sandinista regime, Jimmy Carter lobbied Congress to provide it economic aid, and Ronald Reagan lobbied Congress to provide its enemies weapons.

The United States is motivated by security concerns, but its choices of how, when, and in what ways to respond to a threat require a richer explanation. Within the parameters of the interests and values of the United States, Presidents have considerable latitude in deciding how much attention and priority to give to a particular interest or value. Each Administration's policies reflect a reaction to its predecessor and an independent judgment about which U.S. interests matter most.

Moreover, a new Administration, particularly one that represents a different party from its predecessor, tends at the beginning to overstate differences with its predecessor in order to justify its mandate for change. William Howard Taft condemned the "big stick" of Theodore Roosevelt and announced "dollar diplomacy," which in turn was criticized by Woodrow Wilson, who offered a ringing defense of liberty and democracy. Similarly, Jimmy Carter criticized the covert acts to destabilize governments by his predecessors and identified his Administration with human rights, and Ronald Reagan rebuked Carter for opening the Caribbean to Communism and enunciated a doctrine aimed at overturning leftist governments.

Republicans have been more conservative and anti-Communist, giving higher priority to security and stability and less to human rights and social reform. The choice of instruments reflects these different priorities, with Republicans giving greater weight to military aid, covert actions, military maneuvers and shows of strength, private investment, and bilateral aid, and Democrats stressing diplomacy and negotiations, economic aid, and multilateral institutions. Fundamental debates almost never occur within an Administration. Nixon's policy of supporting Somoza because of his anti-Communism and Carter's of withdrawing support because of human rights were so fundamental to each Administration that the United States could only change direction when either it changed Administrations or events compelled a change in policy.

Perhaps the most important single variable explaining why policies change and why Administrations choose different policies is an Administration's perception of the nature and intensity of the threat that the United States faces. The more distant the threat the more likely an Administration will adhere to its initial principles; the more immediate the threat the more likely the Administration's policy will evolve. As the Cuban and Nicaraguan crises reached a climax, the Eisenhower and the Carter Administrations began contemplating options—such as forcing the dictator's resignation—that they had rejected before.

Threat perception not only explains changes during a single Administration, it also helps to explain the differences between Administrations. Although the Carter Administration was unlikely to have maintained a good relationship with the Sandinista government after finding evidence of its arms transfers to the Salvadorans, it is inconceivable that it would have organized and supported a covert war, as Reagan did. The two Administrations had sharply divergent perceptions of the nature and intensity of the threat. To Reagan, the Sandinistas represented an immediate, grave, Soviet-inspired threat that was testing the will and jeopardizing the interests of the United States. His policies flowed from that definition. To Carter, the Sandinistas represented a Central American revolution; the United States should try to help it and contain it simultaneously.

In addition to a President's ideology and perception of threat, a third factor that is important in explaining why a policy changes is the period in which it occurs. The way policy makers perceive an issue like the Nicaraguan revolution is affected by the general swings in the public mood and by significant international events, such as the Iranian revolution or the Soviet invasion of Afghanistan.

Traumatic events like the Cuban or Nicaraguan revolutions also influence perceptions for a certain period of time. The pace and concern of U.S. policy makers quickens after such traumas. U.S. policy toward Haiti and the Dominican Republic from 1960 to 1964, for example, sought to avoid another Cuba; toward the Philippines and Chile in 1985-86, "another Nicaragua."[16]

These other crises ended differently than Nicaragua and Cuba, but there is no evidence that U.S. policy toward these and almost all other succession crises differed in any significant way. In almost every case, the President feared a power vacuum and rejected the option of pushing the dictator out. Because U.S. policy was similar, the explanation for the different outcomes must reside in the decisions of local actors, who may have been influenced by the previous trauma. Indeed, as one looks at all these crises, local decisions appear central:

- In Cuba in 1958, the support that Castro received from the middle classes and the democratic governments in the region proved more important than U.S. efforts to forge a "third force."
- In the Dominican Republic in 1961, the United States tried to stop the coup against General Rafael Trujillo, but it failed, and the assassination occurred.

- In Haiti in 1961-63, President Kennedy feared another Cuba but was unable to find a formula to replace Duvalier. Nonetheless, the Duvaliers avoided revolution and stayed in power until the son fled in February 1986. When asked whether the United States gave Duvalier "any strong advice to leave," President Reagan said: "No. And he never asked us for any."[17]
- In the Philippines in 1985-86, the crucial events leading to the replacement of Marcos with a democratic government were the elections, the unity of the opposition, their effective strategy to pressure Marcos, and most important, a military coup.
- In Chile from 1977 to 1987, General Augusto Pinochet followed his own schedule for succession despite three different strategies by the United States, one by Carter and two by Reagan.
- And in Nicaragua, the middle class supported by Latin American democratic governments chose to risk a future with the Sandinistas rather than the status quo or a "third force" arrangement proposed by the United States.

Crossing Borders to Explain the Nicaraguan Revolution

U.S. policy does not explain sufficiently either why Somoza fell and the Sandinistas came to power or why the revolution has become radicalized, militarized, and more dependent on the Soviet Union. For a complete explanation, one needs to examine the policies of the other actors. Why did the moderate democrats in Nicaragua and democratic Latin American governments repeat policies that either they or their counterparts followed twenty years before? Why did they support the Sandinistas? Why did their nightmares come true?

Where interests and objectives differ among nations or groups, one expects disagreements and sometimes conflicts. The most difficult and puzzling questions of the Nicaraguan revolution, however, were raised by nations or groups who thought they shared objectives.

- The U.S. government could not understand why Venezuela, Costa Rica, Panama, and Mexico supported the Sandinistas, and these countries could not understand why the United States, which said it did not support Somoza, would not replace him.
- The United States could not understand how or why Nicaraguan moderates would trust the Sandinistas more than they would trust the United States, and the moderates could not understand why the U.S. just did not keep the Cubans out.

· Finally, the U.S. could not understand why its Latin American friends were so quick to eliminate any alternative military pillar to the FSLN, leaving it with a monopoly of power, and several Latin American governments could not understand why the Carter Administration was so obsessed with the Communist specter that it would consider saving the National Guard or proposing an Inter-American Peace Force.

The misunderstandings stemmed from different perceptions of the crisis due to different national experiences. In the case of Latin American nations, the principal pertinent elements in their national experiences derived from their heritage, their recent political history, and their perceptions of the United States and its relationship with Somoza.

HERITAGE. The United States is the product of the northern European enlightenment, individualism, and religious tolerance; Latin America inherited southern Europe's values of hierarchy, centralism, and absolutism. Some attribute the history of militarism and dictatorship to this heritage.[18] Because of this and the late arrival of industrialization, the Latin American state plays a central role in society.

As many of the nations in the region have become democratic, the heritage of militarism has diminished in importance, but nonetheless, its residue is still evident in the fears democrats have of a return to dictatorship and even in the way many democrats define democracy. Latin American democrats tend to give greater emphasis to the ends of social justice; the United States tends to stress due process. Whereas the United States tends to believe that power divided is freedom protected, many Latin Americans tend to believe that power united is necessary for social justice and independence. Therefore, the U.S. Constitution divides, checks, and balances power; Latin America tends to accumulate power in the state as the "protector" of society. Not surprisingly, the concept of "pluralism" is subject to different interpretations in the United States and Latin America.

RECENT HISTORY. In Latin America's experience, however, the last forty years may have been more influential than its four-hundred-year heritage. After the Second World War, a new generation of Latin American leaders, influenced by the Four Freedoms and the social justice of the New Deal, confronted military dictatorships. In Venezuela, Rómulo Betancourt fought with his aide Carlos Andrés Pérez against the dictator General Marcos Pérez Jiménez. When exiled, they stayed in Costa Rica and were protected by José Figueres, and his young assistants Daniel Oduber and Rodrigo Carazo. These leaders conspired with other democrats in the region to overthrow Caribbean dictators, who often called them "Communists."[19]

On assuming the Presidency of Venezuela in 1959, Betancourt declared the military dictatorships of neighboring countries illegitimate. Dominican Rafael Trujillo was his first target, and Betancourt assisted a group of rebels that launched an invasion of the Dominican Republic from Cuba on June 14, 1959. Trujillo put down the rebellion and retaliated by helping right-wing Venezuelan military officers to try to overthrow Betancourt. When Trujillo was assassinated in May 1961, Betancourt rejoiced and in his memoirs, took credit for having prompted the act.[20] Carlos Andrés Pérez felt as strongly about liberating Nicaragua from Somoza as his mentor Betancourt felt about Trujillo.

Unlike Latin democrats, the United States, although often uncomfortable with rightist dictatorships, has never felt threatened by them. U.S. concern has always been focused on leftist governments. Latin American democrats have tended to believe that the United States prefers more obeisant, right-wing dictators to more independent social democrats. Therefore, when the Carter Administration urged its democratic friends in the region not to help the Sandinistas, the Latin governments tended to think that either the United States still supported Somoza or it simply feared social change.

Latin American governments viewed the Sandinistas differently than the United States, partly because they tended to speak mainly with the Terceristas and Pastora, who used the language of social democracy, and also because they were either sympathetic to or supportive of the anti-Americanism of the Sandinistas. The Panamanian and Mexican governments, of course, attached little importance to elections or due process, and emphasized the rhetoric of revolution, anti-imperialism, and social justice.

LIFTING THE WEIGHT OF THE UNITED STATES. The power and presence of the United States in Latin America in the twentieth century has had important and enduring effects on the psychology of the region.[21] Some Latin Americans admire its achievements and look to it for answers; others see the United States as the region's biggest problem. Some feel a certain resentment, anguish, or humiliation because of past U.S. interventions and continuing influence. Many feel a combination of all these feelings, and this is reflected in the different forms that the quest for independence and dignity in Latin America has taken—virulent anti-Americanism on the left, authoritarian nationalism on the right, and a deep, genuine sense of national pride.

Somoza's self-advertisement as a U.S. surrogate offended those in Latin America who were seeking an independent path between subservience and hostility to the United States. Somoza was reported to have told Mexican President Luis Echeverría: "You should envy me. I have no problems. All I have to do is what Washington wants me to do."[22] Both Echeverría and Carlos Fuentes, who reported the story, were astonished that any Latin leader would admit to being a vassal. But by confirming their stereotype of the relationship between the United States and right-wing dictators, Somoza reassured the Mexicans that they were better; they were independent.

Somoza's decline coincided with the ascendancy of Latin America onto the world stage. Panama had just negotiated new treaties on the Canal, and Venezuela and Mexico, awash in billions of petrodollars, extended their foreign policies into the region. At the same time, the Carter Administration consulted them often and encouraged them to play more important roles in the region and the world. These governments were therefore eager to help the Nicaraguan opposition after the death of Chamorro. Many in Latin America viewed Somoza's departure as an opportunity not only to extend democracy but to assert their new power. Removing "Washington's man" was particularly exhilarating.

Carlos Andrés Pérez, Rodrigo Carazo, and Omar Torrijos were not naive about Marxist-Leninists, but their consuming preoccupation was defeating Somoza. Why did they give almost no time or consideration to what would follow? First, they viewed right-wing dictators as a much more serious threat to their interests than Communists. Pérez had fought a military dictatorship, and he felt that the United States did not help in this struggle. Many Latin democrats believed the United States was only concerned about Communists and even helped rightists against democrats.[23] Pérez articulated this frustration best:

> The U.S. is not very knowledgeable. [It] does not know how much blood, how many sacrifices, how much struggle, how much frustration that generations of Latin Americans have gone through. I would never regret having supported the struggle against Somoza, even if the Sandinista movement changes into a communist movement and tries to establish a communist government in Nicaragua because this does not [stain] our moral value . . . in helping the country to free itself from Somoza's dictatorship.[24]

Second, although some governments, notably Mexico, were not worried about leftist regimes, others, like Venezuela, Costa Rica, and Panama, were concerned but skeptical that the Sandinistas would establish a Marxist state. Because Somoza lacked any credibility, his charge that the Sandinistas were "Communists" was dismissed. Many leaders in the region had spoken to the Sandinistas and found them pragmatic. Moreover, the Sandinista strategy of recruiting moderate Nicaraguan leaders left the impression that the Marxist element was being diluted and that a broad national coalition would take power in Nicaragua.

These governments also expected that if they helped the Sandinistas during the revolution, they could gain influence afterward. Pérez also viewed Venezuelan aid as a way to preempt Cuba; he underestimated or did not fully recognize the nature of the Sandinistas' ties to Cuba. The excitement of deposing a hated dictator spread throughout the region and was caught by the foreign journalists who covered the war.[25]

Some leaders in the region believed that the United States would make sure that whatever followed Somoza would be neither Communist nor a threat to the region's (and U.S.) interests. Certainly, this was the view of many Nicaraguan moderates. Ramiro Gurdian, a Nicaraguan businessman and president of the Nicaraguan Union of Agricultural Producers, stated this most clearly: "Many people told us that this was going to be another Cuba, but we did not think it could happen. . . . Surely, the U.S. was not going to let this become another Cuba."[26] It is illuminating to compare that statement to another by a Cuban businessman, who was asked in the 1960s by Philip Bonsal why moderates didn't support an alternative to Castro: "Simple! We had no confidence in any possible Cuban leadership of the anti-Castro forces, and we did not believe that you, the United States, would let Castro get away with it."[27]

Even as the moderates rejoiced over the culmination of Sandino's struggle against the Yankees, many thought the United States would prevent an adverse outcome. Part of the answer to the riddle why the United States and its Latin American friends worked at cross-purposes to undermine each other's compatible objectives is this: All the key actors thought the United States could control everyone else's behavior—except their own.

In other words, Latin American democrats conspired to overthrow Somoza, suspicious and mistrustful in one corner of their minds whether the United States would really permit its surrogate to fall, and confident in another corner of their minds that the United States would not permit the revolution to turn to Cuba. Yet their decisions precluded that. In the end, the middle option disappeared when Nicaraguan moderates allied with the left. Costa Rica, Panama, Venezuela, and to a lesser degree, Mexico effectively shielded Cuba's role. The United States chose to respect its friends' views rather than act unilaterally.

When Carter told the other leaders of his commitment to nonintervention, either they did not believe him, or alternatively, they could not bring themselves to try to persuade him why they felt the principle did not apply to Nicaragua. Of course, neither the United States nor Latin America adheres to the principle when it determines that its interests are threatened. Somoza threatened Latin America's interests, and the Sandinistas were perceived to have threatened those of the United States. It would have been logical to combine both sets of interests, but neither side communicated effectively enough to achieve both goals.

Carter was serious when he talked of the importance of acting with friendly government in the regions. "My inclination from the very beginning," he later said, "was to not act unilaterally for two reasons. First, I was publicly and personally opposed to U.S. intervention in the internal affairs of other countries. . . . And secondly, I was unsure about the accuracy of the information I was getting about Nicaragua. And I had the impression, which may have been erroneous, that a combined assessment by Costa Rica, Panama, Colombia, and Mexico would be more nearly accurate for Central America than our unilateral assessment."[28] Carter was right not to have leaped in front of these other governments or confronted them, but his assumption was questionable. U.S. assessments of the situation had to be different because of different national experiences and interests, and based on subsequent events and even the eventual views of these governments, it would appear that the initial U.S. concern about the Sandinistas was justified.

Unable to Retreat

This explains why the Sandinistas came to power, but it does not explain the radicalization of the revolution, which was not inevitable. Because of the Sandinistas' preconceptions of imperialism, the United States was limited in its ability to influence them positively. The most it could do was not make the situation worse. The Nicaraguan government wanted to diversify its relations, and thus the major opportunities for positive influence rested with Latin American and European governments.

By 1983, however, most of these governments either were disillusioned with the Marxism of the Sandinista leadership, or had serious economic problems of their own. The decline in the price of oil and the rise in debt turned Mexican and Venezuelan policy inward. Many of these governments had their own reasons for lowering their profile and reducing aid to Nicaragua; U.S. pressure gave them an additional reason. The Contadora Group wanted to play a role but was disregarded by two increasingly intransigent actors, the Reagan Administration and the Sandinistas, who seemed determined to collide.

The process through which these two protagonists should find themselves on the precipice of a military confrontation was certainly foreseen. Both sides claimed they wanted to avoid confrontation, yet both contributed to it. Each had a fearful prophecy of the other that connected and came true. The suspicions that each harbored for the other led them to interpret the behavior of the other in the worst possible light. Therefore, each felt the need to take defensive measures, which were interpreted as provocations by the other side. This, in turn, led to deliberate provocations.

By 1983, the Reagan Administration deliberately sought to transfer legitimacy from the Sandinistas to the contras and to isolate Nicaragua from the rest of Central and Latin America. To achieve this goal, moderate leaders in Nicaragua needed to leave and join the armed opposition outside the country. In four years, hardly a long time, U.S. policy had shifted from trying to avoid polarization in Nicaragua to promoting it.

Having committed themselves to the contras, the Reagan Administration could neither retreat nor change direction. In response to a question from Congress about whether he had ever contemplated proposing an alternative approach to the President on Nicaragua or telling him the policy was wrong, Robert McFarlane confessed: "To tell you the truth, probably the reason I didn't is because if I'd done that, Bill Casey, Jeane Kirkpatrick, and Cap Weinberger would have said I was some kind of commie."[29] Inhibited by the fear of looking soft or pink, the Administration was locked into a strategy that could not succeed in Nicaragua or be sustained in the United States; all it could do was hurt Nicaragua and diminish the President's credibility.

What of the Sandinista strategy? The Sandinistas viewed negotiations and tolerance of criticism as a sign of weakness. Either the government was unaware, or it did not care about the effect of its actions on the Congressional debate over funding the contras. At crucial points in the debate, in May 1985 and then in March and May 1986, the Nicaraguan government took actions that strengthened President Reagan's case for aid to the contras. Why? Because as Omar Cabezas, a Sandinista leader, explained: "The only thing they are debating in Washington is how and when to destroy us." Nicaraguan government radio echoed this point: "Nothing good will come from Congress. We must be prepared."[30]

In short, both governments were insecure and distrusted each other so completely that they were unable to consider any way to influence the other except by force. Nicaragua's moderates, who were squeezed to the left during the revolution, were then squeezed to the right by both the Sandinistas and the Reagan Administration.

Philip Bonsal concludes his analysis of the Cuban revolution by suggesting: "A conviction that the United States would take care of the situation sapped the activism of much of the [moderate] opposition."[31] Many Nicaraguan moderates also thought the United States "would take care" of the revolution, but by allying with the FSLN when Somoza was finally ready to leave, they made it difficult for the Carter Administration to assist a democratic transition. Later, by leaving Nicaragua to join the contras, the moderates made it easy for the Reagan Administration to polarize and radicalize the revolution.

THE SIMPLEST way to explain the Nicaraguan revolution and its radicalization is to find a villain. For the Carter Administration, the Nicaraguan moderates lacked the courage to create a democratic alternative; and for these moderates, the Carter Administration lacked the will to depose Somoza and contain the Marxists. For the Reagan Administration, the Sandinistas are the cause of the country's distress; and for the Sandinistas, it is U.S. imperialism. Pointing fingers completes the repetition of the Cuba parallel.

Our purpose, however, is to understand what happened well enough to avoid repetition. To do so, one needs to visualize the Nicaraguan drama as a puzzle, and recognize that identifying, or blaming, the individual pieces is less useful than knowing how they fit together.

Chapter 15

TURNING POINTS

When you are on a circle,
every point is a turning point.
Luis Muñoz Marín

THE WORLD is not a laboratory that will hold still while a social scientist changes a single variable to see if that would produce a different outcome. We know that the U.S. government often failed to accomplish its objective in Nicaragua. We do not know whether other policy ideas that were either rejected or not considered by the U.S. government would have been more successful. It is worth recalling that many options were rejected because they were judged more costly than the decisions that were chosen.

Nonetheless, there were turning points when different decisions—by Anastasio Somoza, the Nicaraguan moderate opposition, the Latin American democratic governments, the U.S. government during the Carter and Reagan Administrations, and finally the Sandinista government—might have fulfilled some dreams and led to fewer nightmares.

In examining alternatives, one should be wary of the power of hindsight and the temptation of subjectivity. It is hard, perhaps impossible, to interpret the past without being influenced by one's conception of the present. If one believes that the current regime in Nicaragua is a threat to the United States, then in reviewing the history, one is likely to think that the United States should have been more forceful and taken "all measures necessary" to prevent the Sandinistas from coming to power, perhaps even defending Somoza or, alternatively, airlifting arms to the Guard after he left.

If one believes that the Sandinista revolution is noble, then one would probably view most of the decisions made by the U.S. government from 1977 to 1987 as malevolent or mistaken and believe that U.S. policy should simply have tried to facilitate and support the revolution or, at the minimum, not have tried to stop it.

Finally, if one believes that the Sandinista revolution is misguided, but not terribly dangerous, then one might wonder why the United States was and is so exercised about Nicaragua.

These three examples help demonstrate the combined trap of sub-

jectivity and hindsight. Although the rest of this book has tried to resist the temptation of viewing events with the benefit of hindsight,
in this chapter I will yield to it, though not completely. Instead of
evaluating the key decisions in terms of what I think should have
been done, I ask whether an alternative might have better served the
interests and objectives of the particular decision maker and whether
a long-term approach could help resolve the outstanding problems
between the United States and Nicaragua.

Different Decisions

Although no single actor is responsible for the Nicaraguan revolution and its aftermath, Anastasio Somoza, Jr., is more responsible
than any other. It was his decision to remain in power, exploit his
country, and fight a war against Nicaragua's youth that decimated
Nicaragua and continues to shape its future. The Sandinistas believed that Somoza was both their worst enemy and their best ally,
and they were right.[1]

In a comment that showed the dynasty's cynicism, Anastasio Somoza, Sr., described Nicaragua's political process to reporters in
1948: "It took 20,000 lives for the Liberals to get into power. It will
take 40,000 to get us out of here."[2] He was prescient. The first and
most important turning point was simply Somoza's decision not to
step down to allow for a peaceful, stable transition. The best way
would have been for him to accept a plebiscite, because that would
have permitted the opposition to organize its own leadership and assume power when it won. If Somoza had stepped aside at any moment before May 1979, he would have saved many lives and much
grief. And from his own perspective, if he had not stayed until the
end, it is possible that today he might be alive and living well in
Miami.

In a nation that has seen its leaders change only by war, Nicaragua's moderates have always been the victims. When Somoza would
not leave, they transferred their only currency—legitimacy—to the
Sandinistas, giving them the patina of respectability that contributed
to their winning the struggle. Had they—the FAO and its associated
groups—remained united and independent of both the Sandinistas
and Somoza, it is conceivable that they could have been the center of
the transitional government after Somoza left, and the possibility of
Nicaragua becoming democratic would have been much greater. In
retrospect, Alfonso Robelo said that the biggest "mistake I made was
to join the Junta."[3] Some, like Robelo, played leading roles in the new

government, but over time most resigned, and many left the country to pursue another round of the armed struggle.

A similar role was played by the governments of Venezuela, Costa Rica, Panama, and, to a lesser degree, Mexico. They provided the weapons, logistical network, but most of all, the legitimacy that permitted a Sandinista military victory. They judged that the only way to dislodge the Somoza dynasty was by helping the Sandinistas. They shielded Cuba's massive involvement in the last month before the victory, and blocked the alternative—a peace force, a transitional government—that the United States proposed at that time. After the Sandinistas came to power, each of these neighboring governments became disillusioned, although to different degrees. Each reduced rather than increased efforts to promote moderation within Nicaragua.[4]

Between October 1978 and November 1984, there were six moments when a different decision by the U.S. government might have been more successful in influencing a change in the Nicaraguan government and permitting a brighter future for U.S.–Nicaraguan relations. In none of these moments, however, was U.S. influence in Nicaragua as strong as it was in the aftermath of the earthquake in 1973-74. At that time Somoza was extremely weak; the opposition relatively strong and united; and there was no serious insurgency. The tradeoff for the United States was simple: either help stabilize Somoza or make U.S. aid conditional on Somoza's acceptance of a genuine democratic process. President Richard Nixon, guided by his Ambassador, Turner Shelton, chose the first option. In comparison, the ability of the United States to influence Nicaragua during the six moments between 1978 and 1984 described below was much smaller.

First, in October and November 1978, during the mediation, if the United States had applied more pressure on Somoza, he might have recalculated the costs and benefits of remaining in power and left. Unfortunately, the debate was framed in such a way that this argument could not win. The issue was whether the United States should try to overthrow Somoza. For the five reasons described in the last chapter, the United States government is unlikely ever to answer that question affirmatively unless the target government is perceived as an ally of a rival power. (In my view, the United States should not overthrow a government of the right or the left.)

The question of when to apply sanctions was a matter of judgment. Vaky and Bowdler wanted to apply them before Somoza made a decision, and Carter and his senior advisers preferred to threaten Somoza first and only apply the sanctions if he rejected the U.S. proposal. We know the sanctions did not have their desired effect in February; the question is whether they would have worked in October or November. I asked Charles Wilson, who was in frequent contact with Somoza in October, what would have been Somoza's reaction then. Without hesitating, Wilson said: "Defiance. Somoza wasn't ready to go until [late June 1979 when] the situation made it impossible to stay." Then, I pressed Wilson whether a different Ambassador or a different approach might not have induced Somoza to leave earlier, and Wilson retreated and conceded that it was possible.[5] Interviews with other friends of Somoza elicited almost the same pattern of response: Somoza would have rejected U.S. pressure, but maybe not. Though I had thought such pressures would not work in October, I now believe the U.S. should have applied gradually escalating pressures beginning in October 1978 to persuade Somoza that the United States was serious about the mediation.

At the second moment—in December 1978—Somoza unintentionally gave the U.S. government the answers to the question of what kind of pressure would affect him and to the dilemma of how to get him to leave without pushing. He sent his cousin Luis Pallais to the State Department to ask three questions: whether Somoza would be permitted to live in the United States if he left Nicaragua, whether he would be extradited, and whether he could retain his assets. In short, he told the U.S. government his three most vulnerable pressure points.[6] The State Department responded matter-of-factly, without informing the White House. In retrospect, this might have been the best moment to resolve the crisis. Had the United States made a favorable answer to Somoza's three questions *contingent* on his accepting a plebiscite or leaving at that time, he might have agreed. (This was the only time that the policy process did not work to pass an important decision to the President, although it is by no means certain that the Administration would have chosen to use this opportunity, and indeed that may have been the reason why the process did not work.)

The third lost opportunity occurred during a four-month period—between March and June 1979. At this time, the U.S. government was exhausted with the subject of Nicaragua and turned to other issues; the moderate Nicaraguan opposition was in despair; Somoza was confident he had weathered the worst; Venezuela was in transition to another government; and Panama and Costa Rica decided to "open the door" for Cuba to help the Sandinistas, as Carlos Andrés

Pérez put it. Only the Sandinistas had a realistic military and political strategy, and that is why they prevailed.

If, however, the United States had moved at almost any point during that period to implement the idea of a transitional government, (which it eventually suggested in late June 1979), it might have worked. If it had sent an Ambassador like Pezzullo in March instead of late June, he might have been able to facilitate the establishment of an Executive Committee while the moderate leadership was still in Managua.

The new reality was the military power of the Sandinistas, which they obtained from late May to July 1979 from Carazo, Torrijos, and Castro. At that time, the United States was unaware of the degree of commitment and the scale of involvement of these governments. U.S. intelligence only detected "the tip of the iceberg."[7] With each piece of information, the United States protested to Torrijos, Carazo, and Pérez and they denied their involvement, probably because they thought the United States would stop them if it knew. But by not knowing the magnitude of the Sandinistas' arsenal, not only was the United States caught behind events, it was denied the chance to put forward the kind of coordinated strategy that could have created a different outcome. Nonetheless, even in the last month, if the United States had given assurances to some moderate leaders and to a credible new leader of the Guard, the Executive Committee might have stood some chance of success. It needs to be repeated that at the time the Administration judged the costs of such a decision to be high and the chances of success, very low.

The fourth moment occurred in the first year of the Reagan Administration, when it decided to respond to Nicaraguan support for Salvadoran rebels by helping the contras rather than by building a coalition of support in the OAS. The OAS was unlikely to have taken strong action, if any, against Nicaragua in 1981, but over the long term, the threat of multilateral sanctions would have been a far more effective deterrent to Nicaragua's external behavior than the contras.

The contras were initially supposed to interdict Nicaraguan arms being sent to Salvadoran rebels, but in December 1981, when the program began, there was little if any evidence that the flow of arms was continuing or significant. Alexander Haig argued that covert support for the contras would only lead to an escalation of militarization in Central America, and he was right. There was an additional reason why this strategy was mistaken: once the Administration committed itself to the contras, it could not "abandon" them without appearing weak.

The fifth moment occurred in late 1983. Armed with the credibility of its invasion of Grenada and its support for the contras, it appears that the Reagan Administration could have negotiated the kind of bilateral security arrangement with Nicaragua that Assistant Secretary of State Enders had first proposed two years before. But by 1983, the Administration had decided that only a change in regime would guarantee a security arrangement, and so it missed the opportunity to wind down the war and contain the revolution.

The sixth moment occurred from June to October 1984 when the U.S. government chose to discourage the moderate opposition from participating in the elections. If these important groups had participated and gained a larger share of the vote (which was possible, since the elections were judged to be fair), the political complexion of the country could have changed. The focus would have shifted from the contras to Nicaragua's internal opposition.

The Sandinista government also had three crucial moments when a different decision could have contributed to their objectives—peace, economic prosperity, and social justice—while permitting a better relationship with the United States. In November 1980, the Sandinistas' decision to support the Salvadoran rebels was a major mistake; the fact that they continue to deny their involvement only compounds the problem, because it sustains the Reagan Administration's argument that they cannot be trusted.

Their second error was not seriously negotiating an arrangement with Enders. For reasons described in Chapter 12, it is by no means clear that the Reagan Administration was any more capable than they were of reaching an agreement at that time, but if they had merely proposed in 1981 what they proposed in 1983, the possibility of an arrangement would have been much greater. It appears that both Enders and Haig were prepared to accept the Nicaraguan revolution provided it was contained—not supporting insurgents or deepening its military relationship with Cuba and the Soviet Union. With the departure of both Enders and Haig, the Sandinistas' prospects of achieving such an agreement declined.

The third missed opportunity for the Sandinistas came during their negotiations with the opposition from early 1984 through the elections and beyond. The Sandinistas have repeatedly dismissed the internal opposition and rejected any dialogue with those in armed opposition, who they argue are just mercenaries of the United States. The International Court of Justice delivered an opinion favorable to the Nicaraguan government in June 1986, but at the same time the court found that the contras did have indigenous roots and branches and were not simply an appendage of the United States.

There are two reasons why it would be desirable for the Sandinistas to find a way to demonstrate to their enemies a willingness to talk, listen, negotiate, and permit their participation in government. First, negotiations could begin to heal the wounds of a decade of war and provide the basis for a genuinely new Nicaragua in which the people would have the option of changing their leaders peacefully. (The Sandinistas would contribute to breaking the cycle of Nicaraguan history if they realized that their refusal to talk with the armed opposition because they are "CIA agents" is equivalent to Somoza's dismissal of his armed opposition as "Communists.") Second, the U.S. Congress is unlikely to approve aid for the contras if the Sandinistas show a willingness to talk to the opposition and permit them a voice in shaping their country's future.

An Alternative to Perdition

We have explored what could have been done to allow more dreams and fewer nightmares to come true. Until now, the United States and Nicaragua have been condemned to repetition, yet the past could have been different. In comparison to rearranging the past, fashioning a different future holds more promise.

For the Reagan Administration, the contras have become more of an obsession reflecting a visceral hatred for a leftist, anti-American regime than an effective instrument to pursue U.S. interests.[8] A more rational policy for the United States should merge a clear definition of U.S. interests with the best means to achieve those interests.

Primary U.S. interests in Nicaragua remain what they have always been: to keep out Soviet–Cuban offensive weapons and prevent Nicaragua from being used by these two countries as a military, naval, or intelligence base. The United States has three legitimate and feasible avenues for pursuing these interests: (1) it could negotiate a bilateral agreement with Nicaragua and/or the Soviet Union on the model of the Kennedy–Khrushchev agreement on Cuba; (2) it could support negotiations of such an arrangement within the context of either a Contadora Treaty or an OAS-wide agreement; or (3) it could obtain bipartisan agreement for a unilateral statement that could be embodied in a Joint Resolution of Congress.

In the past, Latin America's strong support for self-determination and nonintervention would have led most of these countries to reject an agreement that limited a government's right to any international relationship. The Contadora Group's acceptance of U.S. security interests aimed at limiting Nicaragua's relationship with the Soviet

Union and Cuba is therefore extremely significant and offers the best path for achieving U.S. security interests. Although a unilateral approach is less desirable, it has both credibility and legitimacy—given the public acceptance by Contadora of the same aims—and is therefore a satisfactory fall-back strategy. It is highly unlikely that the Soviet Union would ignore or trespass on a clear bipartisan warning not to overstep the bounds of primary U.S. interests in Central America. Indeed, their decision not to deliver advanced MIG aircraft to Nicaragua confirms the point.

The second tier of U.S. interests in Nicaragua is the physical containment of the revolution. Provided the United States helps the other nations of Central America deepen democracy and extend the benefits of development to their poorer people, there is no reason to fear or even be concerned with the Nicaraguan revolution as a model or an "idea." Nicaraguans would have much more to fear from a democratic Central America than Central America has to fear of a revolutionary Nicaragua. The key concern, then, is to preclude Nicaraguan support for insurgencies abroad. The initial rationale of the contra program was to interdict Nicaraguan supplies to insurgents; later, the Administration argued that the contras fulfill the same purpose by diverting Nicaragua's attention and resources. If there were any evidence that the contras had achieved either objective, the program might be more acceptable—but there is not.

The fatal flaw of the contra program is that it transforms the Nicaraguan issue into a bilateral one between the United States and a small Central American nation. In effect, the Administration says that its security interests are the only ones that matter in the region, or that the United States knows how to pursue the security interests of the other nations better than they do themselves. Either way, the Reagan Administration is perceived by the Contadora Group and the other countries in Central America as arrogantly dismissing instead of defending their interests.

Instead of leaping in front of its friends in the region to confront the Sandinistas, the United States would be wiser and more effective if it stepped behind its friends and recognized that they have direct security interests at stake in preventing Nicaraguan support for insurgents, whereas U.S. interests are indirect. Central America, and to a lesser extent Contadora, therefore, have a legitimate concern and incentive to see that Nicaragua does not support insurgencies.

These nations do not have to stop all the weapons flowing out of Nicaragua; all they need to do is produce some evidence that the flow occurs. The United States could negotiate with the Contadora Group an arrangement whereby the U.S. would cease support for the contras in conjunction with Contadora's acceptance of five graduated steps that would be activated the moment such proof was obtained. Then Central America, Contadora, and the United States would bring the evidence to the OAS to seek a condemnation of Nicaragua's support. If Nicaragua's response was inadequate, the Group would escalate pressure by diplomatic isolation, selective economic sanctions, embargo, and finally collective military action. Any lasting agreement would need to include incentives for compliance and automatic sanctions against violations. As Nicaragua has no desire to replicate Cuba's isolation from the hemisphere, this might conceivably be the most effective deterrent and source of leverage.

The third tier of U.S. interests is the support of democratization. There is no doubt that this set of interests has suffered the most because of the contra program. The Nicaraguan government has indicated that the state of siege and other measures of repression would be lifted if U.S. support for the contras were to end. Although one might doubt Nicaragua's assurances, there is no doubt that the war has contributed to the country's polarization and that the ending of the war would eliminate a reason, or a pretext, for repression.

It is possible that some steps toward democratization could be negotiated as part of a general settlement, and indeed, both the Costa Rican and the Contadora plans include important provisions on democratization and national reconciliation. Given Nicaragua's history and the Sandinista ideology, however, one should not be overly optimistic that democracy would arrive quickly or in one piece. Nonetheless, the current path of supporting the contras is clearly a failure; an alternative is unlikely to result in less freedom.

If the United States stopped supporting the contras they would not disappear, but they would become less of a threat and a cause for mobilization, and there would be a greater opportunity for reconciliation. Because of the Iran–contra scandal and public opinion, no future Administration will be able to circumvent a clear Congressional cutoff of aid to the contras. If U.S. support for the contras were phased down and out, then the other governments in Central America would probably reach a modus vivendi with Nicaragua. It is unlikely that U.S. relations with Nicaragua will see much improvement in the near term; the war will leave the small nation with a large hatred.

Nonetheless, the United States has many opportunities to negotiate and achieve its principal concerns more effectively and, of course, at much lower cost, than by escalating its military involvement. The essence of a new strategy would be to substitute the more effective and united influence of Central America and Contadora for the counterproductive weight of the United States.

The Reagan Administration has provided aid to its Central American friends as an incentive for them to isolate Nicaragua. This has not worked as either a political or an economic strategy: Nicaragua has avoided isolation, and billions of dollars of U.S. aid have not stopped the economic deterioration of the entire region. A more effective approach would be to provide incentives for the Central Americans to unite and negotiate their concerns with Nicaragua directly and quietly within a Central American framework. These countries have a political incentive to prevent Nicaraguan support for insurgents, and they have an economic incentive to resolve their differences and invigorate the Central American Common Market. At the same time, the U.S. strategy ought to recognize the special bonds that have been built in recent years between the United States, Costa Rica, and the emerging democracies in Guatemala, Honduras, and El Salvador. What is required is a variation on the Kissinger Commission recommendations that the Reagan Administration and Congress adopted.

In February 1984, based on the Kissinger Commission's recommendations for a multiyear aid program to all of Central America except Nicaragua, President Reagan requested $8.4 billion for the period 1984-89. Congress decided to fund the program on an annual basis, and for the first year, it appropriated 88 percent of the request. Three years later, on March 3, 1987, President Reagan requested an extension of the program to 1992 and a slight increase in funds.[9] The United States has contributed on the average nearly $1 billion per year in economic and military aid to the region since 1982, yet Central America's gross domestic product has declined by about 15 percent from 1981 to 1986 and intraregional trade has dropped from $1.1 billion in 1980 to $370 million in 1986.[10] These facts should underscore that trade and growth cannot begin until the war ends and a new strategy for peace and development begins.

A new proposal should offer the leaders of Central America $5 billion more than proposed by the Reagan Administration, *but only if* they can reach agreement among themselves and with Nicaragua on matters of security and economic integration. This would place significant new leverage in the hands of our friends who are better positioned to use it effectively. To avoid waste and disillusionment, this new plan for the entire region should not start until the shooting stops; it cannot succeed unless all the nations of Central America participate.[11]

Since 1982, the economies of all the nations of Central America have declined, despite massive aid commitments by the United States. All the nations have become more militarized, and their in-

ternal political space and their external autonomy have been reduced. The only exit from the downward spiral of war and depression
is for the United States to trust in the nations of the region to shape
a more positive future for themselves. The Central American Common Market was the principal stimulus for the most dramatic revolution the nations in the region have ever achieved; the lives of the
people in the region can only be improved if that old system is rein-
vigorated.

The United States needs to shift its strategy from the contras to
one that relies on friendly nations in Central America to pursue their
own security and economic interests. The proper role for the United
States is to support these nations, not to fight for them, and to provide incentives for growth and unity rather than for war and division.

Chapter 16

A DIFFERENT ROAD

For what is the value of going to the trouble of remembering
the past which cannot become a present.
Søren Kierkegaard

THE UNITED STATES has at least one thing in common with declining dictators and rising revolutionaries: each has consistently
brought out the worst in the other. They have suspected the worst,
and as Cole Blasier put it so well, no one has been disappointed. The
question is whether we are eternally condemned to repetition, or
whether enhanced awareness of the patterns of the past and some
new ideas might permit a better future. How should the United
States address future crises of political succession and relationships
with revolutionary governments?

Future Crises of Political Succession

THE PROBLEM.   The problem is, by now, familiar. A rightist dictator, who is friendly to the United States, but brutal to his own people, faces a Marxist guerrilla movement, which is inspired by hatred
of the United States and admiration for Cuba. A moderate opposition
wants to change the regime because it despises the dictator and fears
the Marxist radicals. With increasing urgency, moderates demand
that the United States depose the dictator before the situation becomes so polarized that only the Marxists will profit.

Since World War II, this problem of political succession has been
one of the most difficult recurring crises faced by U.S. policy makers.
Most of the cases have been in the Caribbean Basin, where the U.S.
presence is the largest and most problematic, but the United States
has also faced succession crises in the Middle East (Iran) and Asia (the
Philippines and South Korea). A recent study notes that dictators are
staying in power today longer than in the past.[1] The problem, therefore, is more likely to get worse than to go away.

Though crises of political succession have a number of common
elements that permit a single recommended strategy, each has
unique national characteristics. To assist U.S. policy makers in un-

derstanding the differences and similarities among current and past succession crises,[2] a more systematic support system is needed. Currently, the State and Defense Departments have professional historians, but they concentrate more on writing diplomatic or military history than on preparing historical background information useful to the policy maker. Although the policy makers in the Nicaragua crisis were aware of the historical outline of U.S.–Cuban relations and had some, albeit limited, understanding of Nicaraguan history, no one could have recalled the details that might have forced a reevaluation of recommendations. Moreover, the White House, which lacks a historical office, needs one.

As military intervention by the United States is not a recommended option, the United States is simply not in a position to control or even manage a succession crisis. The outcome will depend, first and last, on the decisions of local actors—on the dictator, the military, the moderate opposition, and the radicals. The issue for U.S. policy makers is how to influence the crisis from the margin of events.

CHOICE OF OBJECTIVES. As the crisis unfolds, the United States can choose from four objectives. It can: (1) bolster the dictator; (2) aid the revolutionaries; (3) let events take their course; or (4) promote a democratic transition. In almost every case, the United States government has chosen the fourth option, but just because that path has been taken in the past is not sufficient reason to continue taking it. There are other reasons, however.

The United States has bolstered dictators in cases when strategic interests were perceived as paramount or when an Administration and a dictator viewed the world or a regional crisis similarly. When the middle class, however, rebels against the dictator, option 1 has been discarded by both conservative and liberal Presidents for reasons of both idealism and practicality—the dictator lacks legitimacy and support. Option 3 is discarded when the President realizes that passivity guarantees a negative outcome; the United States may not be able to influence the succession crisis effectively, but if it does nothing, polarization and revolution are the most likely results.

Let us examine option 2 for a moment. Why not help the revolution? Why should the United States be threatened by a revolution when that is also part of its own heritage? Leaving aside that the American revolution was actually a war of independence, the same values and pragmatism that prompt the United States to reject a dictator should also lead to a rejection of most, though not necessarily all, revolutionaries. One needs, first, to examine their cause and, second, to examine the manner in which they make decisions. Since Castro, most revolutionaries in the Caribbean Basin have been Marxist-Leninists, who look to Cuba as a model and to the United States as the enemy. Some revolutionaries conceal this fact, and the United States therefore has to look for other clues to their ends and means.

No nation in the world wants a neighbor that views it as an enemy or has a philosophy of governance that is inimical to its values. Such a neighbor can become a threat either by itself or by inviting in a powerful rival. It is possible that if a hostile group comes to power, it might change or become friendly, but the probability of that occurring is much less than if a known, nonhostile group comes to power.

Mexico prides itself on a principled, defensive foreign policy, but it is acutely sensitive to the possibility of regime change in Guatemala. Though its rhetoric and foreign policy support revolution abroad, Mexico draws the line and opposes revolution in Guatemala, even to the point of assisting the Guatemalan military, one of the most repressive in Latin America, to capture Guatemalan revolutionaries on the Mexican side of the border.[3]

Should the United States be different? Given its substantial power, it should be less insecure (and more consistent) than Mexico. The United States should show restraint and recognize that it has other interests that could be harmed by using "all means necessary" to prevent leftist guerrillas from taking power. But the overall objective ought to be similar: the United States should not help groups that believe the United States is their nation's enemy, and it should oppose them in appropriate, though not in all, ways.

The manner in which a group comes to power matters. If it uses violence, the group is unlikely to have acquired the arts of political compromise and conciliation so essential to a functioning democracy. As Samuel Huntington has written, "except for Costa Rica in 1948, guerrilla insurgencies do not inaugurate democratic regimes."[4] On the other hand, if a group is elected and has to compete for votes against those who are friendlier to the United States, it is more likely to be sensitive to the United States. It is not surprising that both Carter and Reagan emphasized democracy as a "national interest"; it is both an idealistic and a geostrategic objective. In the Caribbean Basin, no democratic government is likely to succeed economically or at the polls if it sustains a determined anti-American posture. In addition, Che Guevara warned budding revolutionaries that they could not succeed against a government that "has come to power through some form of popular vote ... since the possibilities of peaceful struggle have not yet been eliminated."[5]

In brief, the United States ought to pursue option 4: to promote a democratic transition. That means, first of all, that the United States should pursue a human rights policy—one that makes clear to all concerned that dictators do not enjoy the support of the United States even though they may be friendly. The United States should encourage respect for human rights through its bilateral relations, and should also rely on international organizations, such as the Inter-American Human Rights Commission.

While promoting human rights, the United States should not become involved directly in internal political disputes unless and until the human rights problem becomes a succession crisis. Determining that point is, of course, not easy, but one wants to err on the side of caution: not every country with serious human rights problems is in the midst of a succession crisis. Symptoms of a succession crisis include chronic violence, a growing insurgency, and an increasingly politicized moderate opposition.

CHOICE OF POSTURE.   Once a human rights problem becomes a succession crisis in a nation in which the United States historically has had considerable influence, the United States cannot choose to be uninvolved. Even the most rigid noninterventionism by the Franklin Roosevelt Administration was interpreted as helping Somoza. The United States *will* be involved; the issue is how.

The United States can choose between two postures: (1) low-key facilitator: the United States can try to stay in the background of events, discretely contacting all interested parties and assisting them as necessary to resolve the transition problem; or (2) proconsul: the United States can step powerfully and publicly into the chasm separating the dictator and the opposition and try to resolve the dispute. The first option is preferable, because it keeps the local actors in the front of the drama.

But if history is any guide, the United States should not be overly preoccupied by the posture it chooses, because the press and the local political leaders will probably view the United States as a proconsul, regardless. Nonetheless, the United States should repeat publicly and privately to the local leaders that *their* role is central; the United States will assist a process, not control the outcome.

USING POLITICS TO MAKE BETTER POLICY.   Public debate on what the United States should do about the declining dictator is both inevitable and predictable, and it affects policy, albeit indirectly. Liberals will argue that we should dissociate from the dictator and not be afraid of change, and conservatives will insist that we neither abandon old friends nor risk new alliances with Marxists. The tendency within all Administrations—particularly among foreign service officers—is to try to ignore both, dismissing them as extremes with either an axe to grind or a failure to understand the nuances of the case or of U.S. policy. There is some truth to this, of course. In the Nicaraguan case, the Carter Administration heard more from Congressmen Murphy and Wilson on behalf of Somoza and from Tom Harkin on behalf of the Group of Twelve than from everyone else in Congress put together.

A President has to be sensitive to the national debate, but the foreign affairs bureaucracy is generally uninterested or unable to help him develop a political strategy. Instead of pretending that politics has nothing to do with foreign policy, the Executive Branch should take two steps at the beginning of a succession crisis to incorporate the political dimension into the policy process.

First, as the crisis unfolds, the Administration should invite at least one respected senior official who has served a President of the other political party to be briefed regularly or to participate in the policy review process. This person should have contacts and credibility on Capitol Hill, but also, if possible, some experience in the region. One of this individual's primary responsibilities should be to keep the moderates in the other political party informed about what is happening in an effort to obtain their support at crucial moments.[6]

Second, one should recognize that each political party has a comparative advantage in dealing with crises of political succession. Democrats tend to be better at dissociating from rightist dictators; Republicans tend to be better at reassuring them. Both tactics, as we shall see, are needed. Also, Democrats tend to have more credibility with the moderate opposition, which is an asset at times but also raises their expectations, which is a liability. The Republicans exchange the asset for the liability: they have less credibility, but they also do not raise expectations. A good political strategy ought to seek ways that would exploit the comparative advantage of each party for the benefit of the nation.

STRATEGY.   The U.S. strategy should be directed at the following targets, in order of priority: (1) the dictator; (2) the moderate opposition; (3) the military; (4) other governments in the region; and (5) the revolutionaries.

Although the United States will reduce aid and resources to the particular country during the crisis, it is a serious mistake to reduce the size of the U.S. Embassy there. To the contrary, the first step the United States should take after determining the onset of a succession crisis is to increase the number and quality of Embassy personnel, although the total number need not increase by much because AID personnel would probably be reduced. Those offices that ought to receive the highest priority for more people include the political section, the office of the Defense Attaché, and the CIA. A new Ambassador should be appointed to send a new message and to indicate that the U.S. government has decided to give its relations higher priority. The new Ambassador should be an effective political operator, with previous experience in the country or the area. The primary responsibility of the increased number of staff is to expand and maintain contacts with as wide a range of influential people in the country as possible.

The dictator is the principal target of the strategy. The issue is how to persuade him to change from being the problem to helping find a solution. The sooner he accepts that analysis, the faster the crisis will be defused. The better the United States understands the individual, the more likely they will influence him.

The State Department should set up a working group to study the dictator. They should consult with professional psychologists and people with substantial experience in that country. They should interview acquaintances, friends, and enemies of the dictator to learn his strengths, weaknesses, hopes, fears, and vulnerabilities. Which of his experiences have had the most important effect on him? What historical analogies does he tend to use? What are his views of the United States, the President, other leaders? Whom does he trust?

Based on these interviews, the State Department should write a psychological portrait for all the senior officials working on the crisis.[7] Perceptive people who have known the dictator should meet periodically with senior officials to brief them on the situation and to hear the Administration's concerns about the dictator.

A list of all economic and military programs with the country should be compiled, along with a memorandum explaining how each of these programs relates to the dictator's own wealth. In addition, a study should be undertaken of the dictator's investments outside the country—how much, where, and who are the partners?

Senior people outside the government should be encouraged to visit the country to talk to him. (Such initiatives are rarely taken due to bureaucratic reasons.) The only message they should convey is one of concern in the United States; their principal purpose is to explore the state of the dictator's mind and how he might be influenced by U.S. actions. At an appropriate point, one of these people should be tapped to be the President's special envoy.

Based on all of this information, the Administration should begin to draft a strategy to influence the dictator. The strategy should include answers to the following questions: What actions by the United States are most likely to have the most influence on his decisions? Who is most likely to have the most influence on him? If he cannot maintain power, what does he most want to do? Where does he want to go? What, if any, role should the U.S. President play? This draft plan should then be put aside until a specific strategy for succession is developed by the major actors in the country.

The moderate opposition includes all the individuals and groups that are independent of the dictator and prefer a moderate, gradual change in the country to violent revolution. Any dictator who has ruled a country for an extended period is most likely to have exiled, imprisoned, or coopted many of the moderate leaders, leaving the opposition divided, uncertain, suspicious, and often dependent on foreign leaders or governments. For self-serving reasons, both the dictator and the revolutionaries will claim that the moderate opposition is not viable; extremes fear the middle. This is why Somoza began arresting moderate leaders and why the FSLN was so fearful that the mediation would succeed.[8]

The succession crisis in both Nicaragua and the Philippines began with the assassination of the dominant opposition leader. In the Philippines, Aquino's wife had the strength to step into the breach, the political parties had the depth to support her, a competent nonpartisan electoral monitoring organization (NAMFREL) existed, and the country had experience with free elections. Nicaragua was not so fortunate. Generally, when the succession crisis begins, the probability is that the moderate opposition will be a weak reed with either no leaders or too many.

Any successful transition, however, depends on leadership emerging from this group. If the dictator should be the principal target of a U.S. strategy, the cultivation and nurturing of the moderate opposition should be the Embassy's most important and delicate job. It is important because the only viable and durable solution, from the U.S. perspective, must come from the middle. It is an awkward and delicate task because if the opposition leaders appear to have been anointed by the United States, their credibility and effectiveness is weakened. And if, in fact, the United States chooses the leaders, as it has done with the contras, the United States rather than their nation becomes their principal constituency. They know that if the United States can select them, the United States can replace them, and their actions will be shaped more by their desire to please the United States—or the U.S. Congress—than their fellow citizens.

When the moderates turn to the United States for leadership, they should be given encouragement and incentives for unity, but not leadership. Leadership must come from within the country; if it does not emerge, it cannot be created from the outside. The major incentive to unify that the United States can offer the moderates is to make the pace and kinds of pressures against the dictator conditional on the opposition's success in uniting and developing a specific program for succession.

The United States needs to avoid raising the expectations of the moderate opposition. As indicated above, this is an easier job for Republicans than for Democrats. The cost of keeping expectations low is that the United States may look as if it does not care about democracy. Nonetheless, lowered expectations are an essential ingredient. If the hopes of the opposition are dashed too soon, then the possibility of a successful transition is diminished. For a nonviolent transition to succeed, the opposition needs to persevere.

For the opposition to be effective, not only will it need to be united, it will need a few leaders who have the strength and the political space to negotiate with the dictator and make concessions. Elections for a fixed period, say for two years, as the Democratic Alliance did in Chile, can provide a buffer from the constant pressures of different groups. A unified leadership not only undercuts the dictator's argument that the opposition is not a viable alternative but demonstrates that the opposition is capable of governing. As the opposition becomes united, the United States should encourage it to develop an overall strategy for the transition.

The military will normally have been secured by a dictator who has stayed in power for a long time. It will therefore be very difficult for the U.S. military to develop independent relationships. If the military is a personalized institution, like the National Guard in Nicaragua, the problem is compounded. But the military in each nation has its peculiarities, and the United States needs to understand the capabilities and vulnerabilities of each as a political as well as a military institution.

It is important for the United States to remain in contact with all levels of the country's armed forces, but there are serious obstacles to developing these relationships. If the insurgency is serious, the military probably will have committed serious human rights abuses, and the United States will have reduced, suspended, or terminated military aid. Nevertheless, the United States should try to keep its military advisers in place and, if possible, increase the number.

The Ambassador needs to oversee this operation very closely. He or she should have a Military Group Commander who is trusted, and all the military officers should participate in the Embassy's political discussions. Like some foreign service officers, some U.S. defense attachés succumb at times to "clientilism"—explaining foreign views more than representing U.S. policy—but their kind of clientilism is more serious. If the Defense Attaché empathizes with his foreign counterparts who are angry over the cut in U.S. military aid, then the credibility and effectiveness of the overall strategy is undermined. U.S. military officers must deliver the combined message of the U.S. government. The United States should not conspire with the foreign army, but U.S. officers should learn the concerns of their counterparts and explain clearly the U.S. objective—to defeat the insurgency by stopping human rights violations and permitting a democratic transition. The Pentagon should identify several retired U.S. generals who can visit the country periodically for conversations. There is no question that the best interlocutor for the Latin military is the U.S. military, and if this instrument is used carefully, it can be very effective.

Friendly governments in the region should be consulted as a high priority of U.S. policy. This means listening, and, when appropriate, adjusting U.S. policies to take these different perspectives into account. Although this item is listed fourth in the strategy, an Administration ought to aim to cultivate some regional powers from the beginning. It is generally too late to develop a confidential relationship between Presidents when a crisis starts; such a link should already exist. To the extent possible, the President should personally encourage leaders from these governments to play a role—indeed, to play a more important role than that of the United States. If joint approaches are possible, these are preferable. Certainly, any sanctions should be coordinated and, to the extent possible, implemented jointly.

Carter tried to do this, but the Latin American leaders were not ready to coordinate strategy or to confide. The Reagan Administration pursued a unilateral policy toward Nicaragua; its principal contacts were with those Central American governments that are most dependent on U.S. aid. In a future succession crisis, it is worth exploring whether Latin American leaders would want to coordinate strategy.

If the crisis occurs in a subregion, say Central America or the Caribbean, it is important for the United States to demonstrate its interest and support for the small neighboring countries. As the United States reduces its aid to the declining dictator, the United States

should increase aid to the neighbors, particularly if they are democratic, but only if there are no human rights problems.

The revolutionaries have seldom tried to talk with the United
States, which has never devised a strategy to communicate with
them. This needs to be corrected. At some level, the U.S. government
should maintain discrete contacts, but the preferable approach is for
the government to use people outside the government—former Ambassadors, members of Congress, scholars—for two reasons. First,
leaders of the radical left in Latin America have their own problems
communicating with U.S. government officials. Their distrust for
the United States is so great that they often posture rather than talk
frankly.[9] People who are in the U.S. government tend to discount reports they receive from those outside about new initiatives or probes
from a radical government; they assume that if the other government
were really serious, it would communicate the message directly to
the U.S. Embassy. In some cases this might be true, but it is also true
that radicals have difficulty, due to ideology, communicating with
the U.S. government, and therefore any attempt to communicate
with the United States through some other party is worth exploring.

Second, contact from the United States should be outside the government because it does not convey any special U.S. government im-
primatur or legitimacy that could create problems for the moderate
opposition. These contacts should explore the motives, ideas, and
concerns of the revolutionaries and judge the extent to which they
are independent of the Soviet Union and capable of modifying their
hostile view of the United States. To assume that all revolutionaries
in the Caribbean Basin are Marxist-Leninists and indissolubly connected to Cuba and its ally is wrong, but the United States may never
know this if it fails to communicate with any of them.

More important, by failing to understand the revolutionaries, the
United States, in many cases, removes itself from a deeper understanding of the social and economic inequities in many nations. The
structural barriers to social and economic change are formidable in
many small countries, and efforts to organize the poor often meet
with repression. If the United States confines its efforts to half-
hearted advocacy of peaceful change among the middle class in urban
areas, it will not only confirm the radicals' stereotype of the United
States as a status quo power, but worse, it will lose its purpose.

A PLAN, A MISSION, AND AN ELECTION.   Timing for a specific
plan must depend on events in the country, the state of the moderate
opposition, and the views of friendly governments. The plan for a

democratic transition should be drafted primarily by the moderate opposition with the help of friendly governments and the input of the dictator. How this is done depends on the particular country, but an interlocutor or a mediator could be appointed to help.

Elections are the most legitimate and peaceful means to transfer power, and in countries with a history of free elections, like the Philippines or Chile, that is the best path. Elections also permit the moderate opposition to campaign, organize, and broaden its political base.

However, in countries where the dictator has manipulated elections, moderates may be fearful about contesting an election. The problem is how to have a free election on short notice in a country with no or little prior experience. This was the issue that the U.S. government wrestled with in December 1978; though many in the State Department tended to agree with the Nicaraguans that such an election was an absurd projection of North American political culture, they nonetheless looked into how it might be done. They concluded that it would be extremely difficult, perhaps impossible. There did not exist then, nor does there exist today, an international organization that has developed the institutional capability to monitor elections and judge whether they are fair and free.

In the 1980s, as democracy has spread, a number of organizations— for example, the Center for Electoral Assistance and Promotion (CAPEL) of the Inter-American Institute for Human Rights in San José and the International Human Rights Law Group—have observed elections, but their capability is limited and they have had serious problems in obtaining access to countries that are in the midst of questionable elections. It would appear that the world could benefit from an international organization to advise and monitor elections.

The threat of sanctions will probably be necessary to encourage the dictator to hold elections and permit comprehensive international observation. This threat should be communicated to the dictator by a special envoy of the President. If possible, the emissary should be someone the dictator knows and respects; it should be someone who can both reassure the dictator that the United States shares some of his concerns, but be tough enough to explain that the dictator's problem has deep roots and cannot be resolved by small, hesitant steps. The emissary would say that the U.S. President already made a decision on sanctions, but the decision will only be announced if the elections are not held within one or two months. The envoy would provide a detailed sketch of what a transition would look like, and what the dictator could expect if he did or did not permit a free election.

If the elections occur, and are judged fair, then the dictator will have to follow the will of the people, or he will find himself isolated, much as Marcos did. If he wins, and the international organization judges the elections fair, so be it.

Although this strategy seems quite elaborate, involving considerable time, it represents a small fraction of the time that the Carter Administration's highest officials gave to the Nicaraguan crisis, and a minuscule amount of time compared to that given to the Iranian crisis. Moreover, by thinking systematically at the beginning, most of this work could be done by lower-ranking officers with more detachment and under less stress than senior people usually experience during a crisis.

Relating to Revolutionary Governments

If the strategy fails, and the revolutionaries come to power, then U.S. influence is turned inside out. For a period of time, perhaps two years, the opportunities of positively influencing the new government to be moderate and friendly to the United States are negligible at best. The opportunities of negatively influencing the new government are legion. To put the same point differently, the United States cannot easily make the revolutionaries friendlier to the United States or to U.S. interests, but it *can* make them more hostile and intransigent.

This is an extremely difficult point for the American people to accept. If the United States is generous and helpful, the revolutionaries will take it for granted; sometimes, they will criticize the United States for being stingy. They are unlikely ever to express gratitude, which is the minimum the United States expects. If the United States is not helpful or is suspected of destabilizing the regime, that reinforces the leaders' anti-Americanism. It is difficult to sustain a policy of helping a regime that is Marxist and anti-American for any period of time. When Republicans are out of power, they can make it difficult for Democrats to continue such a policy, and when they are in power, they reject the policy. Could a more patient policy by the United States yield a more moderate regime? In at least two cases—the Mexican petroleum nationalization in 1938 and the Bolivian revolution of 1952—Cole Blasier found that a policy of patience by the United States yielded more moderation over time. But in both cases, the foreign governments remained sensitive to U.S. concerns.[10] And, of course, both cases occurred before the Cuban revolution. In neither the Grenadian nor the Nicaraguan case did the leaders display any sensitivity to U.S. concerns, and to them the U.S. response was interventionist, even before it actually was.

However, just because relations are unlikely to be good does not mean that a confrontation is inevitable. Perceptions of each other's behavior were crucial in bringing the United States and the Nicaraguan revolutionary government to a point of confrontation. Comparing U.S. relations with Nicaragua with those with Grenada suggests that a more confrontational policy by the United States is more likely to lead to a radicalization of the regime. The Grenadian regime viewed itself as Marxist-Leninist and tried to mobilize and militarize its people in a struggle against U.S. imperialism. The revolution needed an enemy, but until 1983 the United States did not oblige, and the revolution self-destructed.[11]

In a speech in December 1979, Fidel Castro complained that "a counter-revolution . . . has begun to appear" in Cuba because of the relatively relaxed relationship with the United States during the previous year. He concluded: "Perhaps, in a certain way, we have been needing an enemy; because when we have a clearly defined enemy, engaged in hard-fought combat, we are more united, energetic, stimulated."[12] In the absence of a clear and credible enemy, the Nicaraguans too would have had trouble transforming their plans for a militarized, mobilized society into reality.

The correct policy for the United States, then, is to try to starve the revolutionaries' anti-Americanism, not feed it. Patience is necessary, but the American political system is notoriously impatient. The best fall-back policy is to end the aid, disengage, help neighboring governments, and be alert to any sign that the revolutionary government might strengthen its strategic alliance with the Soviet Union or Cuba or help insurgents in other countries.

U.S. policy makers need to be sensitive to the problem of sequencing. Soon after the revolutionaries come to power, the United States is most ready to negotiate and they are least able. After a couple of years, when the revolutionaries have had to cope with the hard day-to-day problems of helping the poor find jobs, health care, and shelter, some of the revolutionaries may be ready to negotiate seriously and strike a new relationship. By this point, U.S. policy has hardened. What is needed then is an interlocutor to lay the ground between the two sides and find confidence-building exercises that could start to build trust before negotiations begin. Supporting an insurgency against the government locks both governments into permanent hostility.

In the longer term, there is the question whether Marxist revolutionaries will ever fade away or can ever change or, alternatively,

whether the United States could change in a way that would influence the thinking of these revolutionaries. It would be a mistake for
the United States to assume that it could do nothing to affect the
mind-set of Marxist revolutionaries, but it would be an illusion to
think that the United States could change their views anytime soon.
What is needed is a dialogue, directly and through interlocutors.

The United States needs to demonstrate to all those on the left in
Latin America that it can live with—indeed, that it welcomes—genuine social change and justice in Latin America. Very few on the
Latin American left believe this; most believe that the major reason
that the United States will not accept revolution in Latin America is
because the United States is a status quo, capitalistic power that opposes social change and equity. This conclusion is drawn from numerous examples when the U.S. government defended the interests
of U.S. multinational corporations, and also from U.S. efforts to overthrow or destabilize two leftist democratically elected governments—in Guatemala in 1954 and Chile in 1970. These were historical errors of grave consequence to U.S. interests.

The credibility of U.S. support for democracy depends on whether
the United States demonstrates its support for democratic outcomes
when the left wins. To prove that the basis of U.S. concern with leftist regimes is their military relationship with Cuba and the Soviet
Union and their antagonism to the United States, the United States
needs to identify ways to manifest its support for social change in
that country.

A Long-Term Approach: A New American Community

The strategy suggested thus far in this chapter for the United
States to try to influence political transitions and to forge less unproductive relationships with revolutionary governments has involved
recommendations of a short-term, tactical nature. What are longer-
term ideas for the kinds of institutions, attitudes, and procedures
that the inter-American community needs to deal more effectively
with future challenges?

One of the most intractable problems that has challenged the international community in the postwar period is intranational violence that becomes connected to the East–West struggle. Two ways
to resolve the problem are to contain the competition between the
United States and the Soviet Union or to contain or settle conflicts
within the developing nation. When all groups within a nation be-

lieve the procedure for changing leaders and settling disputes is fair, then disputes are insulated.

How to attain a smooth process of political succession? Although the influence of the United States in the Caribbean Basin remains predominant, no long-term strategy can succeed unless it takes into account two trends. First, Latin American nations are increasing control over their internal affairs and extending their influence outside their nations. The debt crisis has temporarily slowed and, perhaps in a few cases, reversed this, but the trend has deep roots and genuine aspirations based on the need for national dignity and respect.

The second trend is the increasing democratization of Latin America and the Caribbean. In 1975, there were only two Latin nations in South America that were democratic. Ten years later, there were only two that were not democratic. The trend toward democracy represents a statement by Latin America that the system by which the people choose their leaders by periodic elections under the rule of law is the best—or in Churchill's words, the least worst—for settling disputes and transferring power.

These two trends offer an opportunity for the emerging democracies of Latin America and the United States to forge an agreement on a New American Community that would coordinate a single approach to democracy. The most effective long-term solution to crises of succession, violent change, and U.S. intervention in the Americas is to expand and consolidate democracy in the Americas. The elements of this approach would respond to the four stages of the succession crisis: (1) isolation of the dictatorship; (2) facilitating the dictator's exit; (3) assisting in the transition toward free elections; and (4) aiding the consolidation of democracy.

1. ISOLATING THE DICTATORSHIP: A NEW BETANCOURT DOCTRINE. Before Woodrow Wilson ever mentioned the goal of making the world safe for democracy, Carlos Tobar, an Ecuadorean diplomat, devised a practical way to strengthen democracy internationally. He recommended that governments deny recognition to a regime that comes to power by violent means until it holds a free and popular election. The Tobar Doctrine was imbedded in the Central American treaties that emerged from the Washington Conference in 1907.[13]

Fifty years later, the President of Venezuela, Rómulo Betancourt, rejuvenated and modernized the doctrine. He urged nonrecognition of de facto regimes and their expulsion from the OAS. His proposal failed then because most of the OAS members were still dictatorships, but as democracy has expanded in the Americas, the chance has improved that some variation on the Betancourt Doctrine could be adopted. The democratic countries could devise coordinated strategies to deal with dictatorships in crises of political succession. The moral weight of such a group would give it considerable influence.[14]

2. THE DICTATOR'S EXIT: THE ELBA ISSUE.   Should the United States and other democratic governments set aside a single, post-fantasy island where fallen dictators can flee and fade away? In almost every case, the continued existence of the dictator creates problems for the new government, the United States, and the dictators themselves. Few fallen dictators have found a tranquil place to live out their days, and this cannot help but affect the decisions of incumbent dictators.

Would the decision be easier if the dictator were guaranteed an "Elba"? The answer is probably yes, but the dilemma is how to create an incentive for their departure without rewarding them for their brutality and corruption. One does not want to permit or condone a dictator who takes millions or billions of dollars and leaves his country impoverished. In the end, the best strategy is probably to negotiate on a case-by-case basis and to secure departure by guaranteeing as little as necessary.

3. SECURING THE TRANSITION: AN INTERNATIONAL ELECTION-MONITORING ORGANIZATION.   Elections are not always the answer; in many countries where they are manipulated, they are the problem. Assuming the democratic governments can persuade a dictatorship to hold elections, the only way to guarantee the participation of the opposition is with a nonpartisan, international mechanism that can monitor and judge the fairness of an election. Such an organization needs to define its mandate broadly, visiting the country for an extended period before, during, and after the election. Such an organization should be composed of representatives from dozens of countries with an advisory board of former Presidents from throughout the Americas. It should not be a U.S. group or even U.S.-based.

It would also be desirable for all democratic countries to invite this group automatically to all elections, leaving it to the discretion of the organization to choose which ones to monitor. The reports that this group issued at the conclusion of the election would be authoritative. Perhaps the OAS could review these reports as they do with the reports of the Inter-American Human Rights Commission.[15]

4. CONSOLIDATION OF DEMOCRACY.   After an election, a new democracy may experience a period of exuberance and national support, but that fades, and the success of democracy sometimes hinges on the popularity of the leaders in power. There are numerous ways that the New American Community of democratic nations could help one another to prevent a retreat to dictatorship. First, the nations could consider ways to formalize their mutual reinforcement for democracy with either an amendment to the OAS or a new treaty to defend democracy collectively. Elected leaders of nations that are party to the treaty and are overthrown would have the legal right to request collective action to restore the democratic system.

Second, the democratic governments could promote the use of a Council of Freely Elected Heads of Government, composed of some former and current Presidents and Prime Ministers of North and South America. Such a group could lend its moral influence to help those who are fighting for democracy or struggling to maintain it.[16] Whenever a democratically elected President judged democracy in his country to be threatened, he or she could invite advice and support from this Council. Members of the Council could visit the threatened democracy and meet with leaders of all factions to try to heal the divisions and reinforce the democracry.

A Positive, Mutually Fulfilling Prophecy

Are we condemned to repetition? No, but the beliefs that have led to the repetition of past mistakes remain compelling to many. These old beliefs need to be replaced by two other thoughts. First, the United States and revolutionaries need to rethink the patterns of their past conflicts, and second, big nations like the United States and small ones like Nicaragua need to discard stereotypes and find a new, less destructive relationship.

The relationship between the United States and revolutionaries will always be difficult, but the first step toward improving it is to recognize that responsibility for the dispute is shared by both sides, and the conflict will end only when *both* change their attitudes. Of course, not only do suspicions prevent that from occurring, but the distrust leads each to interpret the other's behavior in a way that exacerbates the conflict. Both are imprisoned—or because of exaggerated perceptions, imprismed—in a dilemma from which they cannot extricate themselves.

Each has a prophecy of the other—the United States suspects the revolutionaries are Marxist-Leninists who will invite the Soviet Union into the region, and the revolutionaries suspect that the United States will undermine their revolution. One problem is that the prophecies may be partly accurate. Each contains some truth that is serious and negative and compels the other to prepare for the possibility that the statement could become completely true. Because the revolution's survival is at stake, revolutionaries prepare against U.S. attacks, and because the revolution is weakest at its beginning, the United States has often decided that this may be the best time to confront it. Secondly, the two prophecies are connected. Even if one side tries to suppress its suspicions and temporarily discard its negative prophecy of the other, as the United States tried to do in Nicaragua, the other side will offer sufficient grounds to reinvoke the suspicions.

It is precisely because the prophecies have some basis in reality that they cannot be dismissed, and it is because they are connected that one side cannot escape by itself. Nevertheless, interlocutors can use confidence-building steps to smooth the edges of distrust, while trying to replace the negative pattern with a positive prophecy that could also be mutually reinforcing. The United States could recognize the need of the revolutionaries for dignity and equity, and the revolutionaries could accept U.S. security concerns.

James Rosenau defined international relations as "the politics of national adaptation."[17] With respect to the United States and Nicaragua, both have been compelled to adapt to each other. The larger nation has had the advantage of strength and confidence, but the smaller nation has been able to compensate for that because the United States has not used direct force since the 1930s, and Nicaragua has been playing on its own turf. This has brought more balance to the competition than anyone perceived or thought possible.

At the same time, both nations have engaged in a confusing game of self-deception. The United States claimed it was not interfering even while it tried desperately to shape the result. Nicaraguans complained that the United States was deciding their future even while they shaped their own destiny.

Old myths, the product of a misperceived history, continue to haunt the present and limit the possibilities for future cooperation. The future of U.S.–Nicaraguan relations, however, will improve on the past only when the two nations decide to stop repeating it.

Chapter 17

EPILOGUE: THE CENTRAL

AMERICAN OPENING

"[To the two superpowers:] Let Central Americans decide
the future of Central America. Leave the interpretation and
implementation of our peace plan to us. Support the efforts
for peace instead of the forces of war in our region."[1]

Oscar Arias, Costa Rican President
December 10, 1987, Oslo

THE U.S. GOVERNMENT was set to close down at 12:01, Monday
morning, December 21, 1987, unless Congress and the President
agreed to an omnibus appropriation bill. Through the weekend, the
President's staff and Congressional leaders cajoled each other until
they were left with the issue of aid to the contras. Congress opposed
the aid, but President Reagan pledged to veto the $608 billion bill
and bring the government to a halt unless $8 million of contra aid
was in it. White House Chief of Staff Howard Baker, Jr., told House
Speaker Jim Wright: "This is the President's last year, and he isn't
willing to lose the contras on his last vote, and he is willing to stay
here through Christmas."[2] The contra issue had become so central
to the President that during the nights before Christmas, a minor
decision on that issue alone determined whether the lights would
stay on or go off in the government of the world's most powerful
nation.

Congress had encountered an immovable object of Presidential
determination. "I make a solemn vow—as long as there is breath in
my body," President Reagan told the hushed delegates at the OAS
in October, "I will speak and work, strive and struggle, for the cause
of the Nicaraguan freedom fighters."[3] And so he did. In the end,
Congress deferred to the President and added $8 million to the
budget for aid "but no arms" for the contras. The President wanted
much more, but he settled for that and a promise that Congress
would vote again on February 3, 1988. The government kept running and so did the contras.

This midnight debate on contra aid was yet another example of
the tragic polarization afflicting both the United States and Nica-

ragua. Part of Washington argued that only the Resistance could bring peace and freedom to Central America, and the other part was convinced that supporting the contras would guarantee continued war and less freedom. Nicaragua was divided between those who supported and those who opposed the Sandinista revolution. A Gordian knot connected the two struggles, with events in Nicaragua influencing the Congressional debate on the contras and the vote on aid shaping politics in Managua.

The four newly elected Central American Presidents stepped between these two protagonists to try to untie this knot. Although the contra war was aimed at Managua, it was also hurting their countries, and this was one of the reasons why they negotiated and signed the peace plan in Guatemala on August 7, 1987, that had been first proposed by Costa Rican President Oscar Arias six months before. They were joined by the Nicaraguan President in an effort to affirm their regional identity, assert control over their destinies, and try to cage the dogs of war.

Because the debate in Congress was so evenly divided, Central Americans for the first time in history had an opportunity to influence U.S. policy toward them in a decisive way. The rhetoric of the debate obscured this reversal of the traditional pattern of influence, and thus few recognized or understood its significance, but the effect was unmistakable. From the signing on August 7, President Reagan used every opportunity to try to persuade Congress to vote military aid for the Resistance, but Congress refused because the majority believed correctly that the Central American peace plan would have failed if such aid were provided.

Thus, just as the warmakers in Washington and Managua provided a steady flow of provocations to justify each other's belligerence, the peacemakers in Central America and in Congress began to help each other. But progress toward peace was hampered by distrust in the region and the unwillingness of the United States and Nicaragua to communicate, let alone negotiate.

The Sound of Hearings

When the joint Congressional hearings on the Iran–Contra affair opened on May 5, 1987, the American people were half hoping for the excitement of another "Watergate" and half fearing the consequences if it occurred. The nation was anxious to find out if the President had violated the law, and yet no one—not even the most zealous Democrat—wanted to witness another impeachment or constitutional crisis. Nonetheless, the Constitution defined Congress's role, and the legislators played it: to check the Executive and restore the balance in the system.

The hearings were made for television. Major General Richard Secord started by describing how the "Enterprise" that he managed had begun and worked. Secord marked the trail that led to Lieutenant Colonel Oliver North, who had first asked him to set up the Enterprise in early 1984. A handsome, boyish-looking marine with a chest full of medals, North looked as if he had been sent by central casting. He soon captured the afternoon soap opera audience with a voice that cracked at emotional moments and an ability to talk about himself in the third person without grinning. Protective of his family and country, Oliver North acted the part of the all-American hero that Ronald Reagan had loved to play in the movies. Instead of being contrite for misleading Congress and breaking the law, North was unabashedly proud, and while pledging fealty to the President, he was defiant to the point of insulting the Congress:

> If the Commander-in-Chief tells this Lieutenant Colonel to go stand in the corner and sit on his head, I will do so. . . . The Congress is to blame because of the fickle, vacillating, unpredictable, on-again-off-again policy toward the Nicaraguan democratic resistance. . . . In my opinion, these hearings have caused serious damage to our national interests. Our adversaries laugh at us, and our friends recoil in horror.[4]

North said that William Casey had first given him the idea in early 1984 for a covert entity operating outside the bounds of government and accountability that "you could pull off the shelf and use [and] that was . . . self-sustaining."[5] This Enterprise served to maintain the contras after Congress stopped the funds. Under oath, North told Congress that he "sought approval of my superiors for every one of my actions, and it is well documented."[6] However, after North's electric performance, few stayed tuned to watch his two superiors deny his testimony. Robert McFarlane described North's allegation that he had approved the operations of the Enterprise as "untrue [and] unthinkable." Admiral John Poindexter, who succeeded McFarlane as National Security Adviser, knew more, but he also made clear that he did not approve all of North's actions. North admitted that he had shredded the documentation, and CIA Director William J. Casey, who appeared to be the mastermind and the man with all the secrets, died the day that the hearings began.

The Watergate question at the center of the hearings therefore gravitated to Poindexter. Had he informed Reagan of the diversion of profits from Iranian arms sales to the contras? Poindexter's name, his choice of a dark suit instead of a uniform, his pipe, and his blandness offered a sharp contrast with North's demeanor. And, typically, rather than burst the balloon of expectation, as North would have done, Poindexter nonchalantly let the air out in a slow, matter-of-fact manner that denied the audience the chance to savor the end of the drama. On his first day on the stand, he told the Committee: "Although I was convinced that we could properly do it [support the contras through the Enterprise with profits from arms sales] and that the President would approve it if asked, I made a very deliberate decision not to ask the President so that I could insulate him from the decision and provide some future deniability for the President if it ever leaked."[7] That was it. The President then said he would not have approved it, and the scandal was contained. The President was responsible, but not culpable.

Still, the Committees' final report leaves the reader with a sense of horror over the activities condoned by President Reagan. One example will suffice: the Administration explored with the government of South Africa and with Panama, then run by a major international drug trafficker, ways to cooperate in supporting the contras.[8] The report condemned the Administration's actions, even while acknowledging that it did not have all of the evidence:

> In light of the destruction of material evidence by Poindexter and North and the death of Casey, all of the facts may never be known. The Committees cannot even be sure whether they heard the whole truth or whether Casey's 'fall guy' plan [to cover up the Enterprise's operations and protect the President] was carried out at the public hearing. But enough is clear to demonstrate beyond doubt that fundamental processes of governance were disregarded and the rule of law was subverted.[9]

The lesson that many in the Reagan Administration had drawn from Watergate was that Nixon's only wrong was his failure to burn the tapes. In the contra scandal, North and others destroyed the evidence. "I think I shredded most of that," North playfully told the Committee. "Did I get them all?"

The Administration circled the wagons and kept the President in power, permitting him yet another fight on behalf of his freedom fighters. By the time that Congress's report was issued on November 18, the *New York Times* agreed with the White House assessment: "Worst is Past for President: Damage to Reputation Was Done Long Ago."[10]

Peace Plans

With the luck of an Irish President, North's secret operation to aid the contras unravelled after it was no longer needed. On October 1, 1986, four days before Hasenfus' plane crashed, the Administration finally had authority to provide $100 million of military and economic aid to the contras. During much of the succeeding year, while the White House jousted with Congress over the legality of helping the contras two years earlier, the CIA quietly and legally shipped arms and other supplies to the Resistance. But the Administration never took its eye off the need to seek more funds before October 1, 1987, and it stayed alert to any opportunity to persuade the swing votes in Congress—30-50 conservative Democrats from the South and Midwest—that were needed to approve the aid.

The President soon found that he had to contend with the wily Jim Wright, a moderate Texas Democrat, who was elected Speaker of the House in January 1987. Unlike his predecessor Tip O'Neill, whose knowledge of Central America came mainly from Maryknoll priests,[11] Wright spoke some Spanish and had considerable experience in the region. Since each vote on contra aid split the Democratic Party on ideological and geographical grounds, Wright tried to negotiate a compromise that would prevent repeated votes and keep the party together. The problem was to construct a bridge between the President, who believed that the contras were the solution, and the bulk of his party, who opposed the contras and supported negotiations.

On the eve of a Summit among Central American Presidents, Wright and Reagan tried to outsmart each other, but both failed. Wright wanted the President to negotiate with the Sandinistas, and the Administration wanted Wright to support aid to the contras. Together, they sewed these two goals into a crazy-quilt: the White House accepted negotiations with Nicaragua in return for setting a deadline of September 30, the end of the fiscal year. If the Sandinistas did not agree to a cease-fire by then, the Administration thought that Wright would have no alternative but to accept its proposal for more aid. This Reagan–Wright plan was presented to Congressional leaders on August 4, but there was not time to send it formally to the Central American Presidents.[12]

There was something strange about a peace plan for Central America that represented a compromise between the two ends of Pennsylvania Avenue, but the irony went a step further because the proposal came apart even before it came together. Daniel Ortega trumped the plan by immediately accepting direct, unconditional talks with the United States. Wright expressed delight, but the Administration rejected Ortega's acceptance, insisting that he should talk with the contras. The Administration and the Speaker were still bickering over how to interpret "their" plan when the Central Americans startled the world by showing that they too could make peace.

The five Central American Presidents arrived in Guatemala City on August 6 with the differences between them so deep that there was some question whether they could remain in meetings together for two days. Presidents Napoleón Duarte of El Salvador and Daniel Ortega of Nicaragua each represented a government that aided guerrillas fighting the other's government; they considered each other enemies. Duarte was also upset with Reagan's plan because it seemed only concerned with Nicaragua; he was determined to refashion the Arias plan so that it would force Nicaragua to recognize his legitimacy and end its support for the Salvadoran rebels.[13] Honduran President Azcona was squeezed between his military and the United States; U.S. aid kept the military from overthrowing him but also prevented him from being independent. A last-minute peace proposal by his government was widely seen as an American ploy. A senior Costa Rican official later described that proposal together with the Reagan–Wright plan as a "sabotage attempt" by the United States to undermine the Arias plan.[14]

The two Presidents with the most democratic credentials and distance from the Nicaraguan conflict were also men of great integrity and strength; together they turned the Arias plan into the Guatemala Accord. Vinicio Cerezo had been exiled by the Guatemalan military but had returned to win election and take office in January 1986. Oscar Arias had taken office in May 1986. Like his predecessor, he pledged Costa Rica's neutrality, but unlike his predecessor, he meant it. He closed the southern front of the contra war, sending Oliver North's operatives into a tizzy. In September 1986, the Costa Rican security forces raided one of the contras' bases in northern Costa Rica, and a secret cable was sent to Washington: "Alert Ollie [that] Pres. Arias will attend Reagan's dinner in New York Sept. 22. Boy needs to be straightened out by heavy weights."[15] Reagan did not prevail upon Arias, and Daniel Ortega began to take notice. Despite deep philosophical differences, Arias and Ortega began to develop a relationship of respect that made the eventual acceptance of Arias' plan possible.

The Accord contained provisions for democratization—freedom

of the press and media, an end to states of emergency, a general amnesty—and regional security, including cease-fire negotiations and the end of support to insurgent groups. The security provisions would be subject to an elaborate system of verification—including on-site inspections. Some of these steps would have to be implemented simultaneously; all of them, within 150 days. In addition, the Accord included Cerezo's proposal for a Central American Parliament.

By focusing on democratization and internal reconciliation, the Accord proved its genius, slicing through the cord that had tied internal strife to international intervention for 160 years of Central American history. All five Presidents had strong reasons to agree to the Accord provided that everyone agreed and implemented it. Their economies were failing; the military and guerrillas threatened several of them; they knew that, without peace, they could not govern, and their countries could not develop. All wanted to end external support for insurgencies, but only if the provisions were verifiable and effective. Also lurking behind their discussion was the ghost of Central American unity, as well as the pride that an agreement would represent the "coming of age of Central America," in the words of the Costa Rican Foreign Minister.[16]

Ortega, who sat at the center of the crisis, had additional reasons to sign. He could not afford to antagonize Arias and Cerezo or permit his government to become isolated from the rest of Central or Latin America. The Sandinistas were obsessed with the invasion of Grenada and concluded that it had occurred for two reasons: internal division and an invitation from Grenada's neighbors. The chances of a U.S. invasion of Nicaragua would increase if its neighbors united in perceiving Nicaragua as a threat to their security. More immediately, the war had grown worse during the year. The contras' strength had increased because of $100 million in U.S. aid. Soviet helicopters were less effective now that the contras were using Red-Eye missiles. Soviet oil was reduced, inflation was soaring above 1,000 percent, and the economy was collapsing.

Ortega was practical, but he was also proud. If Arias had not demonstrated his independence from the United States and his willingness to deal respectfully with the Sandinistas, Ortega probably would have played with the Accord without really committing himself to it, much as he had done with Contadora. Reagan could have been expected to assist him by refusing to stop aid to the contras. But, instead, Ortega not only signed the Accord but he took risks to make it work. In brief, without Arias and his plan, the war in Nicaragua probably would have been unchanged, and the political space and the prospects of democracy would have continued to diminish, as they had since the beginning of the contra war.

Another possible reason why Ortega agreed to the Accord was that he might not have fully grasped its significance at first. To him, the plan was an instrument to end U.S. aggression and a historic moment because "the Central American Presidents have taken an independent position without foreign influence." In describing the provisions for democracy, however, he said that Nicaragua had already instituted them with the revolution in 1979: "We are not speaking about anything new."[17] Oscar Arias called Ortega soon after that statement to make sure Ortega understood that opening La Prensa and the radio stations were not options, as he had said, but rather some of the democratization steps required of him.[18]

The Accord had put the two protagonists on the spot; it divided the Sandinista government, and it exacerbated contradictions within the United States. The White House first said it was "encouraged" by the plan, but then the conservative wing of the Republican Party, fearful that the contras would be abandoned, unleashed a terrific campaign that caused the President to flip-flop. Despite the plan's demand that the United States stop aiding the contras, President Reagan reassured his conservative supporters, "I am totally committed to the democratic resistance—the freedom fighters," and he described the plan as "fatally flawed." George Bush criticized the plan for putting too much faith in the Sandinistas and, resurrecting a Watergate phrase, said the contras should not be left "twisting in the wind."[19]

The discordant sounds were evidence of a battle royal within the Administration. Philip Habib, the President's Special Envoy to Central America, argued that the Accord offered the United States an opportunity to broker an agreement, but others were more concerned that the peace plan was a mirage that would reduce support for the one strategy that could change the Nicaraguan government—the Resistance. Habib lost the argument and resigned. Abrams, who prevailed, recalled the U.S. Ambassadors from the five Central American countries to discuss why they had been surprised by the Accord and how it could be blocked without the United States getting blamed. With his special flair, Abrams gave the Ambassadors copies of the 1973 Paris accords to end the war in Vietnam, reminding them that it was violated within two years. The Ambassadors were instructed to return and "convey doubt" about the plan.[20]

Anxious to renew aid to the contras, the Administration first tried to resurrect the Reagan–Wright plan, but when Wright insisted that plan had been superseded by the Guatemalan Accord, the Administration began to stress the continued Soviet buildup in Nicaragua and the untrustworthiness of the Sandinistas. Reagan himself spoke on "Nicaragua Libre," the contra radio station, and said: "The Sandinistas have agreed that the repression must stop at the same time the fighting stops. The Sandinistas have told us that before, but no one believes the Sandinistas anymore. Simultaneity must mean freedom up front or no deal."[21]

The Sandinistas were also divided, and Ortega confided to Arias and Cerezo that that was one of the reasons for his trip to Havana on August 12 and "an extraordinary meeting of the FSLN National Directorate with the members of the Sandinista Assembly" on August 17. As a result of that meeting, the Directorate finally decided to back Ortega and Ramírez, the only ones speaking out for the Accord, and to commit to changes that would not have been considered one month before.[22] They established a four-member National Reconciliation Commission with three non-Sandinista members, headed by none other than Cardinal Obando y Bravo, the symbol of the opposition. Daniel Ortega announced that two priests, Bismarck Carballo and Bishop Pablo Antonio Vega, who had been exiled, could return. Two human rights leaders, who had been arrested in the first demonstration after the signing of the Accord, were released, and other demonstrations were permitted.

Tomás Borge, who had arrested the human rights leaders, kept his reservations to himself, refusing to be interviewed by *New York Times* correspondent Stephen Kinzer for nearly four months. He was biding his time, waiting for the Accord to fail, but the other Comandantes were serious. On September 15, Kinzer reported that the repeated public pledges and actions by the Sandinista leadership had created in Managua "a mood of expectation unseen since the Sandinistas swept into power eight years ago."[23]

Arias and his Foreign Minister Rodrigo Madrigal oversaw this democratization process in Nicaragua. At their behest, *La Prensa* began publishing without any censorship on October 1. Each time the Nicaraguans took a positive step, Arias called on the United States to suspend its support for the contras and give Central America "political space" to make the negotiations succeed. Arias went to Washington to state his case directly. In a chilling confrontation with Reagan at the White House, Arias recalled telling him: "We agree on the ends but we disagree on the means. You want democracy in Central America by imposing it with bullets. I want democracy by imposing it with votes."[24] Wright had invited Arias to address a Joint Session of Congress, but Reagan vetoed it, and so he spoke only to the Democratic caucus: "It is time to focus on the positive. . . . Let us restore faith in dialogue and give peace a chance. Let us not allow fear to prevail."[25]

By the perverse logic that had come to characterize the relationship, every positive step by the Sandinistas upset the Reagan Administration, and every negative step was applauded. When the human rights leaders were arrested, the State Department declared: "This shows that one should not place too large a bet on Sandinista good faith." Though three of four members of the Reconciliation Commission were democrats, State's view was that the Sandinistas "stacked the Council in their favor." At the United Nations on September 21, President Reagan called the steps taken by Managua "a fraud." On the same day that Arias asked Washington to stress the positive, the State Department described a series of actions including La Prensa's opening as "cosmetic gestures," and a few days later, Reagan called them "Potemkin reforms." When the Nobel Prize Committee announced on October 13 that Arias had been awarded the prize, the Republicans in Congress were distressed. Representative Newt Gingrich of Georgia called the award "saddening." Wright held that it precluded new aid for the contras, but George Shultz said that the Administration would still seek $270 million before Thanksgiving.[26]

The first hurdle to implementation of the Guatemalan Accord came on November 5, ninety days after the signing. The behavior of the actors as the date approached revealed their concealed preferences and the inherent difficulty of reaching peace in the region. Using the prestige gained by the Nobel Prize, Arias called on the Sandinistas to open talks with the contras on a cease-fire, and he asked the Reagan Administration to end aid to the contras.

Trying to do as little as necessary, Ortega first insisted on negotiating with the contra field commanders rather than their leaders, but he relented on November 5. Ortega accepted indirect talks with the contras but made clear that "this must not be confused with political dialogue with the contra leadership to negotiate power, because we have never done that, we are not doing it, and we will never do it." He later named Cardinal Obando as the mediator and announced that he would release 981 political prisoners. Ortega promised also to declare a general amnesty and lift the state of emergency as soon as Honduras dismantled the contra bases. Arias responded by describing the end of support for insurgents as "an indispensable element to achieve stable and lasting peace in the region." And the Reagan Administration replied in its customary way: asking Congress to renew aid.

The decision to begin talks with the contras was a painful reversal by Ortega, and that is evident in the feeble, half-hearted way it was implemented. To try to underscore that the contras were illegitimate, Ortega first sought Americans to participate in the talks on their side; then, when that effort failed, he appointed an American and a German as Nicaragua's representatives to the talks. The moves were childish, and eventually he abandoned them.

President Reagan refused to meet Ortega during his trip to Washington, but Wright saw him and tried to facilitate direct talks with the contras and Cardinal Obando. The Reagan Administration saw this, incorrectly, as a maneuver to avoid Sandinista talks with the contras and criticized the Speaker sharply.

The Soviet Peace Threat

Ronald Reagan, the man who had called the Soviet Union "the evil empire" and derided negotiations with the Soviets as fool's play, signed a nuclear arms control treaty with General Secretary Mikhail Gorbachev in Washington. Their meetings in December covered the full gamut of U.S.–Soviet relations. Since the Administration had criticized the Guatemalan Accord for neglecting the problem of Soviet military aid and advisers in Nicaragua, one would have expected this subject to be an important agenda item. What was said and not said on Nicaragua was heavy with unintended symbolism.

Notwithstanding his rhetoric about democracy, President Reagan's principal concern in Nicaragua was, legitimately, the Soviet tie to the Sandinistas. His first Assistant Secretary Thomas Enders had discussed this issue with the Nicaraguan government in 1981, but found them uninterested in negotiating what they then perceived as a limit on their sovereignty. Two years later, for many reasons (one of which was the contras), the Sandinistas were ready to negotiate about U.S. security interests, but by then, President Reagan was no longer willing. The Administration had committed itself to the contras and had concluded that only a fundamental change in the Nicaraguan regime could protect U.S. security interests. Elliott Abrams articulated the rationale for this position clearest: "It is preposterous to think we could sign a deal with the Sandinistas to meet our foreign policy concerns and expect it to be kept. The only guarantee that security agreements that are made will stick is internal democracy."[27] Negotiations therefore were ruled out.

For similar reasons, the Administration was slow to negotiate arms control with the Soviet Union, but when a new generation assumed leadership there, new opportunities arose, and the Administration, to its credit, seized them. Ironically, its success in negotiating a treaty with the Soviet Union made it more difficult, not easier, to negotiate with Nicaragua or even on the subject of Nicaragua. Reagan was accused of being a "useful idiot" of the Soviets by Republican conservative leader Howard Phillips, and if Reagan had shown the smallest sign of abandoning the "freedom fighters," who had become an icon in the conservative firmament, he might have risked dividing the party. Since negotiations were extremely risky anyway, with a low probability of success, the safest approach politically and geopolitically was to side-step talks and rally around the Resistance.

Therefore, Reagan did not even mention Nicaragua in his meetings with Gorbachev, nor did he respond when Gorbachev, according to Reagan, "told me that he wants to go forward with the [Arias] peace plan, and he would withhold aid from the Sandinistas in order to do so."[28] That the Administration failed to respond or explore these issues was all the more revealing when it uncorked a Nicaraguan defector on December 10, while Gorbachev was still in Washington. On condition that they not publish articles until December 14—after Gorbachev had left—several reporters were invited into Elliott Abrams' office to interview Major Roger Miranda Bengoechea, who had left Nicaragua two months before.

Miranda had fought in the revolution and served as a personal assistant to the two senior military figures of the Nicaraguan government, Humberto Ortega and Joaquin Cuadra Lacayo. He knew the innermost secrets of the Nicaraguan military, and indeed he took with him a report of the army's capabilities and requirements for the next decade. The document assumed that the contras— called "mercenaries"—would be defeated by 1990, but five dangerous years would follow when an American invasion would become most likely. For that reason, the report recommended an expansion of Nicaragua's military forces through 1995 to 80,000 regular armed forces and a people's militia of 420,000 people. The motive for this expansion is unequivocal: to "more convincingly avert the possibility of a direct invasion by American troops and assure their defeat, should the invasion occur."

The report describes the fighting against the contras as having been so fierce that the Sandinistas had exhausted all the Soviet arms provided under the five-year plan in just three years, from 1985 to 1987. The Soviet Union was not as forthcoming or reliable a supplier as the Administration contended. The Soviets had promised MIG-21's in 1981, but had reneged on the promise.[29]

Besides providing the report, which appeared authoritative, Miranda had much to say. Probably most embarrassing to the Sandinista leadership was his disclosure that Humberto and Daniel Ortega, Tomás Borge, and Jaime Wheelock all had secret Swiss bank accounts. His information on Humberto's bank, the account number, and the value ($1.5 million) was the most credible as he had managed the account. Miranda said that Bayardo Arce coordinated a group called "The Bureau," which assisted the Salvadoran and Guatemalan insurgencies and was prepared to launch a regional war if the United States ever attacked Nicaragua. In September 1987, Salvadoran guerrilla leader Joaquin Villalobos requested that Nicaragua train his soldiers to use portable anti-aircraft weapons, and according to Miranda, a group of 15 rebels was being trained in Nicaragua for a 35-day course when he defected.

The Administration made good use of the information. Humberto Ortega was so stung by the allegations that he angrily announced the right of the Nicaraguan people to expand its army to 600,000, not 500,000 as Miranda had said. Humberto also indirectly confirmed the report about the Salvadorans with a transparent threat that if they received missiles, it would be because of U.S. "irresponsibility" for giving them to the contras. The real point of his remarks, however, was lost in the U.S. report of them. What he was trying to do was to exaggerate Nicaraguan military capabilities in order to discourage U.S. intervention: "This is no Grenada. They [the Yanquis] better not think they can come here and finish this up in 2 or 3 days. It will not be like that, no sir."[30]

The recurring themes of the relationship continued to reverberate. Humberto's defensiveness sounded provocative in Washington, and together with Miranda's disclosures and President Arias' expressions of concern about Nicaragua's plans, the Administration found itself in striking distance of obtaining aid.[31] If Reagan were so concerned about Miranda's revelations of increasing Soviet military support for Nicaragua, why did he not pursue this issue with Gorbachev? "You don't understand," a senior State Department official explained to a reporter, who asked a similar question: "Miranda was for the press and Congress, not for Gorbachev."[32] The Administration believed that the best way to pursue U.S. security interests was by supporting the contras, not by negotiations.

In the omnibus appropriation bill passed as Christmas approached, Congress approved $8.1 million of aid to the contras. Since the aid was "humanitarian" rather than military, Congress fudged the Guatemalan Accord's requirement to stop support by January 15. The Nicaraguans thus had an excuse: why should they fully comply with the plan if the United States was not complying? Because this question was so central to the peace process, to which all the Central Americans were committed, it was dodged.

Judgment Day

Preparations for the Summit of Central American Presidents in San José on January 15 followed the rhythm of previous encounters. In advance of the meeting, President Arias took the one step required of Costa Rica in the plan: he expelled all the contra political leaders from San José. Three of the four Nicaraguan members of the Reconciliation Commission expressed disappointment with the inadequate steps taken by the Sandinista government with regard to internal dialogue or negotiations with the contras. Instead of responding to these concerns from his people, President Ortega addressed the American audience by writing an article in the *New York Times*. Reversing a previous position, he pledged that he would "turn over the government" if the opposition won an election, although he said nothing about turning over the military. He also repeated his pledge that "if we receive sufficient security guarantees from Washington, we will not maintain a large army or unnecessary armaments," and within the context of a region-wide agreement, he would accept "a mutual ban on all offensive foreign military bases [and would] actively prevent the use of our territory to threaten or subvert any country in the world."[33]

While the key parties were offering new promises, the Reagan Administration repeated an old threat. General Colin Powell, Reagan's sixth National Security Adviser, travelled to each country in Central America except Nicaragua and told the Presidents that if they failed to condemn the Sandinistas in San José, contra aid would probably lose, and so too would aid to their countries. The heavy-handed warning was all the more remarkable because Powell had it published when he returned to Washington.[34] The Defense Ministers of Guatemala, El Salvador, and Honduras also met on the eve of the Summit to discuss strategy and urge their Presidents to take a hard position in San José.

In recognition of the contribution of Contadora, the Central Americans had asked the four governments to organize an International Verification and Follow-up Commission (CIVS) to prepare a report on the extent of the five governments' compliance before January 15. The report concluded that substantial progress had been made, but that the job was not complete. The report was impartial but critical of almost all of the countries, and perhaps for that reason, the Central Americans disbanded the Commission after the meeting. The report was tougher on Nicaragua than on any other country, criticizing it for not including representatives of the Resistance on the Reconciliation Commission, for failing to sustain a dialogue with the internal opposition or begin one with the Resistance, for continuing its people's tribunals, for offering only a partial amnesty, and for not lifting the state of emergency. Its comment on U.S. policy was blunt: "Despite calls made by the Central American Presidents, the U.S. government's policy and practice of providing military assistance to irregular forces that operate against the Nicaraguan government still persists. The definite suspension of this assistance is an essential requirement for the success of the peace efforts as a whole."[35] The Commission also recommended establishing "mobile units" of international representatives in each of the five countries to ensure compliance with the Accord by on-site inspections, especially of the security commitments like the cease-fire and the end of support for insurgents.

After two days of talks, the five Presidents issued a Joint Declaration calling on all parties to "immediately fulfill" the remaining commitments, especially those related to democratization. The Reconciliation Commissions in each nation were given the primary responsibility for compliance, but the Presidents also instructed the Foreign Ministers to meet soon to discuss "verifying, controlling, and following up on all the commitments."[36]

Daniel Ortega apparently felt most of the heat, and he called a press conference immediately following the issuance of the Joint Declaration on January 16. Ortega announced a series of measures that were required by the Accord but that he had previously conditioned on the end of U.S. support for the contras. He ended the state of emergency, agreed to direct talks with the contras, and promised to release 3,000 former National Guardsmen from prison if any country accepted them. These were significant steps, particularly the decision to begin direct talks with the contras, but there was a smallness about these large decisions that revealed Ortega's ambivalence and left his adversaries legitimately uncertain of his intentions. Whereas the Verification Commission's report and the Joint Declaration stressed the need for political dialogue, Ortega sharply circumscribed the talks with the contras so as to focus "exclusively" on the cease-fire. "In order to have a political dialogue," he said, "the contras must first lay down their arms and accept the civilian option."[37] But in his dismissal of a substantive and serious dialogue with the internal opposition in December, Ortega did not instill much confidence as to what, if anything, would be discussed after the contras surrendered their arms.[38]

Similarly, Ortega referred to the contras in the most derogatory terms just because they had asked the Sandinista delegation to include Nicaraguans. (It had been composed of an American lawyer and a German Social Democrat.) Ortega conceded in his customary manner: "To prevent the contra movement—which is the instrument of U.S. policy—from devising pretexts, and to make another effort to attain a cease-fire agreement, we have now decided to include a Nicaraguan official in the Nicaraguan delegation." Ortega was still unwilling to accept that his adversaries were Nicaraguans with legitimate concerns.

From the outside, Ortega's approach seemed half-hearted and petty—giving with one hand, but holding back with the other—but from within the Sandinista party, his reversal on direct talks to the contras probably shocked the cadre, requiring him to preserve some part of his previous position. A personality clash between Ortega and Tomás Borge seemed to intersect with a genuine debate on how the revolution could best be preserved, with Ortega characteristically calling for adaptation, and Borge arguing that concessions to the contras would demoralize the party faithful and make the revolution more vulnerable. The debate among the Sandinistas played itself out in the form of contradictory policies that hurt them and helped Reagan persuade Congress.

On the road from Esquipulas II, every step toward liberalization by Ortega coincided with a step backwards by Borge. Within days of the Accord's signing, Borge's police harshly broke up a demonstration in Managua and arrested several human rights leaders. When Ortega announced direct talks with the contras on January 16 in San José, the police in Managua arrested four opposition leaders. When Ortega returned to Managua two days later to abolish the people's tribunals and end the state of emergency, the police arrested five more opposition leaders, and *Barricada*, the FSLN newspaper, warned that Ortega's decisions to restore civil rights "should not be misinterpreted as a blank check for irresponsibility and subversion." Stephen Kinzer, the *New York Times* correspondent in Managua, was told by "an official close to Mr. Ortega that those reports [that Borge had ordered the arrests without consulting Ortega] were accurate." This was the first time that the private differences between the Comandantes had been made public.[39]

The Reagan Administration, of course, chose to interpret these

contradictory events differently, highlighting the arrests as still another reason why the Sandinistas should not be trusted. "Without
the freedom fighters," said President Reagan, "the hope of democracy in Nicaragua would be lost."[40] And yet the Administration realized that the progress made by Nicaragua and the rest of Central
America toward democracy decreased its chance to secure *any* aid
for the Resistance, let alone the proposed $270 million. As it moved
to adapt to this reality, the Administration found itself under attack
from its right. The *Wall Street Journal* warned that if the Administration reduced its request to aid the contras, "We may be on the
brink of handing over Nicaragua to a communist government. . . .
The future of Nicaragua will be decided this weekend in the Reagan
White House." The editorial ended sarcastically: "We hope Mr. Reagan will participate in those discussions."[41]

The crucial vote on aid occurred in the House of Representatives
on February 3, 1988. To persuade the swing votes, the Administration scaled down its proposal from $270 million to just $36 million.
Ten percent was for ammunition, and that amount would be suspended until March 31 pending the cease-fire negotiations. The entire package would sustain the contras until July when the President would make a new request. On the night of the vote, President
Reagan addressed the American people on television. He argued
that pressure had worked on the Sandinistas, and that this was not
the time to let up on it. The Democratic response was given by Rep.
Lee Hamilton. He stressed the importance of supporting the peace
process by ending aid: "Seven years of contra war have not achieved
what the peace plan has achieved in six months. . . . The President's
request will cripple, if not destroy, the peace process. It will lead
toward more war, more repression, less democracy, and more Soviet
aid."[42]

The debate the next day showed the deep polarization that divided America on Nicaragua. One Congressman after another rose
either to denounce the Sandinistas as a Communist scourge that
needed to be excised or to criticize the Reagan Administration as
the major problem in the region. The White House lost the vote by
a narrow margin, 219-211, because of the Accord and because Jim
Wright proved more adept than the Administration at finding a
compromise between those who wanted to support the Accord and
those who did not want to abandon the contras. He did so by promising an alternative "humanitarian" package for the contras.

President Arias applauded the vote, saying that Nicaragua had
"no more excuses" for not complying fully with the Accord. With
regard to Wright's proposed alternative, Arias said this "would not
be a violation of the peace accord. It is military aid that is prohibited

and not humanitarian aid."[43] This was an important but subtle point, suggesting that Arias valued the contras as a lever to move the negotiations forward, but opposed military aid as a roadblock that would halt negotiations and preclude acceptance of his plan. Wright had grasped this point, but Reagan had not.

Ortega had previously indicated that "one single additional dollar for the contras, regardless of whether it is termed humanitarian aid or not, would be a dollar used to kill the Central American agreements." But he chose not to repeat that charge after the House vote; instead, he congratulated "the majority of the House" for voting "for a peaceful solution to the . . . conflict." The rest of his comments, however, suggested a perspective quite different from Arias'. Claiming that Nicaragua was already "complying with each and every point" of the plan, he described how its neighbors—especially Honduras because of the contra bases—were not in compliance. He went even further, telling Nicaraguans that they lived "in a complete democracy. Now we do enjoy total freedom of expression."[44]

The Sandinistas' opponents were not prepared to concede that point. Direct negotiations between the Resistance and the Sandinista government began on January 28, but were deadlocked from the start. The Sandinistas wanted to discuss the technical details of a cease-fire, while the contras wanted to be assured of political guarantees before they gave up their weapons.

Democrats and Republicans were having no more success in reaching agreement. Wright proposed a package of $30.8 million of food, clothing, and medical aid to the contras, but the Republicans, disturbed about Wright's tactics and wanting a guarantee of a quick vote on military aid if the negotiations broke down, defeated it on March 3, 216-208. The Republican decision was yet another example of the way that frustration often turns rational decision-makers into shortsighted spoilsports. Had the Republicans voted for the aid, the result would have been an extraordinarily broad, bipartisan message of support to the contras. Moreover, the vote against Wright proved to be a vote against any aid to the contras as the Republicans failed to gain agreement for a new package.

This was also the end of the dry season in Nicaragua, and the Sandinistas decided to launch a major campaign against the contras. Hoping perhaps to finish the contras and capture their arms stockpile, Sandinista troops pursued the contras into Honduras. When the Administration received reports that Nicaragua's campaign might succeed, it responded energetically. On March 16, Reagan announced he was sending 3,200 troops to Honduras to bolster Honduras. The troops would also protect both the contras and their arms stockpile. Coincidentally, the announcement of the dispatch of the 82nd Airborne occurred at the same time that Oliver North, John Poindexter, Richard Secord, and Albert Hakim were indicted on twenty-three counts of defrauding the federal government, embezzling U.S. funds, destroying documents, and obstructing a Presidential inquiry. Several days before, Robert McFarlane had pleaded guilty to charges of lying to Congress.

As the war seemed to accelerate to its most dangerous phase, and U.S. troops moved to within fifteen miles of the Nicaraguan border, the Sandinistas continued their awkward two-step on negotiations—for every two steps forward, they took one backwards and one sideways. They raised the level of their delegation to be led by Minister of Defense Humberto Ortega and permitted talks in Nicaragua, but they then dismissed Cardinal Obando as a mediator and scheduled the meeting before the contras were ready.

From these contradictory moves and apparent incoherence, a pattern began to emerge. The battles showed that the Sandinistas were strong but not strong enough to erase the contras. As long as the war continued, the economy, which had plummeted in 1987, could not improve. By denying military aid to the contras, Congress gave the Sandinistas more face-saving space to make serious concessions without them appearing to surrender. At the same time, after watching Democrats and Republicans bicker over aid, the contras realized that they could not take U.S. support for granted. In brief, both sides had compelling reasons to negotiate more seriously than they had before. Interestingly, both may have been moved closer by their interests in asserting their independence of the United States.

The agreement signed in Sapoá on March 23, 1988 was historic— the first time the Nicaraguan government and its armed opposition faced each other without an American mediator and reached a compromise that began by recognizing the legitimacy of the other. The agreement's importance was less in what it achieved than in the risks that each side assumed. The contras agreed to move their forces to specified enclaves where they would be vulnerable and their true strength could be ascertained. During the cease-fire period, the contras agreed to reject any military aid, although the Reagan Administration seemed close to obtaining some in the aftermath of the Nicaraguan invasion of Honduras. (The Nicaraguans asked the United Nations to send a team to the border to confirm they had not crossed it, but the team found that they had.[45]) The Reagan Administration had rejected efforts by Democrats to channel aid to the contras through "neutral organizations," but the contras accepted that. Most important, the Resistance defined a realistic negotiating agenda by accepting the Constitution and President Daniel Ortega's incumbency until 1990. The next round of negotiations would more profitably focus on ways to guarantee the full participation of all Nicaraguans in elections for municipalities and the Central American Parliament.

In accepting the contras and permitting them to keep their weapons during negotiations, the Sandinista leadership reversed two of their most sacrosanct positions. The government "guaranteed unrestricted freedom of expression," accepted a gradual but unconditional amnesty, invited the contra leadership to Managua for talks on political issues and not just a cease-fire, and accepted an ongoing role by the Organization of American States and Cardinal Obando to verify this and other agreements.

The Reagan Administration was trapped once again in an awkward position. If it embraced the Sapoá agreement, the Administration would have contradicted its argument that military aid to the contras was essential to a good agreement. If it opposed the agreement, it would appear to be even more hard-line and intransigent than the contras. The Reagan Administration therefore responded much as it had to the Guatemalan Accord. It confessed surprise, officially welcomed the agreement, but privately expressed skepticism and applied pressure to the contras to harden their negotiating posture.

Congress responded warmly to the initiative, as it had to the Guatemalan Accord. Wright assembled a $47 million package of aid that included $17.7 million of food, clothing, and medical aid to the contras to be delivered by "neutral organizations"; an equal amount to finance a special program for the children who were victims of the war; and $10 million for the verification commission. The package passed the House by a vote of 345-70 on March 30 and the Senate by a vote of 87-7 the next day.

The Prospects for Reconciliation

The decision by the five Presidents of Central America to sign the Guatemalan Accord on August 7, 1987, was a landmark in Central American history. It changed the terms of the debate within the region and the United States. Before the signing, the only movement was toward militarization and war. Afterwards, one could measure progress toward democracy and peace. The signing was the result of a confluence of events. War, depression, continuing threats of militarization, the Reagan Administration's relentless pressure, and the break-down of the Nicaraguan economy—these factors pressed the Presidents to search for an exit and to avoid being blamed for not finding one. During the previous five years, these factors had had the opposite effect, reducing political space and increasing repression. They led to a different direction in 1987 because two men opened a window for their colleagues to crawl through. Oscar Arias and Vinicio Cerezo forged a peace plan and persuaded their colleagues that the alternative was untenable.

By constructing a framework that would require each Central American nation to comply with each principle at the same time, Arias placed the burden on the country that refused to comply. Even Ortega recognized that this approach was a leap beyond Contadora. He could never accept a political dialogue imposed from Washington, but he could accept one that was proposed by Central Americans and accepted as part of a broader region-wide agreement. One measure of the risk he took for peace was the public split that occurred within the FSLN Directorate.

The one crucial piece of the puzzle that the Central Americans could not insert themselves was an end to U.S. support for the Resistance, and President Reagan's support was nonnegotiable. Nonetheless, the steps by Nicaragua toward peace convinced the few Congressmen whose minds were still open on this issue. In this sense, Central America had a decisive impact on U.S. policy. Convinced that the region's Presidents were serious and making progress, Congress took the political risk that Arias had requested: it suspended military aid long enough to permit negotiations to proceed. The risk was rewarded with the Sapoá agreement.

Still, the questions for the United States remained unanswered: could it develop a strategy that would serve its three interests—strategic, regional security, and democracy—in Nicaragua? Would it seek to reinforce or undermine local efforts to negotiate peace and freedom? The Democratic and Republican Parties reflect the region's polarization. It was no coincidence that in 1988, no Democratic Presidential candidate supported the contras, and no Republican opposed them. Each party pressured and inhibited the other; the United States, in brief, remained divided on this issue.

Sapoá was not the end of the road; it was a stop on a long journey, one which would continue up hills and down valleys, from brief moments of euphoria to long periods of disillusionment. Until the opposition believes it can win power legally and peacefully, armed struggles will continue, and local parties will always seek help from outside.

This pattern cannot be broken easily. Internal strife can only be insulated from international intervention when the local government earns the trust of its opposition, and the superpowers show respect for regional governments. When this occurs, Nicaragua's future and its relations with the United States will improve on its past, and it will be easier to make peace in Central America than to make war.

Selected Abbreviations

Andean Pact	Economic association of five countries (Venezuela, Colombia, Peru, Ecuador, and Bolivia), which also played a political role in Nicaragua
ARA	Bureau of American Republic Affairs (Latin America and the Caribbean), Department of State
Contadora	Panamanian island where foreign ministers of Mexico, Venezuela, Panama, and Colombia met in January 1983 to begin peace negotiations on Central America
Contras	Counter-revolutionaries; see FDN
COSEP	Superior Council of Private Enterprise; main business association in Nicaragua
Directorate	Nine-member political-military leadership of the FSLN. Established in Havana in March 1979. Composed of three leaders or Comandantes from each of the three FSLN factions
ExCom	Executive Committee. Carter Administration's proposal in June 1979 for a transitional government to take power from Somoza and negotiate a cease-fire with the San José Junta
FAO	Broad Opposition Front; a coalition initially representing sixteen groups that negotiated during the mediation
FDN	Nicaraguan Democratic Force. The main group of contras; established in 1981. Later part of United Nicaraguan Opposition (UNO) and subsequently Nicaraguan Democratic Resistance
FMLN	Farabundo Martí National Liberation Front; coalition of Salvadoran revolutionary groups
FSLN	Sandinista National Liberation Front; or Frente. Established in 1961. By 1975, split into three factions or "tendencies": Prolonged War (GPP), led by Tomás Borge, Henry Ruiz, and Bayardo Arce; Proletarian Tendency (TP), led by Jaime Wheelock, Luis Carrión Cruz, and Carlos Núñez; and Terceristas, led by Daniel and Humberto Ortega and Víctor Tirado. These nine became the Directorate

GRN   Government of National Reconstruction. Led by
                       San José Junta, which was announced on June 16,
                       1979. The GRN formally assumed power on July
                       20, 1979

Group of Twelve   Twelve apparently independent businessmen,
                       lawyers, and priests. In October 1977 demanded
                       that the FSLN be part of any new government.
                       Also referred to as "the Twelve"

Guard   The National Guard of Nicaragua

HA   Bureau of Human Rights, Department of State

IAHRC   Inter-American Human Rights Commission of
                       the OAS

Junta   See GRN

NSC   National Security Council

OAS   Organization of American States

PG   Provisional Government established in San José,
                       led by five-member Junta. Became GRN

PRC   Policy Review Committee. One of two commit-
                       tees of NSC; generally chaired by State Depart-
                       ment

SCC   Special Coordination Committee of NSC. Chaired
                       by National Security Adviser Zbigniew Brzezin-
                       ski. Mini-SCC was chaired by his Deputy, David
                       Aaron

Chronology

1936-56	Rule of Anastasio Somoza García (Tacho I)
1956-66	Presidency and indirect rule of Luis Somoza
1966-79	Presidency and indirect rule of Anastasio Somoza, Jr. (Tacho II)
1961	Establishment of FSLN
1972	Earthquake shakes Managua
1974	FSLN takes hostages at Christmas party; Somoza imposes state of siege

1977

January 20	Inauguration of Jimmy Carter as President
July 28	Anastasio Somoza's heart attack
September 19	Somoza repeals state of siege
October 13-15	FSLN raids; Group of Twelve established

1978

January 10	Murder of Pedro Joaquín Chamorro; general strike
August 1	Disclosure of Carter letter to Somoza
August 22-24	Edén Pastora takes over National Palace
August 25	General strike; insurrection; arrest of moderates
September 4	First NSC (mini-SCC) meeting on Nicaragua; recommends support for Costa Rican mediation
September 22	U.S. warns Panama about bombers and expanding war
September 23	OAS resolution indirectly endorses mediation
October 6	Mediation team arrives in Managua
November 14	Carter decides to propose negotiating terms for a free plebiscite rather than force out Somoza
December 4	Luis Pallais presents three questions about Somoza's departure
December 9	FSLN announces unity agreement in Havana; condemns plebiscite
December 20	Mediation team presents detailed plebiscite proposal; Bowdler delivers ultimatum to Somoza

1979

February 8	State Department announces sanctions against Somoza
May 16	Costa Rica assures U.S. of no arms trafficking; at same time, finalizes arrangements for direct Cuban flights, which delivered over 30,000 pounds of arms in 21 flights between late May and July 19
May 20	Mexican President breaks relations with Nicaragua after meeting with Fidel Castro and Rodrigo Carazo
May 29	Sandinista force of 300 enters Nicaragua from south to begin "final offensive"
June 5	Torrijos and Royo of Panama pledge not to interfere in Nicaragua's affairs
June 12	Carter approves PRC recommendation to consult with Latin America on plan to link Somoza departure with peace force and transitional government
June 15-18	Carter summit meeting with Brezhnev in Vienna
June 16	Andean Pact announcement of "state of belligerency," recognizing FSLN as coequals; five-member Junta announced in San José; Pastora's second invasion
June 20	ABC newsman Bill Stewart killed by Guard
June 21	Vance speech to OAS links Somoza departure with peace force and transitional government
June 22	Carter rules out unilateral intervention
June 23	OAS resolution calls for replacing Somoza regime with a democratic government
June 23–July 1	Tokyo summit; Carter state visit to Japan and Korea
June 24	Carter makes support for Guard conditional on obtaining some international support, but approves proposal to designate a Guard Commander and encourage an Executive Committee as transitional government
June 25	SCC recommends two-pillar strategy: influence the Junta while trying to establish an ExCom
July 2	Carter decides to seek new Guard Commander and expand Junta; ExCom idea dropped
July 3	Secret meeting with Torrijos, who agrees to try to persuade FSLN of July 2 plan
July 3-14	Junta rejects plan. Carter goes to Camp David for domestic summit and energy speech preparation

July 17-19	Somoza leaves; Urcuyo becomes President; agreement breaks down. Amb. Pezzullo, then Urcuyo leave
July 20	Junta of the Government of National Reconstruction is sworn into office
September 24	Carter meets with Junta in White House
November 9	Carter seeks supplemental aid request of $75 million for Nicaragua

1980

April	FSLN negotiations with COSEP; resignation of Robelo and Chamorro from Junta
July 19	Castro gives main speech at first anniversary of revolution
September 12	Carter signs certification to disburse aid to Nicaragua
November	Reagan landslide; FSLN decides to support Salvadoran rebels massively

1981

January 19	Carter suspends aid to Nicaragua
April 1	After gaining agreement to stop arms flow, State Department announces termination of aid
August-October	Enders negotiation on security guarantees; fails
November 17	Reagan decides to support contras

1982

March 14-15	FSLN declares state of emergency in response to first major contra attack

1983

October	Invasion of Grenada by U.S. and Caribbean forces

1984

October 1	Aid to contras halted by Congress; NSC-directed operation under North supports contras
November	Reagan wins reelection; Daniel Ortega wins in Nicaragua

1985

August	Congress approves $27 million in humanitarian aid for contras but continues ban on military aid

1986

June 27	International Court of Justice finds U.S. in breach of international law for helping the contras

October   New law provides $100 million (70% for arms) for Nicaraguan resistance

November   Poindexter and North of NSC resign; investigations into diversion of funds to contras begin

1987

February 27   Tower Commission report describes elaborate private operation run by North of NSC to aid contras

May 5   Joint Hearings on the Iran–Contra issues by Senate and House Select Committees begin

May 7   Contras reorganize themselves for fourth time in four years as Nicaraguan Democratic Resistance

August 7   The five Central American Presidents meet in Guatemala and sign a peace Accord first proposed by Costa Rican President Oscar Arias that stresses democratization and regional security

November 5   Nicaraguan President Daniel Ortega accepts indirect talks with the Resistance to be mediated by Cardinal Obando. He also releases 981 political prisoners and promises to lift the state of emergency when Honduras closes the contra bases

December 21   Congress votes $8.1 million in nonlethal aid for the Resistance to last until February 29

1988

January 16   Five Central American Presidents meet in San José and pledge to implement remaining obligations under the Guatemalan Accord. Verification Commission asks U.S. to end military aid to the contras. Ortega agrees to direct talks with the contras and lifts the state of emergency

February 3   The House of Representatives rejects President Reagan's request for military aid to the contras

March 3   Republicans reject Democratic plan to provide $30.8 million in humanitarian aid to the Resistance by 216-208. Aid to contras ends

March 12-17   Robert McFarlane pleads guilty to lying to Congress; North, Poindexter, Secord, and Hakim are indicted. Reagan sends 3,200 troops to Honduras in response to Nicaraguan incursion

March 23   Nicaragua and Resistance sign agreement at Sapoa for a two-month cease-fire and political dialogue. Contras reject military aid, accept humanitarian aid through "neutral organizations," and can keep arms during negotiations

March 31   Congress approves $17.7 million in humanitarian aid to contras; same amount for children hurt by war; and $10 million for verification commission

Notes

Preface

1. Sandinista Comandante Dora María Tellez held a press conference in Panama that day. It was published by the Foreign Broadcasting Information Service, *Daily Report* [hereafter *FBIS*], September 2, 1978, pp. N4-5, annex 2. Somoza's interview with ACAN-EFE was republished in *FBIS*, September 5, 1978, p. P2.

2. Charles A. Krause, "Nicaraguan Rebels Losing Key Support," *Washington Post*, March 17, 1979, p. A20.

3. Lenin's prediction is cited by Hans J. Morgenthau, *Politics among Nations* (New York: Alfred A. Knopf, 1973), p. 22; Daniel Ortega's is in his interview with WGBH in Managua, June 4, 1984.

Chapter 1

1. Few books or articles written about Nicaragua since the 1960s in English or Spanish fail to mention some variation of this comment. Some authors have modified the comment, and some have suggested that Roosevelt used it to refer to Dominican dictator Rafael Trujillo. The most commonly used story is that Roosevelt said this of Somoza on the eve of Somoza's visit to Washington in 1939.

2. I did my own search of the published documents of FDR before interviewing Donald Schewe, former Assistant Director of the Franklin D. Roosevelt Library and currently Director of the Carter Presidential Library, October 10, 1986, Atlanta. Arthur M. Schlesinger, Jr., one of the foremost historians of the Roosevelt era, wrote me that he has "never been able to find any source for the alleged FDR statement, and I suspect it is apocryphal" (letter to the author, March 30, 1987).

3. Visiting Americans commented about the Somoza family's use of "quaintly antiquated American slang which they laced with obscenities portraying a 1930s B-picture tough-but-nice-guy image." Bernard Diederich, *Somoza and the Legacy of U.S. Involvement in Central America* (New York: E. P. Dutton, 1981), p. vii.

4. This story is recounted by Diederich, *Somoza*, p. 212. Transcendental meditators believe they emit "positive unity force fields,"

which can, among other things, reduce crime rates, traffic accidents, and global tensions. Andrew Malcolm, "Iowa Town Contemplates Pitfalls of Being Meditators' Utopia," *New York Times*, January 1, 1984, p. 14.

5. *FBIS*, September 5, 1978, p. 1. Also published in *Washington Star*, September 4, 1978.

6. Jeane Kirkpatrick, "U.S. Security and Latin America," *Commentary*, January 1981, p. 36. Her other article was "Dictatorships and Double Standards," *Commentary*, November 1979.

7. William LeoGrande, "The Revolution in Nicaragua: Another Cuba?" *Foreign Affairs* (Fall 1979): 28; Tom Farer, "At Sea in Central America: Can We Negotiate Our Way to Shore?" in *Central America: Anatomy of Conflict*, ed. Robert Leiken (New York: Pergamon, 1984), pp. 282-83; Shirley Christian, *Nicaragua: Revolution in the Family* (New York: Random House, 1985). Three other books argue the United States should have overthrown Somoza and might have, if it had understood the situation better: Thomas G. Walker, *Nicaragua: The Land of Sandino* (Boulder: Westview Press, 1981); John A. Booth, *The End and the Beginning: The Nicaraguan Revolution* (Boulder: Westview Press, 1982); and George Black, *Triumph of the People: The Sandinista Revolution in Nicaragua* (London: Zed Press, 1981). All are sympathetic to the revolution and critical of U.S. policy.

8. Richard R. Fagen, "Dateline Nicaragua: The End of the Affair," *Foreign Policy*, no. 36 (Fall 1979): 188.

9. LeoGrande, "Revolution in Nicaragua," pp. 37-38.

10. Fulgencio Batista y Zaldivar, *Cuba Betrayed* (New York: Vantage Press, 1962); Anastasio Somoza, Jr., as told to Jack Cox, *Nicaragua Betrayed* (Boston: Western Islands, 1980).

11. Castro advised the Sandinistas not to repeat the mistakes he made at the beginning of his revolution. *New York Times*, July 9, 1980, p. 10.

12. Cited in "Reagan Warns: No More Cubas in the West," *The News* (Mexico City), June 9, 1986, p. 1.

13. Richard Neustadt and Ernest May have proposed numerous ways policy makers could improve their decisions if they learned from Santayana and history. *Thinking in Time: The Uses of History for Decision-Makers* (New York: The Free Press, 1986).

14. Bryce Wood, *The Making of the Good Neighbor Policy* (New York: Columbia University Press, 1961), p. 64.

15. The following chronology on the Cuban revolution and the U.S. response to it has been reconstructed from many sources, but the following have been most useful: Richard E. Welch, Jr., *Response*

to *Revolution: The United States and the Cuban Revolution, 1959-61* (Chapel Hill: University of North Carolina Press, 1985); Hugh Thomas, *Cuba: The Pursuit of Freedom* (New York: Harper and Row, 1981); Cole Blasier, *The Hovering Giant: U.S. Responses to Revolutionary Change in Latin America* (Pittsburgh: University of Pittsburgh Press, 1979); and Philip W. Bonsal, *Cuba, Castro, and the United States* (Pittsburgh: University of Pittsburgh Press, 1971).

16. Thomas, *Cuba*, p. 958.

17. Blasier, *Hovering Giant*, p. 22.

18. Thomas, *Cuba*, p. 965.

19. Figueres's involvement is documented in a Senate hearing. See U.S. Senate, Committee on the Judiciary, *Communist Threat to the U.S. through the Caribbean: Hearings before the Subcommittee to Investigate the Administration of the Internal Security Act and Other Internal Security Laws, Part 8*, January 22, 23, 1960, pp. 447-54. Pérez noted his help in his interview with WGBH, May 2, 1984, New York City.

20. WGBH interview with José Figueres, June 8, 1984, San José.

21. Thomas, *Cuba*, p. 1005.

22. Cited in ibid., pp. 1015-16.

23. Thomas, *Cuba*, p. 1018.

24. Ibid., p. 1028.

25. Welch, *Response to Revolution*, p. 62.

26. Some correspondents also noted the similarities. Don Bohning, "Nicaragua 1978, Cuba 1958—Parallels Are Striking," *Miami Herald*, September 6, 1978.

27. For one example, see "Forum: Why Are We in Central America? Can the U.S. Live with Latin Revolution? The Dilemmas of National Security," *Harper's*, vol. 268, no. 1609, June 1984, pp. 35-48.

28. Walter LaFeber, *Inevitable Revolutions* (New York: W. W. Norton, 1983), p. 15.

29. For a perceptive essay on the nature of revolution, see Chalmers Johnson, *Revolutionary Change*, 2d ed. (Stanford: Stanford University Press, 1982).

30. Both theses—that revolutions are inevitable and resisted by the United States and the bourgeoisie—are developed by Walter LaFeber in *Inevitable Revolutions*.

31. I have examined the issues related to how events in Central America could affect the national security of the United States in several other papers. See "Our Real National Interests in Central America," *The Atlantic*, July 1982, pp. 27-39; and "U.S. National Security and Latin Revolutions: Imprismed," written for the World Peace Foundation, December 1, 1986.

32. Even in the case of "revolutionary" Grenada, U.S. policy was not negative at the beginning. See Robert Pastor, "Does the United States Push Revolutions To Cuba? The Case of Grenada," *Journal of InterAmerican Studies and World Affairs* (April 1986).

33. LaFeber, *Inevitable Revolutions*, p. 230.

Chapter 2

1. Carlos Fonseca Amador, *Nicaragua: Hora Cero*, first published in *Tricontinental*, no. 14, 1969; excerpts reprinted in Tomás Borge et al., *Sandinistas Speak* (New York: Pathfinder Press, 1982), p. 29.

2. David Richard Radell, *An Historical Geography of Western Nicaragua: The Spheres of Influence of León, Granada, and Managua, 1519-1965*, cited in Walker, *Nicaragua: The Land of Sandino*, pp. 10-12.

3. Franklin D. Parker, *The Central American Republics* (New York: Oxford University Press, 1971), pp. 219, 66.

4. Thomas L. Karnes, *The Failure of Union: Central America, 1824-1975* (Tempe: Arizona State University, 1976), p. 94. The civil wars in Nicaragua were typical of the entire region. In the same period, El Salvador had 40 battles and 23 different Presidents; Honduras, 27 battles and 20 Presidents; Guatemala, 51 battles and 18 Presidents.

5. Richard Millett, *Guardians of the Dynasty: A History of the U.S.-Created Guardia Nacional de Nicaragua and the Somoza Family* (Maryknoll, N.Y.: Orbis Books, 1977), p. 16.

6. For a description of the U.S.–British competition in Central America, see Karnes, *Failure of Union*, ch. 5, pp. 96-125; Parker, *Central American Republics*, pp. 234-35; and Samuel F. Bemis, *The Latin American Policy of the U.S.: An Historical Interpretation* (New York: Harcourt, Brace and Company, 1943), pp. 103-108.

7. Proclamation of President Franklin Pierce, December 8, 1855, in *Messages and Papers of the Presidents, 1789-1897*, ed. James D. Richardson (Washington, D.C.: GPO, 1897), pp. 388-89.

8. William O. Scroggs, *Filibusters and Financiers* (1916; reissued New York: Russell and Russell, 1969), pp. 166-67.

9. See Laurence Greene, *The Filibuster* (New York: Bobbs-Merrill, 1937), pp. 137, 200-201; Scroggs, *Filibusters*, pp. 166-72.

10. See Dana G. Munro, *The Five Republics of Central America: Their Political and Economic Development and Their Relations*

with the United States (New York: Oxford University Press, 1918), ch. 4.

11. Millett, *Guardians*, pp. 19-22.

12. Munro, *Five Republics*, p. 90.

13. "Letter transmitted from the Nicaraguan Minister to Secretary of State Richard Olney," 1895, cited in Wilfrid Hardy Callcott, *The Caribbean Policy of the United States, 1890-1920* (Baltimore: The Johns Hopkins Press, 1942), p. 77.

14. Bemis, *Latin American Policy*, p. 145.

15. For a good description of the Washington conference and an evaluation of the effectiveness of the treaties on peace in the region, see Karnes, *Failure of Union*, pp. 188-203; and Munro, *Five Republics*, pp. 206-226.

16. Millett mentions the Canal negotiations (*Guardians*, p. 23). Karl Berman doubts these occurred, but notes the railroad contract. *Under the Big Stick: Nicaragua and the United States Since 1848* (Boston: South End Press, 1986), p. 150.

17. Actually, Estrada provoked U.S. intervention with a clever ruse. As governor of the province, Estrada informed the U.S. Consul that his efforts to resist an attack by Zelaya's soldiers prevented him from protecting U.S. citizens in the area. Though self-serving, the statement was credible, and given the norms of the times, the Consul was compelled to ask the Marines to provide the protection. See William Kamman, *A Search for Stability: United States Diplomacy toward Nicaragua, 1925-1933* (Notre Dame: University of Notre Dame Press, 1968), p. 10.

18. Dana G. Munro, *Intervention and Dollar Diplomacy in the Caribbean, 1900-21* (Princeton: Princeton University Press, 1964), pp. 176-86.

19. Harold Norman Denny, *Dollars for Bullets: The Story of American Rule in Nicaragua* (New York: Dial Press, 1929), p. 7.

20. Callcott, *Caribbean Policy*, pp. 280-85; Millett, *Guardians*, pp. 26-30.

21. For a description of the extensive involvement by the United States in restructuring the finances of the Nicaraguan government, see Department of State, *The United States and Nicaragua: A Survey of the Relations from 1909-1932*, Latin American Series no. 6 (Washington, D.C.: GPO, 1932), pp. 12-28.

22. Dana G. Munro, *The United States and the Caribbean Republics, 1921-33* (Princeton: Princeton University Press, 1974), pp. 159-66. The United States was so involved in Nicaragua's affairs that an American refused to reimburse the Nicaraguan President for his expenses ($446) in hosting a reception.

23. Ibid., p. 162.

24. The United States tried to follow this formula even when it was not in its interests because it did not want to contribute to undermining the treaties (as it had done with the Central American court established by the 1907 treaties). Ibid., pp. 118-19, 193. See also Thomas M. Leonard, *U.S. Policy and Arms Limitation in Central America: The Washington Conference of 1923* (Los Angeles: California State University, Occasional Papers no. 10, 1982).

25. Munro, *United States and the Caribbean Republics*, p. 218.

26. Calvin Coolidge, *Message to Congress: The Conditions and the Actions of the Government in the Present Disturbances in Nicaragua* January 27, 1927.

27. Henry Stimson, *American Policy in Nicaragua* (1927; reprint New York: Arno Press, 1970), p. 42.

28. Ibid., p. 57.

29. See Stimson, *American Policy*, pp. 84-87; Munro, *United States and the Caribbean Republics*, p. 247.

30. See Neill Macaulay, *The Sandino Affair* (Chicago: Quadrangle Books, 1967); Gregorio Selser, *Sandino* (New York: Monthly Review Press, 1981); Millett, *Guardians*, pp. 63-65, 87.

31. In a study of this and other U.S.-supervised elections in Latin America, Theodore Wright argues that an election might be fair but could not be considered completely "free" when it is supervised by a foreign military presence. See his "Free Elections in the Latin American Policy of the United States," *Political Science Quarterly* 74 (1959).

32. Millett, *Guardians*, p. 136.

33. Ibid., pp. 137-38, 183.

34. Secretary of State Cordell Hull initially rejected the request for a statement because he did not want to "dignify such absurd stories by issuing a denial," and because the United States wanted to remove itself from Nicaraguan internal affairs. See U.S. Department of State, *Foreign Relations of the United States* [hereafter *FRUS*], 1934, vol. 5, "Policy of the U.S. Not to Interfere in Nicaraguan Internal Affairs," pp. 526-58.

35. Millett, *Guardians*, pp. 146, 153, 155.

36. *FRUS*, 1934, vol. 5, "The Secretary of State to the Minister in Nicaragua [Lane], February 26, 1934, pp. 538-39.

37. *FRUS*, 1935, vol. 4, "Memorandum by the Assistant Chief of the Division of Latin American Affairs [Beaulac]," reporting on conversation with Dr. Sacasa," October 1, 1935, pp. 877-79.

38. *FRUS*, 1935, vol. 4, "The Minister in Nicaragua [Lane] to the Secretary of State," May 14, 1935, pp. 855-61.

39. This part of the historical record captures the ambiguity and hesitancy of U.S. policy in its title, "Efforts to Discourage President Somoza's Bid for Re-Election in 1947, While Maintaining a Policy of Non-Interference in Nicaragua's Internal Affairs," *FRUS*, 1945, vol. 9, p. 218.

40. The opposition urged the State Department to protest the fraud, but to no avail. *FRUS*, 1947, vol. 8, "Telegrams from Secretary of State to Embassy in Nicaragua and from Embassy to the Secretary of State," April 8 and 23, 1947, pp. 846-47.

41. Author's telephone interview with Maurice Bernbaum, Washington, D.C., July 24, 1985. Bernbaum was the Chargé at the time.

42. *FRUS*, 1947, vol. 8, "Telegrams from the Chargé in Nicaragua to the Secretary of State," May 9, 24, and 26, 1947, pp. 848-53.

43. *FRUS*, 1947, vol. 8, pp. 40, 589, 859-65.

44. *FRUS*, 1947, vol. 8, "Memorandum of Conversation, by Assistant Secretary of State Armour," August 24, 1947, pp. 871-72. During this time, U.S. Chargé Maurice Bernbaum is reported to have called Somoza's son (Tacho II) and asked when his father would leave. The elder Somoza returned the call, enraged: "This is my country. Where do you want me to go? You come and take me out!" Cited in Diederich, *Somoza*, p. 30.

45. Two decades before, on January 2, 1947, Undersecretary of State Robert Olds wrote that Central American "governments which we recognize and support stay in power, while those which we do not recognize and support fall." Cited in Millett, *Guardians*, p. 52. The failure to unseat Somoza by nonrecognition was one of several cases that ended the nonrecognition policy. See Thomas M. Leonard, "The Decline of the Recognition Policy in United States–Central American Relations, 1933-49," Occasional Paper 49, Florida International University, July 1985.

46. Charles Ameringer has examined the rise of democrats in the Caribbean area in three works, from which the next sections of this chapter borrow: *The Democratic Left in Exile: The Antidictatorial Struggle in the Caribbean, 1945-1959* (Coral Gables: University of Miami Press, 1974); *Don Pepe: A Political Biography of José Figueres of Costa Rica* (Albuquerque: University of New Mexico Press, 1978); "The Thirty Years War between Figueres and the Somozas," *Caribbean Review* 8, no. 4 (Fall 1979).

47. *FRUS*, 1952-54, vol. 4, *The American Republics* (Washington, D.C.: GPO, 1983), September 29, 1952, pp. 1372-75. In light of the Eisenhower Administration's decision in 1953 to overthrow the Arbenz government, the State Department's reasons for rejecting the idea in 1952 are interesting: it violated international law, and "we

would find it difficult to fight aggression in Korea and be a party to it in this hemisphere" (p. 1374). Actually, one of Truman's aides thought the plan had merit, and persuaded the President. Truman instructed the CIA to proceed with the conspiracy, but when Secretary of State Acheson learned of it, he convinced the President to abort the mission. Stephen Schlesinger and Stephen Kinzer, *Bitter Fruit: The Untold Story of the American Coup in Guatemala* (Garden City, N.Y.: Doubleday, 1982), p. 102.

48. *FRUS*, 1952-54, vol. 4, "Memorandum by the Secretary of State to the President," May 1, 1952, pp. 1369-71.

49. Ibid., "The Ambassador in Nicaragua [Whelan] to the Department of State," March 6, 1953, pp. 1375-77. Whelan, a former Republican Party chairman from North Dakota, was appointed by President Truman in 1951 as part of a deal with Senator William Langer, Chairman of the Judiciary Committee, who threatened to delay the Administration's legislation until Truman appointed a North Dakotan to an Embassy. Albert M. Colegrove, "Nicaragua: Another Cuba?" *The Nation*, July 1, 1961, pp. 6-9.

50. For the negotiation and signing (April 23, 1954) of the military aid agreement, see *FRUS*, 1952-54, vol. 4, p. 1378. On the Guatemalan chronology, see Schlesinger and Kinzer, *Bitter Fruit*, p. 113.

51. *FRUS*, 1952-54, vol. 4, p. 1389; Ameringer, *Don Pepe*, pp. 119-22; Millett, *Guardians*, pp. 213-14.

52. Cited in John D. Martz, *Central America: The Crisis and the Challenge* (Chapel Hill: University of North Carolina Press, 1959), p. 199.

Chapter 3

1. Millett, *Guardians*, p. 225; Ameringer, "Thirty Years War," p. 40. Chamorro and Lacayo were freed by the end of 1960.

2. Interviews (both author's and WGBH) with Edén Pastora (November 14, 1983 [author]; July 1, 1984 [WGBH]; both Washington, D.C.) and Tomás Borge (August 4, 1983 and February 8, 1986 [author]; June 3, 1984 [WGBH]; all Managua). The origins of the FSLN are not clear. Pastora predictably tends to enlarge his role, and the current leaders of Nicaragua, Borge and the Ortegas, tend to omit or discount Pastora's role. A Senate Foreign Relations Committee study in 1969, however, indicated that the Frente Liberación Nacional had been founded first in Havana, giving some credibility to Pastora's claim that he inserted the word "Sandino" into the Frente's name. U.S.

Senate Committee on Foreign Relations, *Survey of the Alliance for Progress*, April 29, 1969, p. 233.

3. Carlos Fonseca Amador, "El Aporte Revolucionario de Sandino," from *Escritos*, in *Nicaragua: La Estrategia de la Victoria* (Mexico: Editorial Nuestro Tiempo, 1983), pp. 71-72.

4. Millett, *Guardians*, p. 227.

5. See the description in his memoirs of his trip to South America in 1958, where he attributes the demonstrations against him to Communist agitators. Richard Nixon, *RN: The Memoirs of Richard Nixon* (New York: Grosset and Dunlap, 1978), pp. 186-92.

6. Author's conversation and correspondence (December 3, 1982) with James Cheek, who was political counselor in the U.S. Embassy in Managua at the time. Cheek risked the Ambassador's displeasure by sending his reports to the State Department by the dissent channel. He later received a special award from the department for these reports.

7. Author's interview with Max Kelly, February 13, 1984, Miami, Florida.

8. Cited in Diederich, *Somoza*, p. 24.

9. Somoza, *Nicaragua Betrayed*, p. 58.

10. Diederich's book is an excellent portrait of the two sides of Anastasio Somoza—a man who was relaxed with Americans and authoritarian to Nicaraguans who were not members of his family. A similar characterization of the man was made by two Nicaraguans who worked closely with Somoza, but who asked not to be identified.

11. The book was published by the John Birch Society in English just before the Presidential election in 1980. In a press conference on August 24, 1978, in Managua, Somoza was asked whether he viewed Carter's policy as a betrayal. He answered: "I am a politician, and I recognize that every adminstration has different attitudes. Therefore I do not consider a change in the attitude of the United States government a betrayal. We both have to adjust to our new relations." Unclassified Cable from U.S. Embassy, Managua to Secretary of State, 26 August 1978, Managua 3997, "Somoza's Press Conference."

12. Somoza, *Nicaragua Betrayed*, p. 55.

13. Ibid., p. 209. Although the human rights situation in Nicaragua was not as bad as in many countries of the Southern Cone, Amnesty International's Annual Report for 1975-76 noted "many reports of arbitrary arrest, torture, and disappearance." Cited in *Human Rights Reports*, prepared by the Department of State, submitted to the U.S. Senate Committee on Foreign Relations, March 1977, p. 134.

14. Somoza, *Nicaragua Betrayed*, p. 58.

15. This and subsequent information on the Ford Administration's policy toward Nicaragua was obtained in an interview with William D. Rogers, Assistant Secretary of State for Inter-American Affairs (1974-76) and Under Secretary of State for Economic Affairs (1976), May 22, 1985, Washington, D.C.

16. Interview with William D. Rogers, May 22, 1985, Washington, D.C.

17. Somoza, *Nicaragua Betrayed*, p. 58. Somoza also noted the award to James Cheek and the Congressional hearings on human rights in Nicaragua as other signs that public opinion in the United States might be beginning to turn against him.

18. Stephen Kinzer, "Sandinistas Mark Raid That Presaged Victory," *New York Times*, January 7, 1985, p. A4.

19. WGBH interview with Tomás Borge, June 3, 1984, Managua. Humberto Ortega agrees that this was "the most important operation carried out by the Front. . . . For the first time, the Sandinistas' revolutionary views were broadcast on TV and radio." "Interview with Humberto Ortega," in Borge et al., *Sandinistas Speak*, p. 55.

20. Author's interview with Alfredo César, April 9, 1984, Washington, D.C.

21. Many of the original Sandinista leaders were writers and poets, and there is ample literature to identify their world view. In English, the most accessible compendium is the short book *Sandinistas Speak* (New York: Pathfinder Press, 1982), which includes the translated and edited speeches and writings of Carlos Fonseca and others. In particular, see the 1969 program of the FSLN and excerpts from Fonseca's *Zero Hour*, pp. 13-42. For a discussion of the significance of U.S. interventions in the history of Nicaragua, see the excerpt from Fonseca's book and the speech by Daniel Ortega also in that volume. For a discussion of the importance of U.S. imperialism in defining Nicaragua's economic problems, see Jaime Wheelock Román, *Imperialismo y Dictadura: Crisis de una Formación Social*, 6th ed. (Mexico: Siglo Veintiuno Editores, 1982), originally published 1975. For an overall analysis, see David Nolan, *The Ideology of the Sandinistas and the Nicaraguan Revolution* (Coral Gables: University of Miami, 1985).

22. This early history is recounted by Carlos Fonseca, who excused this "grave error" by suggesting that "the Marxist leadership [in Nicaragua] did not possess the necessary clarity" of thought at the time. In Borge et al., *Sandinistas Speak*, pp. 31-32.

23. Cited in Selser, *Sandino*, p. 97. Neill Macaulay describes the break between Sandino and the Communists in *The Sandino Affair*, pp. 158-60.

24. WGBH and author's interviews with Edén Pastora, November 14, 1983 (author), Washington, D.C.; July 1, 1984 (WGBH), Washington, D.C.

25. WGBH interview with Daniel Ortega, June 4, 1984, Managua.

26. Humberto Ortega Saavedra, *50 Años de Lucha Sandinista* (Managua: Ministerio del Interior, 1980), but originally written in 1976. At the conclusion of his book, the Sandinistas are confronting the combined forces of Central America, plus advisers from the United States, Brazil, Colombia, and exiles from South Vietnam (p. 120). Also, see Humberto Ortega in Borge et al., *Sandinistas Speak*, p. 57.

27. WGBH and author's interviews with Tomás Borge, August 4, 1983 (author), Managua; June 3, 1984 (WGBH), Managua.

28. The interviews were with Henry Ruiz from the GPP, Daniel Ortega from the Terceristas, and Jaime Wheelock Román of the TP, in *Latin American Perspectives* 6, no. 1 (Winter 1979): 108-128.

29. *Latin American Perspectives*, p. 115.

30. Ibid., p. 118.

31. This is Jaime Wheelock Román's conclusion at the end of his study of the Nicaraguan economy. See his *Imperialismo y Dictadura*, 6th ed., pp. 195-96.

32. The Nicaraguan case offers an almost classic fit with the thesis developed by Samuel P. Huntington that revolution "is most likely to occur in societies which have experienced some social and economic development and where the processes of political modernization and political development have lagged behind the processes of social and economic change." *Political Order in Changing Societies* (New Haven: Yale University Press, 1968), p. 265.

33. U.S. Agency for International Development, *U.S. Overseas Loans and Grants*, July 1, 1945–September 30, 1978, p. 56.

34. All of the statistics in this section are from World Bank, *World Development Report, 1980* (New York: Oxford University Press, 1980); this from pp. 112-13.

35. Harry W. Strachan, *Family and Other Business Groups in Economic Development: The Case of Nicaragua* (New York: Praeger, 1976), p. 116.

36. Richard Feinberg and Robert Pastor, "Far From Hopeless: An Economic Program for Post-War Central America," in *Central America*, ed. Leiken, p. 195. Nicaragua's development progress during this period was typical of most of Central America.

37. Robert W. Fox and Jerrold W. Huguet, *Population and Urban Trends in Central America and Panama* (Washington, D.C.: Inter-American Development Bank, 1977), pp. 53, 160.

38. *New York Times*, July 22, 1979, p. III, 1.

Chapter 4

1. Cited in U.S. House Appropriations Committee, *Foreign Assistance and Relations Programs Appropriation Bill, 1978*, Report no. 95-417, June 15, 1977, p. 65.

2. For a description and analysis of Carter's policies, see Robert Pastor, "The Carter Administration and Latin America: A Test of Principle," in *U.S. Policy toward Latin America: Quarter-Century of Crisis and Challenge*, ed. John D. Martz (Lincoln: University of Nebraska Press, 1988).

3. For the Congressional origins of the human rights policy, see Robert Pastor, *Congress and the Politics of U.S. Foreign Economic Policy* (Berkeley: University of California Press, 1980), pp. 301-321. Also see Congressional Research Service, Library of Congress, *Human Rights and U.S. Foreign Assistance: Experiences and Issues in Policy Implementation (1977-78)*, for the U.S. Senate Committee on Foreign Relations, November 1979 [hereafter, Senate Human Rights Report].

4. Author's interview with Alfonso Robelo, May 3-4, 1983, San José, Costa Rica. Curiously, Somoza himself acknowledges this side of Solaun: "I'll say this for Mr. Solaun, he did his best. However, he was not forceful enough and he didn't have the clout to impress his superiors in the State Department." Somoza, *Nicaragua Betrayed*, p. 70.

5. WGBH interview with John Murphy, May 15, 1984, Danbury, Connecticut.

6. Author's interview with Alan Riding, May 13, 1983, Washington, D.C.

7. Alan Riding, "Nicaraguan Bishops Accuse Government of Resorting to Widespread Torture," *New York Times*, March 2, 1977, p. 1.

8. *Human Rights Reports*, prepared by the Department of State, submitted to the U.S. Senate Committee on Foreign Relations, March 1977, pp. 133-34.

9. For more detail on Somoza's lobbying activities, see Lars Schoultz, *Human Rights and U.S. Policy toward Latin America* (Princeton: Princeton University Press, 1981), pp. 58-64; and Diederich, *Somoza*, pp. 130-35. Both authors tend to exaggerate the importance of the lobbyists, taking their self-promotional boasts at face value.

10. WGBH interview with John Murphy, May 15, 1984, Danbury, Connecticut. Murphy, who had served nine terms in the House, was indicted on June 18, 1980, on conspiracy and bribery charges result-

ing from the FBI's ABSCAM investigation. He lost his seat in the November election, and was subsequently convicted and served sixteen months in Federal prison.

11. My conclusions about Wilson's motivations are based on numerous conversations with him during this period, and a telephone interview on July 31, 1985. When asked by a journalist whether Somoza was too corrupt and repressive to warrant military aid, Wilson said: "I think that's real bullshit, and you can quote me in your little family newspaper." "Charlie Wilson: What's He Done for Nicaragua Lately?" *Texas Observer*, September 23, 1977, pp. 1-2, 22.

12. Amnesty International's report was extremely critical of the abuses of the National Guard from December 1974 to January 1977. However, by the time of the release of the report, in August 1977, the Catholic Church in Nicaragua acknowledged that Somoza had ended the abuses. One source judged by Alan Riding to be credible said: "Since March, we haven't received any reliable report of a massacre. The National Guard has definitely been told to clean up its act." *New York Times*, August 16, 1977, p. 6.

13. Diederich, *Somoza*, pp. 136-38. Somoza claims his attack occurred while doing his daily Canadian Air Force exercises. Somoza, *Nicaragua Betrayed*, pp. 72-73.

14. Somoza, *Nicaragua Betrayed*, pp. 72-73; Diederich, *Somoza*, p. 139. Somoza, who was never accused of spending his own money extravagantly, complained in his memoirs that the flight cost him $30,000 and took seven hours.

15. Author's interviews with Max Kelly, Somoza's personal aide, February 13, 1984, Miami, Florida; and with Luis Pallais, October 16, 1985, Miami.

16. This account is based on an interview with Daniel Oduber, May 19, 1984, Falmouth, Massachusetts. In his memoirs, Somoza alleges that I told Oduber in June 1977: "When are we going to get that son of a bitch up to the north out of the presidency?" Oduber confirmed that I had not said that, but Oduber also acknowledged that he tried to use my remarks as a lever to get Somoza to leave.

17. John Goshko and Karen DeYoung, "U.S. Aid to Nicaragua: 'Garbled' Human Rights Message," *Washington Post*, October 24, 1977, p. A1; and Karen DeYoung, "Nicaragua Denied Economic Aid, Gets Military," *Washington Post*, October 5, 1977, p. A10.

18. Chilean writer Marta Harnecker did an extensive interview with Humberto Ortega that was first published in *Granma*, January 27, 1980, entitled, "La Estrategia de la Victoria." It is a remarkably candid and credible description of the Sandinistas' political-military

strategy to gain power. I cite from the English translation in Borge et al., *Sandinistas Speak*, p. 56 [hereafter H. Ortega, "Strategy"].

19. Author's interview with Tomás Borge, August 4, 1983, Managua.

20. H. Ortega, "Strategy," p. 59.

21. These raids were later described by several of the Sandinista combatants in a book of interviews by Pilar Arias, *Nicaragua: Revolución, Relatos de Combatientes del Frente Sandinista* (Mexico: Siglo Veintiuno Editores, 1981), pp. 134-39. The attacks involved very few Sandinistas but were judged a success by one, José Valdivia, "because it received great international news."

22. Somoza, *Nicaragua Betrayed*, p. 86.

23. Alan Riding, "Nicaraguan Rebels Deny Marxist Aim: Guerrillas Seek Broad Support and Vow Free Elections If Bid to Topple Somoza Succeeds," *New York Times*, October 26, 1977, p. 9.

24. Cited in Luigi Einaudi, ed., *Beyond Cuba: Latin America Takes Charge of Its Future* (New York: Crane, Russak, and Co., 1974), p. 30.

25. The statement was circulated in Washington the day of the announcement. A variation on the statement can be found in *The Central American Crisis Reader*, ed. Robert S. Leiken and Barry Rubin (New York: Summit Books, 1987), pp. 172-73.

26. Sergio Ramírez explains the origin of the Group of Twelve in an interview in Arias, *Nicaragua: Revolución*, pp. 129-33, supplemented by an interview with the author, February 8, 1986, Managua.

27. Author's interview with Arturo Cruz, October 2, 1986, Atlanta.

28. WGBH interview with Edén Pastora, July 1, 1984, Washington, D.C.

29. WGBH interview with José Figueres, June 8, 1984, San José, Costa Rica.

30. Author's interview with Alfonso Robelo, July 29-30, 1983, San José, Costa Rica.

31. That was the conclusion of Gary Sick, *All Fall Down* (New York: Random House, 1985), p. 34.

32. Author's interview with Pedro Joaquín Chamorro Barrios, July 26, 1983, San José, Costa Rica. The Sandinista government held a trial, and in June 1981, found a Miami-based Cuban exile, Pedro Ramos, and eight Nicaraguans guilty of Chamorro's murder. *La Prensa* had published a series of articles exposing Ramos for corruption shortly before Chamorro's murder. *Latin America Weekly Report*, June 26, 1981, p. 12.

33. WGBH interview with Carlos Andrés Pérez, May 2, 1984, New York City.

34. *Public Papers of the Presidents of the United States, Jimmy Carter, 1977*, vol. II, p. 1296.

35. See, for example, Robert G. Kaiser, "Brzezinski, Vance Are Watched for Hint of a Policy Struggle," *Washington Post*, March 28, 1977, p. A2.

36. Zbigniew Brzezinski, *Between Two Ages: America's Role in the Technetronic Era* (New York: The Viking Press, 1970), p. 288.

37. Zbigniew Brzezinski, "America in a Hostile World," *Foreign Policy*, no. 23 (Summer 1976): 96.

38. In October 1976, Vance prepared a detailed memorandum for Carter setting out specific goals and priorities for U.S. foreign policy. The memorandum is reprinted as Appendix I in Vance's memoirs. The section on Latin America resembles the comments of Brzezinski and the reports of the Linowitz Commission on U.S.–Latin American Relations. See Cyrus Vance, *Hard Choices* (New York: Simon and Schuster, 1983), pp. 451-52.

39. For the two views on this issue, see Vance, *Hard Choices*, pp. 84-88; and Zbigniew Brzezinski, *Power and Principle: Memoirs of a National Security Adviser, 1977-1981* (New York: Farrar, Straus, Giroux, 1983), pp. 178-85.

40. Author's interview with Alfonso Robelo, July 29-30, 1983, San José, Costa Rica.

41. In retrospect, the last comment was revealing, because both the moderate opposition and Somoza were then seeking U.S. involvement in Nicaragua, albeit on different sides. Only the Sandinistas, who viewed the United States as the enemy, wanted it to be neutral.

42. Author's interview with General José Antonio Olavarría, Deputy Director of Venezuela's National Security Council (1977-81), December 14, 1986, Casa de Campo, Dominican Republic.

43. WGBH interviews with Edén Pastora, July 1, 1984, Washington D.C.; and with Carlos Andrés Pérez, May 2, 1984, New York City.

44. The Administration did request $150,000 for military training, but this is separate from military aid. For the first time since the military program began, Somoza's government did not officially request military aid for the 1979 fiscal year budget. Senate Human Rights Report, pp. 193-95.

45. John M. Goshko, "U.S. Frees Aid to Nicaragua in a Policy Reversal," *Washington Post*, May 16, 1978, pp. A1, 18.

46. In a speech he gave to the OAS on June 21, 1978, Carter himself had written the italicized part of the following sentence: *"We prefer to take actions that are positive,* but where nations persist in serious

violations of human rights, we will continue to demonstrate that there are costs. . . ." *Public Papers of the Presidents, Jimmy Carter, 1978*, vol. I, pp. 1141-46.

47. Somoza devotes an entire chapter of his book to the letter, which had an extraordinary roller-coaster effect on him. He first saw it as a sign he had won over Carter, but on reflection, saw it as another attempt to undermine him. Somoza, *Nicaragua Betrayed*, ch. 10. The letter is reproduced on pp. 276-77.

48. Author's interview with Max Kelly, a Nicaraguan adviser to Somoza since his graduation from West Point in 1970, February 13, 1984, Miami, Florida. Murphy confirmed this point in his interview with WGBH, May 15, 1984, Danbury, Connecticut.

49. Somoza, *Nicaragua Betrayed*, pp. 137-38.

50. Both Pérez (WGBH interview) and Somoza (*Nicaragua Betrayed*, pp. 138-44) have described the meeting in ways that add to the other's account without contradicting it. I have also been able to confirm other aspects of the conversation with Manolo Reboso, a Cuban-American who accompanied Somoza on the trip; Max Kelly; and with Carlos Andrés Pérez on September 22, 1982.

51. Somoza, *Nicaragua Betrayed*, pp. 137-38.

52. WGBH interview with Carlos Andrés Pérez, May 2, 1984, New York City.

53. Correspondence with the author from Jimmy Carter, August 19, 1985.

54. These are the words used by Vance's special assistant, who called Goshko to try to identify the leaker. Author's interview with John Goshko, June 24, 1985, Washington, D.C.

55. "Somoza Letter Called Joint Effort," *Washington Post*, August 2, 1978, p. A7. The literature on U.S. policy toward Nicaragua has, without exception, used the first Goshko article, rather than the clarification, and has described it as "congratulatory." For example, Booth, *The End and the Beginning*, p. 130; Walker, *Nicaragua: The Land of Sandino*, p. 112. Lars Schoultz suggested it undermined Carter's entire human rights policy; see Schoultz, *Human Rights and U.S. Policy toward Latin America*, p. 117.

56. Somoza, *Nicaragua Betrayed*, pp. 146-47. See also Diederich, *Somoza*, pp. 172-73. Diederich cited a Somoza aide, who said that Somoza's final reaction to the letter was that "Carter was telling Tacho he ran a dictatorship."

57. Diederich describes how. *Somoza*, pp. 177-83.

58. Diederich, *Somoza*, p. 184. This was the consensus of virtually all the reporters who covered the event.

59. Tad Szulc, "Rocking Nicaragua: The Rebels' Own Story," *Washington Post*, September 3, 1978, p. C1.

60. Author's interviews with Edén Pastora, November 14, 1983, Washington, D.C.; Tomás Borge, August 4, 1983, Managua; and Rafael Solís, Secretary to the Council of State, August 2, 1983, Managua.

61. H. Ortega, "Strategy," in Borge et al. *Sandinistas Speak*, p. 69.

62. Karen DeYoung, "Nicaragua Reports It Has Suppressed Anti-Somoza Plot," *Washington Post*, August 29, 1978, p. A12.

63. Diederich, *Somoza*, p. 197. Richard Millett's sources in Nicaragua led him to conclude that Somoza had Allegret killed (author's interview, Atlanta, February 23, 1987), but both Lt. Col. James McCoy, the U.S. Military Attaché, and Luis Pallais insisted that Allegret was not plotting against Somoza, and Somoza did not have him killed. Author's interviews with McCoy and with Pallais, both October 16, 1985, Miami, Florida.

64. "Church in Nicaragua Urges Somoza to Quit to Quell Civil Unrest," *New York Times*, August 5, 1978, p. A22.

65. Luis Pallais, the President of the Nicaraguan Congress, revealed the existence of this special force in an interview with WGBH, May 17, 1984, Miami, Florida.

66. H. Ortega, "Strategy," in Borge et al., *Sandinistas Speak*, pp. 66, 62.

67. Somoza's interview was with ACAN-EFE, but republished in *FBIS*, September 5, 1978, p. P2. The interview with Dora María Tellez was published by *FBIS*, September 5, 1978, pp. N4-5, annex 2.

68. Alan Riding, "In Nicaragua, This May Be the Twilight of the Somozas," *New York Times*, October 30, 1977, p. IV, 3.

Chapter 5

1. Cited in Murray Marder, "Panel Predicted Shah's Ouster," *Washington Post*, December 23, 1984, p. A11.

2. Harold Milks, " 'Somoza or Communism,' Nicaraguan Leader Warns," *Arizona Republic*, September 5, 1978, reprinted in *Congressional Record*, House, September 6, 1978, p. H9068.

3. These characterizations of Vaky's views are the result of years of conversations with him, a long interview on July 24, 1985, Washington, D.C., and his comments on a draft of this manuscript.

4. For a good description of the way the NSC was organized under President Carter, see Brzezinski, *Power and Principle*, pp. 57-63.

5. *Public Papers of the Presidents of the United States, Jimmy Carter, 1978,* vol. II, p. 1521.

6. Correspondence with the author from Jimmy Carter, August 19, 1985. Carter's recollection is based on his diary.

7. Author's interview with Rodrigo Carazo Odío, July 30, 1983, San José, Costa Rica.

8. Correspondence with the author from Viron Peter Vaky, September 8, 1986.

9. His speech is in the *Department of State Bulletin,* January 1979, pp. 57-58.

10. Author's telephone interview with William Jorden, March 12, 1987.

11. This is an excerpt from Carter's diary, which he sent to the author August 19, 1985. These events were reconstructed from the author's interviews with Gabriel Lewis Galindo (many occasions), Viron Peter Vaky (many occasions), and Zbigniew Brzezinski (July 17, 1985, Washington, D.C.).

12. The President's statement is in *Public Papers of the Presidents of the United States, Jimmy Carter, 1978,* vol. II, pp. 1596-1602.

13. White House transcript of "Interview with Zbigniew Brzezinski for Latin American Editors," September 22, 1978.

14. For a brief biographical sketch of Torrijos, see my article, "Remembering Omar Torrijos: Ode to Omar," *The New Republic,* August 15, 1981.

15. Author's interview with Carlos Andrés Pérez, Washington, D.C., September 22, 1982. Gabriel Lewis also filled in some of the gaps of this story in an interview in Panama on December 28, 1982.

16. Author's interview with Gabriel Lewis Galindo, December 28, 1982, Panama.

17. The entire published record of the mediation and its origins is compiled in the *Report to the Secretary of State on the Work of the International Commission of Friendly Cooperation and Conciliation for Achieving a Peaceful Solution to the Grave Crisis of the Republic of Nicaragua,* 1979.

18. Excerpts from the meeting are reproduced in Somoza's memoirs, *Nicaragua Betrayed,* pp. 313-24. The meeting, however, is incorrectly dated as occurring in November.

19. Author's interview with William D. Rogers, May 22, 1985, Washington, D.C. Christopher does not recall these points, nor does he remember whether he or Vance spoke to Carter about it (letter to the author, December 10, 1986). Carter also does not recall this exchange. I would judge that only Rogers focused on these conditions, which went considerably beyond the Administration's position at that time. Rogers had also set a stiff condition when he assisted ne-

gotiations on Panama, and then he had acquiesced when it was violated. See William Jorden, *Panama Odyssey* (Austin: University of Texas Press, 1984), p. 579.

20. Somoza, *Nicaragua Betrayed*, p. 318.

21. Correspondence with author from Viron Peter Vaky, September 8, 1986.

22. *New York Times*, September 26, 1978, p. 56.

23. *FBIS*, October 5, 1978, p. 9.

24. Somoza, *Nicaragua Betrayed*, p. 216.

25. Author's interview with Edén Pastora, November 14, 1983, Washington, D.C.

26. Alfonso Robelo said in an interview printed in the *Washington Star*, September 25, 1978: "Somoza's resignation is the solution."

27. H. Ortega, "Strategy," in Borge et al., *Sandinistas Speak*, p. 72.

28. Interview with Sergio Ramírez, in Arias, *Nicaragua: Revolución*, p. 169.

29. Author's interview with Tomás Borge, August 4, 1983, Managua.

30. Gale McGee recounted this conversation for me on September 5, 1978. It was the only bright spot that day.

31. See, for example, the testimony of Stanford University Professor Richard Fagen before the Senate Foreign Relations Committee, *Latin America*, October 4-6, 1978, pp. 35-36. Church groups in the U.S. were reflecting the changes occurring in the churches in Latin America. See James R. Goff, "Latin American Churches Want Somoza to Resign," *Washington Post*, October 13, 1978.

32. William P. Bundy, "Who Lost Patagonia? Foreign Policy in the 1980 Campaign," *Foreign Affairs* (Fall 1979): 6.

Chapter 6

1. Author's interview with Alfonso Robelo, July 29-30, 1983, San José, Costa Rica.

2. Sergio Ramírez described this in an interview with Arias, *Nicaragua: Revolución*, pp. 170-71.

3. Ramírez interview in Arias, *Nicaragua: Revolución*, p. 171.

4. Correspondence with the author from Viron Peter Vaky, September 8, 1987.

5. After the IMF vote on November 1, Somoza communicated a message to me through Reboso that he considered the vote "an act of hostility," and if we kept behaving like that, he would "no longer consider the U.S. a friend."

6. Richard Millett reports considerable unhappiness among junior

officers when Somoza first assigned Gutierrez abroad. *Guardians*, pp. 227-28.

7. Somoza, *Nicaragua Betrayed*, pp. 219-20.

8. This is Vaky's recollection of what Bowdler told him.

9. Career officials are sometimes accused of "clientilism"—defending the positions of foreigners—rather than advancing the positions of the United States, and political appointees are often accused of "tunnel vision"—projecting U.S. values abroad where they don't fit. Both charges have some validity, but miss the pivotal question of *which* foreign interests a career official chooses to defend—a dictator, the middle class, the poor?—and which U.S. values a political appointee attaches highest priority to.

10. It is significant that Vance's decision to omit a State Department recommendation because he disagreed with his line officers occurred in the middle of Carter's term. The longer an Administration is in office, the more the Cabinet Secretaries are drawn to their department's institutional perspective, widening the gap between the department and the President and the NSC.

11. Correspondence with the author from Jimmy Carter, August 19, 1985. Though Shirley Christian did not speak with either Carter or Bowdler, she reports that Carter asked Bowdler whether Somoza was a "moral man." (*Nicaragua: Revolution in the Family*, p. 77). Carter does not recall asking such a question, and Bowdler would not comment on the conversation.

12. Author's interview with Viron Peter Vaky, July 24, 1985, Washington, D.C. On reflection, Vaky thought he might have missed the significance of Pallais' questions at the time because of the "noise" of other events and distractions.

13. Author's interview with Luis Pallais, October 16, 1985, Miami, Florida.

14. "Communiqué to the Nicaraguan People from the National Directorate of the FSLN-GPP, PC of the FSLN-TP, General Staff of the War Resistance, FSLN-Insurrectional," December 9, 1978, published in *Latin American Perspectives* 6 (Winter 1979): 127-28. Ramírez later said: "If the plebiscite had occurred, it would have been an opportunity—imperialism's last—to unseat Somoza and preserve Somocismo." In Arias, *Nicaragua: Revolución*, p. 170.

15. Author's interview with Edén Pastora, November 14, 1983, Washington, D.C.

16. Author's interview with Luis Pallais, October 16, 1986, Miami, Florida. Pallais' account that Somoza was serious about a plebiscite until the third week in December is credible because he was the only

one of Somoza's entourage to admit that Somoza deliberately decided against the plebiscite at the time of the Cabinet meeting.

17. Somoza, *Nicaragua Betrayed*, p. 328. Citations come from the transcript of the tape that Somoza took of the conversation.

18. Somoza wanted to change the simple question of whether he should remain in office to a two-part question: Should Somoza complete his constitutional term? Should a national constituent assembly be convened? Other than the fact that the relationship between the two questions is uncertain and confusing, particularly for a barely literate campesino, the second question leaves open the possibility that Somoza could manipulate and control the constituent assembly if he were to fail to win approval on the first question. For that reason, the FAO rejected this question.

19. Author's interviews with Jimmy Carter, January 28, 1982, Plains, Georgia, and October 11, 1984, Panama; WGBH interview with John Murphy, July 31, 1985, Danbury, Connecticut. Several writers, such as Shirley Christian (*Nicaragua: Revolution in the Family*, pp. 87-88) and William LeoGrande ("Revolution in Nicaragua," p. 35), have suggested that Murphy's influence on the Canal legislation constrained Carter on Nicaragua. Christian even insinuates that there might have been a deal on the two issues between the two men. She offers no evidence, however, and both men deny it.

20. Author's interview with Jimmy Carter, October 11, 1984, Panama; correspondence dated on August 19, 1985. Carter also said that he never saw any evidence that Murphy was successful in convincing Somoza. Somoza, *Nicaragua Betrayed*, p. 226.

21. Somoza, *Nicaragua Betrayed*, p. 226.

22. Letter from Rep. John Murphy to President Jimmy Carter, January 22, 1979; response from Secretary of State Cyrus Vance on February 10, 1979. Carter Presidential Library, Atlanta.

23. The announcement is in the *Department of State Bulletin*, April 1979, p. 66. It was a mistake to include the Peace Corps in the announcement. Although the rationale for withdrawing them was that we feared for their safety in another round of violence, inclusion of the Peace Corps unintentionally politicized an organization whose strength remains its neutrality and autonomy.

Chapter 7

1. H. Ortega, "Strategy," in Borge et al., *Sandinistas Speak*, pp. 77-79.

2. Author's interview with Viron Peter Vaky, July 24, 1985, Washington, D.C.

3. Author's interview with Alfonso Robelo, July 29-30, 1983, San José, Costa Rica. Pastora was referring to the FSLN's unity agreement in December in Havana.

4. Cited in Diederich, *Somoza*, pp. 235-36.

5. Cited in Diederich, *Somoza*, pp. 230-31.

6. *Washington Post*, March 17, 1979, p. A20

7. Karen DeYoung, "Sandinistas Try Pulling Together to Bring Down Somoza," *Washington Post*, April 5, 1979, p. A22.

8. Author's interview with Alfonso Robelo, July 29-30, 1983, San José, Costa Rica.

9. Author's interview with Rodrigo Carazo Odío, July 30, 1983, San José, Costa Rica.

10. For an excellent summary of the involvement of international organizations in the Nicaraguan crisis, see Dennis R. Gordon and Margaret M. Munro, "The External Dimension of Civil Insurrection: International Organizations and the Nicaraguan Revolution," *Journal of Inter-American Studies and World Affairs* 25 (February 1983): 59-81.

11. H. Ortega, "Strategy," in Borge et al., *Sandinistas Speak*, p. 77

12. Author's interview with Rodrigo Carazo Odío, July 30, 1983, San José, Costa Rica.

13. Asemblea Legislativa, San José, Costa Rica, Comisión de Asuntos Especiales, *Informe Sobre el Trafico de Armas, Primera Parte, Epe 8768*, 14 Mayo 1981, pp. 16-18, 5 [hereafter Costa Rican Arms Report]. The commission was established on June 25, 1980, after some of the arms originally imported for the Sandinistas were discovered to have been sent to the Salvadoran guerrillas. The principal concern of the commission, which was modeled on the Watergate investigation, were allegations that high officials in the Carazo Administration may have made money as middlemen for the arms shipments. It is interesting that the final report condemned Carazo for *not informing* the Costa Rican people, but he was not condemned for aiding the Sandinistas, because in 1981 Costa Ricans were still proud of their nation's role in overthrowing Somoza.

14. Author's interview with Viron Peter Vaky, July 24, 1985, Washington, D.C.

15. WGBH interview with Carlos Andrés Pérez, May 2, 1984, New York City.

16. Ibid., and confirmed in Pallais interview with WGBH, May 17, 1984, Miami Florida.

17. Carlos Andrés Pérez recounted his view of the conversation in an interview with the author, January 28, 1987, Atlanta.

18. Author's interview with Arístides Calvani, January 22, 1985, Washington, D.C.

19. Author's interview with General José Antonio Olavarría, December 14, 1986, in Casa de Campo, Dominican Republic. Olavarría was Deputy Director of Venezuela's National Security Council, which was responsible for shipping the arms.

20. Author's interview with Carlos Andrés Pérez, January 28, 1987, Atlanta.

21. This information was confirmed by the Costa Rican Legislative Commission. See Costa Rican Arms Report, pp. 10-11.

22. Costa Rican Arms Report, pp. 19-20. Edén Pastora said he received several large shipments of arms that Jaime Wheelock purchased in Portugal. Cited in Claribel Alegría and D. J. Flakoll, *Nicaragua: La Revolución Sandinista* (Mexico: Serie Popular Era, 1982), p. 372

23. Author's interview with Rodrigo Carazo Odío, July 30, 1983, San José, Costa Rica.

24. Walker, *Nicaragua: The Land of Sandino*, p. 38.

25. The report was later leaked and reprinted in the *Congressional Record*, Senate, May 19, 1980, pp. 11653-55. Whether the Cuban assessment was disinformation or simply wrong is not known.

26. The following account is a composite taken from many sources. Most important were the author's interviews with Santiago Roel, Mexican Foreign Minister (1976-79) and José Juan De Olloquí, Under Secretary of Foreign Relations of Mexico (1976-79), both on June 13, 1986, Mexico City; interview with Jorge Castañeda G., a former adviser to the Foreign Ministry (August 25, 1986, Mexico City), and his article, "Don't Corner Mexico," *Foreign Policy* (Fall 1985); and many other interviewees, who asked to remain anonymous.

27. Alan Riding, "Castro, Citing Blockade, Lays Poor Relations to the United States," *New York Times*, May 19, 1979, p. 2.

28. The irony of the juxtaposition of that decision with the Castro visit was that Mexico had rejected the decision by the OAS to break diplomatic relations with Cuba in 1964 because of Mexico's adherence to the Estrada Doctrine, which calls for relations with all regimes regardless of ideology.

29. Cited in Marlise Simons, "Mexico Leads Major Regional Effort to Isolate Somoza," *Washington Post*, May 23, 1979. p. A17.

30. Cited in *New York Times*, May 30, 1979, p. A3.

31. See, for example, two articles by Alan Riding in the *New York Times*: "Nicaraguans Brace for Fresh Violence: Rebels Plan New Of-

fensive as Bid to Set Up a Vote on Somoza's Rule Appears to Collapse," January 17, 1979, p. 7; and "Nicaragua on Edge as Rebels Prepare," March 21, 1979, p. 2.

32. "Nicaragua's Military Says It Broke Rebel Offensive," *New York Times*, June 1, 1979, p. A7.

33. The key elements of both letters were reprinted in Fred Barnes, "Royo Assures Carter Panama Won't Intervene in Nicaragua," *Washington Star*, June 10, 1979.

34. Shirley Christian's sources told her that was the case (*Nicaragua: Revolution in the Family*), pp. 95-96. In addition, the Costa Rican Legislative Commission confirmed that by late May, Pastora was receiving arms in Costa Rica directly from Cuba.

35. Graham Hovey, "Panama Is Accused of Aiding Sandinistas," *New York Times*, June 7, 1979, p. 3.

36. Office of the White House Press Secretary, "Remarks of the President at a Briefing for Members of Congress on the Panama Canal Implementing Legislation," June 11, 1979.

37. Declassified cable from the U.S. Secretary of State to all American Republic Diplomatic Posts, 15 June 1979, State 153522, "OAS Action on Nicaragua."

38. Somoza acknowledged the symbolic and real importance of the recall of the Israeli ship. *Nicaragua Betrayed*, p. 239.

39. Carter's popularity sank to a rating lower than Nixon's had been two months before he resigned. Political instability in Iran and the strengthening of OPEC led to a shortage of gasoline, a rise in prices, and the beginning of hyperinflation in the United States.

40. Author's interviews with Alfonso Robelo, July 29-30, 1983, San José, Costa Rica; and with Tomás Borge, August 4, 1983, Managua.

41. For a description of these events, see Karen DeYoung, "Andean Nations Provide Sandinistas a Diplomatic Opening," *Washington Post*, June 18, 1979, p. A20.

Chapter 8

1. Tomás Borge told me this was the reason he opposed an OAS meeting. He admitted his surprise with its outcome. Author's interview with Tomás Borge, August 4, 1983, Managua.

2. *Public Papers of the Presidents of the United States, Jimmy Carter, 1979*, vol. II, p. 1092.

3. Alan Riding, "Rebels in Nicaragua Name Five to Form Provisional Junta," *New York Times*, June 18, 1979, p. 1.

4. Quoted in William Long, "Key Rebel Dreams of New Nicaragua with 'Democracy,' " *Miami Herald,* June 23, 1979.

5. Quoted in Bernard Diederich, "New Nicaragua Front: Rebels Deny Cuba Tie," *Washington Star,* June 24, 1979.

6. Author's interview with Carlos Andrés Pérez, January 28, 1987, Atlanta.

7. Author's interview with Viron Peter Vaky, July 24, 1985, Washington, D.C.

8. For his speech and the final resolution, see *Department of State Bulletin,* August 1979, pp. 56-59.

9. Portions of the secret session on June 20 were published in the *Congressional Record* on July 17, 1979, pp. H6054-6064. Wright's statement was on p. H6059. On June 21, the House voted narrowly to keep the two issues separate, and to pass Murphy's bill to implement the Canal treaties by a vote of 224 to 202. Carter had correctly judged at his lunch on January 19 that Murphy's bill to set up an organization to operate the Canal would be the only feasible vehicle for implementing the treaties. Even though the bill caused problems with Panama and was not fully consistent with the spirit of the treaties, the most likely alternatives were either no bill or something much worse.

10. "A Painful Decision for Carter: President's Belief That Disaster May Be Imminent in Nicaragua Overturns Nonintervention Resolve," *New York Times,* June 22, 1979, p. 1.

11. Author's interview with Jorge Castañeda G., son and adviser to the former Foreign Minister. August 25, 1986, Mexico City.

12. That "creeping intervention" culminated in a Soviet invasion in December 1979. For Brzezinski's views, see his *Power and Principle,* p. 426.

13. These quotes are from Zbigniew Brzezinski's diary—as read to me—in an interview on July 17, 1985, Washington, D.C. For the meeting on June 22, and others that I did not attend, his recollections are the only ones available. I have checked with three other participants—Carter, Vance, and Brown—and they do not recall what was said.

14. For the resolution, see *Department of State Bulletin,* August 1979, p. 58. The Inter-American Human Rights Commission later described the resolution in the following terms: "For the first time in the history of the OAS and perhaps for the first time in the history of any international organization, [the resolution] deprived an incumbent government of a member state of the Organization of legitimacy, based on the human rights violations committed by that government against its own population." Organization of American

States, Inter-American Commission on Human Rights, *Report on Nicaragua*, June 30, 1981, p. 2.

15. Diederich, *Somoza*, p. 281.

16. Somoza, *Nicaragua Betrayed*, pp. 263-67.

17. Cable from U.S. Embassy, Managua, to the Secretary of State, 24 June 1979, Managua 2787, "Message to the FAO." This is one of a number of secret cables that have recently been declassified. They offer a clearer view of developments during this period than was possible to reconstruct from the memories of several of the participants. These cables are available at the National Security Archive in Washington, D.C.

18. Somoza had the tapes of four of his conversations transcribed and included in his book. Pezzullo said they appear accurate but "doctored"—portions put in different order, some of Pezzullo's questions read as if they were his statements, and vice versa. Author's interview with Lawrence Pezzullo, July 30, 1985, New York City; Somoza, *Nicaragua Betrayed*, pp. 333-82.

19. The parallels are striking. In Cuba, Batista blocked the release of Col. Barquín—a comparable figure—from prison in 1958 for the same reason. More recently, the Shah of Iran prevented the return of General Jam, who could have been a credible transitional Minister of Defense. Sick, *All Fall Down*, pp. 120-21.

20. Author's telephone conversation with Ambler Moss, Jr., August 1, 1985.

21. The account of the Embassy and Managua is a composite based on declassified cables and the author's interviews with Lawrence Pezzullo, July 30, 1985, New York City, and several staff members from the Embassy in Managua.

22. Author's interview with James L. McCoy, October 16, 1985, Miami, Florida.

23. Declassified cable from U.S. Embassy, Managua, to Secretary of State, 28 June 1979, Managua 2861, "FAO Communique."

24. Declassified cable from U.S. Embassy, Managua, to Secretary of State, 28 June 1979, Managua 2870, "The Current Scene."

25. Declassified cable from U.S. Embassy, Managua, to Secretary of State, 28 June 1979, Managua 2876.

26. Declassified cable from U.S. Embassy, Managua, to Secretary of State, 29 June 1979, Managua 2887, "Meeting with Red Cross President."

27. Declassified cable from Secretary of State to U.S. Embassy, Managua, 29 June 1979, State 167430, "Discussion with G-12 Member Arturo Cruz."

28. Author's interview with Jimmy Carter, October 11, 1984, Panama.

29. Declassified cable from U.S. Embassy, Managua, to Secretary of State, 30 June 1979, Managua 2914, "National Guard Survival."

30. Declassified cable from U.S. Embassy, Managua, to Secretary of State, 30 June 1979, Managua 2919, "Nicaraguan Scenario."

31. Author's interviews with Alfonso Robelo, July 29-30, 1983, San José, Costa Rica; and Alfredo César, April 9, 1984, Washington, D.C. The statements that follow are based on those interviews as well.

32. In San José and Managua, the public learned of the *New York Times* disclosure of the "U.S. Plan" on June 29, and Washington learned of their reaction on June 30, 1979, the same day that Pezzullo's two cables on the ExCom and the Guard arrived.

33. Torrijos told me this at the time.

34. For much of Torrijos' thinking during the trip, and also for his behavior, I rely on my own impressions at the time and interviews with Ambassador Gabriel Lewis, who accompanied Torrijos, and Ambassador Ambler Moss, Jr.

35. Gabriel Lewis later told me this story, which sounded more credible than the one he had told me that evening when I received his phone call in the White House.

36. This is my interpretation of the meetings.

37. This, like the other references, is directly from Brzezinski's diary.

38. WGBH interview with Lawrence Pezzullo, May 15, 1984, New York City.

Chapter 9

1. Author's interview with Tomás Borge, August 4, 1983, Managua. Interviews with Borge, Robelo, and Alfredo César were helpful in reconstructing the negotiations with the Junta at this time. Carlos Andrés Pérez, who was involved in the negotiations, recalled that Robelo said "he would resign if the Junta is enlarged because the idea originated in the White House. Then, Borge rejected Robelo's statement . . . [and] Ortega supported Borge." Pérez explained that an article in the *Washington Post* that had been reprinted in Central America, indicating that the expansion of the Junta was a U.S. idea, made the moderates more intransigent. Author's interview with Carlos Andrés Pérez, January 28, 1987, Atlanta.

2. Interview with Sergio Ramírez in Arias, *Nicaragua: Revolución*, p. 201.

3. Declassified cable from U.S. Embassy, Managua, to Secretary of State, 6 July 1979, Managua 3633, "Negotiations with FSLN."

4. These negotiations are the composite of interviews by the author with Ambler Moss, Jr., U.S. Ambassador to Panama, telephone conversation, August 1, 1985; William Bowdler, July 23, 1985, Sharps, Virginia; Marvin Weissman, U.S. Ambassador to Costa Rica, July 17, 1985, Washington, D.C.; and Lawrence Pezzullo, December 16, 1982, Washington, D.C.

5. Author's interview with Rodrigo Carazo Odío, July 30, 1983, San José, Costa Rica.

6. Author's interviews with Gabriel Lewis and Ambler Moss, Jr. Both used the cited words to describe Torrijos's often-stated belief.

7. Karen DeYoung, "Somoza agrees to Quit, Leaves Timing to U.S.," *Washington Post*, July 7, 1979, pp. A1, 3. Most people in Nicaragua and most of the leadership of the Guard were unaware of this report. Author's interview with Col. Carlos Agurto, October 22, 1985, Miami, Florida.

8. Cited in *New York Times*, July 14, 1979, p. 2; and *Newsweek*, July 23, 1979, p. 56.

9. Karen DeYoung, "Nicaraguan Rebels Call for Military Including Guardsmen,"*Washington Post*, July 12, 1979, p. A21; also see *New York Times*, July 12, 1979, p. 14. The *Post* article also referred to the detailed economic and social plans written by a wide range of Nicaraguans—including international civil servants and businessmen. These plans were being disseminated by the Junta.

10. Author's interview with Carlos Andrés Pérez, January 28, 1987, Atlanta. Carazo confirmed this was Pérez's idea.

11. For the full text of the Junta's letter to the OAS, see Organization of American States, Inter-American Commission on Human Rights, *Report on the Situation of Human Rights in the Republic of Nicaragua*, June 30, 1981, pp. 4-6.

12. Carazo wanted the United States to rely more on Pastora, as he was doing, but at the same time he recognized that Pastora didn't trust the United States. Author's interviews with him (July 30, 1983, San José, Costa Rica) and Pastora (November 14, 1983, Washington, D.C.).

13. Stephen Gorman and Thomas W. Walker, "The Armed Forces," in *Nicaragua: The First Five Years*, ed. Thomas W. Walker (New York: Praeger, 1985), p. 100.

14. Military contacts between U.S. and Latin American officers have always been subject to the widest divergence in perceptions because both sides project their own institutions onto alien landscapes. The U.S. military meticulously avoids politics at home and abroad.

U.S. officers are aware that their Latin counterparts often play pivotal political roles, but they still relate to them in the direct, matter-of-fact manner that they relate to each other. Latin military officers similarly assume that their U.S. counterparts are as powerful in the United States as Latin American officers are in their countries. Leaders as different and as politically sophisticated as Omar Torrijos and Anastasio Somoza Debayle both thought the Pentagon played a much larger, if not the only role in the policy process.

15. Defense Attaché James L. McCoy denied this was the case, although he also mentioned that he knew of one case—described below—when Somoza personally called the U.S. Army Chief of Staff. Author's telephone conversation with McCoy, August 15, 1985.

16. Author's interviews with James L. McCoy, August 15, 1985 (telephone conversation), and October 16, 1985, Miami, Florida. McCoy's statement illustrates the chasm that separated the Embassy from Washington. Washington policy makers would never have been concerned about importuning Somoza, but would have been outraged had they learned that Somoza's son threatened an Embassy official.

17. Author's telephone conversation with James L. McCoy, August 15, 1985.

18. The following account of the conversation is based on the author's interview with Lawrence Pezzullo, July 30, 1985, New York City.

19. Karen DeYoung, "Somoza Agrees to Quit, Leaves Timing to U.S.," *Washington Post*, July 7, 1979, p. A1.

20. Author's interview with James L. McCoy, October 16, 1985, Miami, Florida.

21. This is Pezzullo's explanation for why he gave lower priority to the Guard. In a cable he sent on July 7 (Managua 3039), Pezzullo acknowledged that he had left the responsibility for preserving the Guard after Somoza's departure with Somoza, who "had not yet done so."

22. Author's interview with Lawrence Pezzullo, July 30, 1985, New York City.

23. "Nicaraguan Rebels Say U.S. Is Ready to Back Regime Led by Them," *New York Times*, July 16, 1979.

24. Author's interview with Col. Carlos Agurto, who commanded three battalions of the Guard at the time. October 22, 1985, Miami, Florida.

25. Luis Pallais described the purpose of the trip in an interview with the author, October 16, 1985, Miami, Florida.

26. From the nature of the request, it appeared that the other Cen-

tral American generals were going through the motions and were seeking to elicit a negative reply.

27. Author's interview with Lawrence Pezzullo, July 30, 1985, New York City.

28. WGBH interview with Francisco Urcuyo Maliaños, May 18, 1984, Miami, Florida, and his book, *Solos* (Guatemala: Editorial Academica Centro Americana, 1979).

29. Author's interview with Lawrence Pezzullo, July 30, 1985, New York City.

30. This is Urcuyo's account (in WGBH interview, May 18, 1984, Miami, Florida). Pezzullo does not recall this conversation. He also does not recall that the Sandinista delegation had even reached Urcuyo. The Urcuyo account is plausible if one believes that Somoza, or someone else, translated Pezzullo's comment that the plan was "unrealistic" into a suggestion that it was a fabrication.

31. Author's interview with Lawrence Pezzullo, July 30, 1985, New York City.

32. Ibid.

33. This represents a composite interpretation of what happened. Author's interview with Pezzullo (July 30, 1985, New York City) and McCoy (October 16, 1985, Miami, Florida), and WGBH interview with Pezzullo (May 15, 1984, New York City).

34. Transcript of WGBH Public Television series, "Nicaragua."

35. This is a composite interpretation based on my interviews, Urcuyo's book (*Solos*), Shirley Christian's book (*Nicaragua: Revolution in the Family*), and WGBH interviews with Pezzullo (May 14, 1984, New York City) and Urcuyo (May 18, 1984, Miami, Florida). There is a considerable amount of inconsistency on the details—for example, who called whom and when. But on the central points of trading insults, and Mejía's aborted trip, there is no disagreement.

36. Author's interview with Lawrence Pezzullo, July 30, 1985, New York City.

37. Interview with Nuñez, cited by Black, *Triumph of the People*, p. 179.

38. Author's interview with Lawrence Pezzullo, December 16, 1982, Washington, D.C.

39. Christian, *Nicaragua: Revolution in the Family*, p. 115.

40. Shirley Christian's interview with Col. Smith (ibid., p. 114), confirmed and developed further in the author's interviews with Pezzullo (July 30, 1985, New York City) and McCoy (October 16, 1985, Miami, Florida).

41. WGBH interview with John Murphy, July 31, 1985, Danbury, Connecticut.

42. Somoza, *Nicaragua Betrayed*, pp. 390-91. Also WGBH interview with Luis Pallais, May 17, 1984, Miami, Florida.

43. WGBH interview with Francisco Urcuyo Malianos, May 18, 1984, Miami Florida.

44. Author's interviews with Alfonso Robelo (July 29-30, 1983, San José, Costa Rica) and Alfredo César, April 9, 1984, Washington, D.C.

45. *New York Times*, July 20, 1979, p. 1.

Chapter 10

1. In his conversation with the Nicaraguan Junta in the White House, September 24, 1979.

2. Cited in Black, *Triumph of the People*, p. 196. Castro's advice was also reported in the *New York Times*, July 9, 1980, p. 10; and the *Washington Post*, November 9, 1980, p. A1.

3. See, for example, Maurice Zeitlin and Robert Scheer, *Cuba: Tragedy in Our Hemisphere* (New York: Grove Press, 1963).

4. For a sophisticated variation on this thesis, see Jorge Domínguez, *Cuba: Order and Revolution* (Cambridge: Harvard University Press, 1978).

5. For a fuller development of all three lessons and a test of one case, see Robert Pastor, "Does the United States Push Revolutions to Cuba? The Case of Grenada," *Journal of InterAmerican Affairs and World Studies* (Spring 1986). Also see W. Anthony Lake, "Wrestling with Third World Radical Regimes," in John W. Sewell, ed., *U.S. Foreign Policy and the Third World: Agenda, 1985-86* (New Brunswick, N.J.: Transaction, 1985).

6. Cited by Blasier, *Hovering Giant*, pp. 208, 300 n. 178; and for an elaboration of this point by Bonsal, see *Cuba, Castro, and the United States*, chapter 17.

7. Kissinger's analysis was reported in an NBC documentary, "The Castro Connection," in September 1980. The left also argues that the middle is illusory, and that the United States should support leftist guerrillas because revolutions will inevitably succeed. For example, see Marlene Dixon and Susanne Jonas, eds., *Revolution and Intervention in Central America* (San Francisco: Synthesis Publications, 1983), and LaFeber, *Inevitable Revolutions*.

8. The United Nations study was cited by Viron Peter Vaky in his testimony before the Subcommittee on Inter-American Affairs of the Senate Foreign Relations Committee, *Central America at the Crossroads*, September 11, 1978, p. 3. Also see Inter-American Human

Rights Commission, *Report on the Situation of Human Rights in the Republic of Nicaragua,* June 30, 1981, p. 155.

9. White House Announcement, "Emergency Aid to Nicaragua," July 27, 1979, reprinted in *Weekly Compilation of Presidential Documents,* July 30, 1979.

10. Reprinted in the *New York Times,* July 26, 1979, p. 14.

11. Author's interview with Edén Pastora, November 14, 1983, Washington, D.C.

12. The FSLN later acknowledged that they did not know how many rebels fought Somoza, but they estimated that at the end there were 3,000–5,000 fighters with some 10,000 muchachos (young boys who joined the fighting). Robert Matthews, "The Limits of Friendship," in North American Congress on Latin America (NACLA), *Report of the Americas,* May-June 1985, p. 25.

13. For conservative fears, see Cleto DiGiovanni, Jr., and Alexander Kruger, "Reports: Central America," *Washington Quarterly* 3 (Summer 1980); for fears from the left, see James Petras, "Whither the Nicaraguan Revolution?" *Monthly Review* 31 (October 1979). For a disappointed Mexican perspective, see Jorge Castañeda, *Contradicciones en la Revolución* (Mexico City: Tiempo Extra Editores, 1980).

14. Gobierno de Reconstrucción Nacional, *1979: Año de la Liberación,* June 18, 1979, Algun lugar de Nicaragua. The document was actually issued in San José, Costa Rica.

15. Author's interview with Alfonso Robelo, July 29-30, 1983, San José, Costa Rica. Arturo Cruz, who became president of the Central Bank, was called to the Junta a couple of weeks after the victory to discuss an issue. To his surprise, he saw "some guys in fancy uniforms" alongside the Junta. "It had not dawned on me," Cruz later said, "until then, that the National Directorate was going to run the country." Christian, *Nicaragua: Revolution in the Family,* p. 122. Cruz had evidently forgotten what he had told the State Department official in his conversation on June 29, 1979. See Chapter 9.

16. Pastora told this story to Christopher Dickey, *With the Contras: A Reporter in the Wilds of Nicaragua* (New York: Simon and Schuster, 1985), pp. 31-32. In late August, the Directorate sent a Comandante to Peñas Blancas to assume command of the forces under Leonel Poveda, one of Pastora's closest friends. Poveda asked the Comandante to wait while he went to Managua and asked Pastora "three times if you are sure you want me to do this." Pastora said yes each time, and Poveda returned home to transfer power and retire from the army. Christian, *Nicaragua: Revolution in the Family,* p. 123.

17. Borge describes the chaos at the beginning of the revolution, and the difficulty that the FSLN had in asserting control. Tomás Borge, "On Human Rights in Nicaragua," in Borge et al., *Sandinistas Speak*, pp. 88-90, 102.

18. "Sandinista Staff Discusses National Security, Defense," *FBIS*, news conference on July 28, 1979, published July 30, 1979, pp. P2-5.

19 The Directorate noted that "we cannot divulge [as much] as we would like" because they recognized the "72-Hour Document" could leak, as it did several months later. Nonetheless, it is an authentic glimpse of the Sandinista perspective. The Department of State translated and published it in February 1986 as "Analysis of the Situation and Tasks of the Sandinista People's Revolution." The following quotes are from this translation.

20. For an analysis of this debate by a former Sandinista official, see Arturo Cruz Sequeira, "The Origins of Sandinista Foreign Policy," in *Central America: Anatomy of Conflict*, ed. Leiken.

21. See Stephen M. Gorman, "Power and Consolidation in the Nicaraguan Revolution," *Journal of Latin American Studies* 13 (1981): 133-49; and Richard Fagen, *The Nicaraguan Revolution: A Personal Report* (Washington, D.C.: Institute for Policy Studies, 1981).

22. Inter-American Development Bank, *Economic Report: Nicaragua*, July 1983, Washington, D.C., p. 3.

23. Tomás Borge, "On Human Rights in Nicaragua," a presentation to the Inter-American Human Rights Commission, October 10, 1980, reprinted in Borge et al., *Sandinistas Speak*, p. 95.

24. Author's interview with Tomás Borge, August 4, 1983, Managua. I discussed the self-fulfilling prophecy with him, noting that if he kept calling Yankees imperialists, they might behave like imperialists. He said *his* words would not be responsible.

25. Pastora's remark is also cited in the article, though my question was omitted. See Warren Hoge, "Nicaraguan Official Warns U.S. on Arms," *New York Times*, August 12, 1979, p. 17.

26. *New York Times*, August 13, 1979, p. 3.

27. Torrijos' views were related to me on July 17, 1979, by a senior U.S. military officer who had just spoken with him.

28. Cruz Sequeira, "The Origins of Sandinista Foreign Policy," in *Central America: Anatomy of Conflict*, ed. Leiken, p. 104.

29. William D. Rogers had several long conversations with Torrijos at this time, and recalls how Torrijos' initial exuberance dissipated as he received reports of the number of Cubans in Nicaragua and the disrespectful way the Panamanians felt they were treated by the Sandinistas. Author's interview with William D. Rogers, May 22, 1985, Washington, D.C.

30. Author's telephone conversation with Lawrence Pezzullo, March 19, 1987. Daniel Ortega was incorrect when he said, "We tried to get weapons from the United States, but our efforts were completely blocked," interview with *Playboy*, September 1983, p. 196.

31. The author learned about this for the first time in an interview with General Olavarría on December 14, 1986, in Casa de Campo, Dominican Republic.

32. U.S. House of Representatives, Subcommittee on Inter-American Affairs of the Foreign Affairs Committee, *Central America at the Crossroads*, September 11-12, 1979, pp. 3-4.

33. Ibid., pp. 28-31.

34. An additional $5-10 million was requested for military aid and training for the Caribbean and a similar amount for Central America. The Administration also sought approval for reprogramming $10 million in aid to the Caribbean.

35. Michael Wormser, "Emergency Nicaraguan Aid Bill Survives House Test," *Congressional Quarterly Weekly Report*, March 1, 1980, p. 594.

36. Ibid.

37. *Congressional Record*, February 11, 1980, p. E496. The Administration had deliberately exceeded the level of U.S. support after the earthquake, and *La Prensa* at least acknowledged this fact.

38. Cited in *Congressional Quarterly Weekly Report*, May 31, 1980, p. 1519.

39. Republican National Convention, *Republican Platform* (Detroit, July 14, 1980), pp. 68-69.

40. *FBIS*, March 10, 1986, p. P15.

41. *FBIS*, "Security Chief Discussed CIA Activities in Country," March 10, 1980, p. P16.

42. Author's interview with Alfonso Robelo, July 29-30, 1983, San José, Costa Rica. Also, see Shirley Christian's excellent description of this crisis (*Nicaragua: Revolution in the Family*, pp. 147-60).

43. Cited in Christian, *Nicaragua: Revolution in the Family*, pp. 149-50.

44. The discussion of this 1980 mediation is from the author's interview with Lawrence Pezzullo, July 30, 1985, New York City.

45. Robelo's speech is in Fagen, *The Nicaraguan Revolution*, pp. 30-32.

Chapter 11

1. Alan Riding, "Reality Transforms Nicaragua's Revolutionists into Pragmatists," *New York Times*, July 20, 1980, p. E5.

2. For Castro's statements, see Alan Riding, "Castro, in Nicaragua, Chides U.S. But Meets Officials," *New York Times*, July 20, 1980, pp. 1, 13. I met with Castro in January 1980 and made this comment to him then, and repeated the point in conversations with his advisers during another visit in June. Similar messages were passed to him by other visitors.

3. For an analysis of the Literacy Crusade and the statistics used here, see Leonor Blum, "The Literacy Campaign: Nicaragua Style," *Caribbean Review* 10, no. 1 (Winter 1981), and Valerie Miller, *Between Struggle and Hope: The Nicaraguan Literacy Crusade* (Boulder: Westview Press, 1985). According to Blum, the teachers' manuals were openly ideological. Even mathematical problems gave examples based on "Yankee imperialist exploitation" and an idealized, equitable Communist system.

4. Ameringer, *Don Pepe*, pp. 153-55. Figueres particularly angered Castro by suggesting that he should give more attention and consideration to U.S. concerns.

5. The speech is reprinted in Robert Leiken and Barry Rubin, eds., *The Central American Crisis Reader* (New York: Summit Books, 1987), pp. 227-29.

6. Robert D. Tomasek, *The Deterioration of Relations between Costa Rica and the Sandinistas* (Washington, D.C.: American Enterprise Institute for Public Policy Research, September 1984).

7. For a description of Mexican foreign policy during this period, see Jorge G. Castañeda, "Don't Corner Mexico," *Foreign Policy*, no. 60 (Fall 1985): 75-90; Bruce Bagley, "Mexican Foreign Policy: The Decline of a Regional Power," *Current History* (December 1983).

8. Christopher Dickey describes the beginnings of the conspiracy to overthrow the Sandinistas and the murder of Bravo in *With the Contras*, pp. 62-67.

9. In a letter to the *Times of the Americas* published on March 25, 1987 (p. 8), Jimmy Carter wrote, "my Administration provided no funding or support of any kind to any contra group fighting against the Sandinista government." Admiral Stansfield Turner, the CIA Director during the Carter Administration, also denied these reports. See Joseph Lelyveld, "The Director: Running the C.I.A.," *New York Times Magazine*, January 20, 1985, p. 25.

10. International Court of Justice, *Case Concerning Military and Paramilitary Activities in and against Nicaragua*, Nicaragua v. United States, Judgment of 27 June 1986, p. 54. [Hereafter ICJ *Judgment.*]

11. Reported in *FBIS*, July 30, 1979, p. P3.

12. Author's interview with Edén Pastora, November 14, 1983, Washington, D.C.

13. The article in *Time* was actually published on September 15, 1980 (p. 55), three days *after* Carter signed the certification.

14. Presidential Determination No. 82-26 of September 12, 1980. *Federal Register*, vol. 45, no. 185, September 22, 1980, p. 62779.

15. The Argentine People's Revolutionary Army (ARP), a small Trotskyite group, later took credit for the assassination. Some ARP leaders had lived in Nicaragua after the revolution, but there is no evidence of direct Sandinista involvement.

16. U.S. House of Representatives, Subcommittee on Inter-American Affairs of the Foreign Affairs Committee, *Hearing: Review of the Presidential Certification of Nicaragua's Connection to Terrorism*, September 30, 1980.

17. An account of the U.S. démarches and the Nicaraguan reaction can be found in Department of State, *"Revolution beyond Our Borders": Sandinista Intervention in Central America*, no. 132, September 1985, pp. 20-21. Author's and WGBH interviews with Lawrence Pezzullo were also helpful in expanding the case.

18. Department of State, *"Revolution beyond Our Borders,"* p. 21.

19. This account is based on the guerrilla documents (this quote is from document "J") in "Communist Interference in El Salvador: Documents Demonstrating Communist Support of the Salvadoran Insurgency," U.S. Department of State, February 23, 1981. The White Paper that was issued with the documents was criticized for its exaggerations and for some errors, but the documents themselves appear authentic. [Hereafter "Guerrilla Documents."]

20. The State Department cited a report that the Salvadoran left had accumulated $50–100 million through kidnappings in 1977-79, and that some of this was passed on to the Sandinistas. Department of State, *"Revolution beyond Our Borders,"* p. 5. Alan Riding told me he had witnessed the delivery of money from Salvadoran guerrillas to some Sandinistas during the revolution. Author's interview, March 13, 1983, Washington, D.C.

21. "Guerrilla Documents," "G," "Informe sobre Viaje."

22. Costa Rica's Special Commission traced at least three plane shipments of arms in 1980 and 1981 from Cuba through Costa Rica to El Salvador, using the same network originally developed by Costa Rica's Minister of Public Security Echeverría. See Costa Rican Arms Report cited in chapter 7; also Alan Riding, "Arms Scandal Is Charged in Costa Rica," *New York Times*, May 21, 1981, p. A3.

23. "Guerrilla Documents," "I" and "J."

24. Department of State, *"Revolution beyond Our Borders,"* p. 7.

25. Cited in Borge et al., *Sandinistas Speak*, p. 103.

26. The story of the Jorge Salazar conspiracy, which began on May 4, 1980, and ended with his murder on November 16, 1980, is told by Shirley Christian, *Nicaragua: Revolution in the Family,* pp. 170-85, and Christopher Dickey, *With the Contras,* pp. 76-82. The account here focuses on the U.S. role, which they do not.

27. *New York Times,* November 10, 1980, p. 5; November 19, 1980, p. 11; December 10, 1980, p. 6.

28. See Flora Lewis, "Except for Latin America, Most Allies and Enemies Are Only Mildly Interested Bystanders," *New York Times,* October 26, 1980. Lewis reported that Central America was "almost paralyzed awaiting the result" of the election, with rightists viewing Reagan as "a kind of savior" and the democratic opposition hoping for Carter. "Only the extreme left say that Carter and Reagan are the same."

29. WGBH interview with Lawrence Pezzullo, May 15, 1984, New York City.

30. "Guerrilla Documents," "K," letter of November 1, 1980.

31. Some of the information gathered at the time was published by the State Department on February 23, 1981, in *Communist Interference in El Salvador.* The most convincing information, however, including the imagery on the Papalonal airstrip, was not revealed until September 1985 in Department of State, *"Revolution beyond Our Borders,"* pp. 7-8. The International Court of Justice accepted the conclusion of Nicaraguan support for the Salvadorans at that time in its *Judgment* of June 27, 1986, p. 86.

32. The principal findings of this intelligence report were declassified and published in Department of State, *"Revolution beyond Our Borders,"* p. 8.

33. This, and other diplomatic correspondence, is summarized in ibid., pp. 21-22, 7 (on Radio Liberación).

34. Ibid., p. 9.

35. See Robert Pastor, "Continuity and Change in U.S. Foreign Policy: Carter and Reagan on El Salvador," *Journal of Policy Analysis and Management* 3 (Winter 1984): 175-90. Among the conditions that the Salvadoran military accepted in January 1981 were the following: specific steps to investigate the murders of the Americans, including permitting involvement by the FBI; greater authority to Napoleon Duarte over military affairs; and the transfer or dismissal of a dozen military officers associated with the repression, including Vice Minister of Defense Carranza.

36. Department of State, *"Revolution beyond Our Borders,"* p. 22.

37. Press conference of Jimmy Carter, February 9, 1986, Managua.

Chapter 12

1. Cited by Ronnie Dugger, *On Reagan: The Man and His Presidency* (New York: McGraw-Hill, 1983), p. 357. Reagan made this remark in 1967 in a speech on Vietnam. Ward Just reported on the speech and wrote that Reagan implied "that the United States should consider promoting wars on Communist territory."

2. Jaime Wheelock, "Nicaragua's Economy and the Fight against Imperialism," speech given to the First International Conference in Solidarity with Nicaragua, Managua, January 26-31, 1981, reprinted in Borge et al., *Sandinistas Speak*, p. 126.

3. Daniel Yankelovich and Larry Kaagan, "Assertive America," *Foreign Affairs: America and the World, 1980*, p. 696.

4. Cited by Dugger, *On Reagan*, p. 351.

5. Ibid., pp. 518-19.

6. For an analysis of the origins, ideology, and policy of the Administration, see Robert Pastor, "The Reagan Administration and Latin America: Eagle Insurgent," in *Eagle Resurgent? The Reagan Era in American Foreign Policy*, ed. Kenneth Oye, Robert Lieber, and Donald Rothchild (Boston: Little, Brown, 1987).

7. Cited by Dugger, *On Reagan*, p. 360.

8. Republican National Convention, *Republican Platform* (Detroit, July 14, 1980), p. 68.

9. In his memoirs, Haig laments the time it took (nearly one year) for President Reagan to decide on National Security Decision Document no. 1, which established the organization and procedures for the National Security Council. Alexander M. Haig, Jr., *Caveat: Realism, Reagan, and Foreign Policy* (New York: Macmillan, 1984).

10. Haig, *Caveat*, pp. 96-97.

11. Cited in John Goshko and Don Oberdorfer, "Haig Calls Arms Smuggling to El Salvador 'No Longer Acceptable,' " *Washington Post*, February 28, 1981, p. A12. Emphasis added.

12. Interviews with Lawrence Pezzullo by WGBH (May 15, 1984, New York City) and by the author (December 16, 1982, Washington, D.C.).

13. Pezzullo's conversations were summarized by the Department of State from diplomatic correspondence and published in Department of State, *"Revolution beyond Our Borders,"* p. 22. Citations reflect the department's summary.

14. In January, when the State Department announced that U.S. aid had been suspended to Nicaragua, Daniel Ortega categorically denied his government's involvement in aiding the Salvadoran guerrillas. *New York Times*, January 23, 1981, p. 3.

15. Author's telephone conversation with Lawrence Pezzullo, March 9, 1987.

16. For the announcement, see *Department of State Bulletin*, May 1981, p. 71. Pezzullo's views were conveyed to me in a conversation on March 9, 1987.

17. This quote is from the Nicaraguan government's record of the conversation, which was submitted to the International Court of Justice. ICJ *Judgment*, pp. 76, 488-95. In addition, the U.S. proposal and record of the conversations can be found in Department of State, *"Revolution beyond Our Borders,"* pp. 21-23.

18. The description of the Sandinista perspective is from Nicaraguan sources in an article summarizing the negotiations by Don Oberdorfer, "U.S., in Secret Dialogue, Sought Rapprochement with Nicaragua," *Washington Post*, December 10, 1981, pp. 1, 12. Department of State, *"Revolution beyond Our Borders,"* pp. 21-23, describes U.S. positions. Additional sources include the author's interviews in Managua in July-August 1983 with Minister of Interior Tomás Borge, officials from the FSLN International Relations Department, and U.S. Embassy personnel.

19. These references are from Oberdorfer, "U.S., in Secret Dialogue." Shirley Christian cites Humberto Ortega's speech, which was given on June 23, 1981, but only became available in September. *Nicaragua: Revolution in the Family*, pp. 191-92.

20. Cited in Oberdorfer, "U.S., in Secret Dialogue." In August 1983, several senior Sandinista officials told me they were prepared to accept a variation on the Enders proposal, which they had previously rejected. That was no longer sufficient for the Reagan Administration.

21. This is from the Nicaraguan record of the conversation. See ICJ *Judgment*, p. 490.

22. The sources for this summary of the debate are: interviews with Administration officials; Haig, *Caveat*, pp. 98-100, 117-40; Don Oberdorfer, "Applying Pressure in Central America," *Washington Post*, November 23, 1983; Roy Gutman and Susan Page, "Central America: The Making of U.S. Policy," *Newsday*, July 31, 1983; and Leslie H. Gelb, "Haig Is Said to Press for Military Options for Salvadoran Action," *New York Times*, November 4, 1981. The Oberdorfer article describes three separate occasions in which Haig tried to persuade the NSC to accept a blockade of Cuba.

23. The authoritative reference to National Security Decision Document no. 17 of November 17, 1981, is in the NSC document "U.S. Policy in Central America and Cuba through FY '84," which was written in April 1982, but leaked and published in the *New York*

Times on April 7, 1983. [Hereafter NSC document (April 1982).] Haig's memoirs (*Caveat*) refer to the discussion without identifying the time. The best, most credible account of the meeting is by Don Oberdorfer, who cited government records. See his "Applying Pressure in Central America," *Washington Post*, November 23, 1983, pp. A1, 10.

24. One official told Oberdorfer that the decision was "a way of letting Al [Haig] down easily." There is no evidence that the group agreed on what constituted "unacceptable" actions by Cuba. ("Applying Pressure in Central America.")

25. Haig described his views in testimony before the U.S. Senate Foreign Relations Committee, *Commitments, Consensus, and U.S. Foreign Policy*, February 7, 1985, pp. 223-24, 242-43.

26. Department of State, *"Revolution beyond Our Borders,"* p. 23. Hector Fabian the leader of an exile training camp in Florida, confirmed the Reagan Administration's decision not to enforce the law in an interview in December 1981. Jo Thomas, "Latin Exiles Focus on Nicaragua as They Train Urgently in Florida," *New York Times*, December 23, 1981, pp. 1, 14.

27. A Presidential Finding is required for a covert action. The reference to the March 9, 1981, finding is in the NSC document (April 1982). That document noted that $19.5 million had been allocated for the covert interdiction program, and recommended an increase to $22 million to cover an expanded program in Guatemala that would begin in 1982.

28. Edgar Chamorro and Jefferson Morley, "Confessions of a 'Contra': How the C.I.A. Masterminds the Nicaraguan Insurgency," *The New Republic*, August 5, 1985, pp. 18-23.

29. Author's interview with Oscar Camilión, Argentine Minister of Foreign Relations (1980-81), December 14, 1986, Casa de Campo, Dominican Republic.

30. Cited by Dickey, *With the Contras*, p. 112. On November 1, Casey met in Washington with General Galtieri, then Argentine Army Chief of Staff (p. 123). Dickey's book and the following are the best sources on the origins of the contras: Nina Serafino, "U.S. Assistance to Nicaraguan Guerrillas: Issues for the Congress," Congressional Research Service, Library of Congress, January 21, 1987.

31. Dickey, *With the Contras*, p. 127.

32. Don Oberdorfer and Patrick E. Tyler, "Reagan Backs Action Plan for Central America: Political, Paramilitary Steps Included," *Washington Post*, February 14, 1982, p. 1. For a history of Congressional objections, see U.S. House of Representatives Permanent Select Committee on Intelligence, "Report 98-122: Amendment to the

Intelligence Authorization Act for Fiscal Year 1983," May 13, 1983. [Hereafter Select Committee 1983 Report.]

33. Jackson Diehl, "State Department Official Sees Role for Argentina in Central America," *Washington Post*, March 10, 1982, p. A18. On March 10, the Administration presented aerial photographs of Nicaraguan military bases as "formal proof" of the threat of Cuba and Nicaragua. *New York Times*, March 10, 1982.

34. Christopher Dickey describes the CIA training of the contras, the bombing of the two bridges, and the views of the senior Administration official. *With the Contras*, pp. 131-32.

35. The story of Pastora's journey from Nicaragua through Panama to Cuba and back was reconstructed from the author's interviews with Pastora (November 14, 1983, Washington, D.C.); Haroldo Monteleagre, former Sandinista Minister (December 4-6, 1981, Washington, D.C.); and members of Panama's National Guard and friends of General Omar Torrijos (in Panama, January 30-31 and December 28, 1982).

36. Shirley Christian, "Rebel Hero Rips Sandinista 'Terror,' " *Miami Herald*, April 16, 1981, pp. 1, 22. Christian includes a copy of Pastora's statement in *Nicaragua: Revolution in the Family*, pp. 319-22.

37. Dickey claims that both the CIA and Pastora understood the value of Pastora's independence, and therefore, the Agency did not press the latter too much in the early period to join the FDN. *With the Contras*, p. 149.

38. For a survey of the alienation of the Atlantic Coast communities from the Sandinista government, see Martin Diskin, Thomas Bossert, Salomon Nahmad S., "Peace and Autonomy on the Atlantic Coast of Nicaragua: A Report of the LASA Task Force on Human Rights and Academic Freedom," *LASA Forum* 16, no. 4 (Spring 1986): 1-18.

39. This quote and subsequent citations are from the Select Committee 1983 Report, pp. 7-8.

40. In a cover story, *Newsweek* reported that the contras were trying to topple the Sandinistas rather than interdict arms. "America's Secret War," November 8, 1982. For a summary of Congressional action, see Nina Serafino, "Summary and Chronology of Major Congressional Action on U.S. Aid to the Anti-Sandinista Guerrillas," Congressional Research Service, Library of Congress, January 28, 1987.

41. Barbara Crosette, "Venezuelan Warns U.S. on Nicaragua," *New York Times*, November 18, 1981, p. A3; Jackson Diehl, "Venezuelan Criticism," *Washington Post*, March 24, 1982. "Public secret" was a

phrase used by José Figueres. Author's interview, February 6, 1986, San José, Costa Rica.

42. Excerpts of the speech were reprinted in the *New York Times*, February 22, 1982.

43. 78% of the U.S. public opposed overthrowing the Nicaraguan government while only 13% favored it. A majority viewed the prospect of becoming entangled in Central America as a greater danger to the United States than the spread of Communism there. See Barry Sussman, "Poll Finds a Majority Fears Entanglement in Central America," *Washington Post*, May 25, 1983, pp. A1, 20.

44. The speech was reprinted in the *New York Times*, April 28, 1983, p. 12.

Chapter 13

1. "Interview," *Playboy*, September 1983, p. 67.

2. See *The Tower Commission Report* (New York: Times Books, 1987), p. 450. Senator Barry Goldwater also discussed the finding in a Senate debate (*Congressional Record*, April 4, 1984, p. 3766).

3. See, for example, the speech by Under Secretary of Defense Fred Iklé, Baltimore Council on Foreign Relations, September 12, 1983; Fred Hiatt, "Weinberger Calls Military Effort in Central America Vital to U.S.," *Washington Post*, September 7, 1983; and especially, "Heat on Central America: The Three Big Words around Washington These Days Are 'Whatever Is Necessary,' " *Newsweek*, June 20, 1983, pp. 18-19.

4. Select Committee 1983 Report, pp. 10-11.

5. Inter-American Development Bank, *Economic Report: Nicaragua*, DES-13, July 1983 (p. 19 for agricultural statistics). For debt statistics, see United Nations Economic Commission for Latin America and the Caribbean, "Preliminary Overview of the Latin American Economy, 1986," Santiago, Chile, December 1986, p. 21.

6. "Interview," *Playboy*, September 1983, p. 64.

7. James P. Wootten, "The Nicaraguan Military Buildup: Implications for U.S. Interests in Central America," Congressional Research Service, Library of Congress, December 18, 1985. "Armed forces" include all active personnel, reserves, militias, and Ministry of Interior forces. In 1985, he estimated there were 62,000 active soldiers. These U.S. estimates are probably high, but the Nicaraguan government does not disclose defense-related information.

8. The lower estimate is from the Nicaraguan Ministry of Defense, cited in Agencia Nueva Nicaragua, "The Defeat of the Counter-Rev-

olution," April 1987. The higher estimate is from U.S. Departments of State and Defense, *The Challenge to Democracy in Central America* (Washington, D.C., June 1986), p. 38.

9. CIA analyst Peter Clement concluded that the Sandinistas' military buildup "seems to be tied to the growth of contra activity." "Moscow and Nicaragua: Two Sides of Soviet Policy," *Comparative Strategy* 5 (1985): 78.

10. Interview with Ambassador Anthony Quainton, February 11, 1984, Miami, Florida.

11. Roger Fontaine, "Choices on Nicaragua," *Global Affairs* 1 (Summer 1986): 113. The FMLN/FDR is the combined military and political leadership of the Salvadoran guerrillas.

12. The President's press conference was published in the *New York Times* the next day, November 4, 1983, p. A16.

13. John Horton, "The Real Intelligence Failure," *Foreign Service Journal* (February 1985): 24.

14. In my interviews in Managua in the summer of 1983, I found considerable progress in the Nicaraguan positions, and the Administration later even described it as "encouraging," even while it condemned the continued military buildup (Hedrick Smith, "Arms Aid to Nicaragua Still Rising, U.S. Says," *New York Times*, October 5, 1983, p. A11).

15. The speech was delivered on May 9, 1984, and reprinted the next day in the *New York Times*, p. A16.

16. David Rogers and David Ignatius, "How CIA-Aided Raids in Nicaragua in '84 Led Congress to End Funds," and "CIA Internal Report Details U.S. Role in Contra Raids in Nicaragua Last Year," *Wall Street Journal*, March 6, 1985. The latter article cites an internal CIA report that documents direct CIA involvement in nineteen separate operations from January 1 to April 10, 1984. National Security Adviser Robert McFarlane later testified that President Reagan personally approved the mining of Nicaragua's harbors. David E. Rosenbaum, "McFarlane States He Briefed Reagan on Contras Often," *New York Times*, May 14, 1987, pp. 1, 7.

17. Arce's remarks were published in *Barricada*, and cited by William I. Robinson and Kent Norsworthy, "Elections and U.S. Intervention in Nicaragua," *Latin American Perspectives* 12, no. 2 (Spring 1985): 84.

18. Statement to the press, reprinted in the *New York Times*, March 29, 1984.

19. Philip Taubman, "U.S. Role in Nicaragua Disputed," *New York Times*, October 21, 1984, p. 12.

20. The two best accounts of these negotiations and the elections

themselves tend to attribute the failure to different sides, though both agree that the Reagan Administration reinforced those who wanted to boycott the election. Robert Leiken ("The Nicaraguan Tangle," *New York Review of Books*, December 5, 1985, pp. 55-64) blames the Sandinistas; the Latin American Studies Association argues that the Coordinadora did not participate "by their own choice, not because of government exclusion" (see Latin American Studies Association, "Report of the Latin American Studies Association Delegation to Observe the Nicaraguan General Election of November 4, 1984," *LASA Forum* 15, no. 4 (Winter 1985).

21. Leiken recounts the meeting. "Nicaraguan Tangle," p. 61.

22. For the results and the State Department's reaction, see Alexander H. McIntire, Jr., *Political and Electoral Confrontation in Revolutionary Nicaragua* (Miami: University of Miami North-South Center, July 1985). For the reaction of the LASA delegation, see LASA, "Report."

23. The letter was reprinted in the *Wall Street Journal*, January 11, 1985.

24. Author's interview with Arturo Cruz, October 2, 1986, Atlanta.

25. Robert J. McCartney, "McFarlane Ends Trip to Five Nations," *Washington Post*, January 20, 1985, p. A19; Philip Taubman, "U.S. Says It Has Halted Talks with Nicaragua," *New York Times*, January 19, 1985, p. 4; "Text of U.S. Statement on Withdrawal from Case before the World Court," *New York Times*, January 19, 1985, p. 4.

26. Reagan made this proposal on April 5, 1985, and it was reprinted in the *Washington Post* that day.

27. For a description of the embargo's origins, see Joanne Omang, "Sanctions: A Policy by Default," *Washington Post*, May 8, 1985. For the Executive Order, see Bernard Weinraub, "Reagan, Declaring 'Threat,' Forbids Nicaraguan Trade and Cuts Air and Sea Links," *New York Times*, May 2, 1985.

28. Gerald M. Boyd, "Reagan Asks Arms Aid for Nicaraguan Rebels," *New York Times*, February 19, 1986, p. 7.

29. Gerald M. Boyd, "Reagan Sees a 'Moral Obligation' by U.S. to Aid Nicaraguan Rebels," *New York Times*, March 11, 1986, p. 1; Doyle McManus, "U.S. Resumes Funding for Rebel Leader Pastora," *Los Angeles Times*, March 12, 1986, p. 1. The Administration discontinued aid to Pastora again after it lost the House vote. Stephen Kinzer, "Nicaraguan Rebel Chief Gives Up Fight," *New York Times*, May 17, 1986, p. 3.

30. A very good analysis of the changes made in each draft of the agreement was done by Nina M. Serafino, "The Contadora Initiative:

Implications for Congress," Congressional Research Service, Library of Congress, May 18, 1987.

31. Author's interview with a senior Peruvian diplomat, May 5, 1986, New York City.

32. Leslie H. Gelb, "Pentagon Predicts Big War If Latins Sign Peace Accord," *New York Times*, May 20, 1986, pp. 1, 6; and Bernard Gwertzman, "State Department Assails the Pentagon over Study of Latin Peace Talks," *New York Times*, May 21, 1986, pp. 1, 6.

33. "Nicaragua Rejects Proposal for Arms Limits in Region," *New York Times*, May 20, 1986, p. 6; Stephen Kinzer, "Nicaragua Balks at Latin Peace Accord," *New York Times*, May 12, 1986, p. 3.

34. For a good analysis of these negotiations, see Bruce Bagley, "Contadora: The Failure of Diplomacy," *Journal of InterAmerican Studies and World Affairs* 28 (Fall 1986): 19-21.

35. "An Interview with Oscar Arias: In the Eye of the Storm," *Newsweek International*, October 6, 1986, p. 52.

36. James Lemoyne, "Costa Rica's Return to Neutrality Strains Its Ties with Washington," *New York Times*, March 22, 1987, p. E2.

37. Stephen Kinzer, "Nicaragua Warms to Latest Peace Plan," *New York Times*, February 22, 1987, p. 10.

38. For a description of the Soviet-sponsored military buildup in Cuba and Nicaragua during the Reagan Administration—unprecedented, according to the Defense Department, since the Cuban missile crisis—see U.S. Department of State and Defense, *The Soviet-Cuban Connection in Central America and the Caribbean* (Washington, D.C., March 1985). For Reagan's estimate on Soviet-bloc aid, see "Text of Reagan Speech on the Contras," *New York Times*, March 17, 1986, p. 8.

39. Gerald M. Boyd, "Reagan Presses for Anti-Sandinista Aid," *New York Times*, June 10, 1986, p. 3. In an interview, Cuban Vice President Carlos Rafael Rodríguez volunteered that there were 800 Cuban military advisers in Nicaragua ("800 Militares Cubanos Colaboran con Sandinistas: Carlos Rafael Rodríguez,"*La Jornada* [Mexico City], May 24, 1986, p. 28).

40. See Jozef Goldblat and Victor Millan, "The Honduras–Nicaragua Conflict and Prospects for Arms Control in Central America," in *World Armaments and Disarmament: SIPRI Yearbook, 1984* (Stockholm: SIPRI), p. 531.

41. Stephen Kinzer, "Nicaraguan Aide Says Embargo Will Bring Closer Ties to Moscow," *New York Times*, May 2, 1985; Theodore Shabad, "Nicaragua Said to Triple Imports from Soviets," *New York Times*, May 12, 1985, p. 2. Canada and Western Europe replaced

some of the U.S. trade. The Soviet Union replaced Mexico as the major source of Nicaragua's oil.

42. United Nations Economic Commission for Latin America and the Caribbean, "Preliminary Overview of the Latin American Economy, 1986," December 1986; and "Notas para el Estudio Económico de América Latina, 1985: Nicaragua," July 4, 1986, pp. 39, 45.

43. The Nicaraguan National Institute for Statistics and Census estimated that from 1981 to December 1986, there were 36,416 Nicaraguan victims (dead, wounded, or kidnapped) of the war. Forty-eight percent were from the Nicaraguan government and people, and 52 percent were from members of the contra forces. Cited in Agencia Nueva Nicaragua, "The Defeat of the Counter-Revolution: An Overview," April 1987, provided by Nicaragua's Embassy to the United States.

44. "Without Liberty There Will Never Be Peace," statements by Violeta de Chamorro and Jaime Chamorro, sponsored by PRODEMCA, Washington, D.C., May 21, 1986, p. 12.

45. Stephen Kinzer, "Sandinistas' Foes Fault Role of U.S.: Opposition in Managua Urges Washington to Do More to Support Its Cause," New York Times, June 25, 1986, p. 6.

46. Cited by Reid G. Miller, "U.S. Aid to Contras Triggers Increase in Repression by Managua," Mexico City News, June 29, 1986, p. 10.

47. Cited in Stephen Kinzer, "Nicaragua Ready to Talk to U.S. on Security, But Not Its Policies," New York Times, February 22, 1986, p. 4.

48. Stephen Kinzer, "Nicaraguans Said to Seek More Soviet Helicopters," New York Times, April 7, 1987, p. 6.

49. Inter-American Development Bank, Economic Report: Nicaragua, July 1983, p. iii.

50. Cited in Philip Taubman, "The C.I.A.: In from the Cold and Hot for Truth," New York Times, June 11, 1984, p. B6; also see Don Oberdorfer and John M. Goshko, "Ex-C.I.A. Analyst Disputes U.S. Aides on Nicaragua," Washington Post, June 13, 1984, pp. A1, 28; Select Committee 1983 Report, pp. 10-11; and ICJ Judgment, p. 86. In 1984, Senator Daniel Patrick Moynihan said: "It is the judgment of the [Senate] Intelligence Committee that Nicaragua's involvement in the affairs of El Salvador, and, to a lesser degree, its other neighbors, continues. . . . [and as compared to 1983, it] has not appreciably lessened." Washington Post, April 10, 1984, cited in ICJ Judgment, p. 485. On the other hand, Col. Humberto Vallatta, Salvador's Naval Commander, explained at a press conference in 1986 that the last arms interdiction that he knew about was in 1981. "Arms Flow

Largely Stopped," *The Times of the Americas*, December 10, 1986, p. 7.

51. A conservative estimate of military aid to the contras totals $142 million ($72 million from 1982 to 1984, $70 million in 1986 and 1987) as compared to $131.6 million in military aid to the five governments of Central America from 1962 to 1980. This does not take into account the $57 million in "nonlethal" military aid to the contras, the fact that all military aid to the contras has been grants (only 60 percent of the aid to Central America has been in the form of grants), or the considerable amount of money that the Administration solicited from foreign governments and private donors. For the data on aid to Central America, see Agency for International Development, *U.S. Overseas Loans and Grants*, July 1, 1945–September 30, 1984, pp. 43, 47, 49, 52, 55.

52. For the judgments, see ICJ *Judgment*, pp. 146-50, and for the reservations of the U.S. judge, Stephen Schwebel, p. 269. Although the key judgments were negative for the United States, the Court also rejected two important Nicaraguan arguments: that it had not supported Salvadoran insurgents and that the contras were solely an instrument of the U.S. government.

53. *Tower Commission Report*, p. 451.

54. David Shipler, "U.S. Again Denies a Nicaraguan Role," *New York Times*, October 16, 1986, p. 4; Stephen Engelberg, "Supply Upsurge to Contras Reported," *New York Times*, October 12, 1986, p. 6. In testimony before Congress, Abrams later admitted he was wrong, but he said that at the time he did not know of NSC involvement.

55. *Tower Commission Report* (February 26, 1987), esp. pp. 51-61, 450-79; U.S. Senate Committee on Intelligence, "Report to the Select Committee on Secret Military Assistance to Iran and the Nicaraguan Opposition," January 29, 1987, pp. 42-63.

56. Joel Brinkley, "Spotlight Falls on the Secret World of a Master Operative," *New York Times*, May 10, 1987, p. IV, 1.

57. This is an excerpt from President Reagan's statement on Taiwan's help, reprinted in the *New York Times*, May 16, 1987, p. 6. President Reagan said Saudi Arabia helped "because they shared our interest in securing democracy in Central America." Gerald M. Boyd, "Reagan Denies Asking Saudis for Contra Aid," *New York Times*, May 13, 1987, pp. 1, 9.

58. "24% Believe Reagan on Contras," *New York Times*, May 24, 1987, p. 10.

59. *Tower Commission Report*, pp. 453-54.

60. Ibid., p. 58.

61. Excerpts from statement by Robert McFarlane to Congressional Committee, reprinted in *New York Times*, May 12, 1987, p. 6.

62. General Secord told this to the Congressional Committee. Cited in David E. Rosenbaum, "Secord Recounts Being Told Reagan Knew of His Work," *New York Times*, May 7, 1987, pp. 1, 6, 7. Secord was told by Poindexter that "not only was he pleased with the work that I had been doing, but the President was as well."

63. President Reagan's address to the nation on June 24, 1986, reprinted by Department of State, Policy No. 850.

64. See Adam Clymer, "Poll Finds Americans Don't Know U.S. Positions on Central America," *New York Times*, July 1, 1983, p. 1; David Shribman, "Poll Finds Fewer Than Half in U.S. Back Latin Policy," *New York Times*, April 29, 1984, p. 1; and "Opinion Outlook," *National Journal*, May 17, 1986, p. 1224. I also looked at various Harris surveys from this period.

65. *National Journal*, May 17, 1986, p. 1224.

66. "Poll: Americans Divided on Nicaraguan Intervention," *Miami Herald*, March 31, 1985, p. 4A.

67. Roger Fontaine, "Choices on Nicaragua," *Global Affairs* 1 (Summer 1986): 101-114.

68. Cited in "Business Dissent: It's Out Front in Nicaragua," *New York Times*, March 31, 1985, p. 6.

Chapter 14

1. In an unusual, candid interview with the *Guardian* of London in April 1983, Victor Volsky, the head of the Latin American Institute in Moscow, complained that the USSR had spent too much money "to send oil to Cuba, two tanks a day for 20 years," and that "we would not like to repeat that" to Nicaragua. Cited by Peter Clement, "Moscow and Nicaragua: Two Sides of Soviet Policy," *Comparative Strategy* 5 (1985): 85.

2. Author's interview with Alfonso Robelo, July 29-30, 1983, San José, Costa Rica.

3. Adolfo Calero, for example, left Nicaragua in December 1982 and subsequently became a leader of the contras.

4. Some in Latin America would view the United States as exploiting instability to serve *its* interests; this is the same point made from a different direction.

5. Whether these objectives are appropriate and whether leftist regimes necessarily must be viewed as adversaries will be discussed in Chapter 16.

6. For a succinct statement of this cycle, see Virginia R. and Jorge I. Domínguez, *The Caribbean* (New York: Foreign Policy Association Headline Series 253, 1981), pp. 76-77.

7. Arthur M. Schlesinger, Jr., "Foreign Policy and the American Character," *Foreign Affairs* (Fall 1983): 1.

8. Lucian W. Pye and Sidney Verba, eds., *Political Culture and Political Development* (Princeton: Princeton University Press, 1965); and Gabriel A. Almond and Sidney Verba, eds., *The Civic Culture Revisited* (Boston: Little, Brown, 1980).

9. Stanley Hoffman, *Gulliver's Troubles or the Setting of American Foreign Policy* (New York: McGraw-Hill, 1968), pp. 87-175.

10. This question was posed but never satisfactorily answered by Raymond Bonner, *Waltzing with a Dictator: The Marcoses and the Making of American Policy* (New York: Times Books, 1987), p. 447.

11. John E. Rielly, ed., *American Public Opinion and U.S. Foreign Policy 1975* (Chicago: Council on Foreign Relations, 1975), p. 22.

12. Cited in Thomas M. Leonard, "The United States and Central America, 1955-60," *Valley Forge Journal* (June 1986): 65.

13. Barry Sussman, "Poll Finds a Majority Fears Entanglement in Central America," *Washington Post*, May 25, 1983, pp. A1, 20.

14. Arthur Schlesinger, Jr., describes a "historic tension in the American soul between an addiction to experiment and a susceptibility to ideology" ("Foreign Policy and the American Character," p. 1). Stanley Hoffmann suggests U.S. policy is a mixture of the engineer's enthusiasm for problem solving and the evangelist's zeal for saving the underprivileged (*Gulliver's Troubles*, pp. 87-175).

15. In the cases of Trujillo and Duvalier, Presidents Eisenhower and Kennedy insisted on virtually impossible conditions before they would consider toppling the dictators. See U.S. Senate, Select Committee to Study Governmental Operations with Respect to Intelligence Activities, *Alleged Assassination Plots Involving Foreign Leaders*, November 20, 1975, pp. 191-205. On Haiti, see Edwin Martin, "Haiti: A Case Study in Futility," *SAIS Review* (Summer 1981); and on the Philippines, see Paul Laxalt, "My Conversations with Ferdinand Marcos, A Lesson in Personal Diplomacy," *Policy Review* (Summer 1986). Laxalt said that President Reagan refused to tell Marcos to resign. Unlike these Presidents, Carter did not promote a rebellion against a leftist government.

In the case of Vietnam, Stanley Karnow, in his book *Vietnam: A History*, commented on why that case might have inhibited future Presidents: "America's responsibility for Diem's death haunted U.S.

leaders during the years ahead, prompting them to assume a larger burden in Vietnam" (New York: Penguin, 1986, p. 278).

16. See, for examples, "Mediation in Chile Termed Essential by U.S. Officials: Review Produces a Consensus for a Major Effort to Avoid 'Another Nicaragua,' " *New York Times*, December 2, 1984, p. 1; and Don Oberdorfer, "U.S. Pressing for Democratic Succession in Philippines," *Washington Post*, March 12, 1985, p. A11.

17. Press conference of President Reagan, *New York Times*, February 12, 1986, p. 10.

18. See Howard Wiarda, ed., *Politics and Social Change in Latin America: The Distinct Tradition*, 2nd ed. (Amherst: University of Massachusetts Press, 1982); Claudio Véliz, *The Centralist Tradition in Latin America* (Princeton: Princeton University Press, 1980).

19. Charles D. Ameringer, *The Democratic Left in Exile: The Antidictatorial Struggle in the Caribbean, 1945-1959* (Coral Gables, Fla.: University of Miami Press, 1974).

20. Charles D. Ameringer, "The Foreign Policy of Venezuelan Democracy," in *Venezuela: The Democratic Experience*, ed. John D. Martz and David J. Myers (New York: Praeger, 1977), p. 338.

21. For a perceptive analysis of the psychology of inter-American relations, see Carlos Rangel, *The Latin Americans: Their Love-Hate Relations with the United States* (New York: Harcourt, Brace, Jovanovich, 1977).

22. Carlos Fuentes, "Give Nicaragua a Chance," *New York Times*, January 18, 1983, p. A27.

23. Although the United States has indeed supported rightists against democrats in cases like Guatemala and Chile, on balance, there are more cases when the United States has helped democrats against dictators or sympathized with democrats but did nothing.

24. WGBH interview with Carlos Andrés Pérez, May 2, 1984, New York City.

25. Shirley Christian wrote that because of the hatred for Somoza, U.S. journalists saw the "Sandinistas through a romantic haze," and "missed or under-reported" the FSLN's behavior, ideology, and ties to Cuba and over-reported the brutality of the Guard. "The story that reporters told—with a mixture of delight and guilt—was the ending of an era in which the United States was proven wrong." Alan Riding and Karen DeYoung, the two reporters that covered the war for the *New York Times* and the *Washington Post*, responded to her point that they failed to see a Marxist future in Nicaragua by arguing, among other points, that Nicaragua was not Marxist. For the dialogue, see Shirley Christian, "Covering the Sandinistas," *Washing-*

ton Journalism Review (March 1982): 33-38; and for the responses, May 1982, pp. 6-7, 56.

My own view is that the journalists did reflect the popular mood in the region and also transposed their adversary mission against the U.S. government to Central America. The reporting therefore played down the Marxist connections of the FSLN before they took power, which made the U.S. government appear obsessed with an irrelevant cold war. Then, after the Sandinistas took power, many in the press focused on the FSLN's Marxism. This made the U.S. government, which was then trying to play down the Marxism in order to obtain aid from Congress, look naive or duplicitous. The press therefore accentuated the view of Nicaraguans that the United States was in the driver's seat.

26. Ramiro Gurdian, "Nicaragua: A View from the Private Sector," *Caribbean Today*, vol. 1, no. 1, December 1983, pp. 5-6.

27. Bonsal, *Cuba, Castro, and the United States*, p. 6.

28. Author's interview with Jimmy Carter, October 11, 1984, Panama.

29. Cited in *Newsweek*, May 25, 1987, p. 19.

30. Stephen Kinzer, "Why Nicaragua Picked a Curious Time to Strike," *New York Times*, March 30, 1986, p. E2.

31. Cited by Blasier, *Hovering Giant*, p. 186.

Chapter 15

1. Recalling the guerrilla struggle of the late 1960s, Henry Ruiz, a Sandinista leader, said: "At one point, we intended to kill Somoza, but this was where Carlos Fonseca's [the founder of the FSLN] great foresight came in. Carlos maintained that Somoza was an invaluable asset who personified all our country's contradictions." Cited in *The Central American Crisis Reader*, ed. Leiken and Rubin, p. 154.

2. Cited in Diederich, *Somoza*, p. 37.

3. Author's interview with Alfonso Robelo, June 30, 1983, San José, Costa Rica.

4. The best case of disillusionment was General Omar Torrijos, who told Jack Vaughan, a former Assistant Secretary of State during the Kennedy Administration and an old friend of his, that "brokering the use of Cubans to depose Somoza . . . [was] the worst political mistake of his career." Jack Hood Vaughan, "Cuba, Mexico: Who's Coopting Whom?" *Wall Street Journal*, June 10, 1983.

5. Author's interview with Congressman Charles Wilson, July 31, 1985, telephone conversation.

6. An analogous incident occurred early in the Nixon Administration when the Soviet Ambassador to the United States met with then National Security Adviser Henry Kissinger and emotionally raised the issue of Chinese aggression. It was the first time, according to Kissinger, that the Nixon Administration considered using the Soviet-Chinese rivalry to the U.S. advantage. Henry Kissinger, *White House Years* (Boston: Little, Brown, 1979), p. 172.

7. In a retrospective memorandum on the crisis, Vaky identified this as one of the three reasons why the Administration failed. The others were the "obduracy of Somoza" and the failure to decide to force out Somoza before entering the mediation.

8. In his testimony before Congress, Robert McFarlane admitted that the Administration had never produced "a thorough and concerted analysis of our Nicaraguan problem [with] a clear definition of U.S. interests." Excerpts in the *New York Times*, May 12, 1987, p. 6.

9. U.S. Department of State, Agency for International Development, and Office of Management and Budget, *Report to the President and Congress: A Plan for Fully Funding the Recommendations of the National Bipartisan Commission on Central America*, Special Report no. 162, March 1987.

10. For trade statistics, see Richard E. Feinberg, "Economic Assistance to Central America," statement to the U.S. Senate Committee on Foreign Relations, March 25, 1987. For aid data, see Jonathan E. Sanford, "Major Trends in U.S. Foreign Assistance to Central America," Congressional Research Service, Library of Congress, April 8, 1986.

11. For a more fully developed proposal along these lines, see Feinberg and Pastor, "Far from Hopeless," in *Central America: Anatomy of Conflict*, ed. Leiken, pp. 208-214.

Chapter 16

1. Richard K. Betts and Samuel P. Huntington, "Dead Dictators and Rioting Mobs: Does the Demise of Authoritarian Rulers Lead to Political Instability?" *International Security* 10, no. 3 (Winter 1985/86): 130.

2. See Neustadt and May, *Thinking in Time*, esp. ch. 3, "Unreasoning from Analogues."

3. Adolfo Aguilar Zinser, "Mexico and the Guatemalan Crisis," in Richard R. Fagen and Olga Pellicer, eds., *The Future of Central America* (Stanford: Stanford University Press, 1983), pp. 161-86.

4. Samuel Huntington, "Will More Countries Become Democratic?" *Political Science Quarterly* (Summer 1984): 213.

5. Che Guevara, *Guerrilla Warfare* (New York: Random House, 1961), p. 2.

6. I do not assume that the strategy of one political party will be acceptable to the more zealous members of the other party, but that it may be to the moderates, and only if the Administration listens closely to them and seeks to incorporate their views into policy.

7. The CIA does psychological profiles of foreign leaders, but they neither address these questions nor serve the kinds of purposes outlined in this section.

8. In El Salvador, both the right and the left persistently describe the other as the only other choice for the country. Neither wishes to acknowledge a moderate option because they know most people would prefer that.

9. In my own experience, I was struck by how different my conversations were with the same Nicaraguan and Grenadian officials after I left the government than when I was a government official. The first conversations deteriorated almost immediately into tiresome, repetitive arguments, while the conversations after I left office were more candid, useful, and informal.

10. Blasier, *Hovering Giant*, pp. 101-150.

11. See Robert Pastor, "Does the United States Push Revolutions to Cuba: The Case of Grenada," *Journal of InterAmerican Affairs and World Studies* (April 1986).

12. Fidel Castro, "Address to the National People's Government Assembly," December 27, 1979, mimeo., pp. 49-55. This secret speech became available in the United States and was the subject of a number of articles in the *Miami Herald*.

13. For an interesting essay on the Tobar Doctrine and why it failed in Central America in the first two decades of the twentieth century, see Charles L. Stansifer, "Application of the Tobar Doctrine to Central America," *The Americas* 23 (January 1967): 251-72.

14. For the development of this proposal and six others for reinforcing democracy in the Americas, see Robert Pastor, "How to Reinforce Democracy in the Americas: Several Proposals," in *Democracy in the Americas: The Swing of the Pendulum*, ed. Robert Pastor (New York: Holmes and Meier, 1988).

15. Some governments view the monitoring of elections as interference in their internal affairs, but the American Declaration of the Rights and Duties of Man adopted with the OAS Charter in Bogotá in 1948 describes periodic elections by secret ballot as one of the basic

rights. The Inter-American Human Rights Commission has an obligation to investigate and report abuses of that and other rights.

16. At a Conference on Democracy at the Carter Center of Emory University on November 17-18, 1986, twelve former and current heads of government from the region—including Carter and Ford, Raul Alfonsin from Argentina, Vinicio Cerezo from Guatemala—announced the establishment of a Council of Freely Elected Heads of Government. The idea is also developed further in my chapter "How to Reinforce Democracy in the Americas," in *Democracy in the Americas*, ed. Pastor.

17. James N. Rosenau, *The Scientific Study of Foreign Policy*, rev. ed. (New York: Nichols Publishing Co., 1980), p. 502.

Chapter 17

1. Excerpts of Arias' address on receipt of the Nobel Peace Prize are in the *New York Times*, December 11, 1987, p. 3.

2. Jonathan Fuerbringer, "Contra Aid Accord Set by Congress and White House," *New York Times*, December 21, 1987, pp. 1, 8.

3. The address was reprinted in the *New York Times*, October 8, 1987, p. 8.

4. Excerpts from testimony, *New York Times*, July 10, 1987, pp. 4-7.

5. North's testimony was reprinted in the *New York Times* on July 11, 1987, pp. 6-7.

6. Excerpts from testimony, *New York Times*, July 8, 1987, pp. 6-7.

7. Excerpts in *New York Times*, July 16, 1987, p. 1.

8. See two articles by Stephen Engelberg in the *New York Times*, "U.S. Planned in '84 For South Africa to Help Contras," August 20, 1987, p. 1; "U.S. Aides Say Panama General Proposed Sabotage in Nicaragua," November 19, 1987, p. 1.

9. U.S. Senate Select Committee on Secret Military Assistance to Iran and the Nicaraguan Opposition and the U.S. House of Representatives Select Committee to Investigate Covert Arms Transactions with Iran, *Iran–Contra Affair: Report of the Congressional Committees* (November 17, 1987), p. 11.

10. Article of that title by Joel Brinkley, *New York Times*, November 19, 1987, p. 1.

11. Tip O'Neill with William Novak, *Man of the House* (New York: Random House, 1987), pp. 367-71.

12. In a press conference on August 6, Guatemalan President Vi-

nicio Cerezo admitted that he and the other Presidents had only learned about the plan the night before from the press.

13. For Duarte's views, see his interview of August 11, 1987, printed in *Foreign Broadcasting Information Service (FBIS)*, August 13, 1987, pp. F1-2.

14. Luis G. Solis-Rivera, Chief of Staff of the Costa Rican Ministry of Foreign Affairs, "Peace and the Future of Central America: A Costa Rican Viewpoint," paper prepared for a conference sponsored by the Friedrich Ebert Foundation, Washington, D.C., October 19, 1987, p. 8. The Honduran proposal was printed in a pamphlet in both Spanish and English and given to the Foreign Ministers just before the Summit. The assumption was that it was written in the United States.

15. The cable appears to be from the CIA station chief. It is reprinted in Joint Hearings Before the House Select Committee to Investigate Covert Arms Transactions With Iran and the Senate Select Committee on Secret Military Assistance to Iran and the Nicaraguan Opposition, *Testimony of Richard V. Secord*, Vol. 100-1, May 5-8, 1987, p. 435.

16. Solis-Rivera, "Peace and the Future of Central America," p. 2.

17. From an interview Ortega gave on August 8, 1987, printed as "Daniel Ortega Discusses Guatemala Summit" in *FBIS*, August 11, 1987, pp. I1-11.

18. Arias later disclosed this and other calls in Stephen Kinzer, "Costa Rican Chief Warns Nicaragua on Press Freedom," *New York Times*, August 12, 1987, p. A6.

19. For Reagan's address, see *New York Times*, August 13, 1987, p. A8; his comment on the plan as "fatally flawed" was in the *New York Times*, September 13, 1987, p. 8; Bush's comment was in Elaine Sciolino, "Latin Peace Plan Is Said to Set Back Help for Contras," *New York Times*, August 11, 1987, pp. 1, 6.

20. The following are all in the *New York Times*: Michael R. Gordon, "Habib Quits Post As Special Envoy," August 15, 1987, pp. 1, 5; Neil A. Lewis, "U.S. Envoys Told to Convey Doubt Over Latin Plan," August 18, 1987, pp. 1, 4; Neil A. Lewis, "U.S. Aide Calls Contras Crucial To Region's Peace," August 19, 1987, p. 4.

21. "Reagan Talks to Contras Over Rebel Radio Stations," *Atlanta Journal-Constitution*, August 25, 1987, p. A13.

22. As he was leaving for Havana, Ortega told the press that he had called "Presidents Arias and Cerezo this afternoon, and informed them about this trip; they reacted positively." The interview is printed in *FBIS*, August 13, 1987, p. I1. The FSLN Communiqué of August 17 is printed in *FBIS*, August 18, 1987, p. I1.

23. Stephen Kinzer, "Nicaraguans and the Winds of Peace," *New York Times*, September 15, 1987, p. 3.

24. Arias' comments are in a radio interview he gave on October 27, printed in *FBIS*, October 29, 1987, pp. 6-7. He also said that he did not believe that Reagan could impose sanctions against his country because of "the prestige we now have in the U.S. Congress."

25. Neil A. Lewis, "Arias Asks U.S. to Give Latin Peace Plan A Try," *New York Times*, September 23, 1987, p. 8.

26. Serge Scheman, "Costa Rica Leader Wins Nobel Prize for Peace Plan: Blow To Contra Aid Seen," *New York Times*, October 14, 1987, pp. 1, 8.

27. Shirley Christian, "Reagan Aides See No Possibility of U.S. Accord with Sandinistas," *New York Times*, August 18, 1985, p. 6.

28. Later a Soviet spokesman protected his boss by suggesting that the proposal was more balanced and innocuous than Reagan had reported—that Gorbachev had merely proposed that both sides "agree on a reciprocal basis . . . to refrain from deliveries of weapons" to Central America. Both quotes are in the *New York Times*. Reagan's statement is cited by John B. Oakes, "Quit Sabotaging the Arias Plan," January 3, 1988, p. E15; and the Soviet statement is in R. W. Apple, Jr., "Contra Issue and Summit," December 17, 1987, p. 9.

29. The report is "Primary Guidelines for Functionally Improving, Strengthening and Equipping the Sandinista People's Army (EPS) for the Period 1988-1990 and Preliminary Guidelines for the Five-Year Period, 1991-1995," written in October 1987. It was distributed by the Department of State. For one report of the interview, see Stephen Kinzer, "Soviet Is Aiding Nicaragua in Buildup, Defector Says," *New York Times*, December 14, 1987, pp. 1, 6. Two months later the *Washington Post* reported that Miranda received $800,000 in rewards, resettlement costs, and a five-year contract for unspecified services. Administration officials would not confirm the amount, but said a large figure was accepted in October when Miranda defected. "Nicaraguan Defector To Get U.S. Payment," *New York Times*, February 5, 1988, p. 6.

30. Humberto Ortega's speech on December 12, 1987, was reported in *FBIS*, December 14, 1987, pp. 16-20.

31. Joel Brinkley, "Congress Is Seen Shifting Toward Aid to Contras," *New York Times*, December 16, 1987, p. 4; and David E. Pitt, "Arias Criticizes Nicaraguan Plan for More Troops," *New York Times*, December 20, 1987, p. 1.

32. Cited in R. W. Apple, Jr., "Contra Issue and Summit," *New York Times*, December 17, 1987, p. 9.

33. Daniel Ortega Saavedra, "More Contra Aid, More Suffering," *New York Times*, January 14, 1988, p. 27; also in the *Times*, James LeMoyne, "Contras Are Given Costa Rican Edict," January 14, 1988, p. 8.

34. Neil A. Lewis, "Four Latin Presidents Cautioned By U.S. on Contras' Fate: Security Adviser Tells Leaders Rebel Failure Could Hurt Their Countries Badly," *New York Times*, January 13, 1988, pp. 1, 6.

35. The text of the report is reprinted in *FBIS*, January 19, 1988, pp. 20-24.

36. The declaration issued on January 16 is printed in *FBIS*, January 19, 1988, p. 4.

37. His interview of January 16 is printed in *FBIS*, January 19, 1988, pp. 16-20.

38. On December 3 and then on the 15th, fourteen opposition political parties asked President Ortega to permit consideration of seventeen constitutional amendments before the legislative term ended so that they could be modified and inscribed, if approved, in 1988. They never received an answer and, as a result, walked out of the national dialogue. See their statements printed in *FBIS*, December 7, 1987, p. 26, and December 16, p. 17.

39. See the following three articles by Stephen Kinzer in the *New York Times*: "Nicaragua Detains Five More Leaders of the Opposition," January 20, 1988, p. 1; "Sandinista Strains: Ortega's Effort to Comply With Peace Pact Points Up Differences Among the Leaders," January 21, 1988, p. 6; and "Ortega Is Said to Face Challenge From Borge in Sandinista Regime," January 24, 1988, p. 7.

40. Joel Brinkley, "Contra Aid Foes Given a Scolding," *New York Times*, January 22, 1988, p. 1.

41. *Wall Street Journal*, January 22, 1988, p. 26.

42. Excerpts of both addresses were in the *New York Times* on February 3, 1988, p. 6.

43. Cited in "Arias: It's Soviets' Turn to Cut Military Aid," *Atlanta Journal-Constitution*, February 7, 1988, p. 3A.

44. Ortega's comment about humanitarian aid was made at his press conference in San José on January 16 (*FBIS*, January 19, 1988, pp. 16-20); his latter comments were printed in *FBIS*, February 5, 1988, pp. 17-24.

45. "Nicaragua Invaded Honduras: Probe by UN Team Concludes," *Atlanta Journal-Constitution*, April 1, 1988, p. 4.

Primary Sources: Interviews

IN ADDITION to many published sources in English and in Spanish, this book has relied on classified documents of the National Security Council and related agencies in the archives of the Carter Presidential library, declassified State Department cables, my own private notes and diary, and interviews with the people listed below. Several of these people have asked that I not cite them specifically in the text of the book.

Although I have relied on interviews as an important source of information, I have used them with care and only when they did not contradict the written record. Memories fade, and in the case of the senior policy makers of the U.S. government, it is unrealistic to expect them to remember the details of most of the events on Nicaragua. Very few have. I have spoken, for example, with the following officials of the Carter Administration: Secretary of Defense Harold Brown, Chairman of the Joint Chiefs of Staff General David Jones, Secretary of State Cyrus Vance, and Deputy Secretary of State Warren Christopher (and received a letter of December 10, 1986), and CIA Director Stansfield Turner. All indicated their desire to be helpful but said that they simply could not recall the events in the Nicaraguan case sufficiently to add much to my research. After a few questions, I realized they were right.

Three policy makers—Jimmy Carter, Zbigniew Brzezinski, and Pete Vaky—were extraordinarily helpful, in large part because their memories were assisted by notes that they wrote at the time. Brzezinski's views were fully and colorfully developed in his diary of the period, and he generously read entire portions, which I transcribed and included in the book.

In addition to those interviews I personally conducted, I have also benefited from reading transcripts of those done by WGBH–Public Television (Boston) for a documentary on Central America. WGBH interviews are so designated below and in the notes. In addition, I traveled to Nicaragua in August 1983 and February 1986 to conduct extensive discussions and interviews with Nicaraguan leaders on the book. The latter trip was enhanced considerably because I also accompanied former President Jimmy Carter and Mrs. Rosalynn Carter in their meetings with Nicaraguan leaders.

For my analysis of U.S. policy during the Reagan Administration, I have relied on published sources and on numerous interviews with about thirty officials from the State Department, the National Security Council, the CIA, and the Defense Department, and a roughly equivalent number of Members of Congress and their aides. Since these interviews, which have been held periodically since the beginning of the Administration, were either informal conversations or were held on condition of anonymity, I have not included the interviewees' names in the list below.

Interviews

Colonel Carlos Agurto, responsible for three battalions of the National Guard (1978-79): October 22, 1985, Miami, Florida.

Maurice Bernbaum, U.S. Chargé in Managua (May 1947–June 1948): Telephone conversation, July 24, 1985, Washington, D.C.

Tomás Borge, one of the founders of FSLN, member of Directorate, and Minister of Interior (July 1979–present): August 4, 1983, Managua; June 3, 1984 (WGBH), Managua; February 8, 1986, Managua.

William Bowdler, President's Special Representative to the Mediation in Nicaragua (October 1978–January 1979), Assistant Secretary of State for Inter-American Affairs (December 1, 1979–January 1981): July 23, 1985, Sharps, Virginia.

Zbigniew Brzezinski, National Security Adviser (1977-81): July 17, 1985, Washington, D.C.

Arístides Calvani, former Venezuelan Foreign Minister, foreign affairs adviser to Venezuelan President Luis Herrera Campins (March 1979–July 1979): January 22, 1985, Washington, D.C.

Oscar Camilión, Argentine Minister of Foreign Relations (1980-81): December 14, 1986, Casa de Campo, Dominican Republic.

Rodrigo Carazo Odío, President of Costa Rica (1978-82): July 30, 1983, San José, Costa Rica.

Jimmy Carter, President of the United States (1977-81): January 28, 1982, Plains, Georgia; October 11, 1984, Panama; March 4, 1985, Atlanta; correspondence, August 19, 1985; numerous other conversations.

Jorge Castañeda Gutman, adviser to Mexico's Ministry of Foreign Relations (1979-82): August 25, 1986, Mexico City.

Alfredo César, Nicaraguan Minister of Reconstruction (1979-80), President of Nicaraguan Central Bank (1980-82), political leader of Nicaraguan Resistance: April 9, 1984, Washington, D.C.

Pedro Joaquín Chamorro Barrios, son of Pedro Joaquín Chamorro, who was assassinated on January 10, 1978, and of Violeta Barrios de Chamorro, who was a member of the first Sandinista Junta; co-editor of *La Prensa* until he left Nicaragua in 1984: July 26, 1983, San José, Costa Rica.

Shirley Christian, *Miami Herald* correspondent in Central America (July 1979–1981): July 14, 1983, Washington, D.C.

Arturo Cruz, member of Group of 12, member of Junta (1980-81), Nicaragua's Ambassador to the United States (June–December 1981), leader of United Nicaraguan Opposition (1985-87): October 2, 1986, Atlanta.

José Figueres, President of Costa Rica (1953-58; 1970-74): June 8, 1984 (WGBH), San José; February 6, 1986, San José, Costa Rica.

José Juan De Olloquí, Mexican Under Secretary for Foreign Relations (December 1976–July 1979): June 13, 1986, Mexico City.

John Goshko, *Washington Post* correspondent: June 24, 1985, telephone conversation.

Moisés Hassán, member of FSLN, member of the first Junta, Vice Minister of Interior: June 4, 1984 (WGBH), Managua.

William Jorden, U.S. Ambassador to Panama (1974-78): March 12, 1987, telephone conversation.

Max Kelly, personal aide and private secretary to Anastasio Somoza, Jr. (1972-73; April 1978–July 1979), also worked in Somoza's businesses: February 13, 1984, Miami, Florida.

Gabriel Lewis Galindo, Panama's Ambassador to the United States (1977-78), close adviser to Torrijos: December 28, 1982, Panama; numerous other conversations.

Lt. Col. James L. McCoy, U.S. Defense Attaché in U.S. Embassy in Managua during the revolution: August 15, 1985, telephone conversation; October 16, 1985, Miami, Florida.

Haroldo Monteleagre, Nicaraguan Vice Minister of Industry and Commerce (July–December 1979), Minister of Reconstruction Fund (April 1980–September 15, 1981); left Nicaragua after that: December 4-6, 9, 1981, Washington, D.C.

Ambler Moss, Jr., U.S. Ambassador to Panama (1978-82): August 1, 1985, telephone conversation; numerous other conversations.

John (Jack) Murphy, nine-term Congressman from New York, who served as Chairman of House Merchant Marine and Fisheries Committee and was close friend of Anastasio Somoza, Jr., convicted for charges stemming from Abscam: July 31, 1984 (WGBH), Danbury Federal Penitentiary, Danbury, Connecticut.

Daniel Oduber, President of Costa Rica (1974-78): February 3, 1983, Washington, D.C.; May 19, 1984, Falmouth, Massachusetts; other conversations.

General José Antonio Olavarría, Deputy Director of the National Security Council, Venezuela (1977-81): December 14, 1986, Casa de Campo, Dominican Republic.

Daniel Ortega, leader of the Terceristas, member of FSLN Directorate, Coordinator of Junta, President of Nicaragua: June 4, 1984 (WGBH), Managua; February 8 and 9, 1986, Managua.

Humberto Ortega, Minister of Defense of Nicaragua (July 1979–present): February 7 and 8, 1986, Managua.

Luis Pallais, President of Nicaraguan Congress and leader of Somoza's Liberal Party, cousin of Anastasio Somoza: May 17, 1984 (WGBH), Miami, Florida; October 16, 1985, Miami, Florida.

Edén Pastora, member of FSLN, Vice Minister of Interior (July 1979–June 27, 1981): November 14, 1983, Washington, D.C. (also participating in interview were Donald Castillo and Carlos Coronel); July 1, 1984 (WGBH), Washington, D.C.

Carlos Andrés Pérez, President of Venezuela (1974–March 1979): September 22, 1982, Washington, D.C.; May 2, 1984 (WGBH); May 2, 1984, New York City; January 28, 1987, Atlanta.

Marcial Pérez-Chiriboga, Venezuela's Ambassador to the United States (May 1979–March 1984): December 14, 1986, Casa de Campo, Dominican Republic.

Lawrence Pezzullo, U.S. Ambassador to Nicaragua (appointed May 17, 1979; presented credentials, July 31, 1979; resigned August 1981): December 16, 1982, Washington, D.C.; May 15, 1984 (WGBH), New York City; July 30, 1985, New York City; numerous other conversations.

Sergio Ramírez, leader of the Group of Twelve, member of the Junta, Vice President: February 7-8, 1986, Managua.

Alan Riding, New York Times correspondent in Mexico and Central America (1971-84): March 13, 1983, Washington, D.C.

Alfonso Robelo, president of COSEP and INDE (1976-79), one of FAO negotiators, member of the first Sandinista Junta (June 1979–April 22, 1980), left Nicaragua in March 1982, leader of Nicaraguan Resistance (contras): May 3-4, 1983, Washington, D.C.; July 29-30, 1983, San José, Costa Rica. Latter interview was also with another leader of contras, Dr. Alvaro Jerez.

Santiago Roel, Mexican Minister of Foreign Relations (December 1976–May 1979): June 13, 1986, Mexico City.

William D. Rogers, Assistant Secretary of State for Inter-American Affairs (1974-76), Under Secretary of State for Economic Affairs (1976): May 22, 1985, Washington, D.C.

Arístides Royo, President of Panama (October 11, 1978–August 1982): January 30-31, 1982, Panama.

Mark Schneider, Deputy Assistant Secretary of State for Human Rights (1977-79): May 27, 1985, Washington, D.C.

Sally Shelton, Deputy Assistant Secretary of State, Bureau of Inter-American Affairs (August 1977–Spring 1979): July 31, 1985, Washington, D.C.

Rafael Solís, Nicaragua's first Ambassador to the United States, Secretary to the Council of State: August 2, 1983, Managua.

Bernabé Somoza, nephew of Anastasio Somoza Debayle: April 1981, Washington, D.C.

Peter Tarnoff, Special Assistant to the Secretary of State and Executive Secretary of the Department of State (1977-81): September 16, 1981, Washington, D.C.

Francisco Urcuyo Maliaños, President of Nicaragua (July 17-19, 1979): May 18, 1984 (WGBH), Miami, Florida.

Viron Peter Vaky, Assistant Secretary of State for Inter-American Affairs (July 1978–December 1, 1979): July 24, 1985, Washington, D.C.; numerous additional conversations and correspondence.

Marvin Weissman, U.S. Ambassador to Costa Rica (1977-80): July 17, 1980, Washington, D.C.

Jaime Wheelock Román, member of FSLN Directorate, Minister for Agrarian Reform: February 9, 1986, Managua.

Charles Wilson, Democratic Congressman from Texas: July 31, 1985, telephone conversation.

Index

Aaron, David, 79, 81-82, 85-86, 88-89, 112, 115, 117-18, 134-35, 151-53, 156-57, 160, 170, 171, 174, 226-27
Abrams, Elliott, 252, 257-58, 391n54
Acheson, Dean, 30, 352n47
Afghanistan, 147, 201, 277
Agency for International Development (AID), 39, 209
Agriculture in Nicaragua, 43-44, 245
Agüerro, Carlos, 40
Agüerro, Fernando, 35-36
Alegrett, José Ivan, 72
Alexander, Clifford, 136
Allende, Salvador, 57
Alliance for Progress, 35, 38, 43
American Convention on Human Rights, 66
Amnesty International, 54, 357n12
Andean Pact, 137-39, 141, 144-45, 162; post-Somoza succession, 147-51; recognition of Junta, 183, 187; Somoza accuses of intervention, 178-79
Anti-Americanism: in Nicaragua, 229, 246; in Latin America, 280-82; among revolutionaries, 308-309
ARA. See Bureau of Inter-American Affairs
Arbenz, Jacobo, 57, 351n47
Arce, Bayardo, 235, 248-49
ARDE (Nicaraguan resistance group based in south), 239
Arévalo, Juan José, 29
Argentina: arms shipments to Somoza, 123-24; support for contras, 237-38; Contadora support group, 251
Argentine People's Revolutionary Army, 380n15
Argüello, Leonardo, 28
Argüello, Rosendo, Jr., 30
Arias, Oscar, 253
Arms shipments: to Sandinistas, 123-24, 127-28, 144-45, 164-65; by the Sandinistas, 217-21, 232, 237

Banking industry (Nicaragua), nationalization, 201
Barnaby, Malcolm, 93

Barquín, Ramón, 10, 370n19
Basic Infantry Training School (EEBI), 55
Batista, Fulgencio, 6, 370n19; ascent to power, 7-8; manipulates elections, 10; similarities with Somoza, 9-10; U.S. pressures for free elections, 8; U.S. support, 270, 272
Bauman, Robert, 209-210, 217
Bay of Pigs invasion, 12; contra effort compared with, 259-60
Bergold, Harry, 236
Bermúdez, Enrique, 216, 238
Bernbaum, Maurice, 351n44
Betancourt, Rómulo, 30, 60, 279-80
Betancourt Doctrine, 311-12
Blasier, Cole, 297, 308
Boland, Edward, 241
Boland amendment, 241-43, 245, 256-59
Bonsal, Philip, 11, 192, 282, 285
Borge, Tomás: 39-40, 57, 71, 95, 171, 199, 201-202, 204-205, 245; arms to Salvadoran guerrillas, 220, 226-27; evacuation of U.S. citizens, 246; expansion of Junta, 371n1; FSLN anthem, 202, 377n24; vs. Pastora, 199, 239; on Sandinista ideology, 35, 41-42, 194, 352n2
Bowdler, William: 92-93, 95, 97-98, 101-102, 103, 105-106, 108, 110-19, 122, 138, 149, 151, 152, 158, 159-60, 165, 168-70, 171, 173, 177, 179, 180-81, 184, 186-87, 214, 226, 271, 288-89
Brazil, 179, 251
Brezhnev, Leonid, 137
Broad Opposition Front (FAO), 64, 68, 120, 122; diagram of, 95-96; Executive Committee proposal, 154-55, 158; general strike, 73; mediation, 85, 94-95, 101-103, 106-20; National Guard survival, 174; OAS resolution, 150-51; as victim, 287. See also Moderates
Browder, Earl, 40
Brown, Harold, 88, 112, 115-16, 147-48, 151-59, 160-61, 218-19
Brunei, 258
Bryan-Chamorro Treaty, 24
Brzezinski, Zbigniew, 83, 102-103, 117-

Library of Congress Cataloging-in-Publication Data

Pastor, Robert A.
Condemned to repetition: the United States and Nicaragua
with a new preface and epilogue, Robert A. Pastor.
p. cm.

Bibliography: p.   Includes index.
1. United States—Foreign relations—Nicaragua.
2. Nicaragua—Foreign relations—United States.
3. United States—Foreign relations—1981-   .
4. United States—Foreign relations—1977-1981.
5. Nicaragua—Politics and government—1979-
I. Title.
E183.8.N5P37 1988   327.7307285   88-12663
ISBN 0-691-02291-7 (pbk.)

Robert A. Pastor is Professor of Political Science at Emory University and Director of
the Latin American and Caribbean Program at Emory's Carter Center. He was Director of Latin American and Caribbean Affairs on the National Security Council from
1977 to 1981. Prior to that, he was Executive Director of the Linowitz Commission on
U.S.–Latin American Relations.

Dr. Pastor received his Ph.D. from Harvard University, and taught at Harvard, the
University of Maryland, and El Colegio de México before coming to Emory. He is the
author of *Congress and the Politics of U.S. Foreign Economic Policy* (University of
California Press, 1980), and the editor of and a contributor to *Latin America's Debt
Crisis: Adjusting to the Past or Planning for the Future?* (Lynne Rienner Publishers,
1987) and *Migration and Development in the Caribbean: The Unexplored Connection* (Westview Press, 1985). He has also contributed 20 chapters to other books and
has written many articles for popular and scholarly journals.